FM 3-04.240 (FM 1-240)

I0167271

Instrument Flight for Army Aviators

April 2007

Headquarters, Department of the Army

*FM 3-04.240 (FM 1-240)

Field Manual
No. 3-04.240

Headquarters
Department of the Army
Washington, DC, 30 April 2007

Instrument Flight for Army Aviators

Contents

DISTRIBUTION RESTRICTION: Approved for public release; distribution is unlimited.

*This publication supersedes FM 1-240, 15 December 1984.

Figures

Tables

Preface

Field manual (FM) 3-04.240 is specifically prepared for aviators authorized to fly Army aircraft. This manual presents the fundamentals, procedures, and techniques for instrument flying and air navigation.

FM 3-04.240 facilitates adherence to Army regulation (AR) 95-1 by providing guidance and procedures for standard Army instrument flying. Aircraft flight instrumentation and mission objectives are varied, making instruction general for equipment and detailed for accomplishment of maneuvers. Guidance found in this manual is both technique and procedure oriented. Aircraft operator manuals provide the detailed instructions required for particular aircraft instrumentation or characteristics. When used with related flight directives and publications, this publication provides adequate guidance for instrument flight under most circumstances but is not a substitute for sound judgment; circumstances may require modification of prescribed procedures. Aircrew members charged with the safe operation of United States Army, Army National Guard (ARNG), or United States Army Reserve (USAR) aircraft must be knowledgeable of the guidance contained herein. This manual applies to all military, civilian, and/or contractor personnel who operate Army aircraft, and adherence to its general practices is mandatory.

The Aeronautical Information Manual (AIM) published by the Federal Aviation Administration (FAA) is not regulatory; however, the AIM provides information that reflects examples of operating techniques and procedures required in other regulations. AIM is not binding on Army aircrews. Furthermore, the AIM contains some techniques and procedures not consistent with Army mission requirements, regulatory guidance, waivers, exemptions, and accepted techniques and procedures. However, AIM is the accepted standard for civil aviation and reflects general techniques and procedures used by other pilots. Much of the information contained in this manual is reproduced from AIM and adapted for Army use. If a subject is not covered in this manual or other Army regulations, follow guidance in the AIM unless mission requirements dictate otherwise.

All figures and tables that display partial or complete navigational excerpts from other publications (such as instrument approach charts, legends, and low-altitude en route charts) are provided for reference only and should not be used in planning for or the conduct of any flight.

This publication applies to the Active Army, the Army National Guard/Army National Guard of the United States, and the United States Army Reserve unless otherwise stated.

The proponent of this publication is Headquarters, United States Army Training and Doctrine Command (TRADOC). Send comments and recommended changes, using Department of the Army (DA) Form 2028 (Recommended Changes to publications and Blank Forms) or automated link (http://www.usapa.army.mil/da2028/daform2028.asp), directly to Commander, U.S. Army Aviation Warfighting Center (USAAWC), ATTN: ATZQ-TD-D, Fort Rucker, AL 36362-5000; or e-mail the Directorate of Training and Doctrine (DOTD) at av.doctrine@us.army.mil. Other doctrinal information can be found on the Internet through Army Knowledge Online (AKO) or by calling the defense switched network (DSN) 558-3551 or commercial (334) 255-3551.

Note. For immediate assistance on issues affecting this FM, contact the Directorate of Training and Doctrine (DOTD), Doctrine Division, at DSN 558-3551, commercial 334-255-3551, or via e-mail at the following address: av.doctrine@us.army.mil.

Unless this publication states otherwise, masculine nouns and pronouns do not refer exclusively to men.

This publication has been reviewed for operations security considerations.

Chapter 1

Flight Instruments and Systems

The efficiency and utility of Army aircraft depend largely on flight instruments and systems accurately depicting what the aircraft is doing in flight and how well its power plants and components are functioning. Important navigation instruments are the magnetic compass, slaved gyro compass system, heading indicator, airspeed indicator, and altimeter. These instruments provide information concerning direction, airspeed, and altitude. The attitude indicator allows the aviator to control the aircraft by showing the attitude of the aircraft in relation to the natural horizon. The performance of an aircraft in a given attitude and with a certain power setting is indicated by the airspeed indicator, heading indicator, altimeter, vertical speed indicator/vertical velocity indicator, and turn-and-slip indicator. Flight instruments are grouped into three systems: pitot-static, compass, and gyroscopic.

SECTION I – PITOT-STATIC SYSTEMS

1-1. Most aircraft instrument panels have three basic pressure-operated instruments: the altimeter, airspeed indicator, and vertical speed indicator (VSI). All three receive the pressures that they measure from the aircraft pitot-static system. Flight instruments depend on accurate sampling of ambient atmospheric pressure to determine the height and speed of aircraft movement through the air, both horizontally and vertically. Ambient atmospheric pressure is sampled at two or more locations outside of the aircraft by the pitot-static system.

Contents

1-2. Static pressure, or still air, is measured at a flush port where air is not disturbed. On some aircraft, this air is sampled by static ports on the side of the fuselage (Figure 1-1). A pitot-static head is a combination pickup used to sample pitot and static air pressures. Other aircraft pick up the static pressure through flush ports on the side of the electrically heated pitot-static head. These ports are in locations proven by flight tests to be in undisturbed air, and they are normally paired, one on either side of the aircraft. This dual location prevents lateral movement of the aircraft from giving erroneous static pressure indications. The areas around the static ports may be heated with electric heater elements to prevent ice forming over the port and blocking the entry of static air.

1-3. Pitot pressure, or impact air pressure, is taken in through an open-end tube pointed directly into the relative wind flowing around the aircraft. The pitot tube connects to the airspeed indicator, and the static ports deliver pressure to the airspeed indicator, altimeter, and VSI (Figure 1-1, page 1-2).

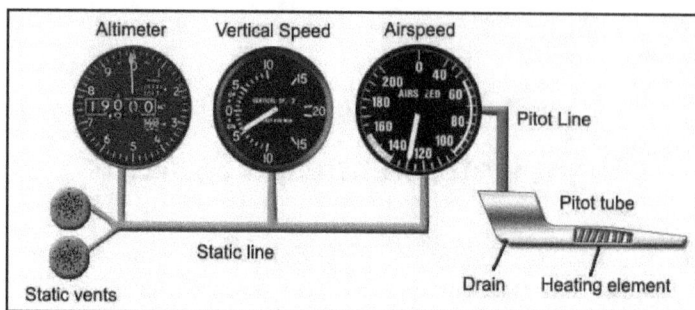

Figure 1-1. Pitot-static head

ALTIMETER

1-4.   An altimeter is an aneroid barometer that measures the absolute pressure of ambient air and displays that absolute pressure in terms of feet or meters above a selected pressure level. The sensitive element in an altimeter is a stack of evacuated, corrugated bronze wafers (Figure 1-2). The air pressure tries to compress the wafers against their natural springiness, which works to expand them. As a result, their thickness changes as air pressure changes.

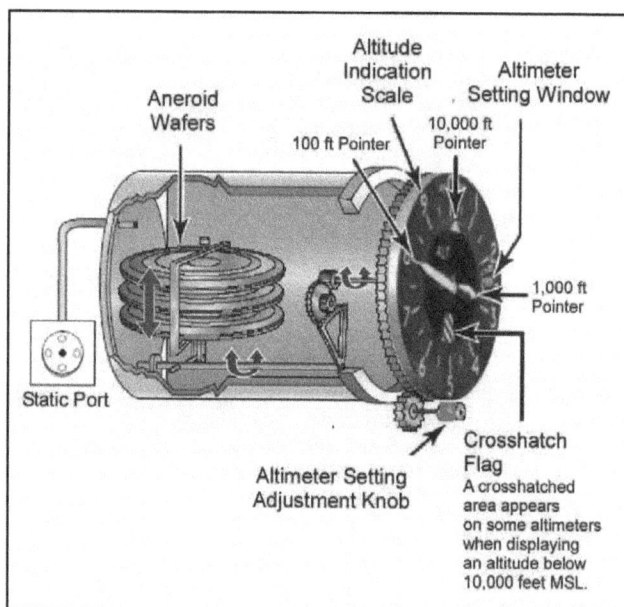

Figure 1-2. Altimeter components

1-5.   An altimeter has an adjustable barometric scale that allows the aviator to set the reference pressure from which the altitude is measured. This scale is visible in the Kollsman window (altimeter setting window) and adjusted by a knob on the instrument. The range of the scale is from 28.00 to 31.00 inches of mercury (Hg), or 948 to 1,050 millibars.

1-6.   Rotating the knob changes both the barometric scale and altimeter pointers in such a way that a change in the barometric scale of 1 inch Hg changes the pointer indication by 1,000 feet. This is the standard pressure lapse rate below 5,000 feet. When the barometric scale is adjusted to 29.92 inches Hg, or 1,013.2 millibars, the pointers indicate the pressure altitude. To display indicated altitude, adjust the barometric scale to the local altimeter setting. The instrument then indicates the height above the existing sea-level pressure.

TYPES OF ALTITUDE

1-7.   The five types of altitude are indicated, absolute, true, pressure, and density. Figure 1-3 compares pressure, true, and absolute altitudes. Indicated altitude is altitude as read on the dial with a current altimeter setting (sea-level pressure) set in the Kollsman window. Absolute altitude is the altitude above the surface or terrain where the aircraft is flying, also called above ground level (AGL). True altitude is the altitude above mean sea level (MSL).

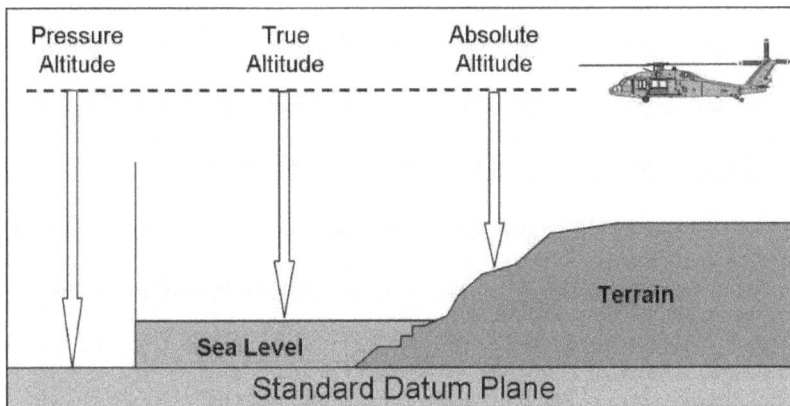

Figure 1-3. Types of altitude

1-8.   Pressure altitude is the height measured above the 29.92-inches-of-mercury pressure level (standard datum plane). If the Kollsman window is set to 29.92 Hg, the hands of the dial indicate pressure altitude. This setting is called the standard altimeter setting. In the United States, the use of pressure altitudes (standard altimeter setting) begins at 18,000 feet. These altitudes are referred to as flight levels (FLs). The following are examples of conversions of altitude in feet to flight levels.

> **Examples of Conversions to Flight Levels**
> 18,000 feet equals FL180; 35,000 feet equals FL350.

1-9.   Density altitude is the altitude for which a given air density exists in the standard atmosphere. If the barometric pressure is lower or the temperature is higher than standard, then density altitude of the field is higher than its actual elevation such as in the following example. Density altitudes can be obtained from many airfield towers or may be computed on the dead reckoning computer (CPU-26A/P).

> **WARNING**
>
> **Because higher density altitude requires a greater takeoff distance and reduces aircraft performance, failure to calculate density altitude could be fatal.**

Example of Density Exceeding Actual Elevation

For Denver, Colorado, with an elevation of 5,500 feet, at a temperature of 100° Fahrenheit (F) and a barometer reading (corrected to MSL) of 29.55 inches of mercury, density altitude is about 10,000 feet.

ALTIMETER ERROR

1-10. An altimeter indicates standard changes from standard conditions; most flying, however, involves errors caused by nonstandard conditions, where the aviator must modify the indications to correct for these errors. Two types of errors are mechanical and inherent.

1-11. A preflight check to determine the condition of an altimeter consists of setting the altimeter pointer to the airport elevation or actual aircraft location altitude, if known, and noting the Kollsman window setting. After obtaining the local altimeter setting, compute altimeter error as described in the following example.

Example Illustrating Difference of Actual and Displayed Altitudes

Set 29.95 with pointer on field elevation; the local altimeter setting is 29.98. This setting causes a difference of 30 feet between actual and displayed altitudes (29.98 – 29.95 = .03, 10 feet for every .01).

1-12. According to the FAA, if the indication is off more than 75 feet from the surveyed elevation, the instrument must be referred to a certified instrument repair station for recalibration. According to current Army operator manuals, aircraft are allowed up to 70 feet from the surveyed elevation. The appropriate operator or maintenance manual should be referenced to confirm which limit is accurate. Differences between ambient temperature and pressure will cause an erroneous indication on the altimeter. Figure 1-4 shows the way that nonstandard temperature affects an altimeter. When the aircraft is flying in air warmer than standard, the air is less dense and pressure levels are farther apart. When the aircraft is flying at an indicated altitude of 5,000 feet, the pressure level for that altitude is higher than in air at standard temperature, and the aircraft flies higher than if the air were cooler. If the air is colder than standard, air is denser and pressure levels are closer together. When the aircraft is flying at an indicated altitude of 5,000 feet, its true altitude is lower than if the air were warmer.

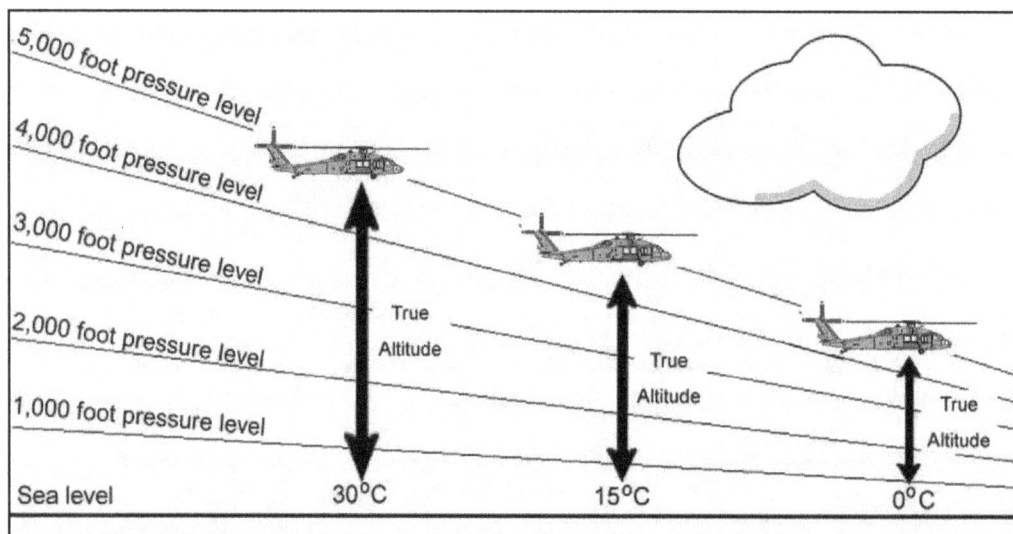

Figure 1-4. Altimeter error caused by nonstandard temperature

1-13. Any time that the barometric pressure lapse rate differs from the standard of inches of Hg per thousand feet in lower elevations, the indicated altitude will be different from the true altitude. Figure 1-5 shows a helicopter at point A flying in air in which conditions are standard; the altimeter setting is 29.92 inches Hg. When the altimeter indicates 5,000 feet, the true altitude is also 5,000 feet. The helicopter flies to point B, where pressure is lower than standard, and the altimeter setting is 28.36 inches Hg; however, the aviator does not change the altimeter to this new altimeter setting. When the altimeter shows an indicated altitude of 5,000 feet, the true altitude, or height above MSL, is 3,500 feet.

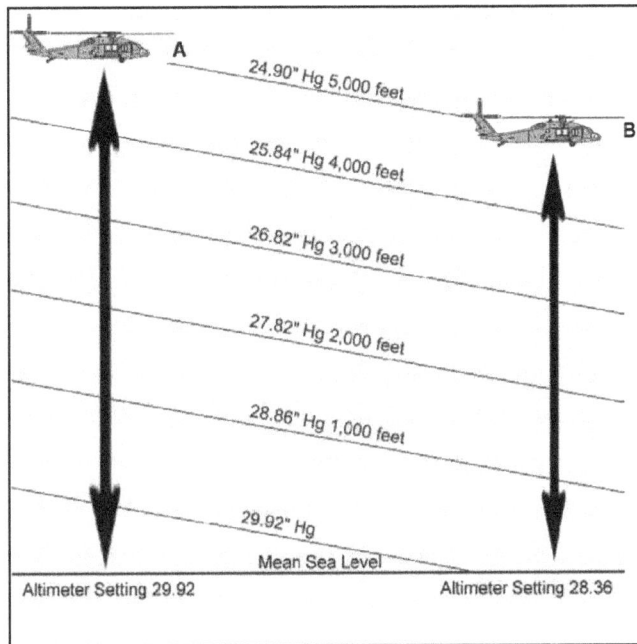

Figure 1-5. Altimeter error caused by nonstandard atmospheric pressure

COLD-WEATHER ALTIMETER CORRECTION

1-14. Pressure altimeters are calibrated to indicate true altitude under international standard atmospheric (ISA) conditions. Any deviation from these standard conditions results in an erroneous reading on the altimeter. This error becomes important when the aviator considers obstacle clearances in temperatures lower than standard because the aircraft's altitude is below the figure indicated by the altimeter. The error is proportional to the difference between actual and ISA temperature and the height of the aircraft above the altimeter setting source. The amount of error is about 4 feet per 1,000 feet for each degree Celsius (°C) of difference. Corrections are only made for decision altitudes (DAs)/decision heights (DHs), minimum descent altitudes (MDAs), and other altitudes inside, but not including, the final approach fix (FAF). The same correction made to DAs/DHs and MDAs is applied to other altitudes inside the FAF. For current cold-weather altimeter correction procedures, refer to the Flight Information Handbook (FIH), section D. An example of cold-weather altimeter correction follows Figure 1-6, page 1-6. The following guidance is an example of how to accomplish the procedure found in the FIH. To ensure adequate obstacle clearance, the values in the chart in Figure 1-6 are—

- Added to the published decision altitude (DA)/DH or MDA and step-down fixes inside the FAF whenever outside air temperature is less than 0 degree C.

- Added to *all* altitudes in the procedure in designated mountainous regions whenever outside air temperature is 0 degree C or less.

- Added to *all* altitudes in the procedure whenever outside air temperature is –30 degrees C or less.

- Added to procedure turn, intermediate approach altitude, and height above touchdown (HAT)/height above airport (HAA) when they are 3,000 feet or more above the altimeter setting source.

TEMPERATURE CORRECTION CHART
Height Above Altimeter Setting

Reported Temp °C	200	300	400	500	600	700	800	900	1000	1300	1500	1800	2000	2300	3000	4000	5000
0	20	20	30	30	40	40	50	50	60	80	90	100	120	130	170	230	280
-5	20	30	30	40	50	60	60	70	80	100	120	140	150	180	230	310	380
-10	20	30	40	50	60	70	80	90	100	130	150	180	200	230	290	390	490
-15	30	40	50	60	70	90	100	110	120	160	180	220	240	270	360	480	600
-20	30	50	60	70	90	100	120	130	140	190	210	260	280	330	420	570	710
-25	40	50	70	90	100	120	130	150	170	220	250	300	330	380	490	660	830
-30	40	60	80	100	120	140	150	170	190	250	280	340	380	430	570	760	950
-35	50	60	90	110	130	150	170	190	220	280	320	390	430	490	640	860	1080
-40	50	60	100	120	150	170	190	220	240	310	360	430	480	550	720	970	1210
-45	60	60	110	140	160	190	220	240	270	350	400	480	540	620	800	1080	1350
-50	60	60	120	150	180	210	240	270	300	390	450	530	590	680	890	1190	1500

HAT/HAA

Figure 1-6. Temperature correction chart (height in feet)

Example of Cold-Weather Altimeter Correction

Published MDA 1,180 feet MSL

HAT 402 (feet)

Temp –30°C

Correction 80 feet

MDA to use: 1,180 + 80 = 1,260 feet MSL

ENCODING ALTIMETER

1-15. An encoding altimeter is also known as an AIMS altimeter. In the term AIMS, A stands for Air Traffic Control Radar Beacon System (ATCRBS), I stands for identification friend or foe (IFF), M represents the Mark XII identification system, and S means system.

1-16. When the air traffic control (ATC) transponder is set to Mode C, the encoding altimeter supplies the transponder with a series of pulses identifying the flight level (in increments of 100 feet) at which the aircraft is flying. This series of pulses is transmitted to ground radar and appears on the controller's scope as an alphanumeric display around the return for the aircraft. The transponder allows the ground controller to identify the aircraft under his control and determine the pressure altitude that the aircraft is flying.

1-17. A computer inside the encoding altimeter measures the pressure referenced from 29.92 inches Hg and delivers this data to the transponder. When the aviator adjusts the barometric scale to the local altimeter setting, the data sent to the transponder is not affected. Figure 1-7, page 1-7, shows an altimeter with a failed encoder displayed by a red blocked code off between the 8 and 9 on the altimeter.

Figure 1-7. Encoding altimeter with a malfunction

RADAR ALTIMETER

1-18. The radar altimeter, also known as an absolute altimeter, measures the height of the aircraft above terrain by transmitting a radio signal, either a frequency-modulated (FM) continuous-wave or a pulse to the ground, and accurately measuring the time used by the signal in traveling from the aircraft to the ground and returning. This transit time is modified with a time delay and converted inside the indicator to distance in feet.

1-19. Most absolute altimeters have a provision for setting a low/high altitude. When the aircraft reaches this height above ground, a light illuminates and/or an aural warning sounds. Aircraft with a flight management system may have a provision for setting a DA/DH or a MDA; when the aircraft reaches this height, a light illuminates and/or an aural warning sounds. For example, the utility helicopter (UH)-60 vertical situation indicator has a DH advisory light that illuminates whenever the radar altimeter is operating and the altitude indicator is at or below the set altitude on the radar altimeter. See the operator's manual for operation of the radar altimeter. A radar altimeter has three main functions:

- Serves as a ground proximity warning device.
- Is an accurate cross-check for the barometric altimeter.
- Indicates absolute height above terrain.

AIRSPEED INDICATOR

1-20. An airspeed indicator is a differential pressure gauge that measures the dynamic pressure of the air through which the aircraft is flying. Dynamic pressure is the difference in ambient static air pressure and total, or ram, pressure caused by motion of the aircraft through the air. These two pressures are taken from the pitot-static system.

1-21. The mechanism of the airspeed indicator in Figure 1-8, page 1-8, consists of a thin, corrugated phosphor-bronze aneroid, or diaphragm, that receives its pressure from the pitot tube. The instrument case is sealed and connected to the static ports. As pitot pressure increases or static pressure decreases, the diaphragm expands. This dimensional change is measured by a rocking shaft and gears driving a pointer across the instrument dial. Most airspeed indicators are calibrated in knots, or nautical miles per hour; some instruments show statute miles per hour, and some instruments show both.

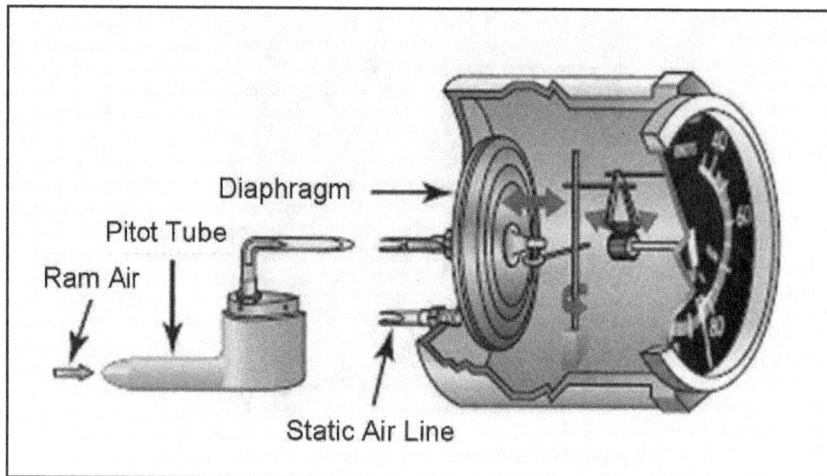

Figure 1-8. Mechanism of an airspeed indicator

1-22. There are four types of airspeed. The four types are indicated, calibrated, equivalent, and true.

- Indicated airspeed (IAS) is shown on the dial of the instrument, uncorrected for instrument or system errors.
- Calibrated airspeed (CAS) is the speed that the aircraft is moving through the air, which is found by correcting IAS for instrument and position errors; the aircraft operator's manual has a chart or graph to correct IAS for these errors and provide correct CAS for various aircraft configurations.
- Equivalent airspeed (EAS) is CAS corrected for compression of air inside the pitot tube; EAS is the same as CAS in standard atmosphere at sea level. As airspeed and pressure altitude increase, the CAS becomes higher and a correction for compression must be subtracted from CAS.
- True airspeed (TAS) is CAS corrected for nonstandard pressure and temperature; TAS and CAS are the same in standard atmosphere at sea level. Under nonstandard conditions, TAS is found by applying a correction for pressure altitude and temperature to CAS. Aircraft equipped with TAS indicators have a temperature-compensated aneroid bellows inside the instrument case. The bellows modifies the movement of the rocking shaft inside the instrument case so that the pointer shows actual TAS; the TAS indicator provides TAS and IAS. These instruments have a conventional airspeed mechanism with an added subdial visible through cutouts in the regular dial. A knob on the instrument allows rotation of the subdial and alignment of an indication of the outside air temperature with the pressure altitude being flown; this alignment causes the instrument pointer to indicate TAS on the subdial.

1-23. In addition to the four airspeeds above, aviators must also consider and calculate ground speed. Ground speed is the speed of an aircraft relative to the surface of the earth. Ground speed is TAS corrected for wind.

VERTICAL SPEED INDICATOR

1-24. The VSI (Figure 1-9, page 1-9) is also called a vertical velocity indicator (VVI) and was formerly known as a rate-of-climb indicator. The VSI/VVI is a rate-of-pressure change instrument that indicates any deviation from a constant pressure level.

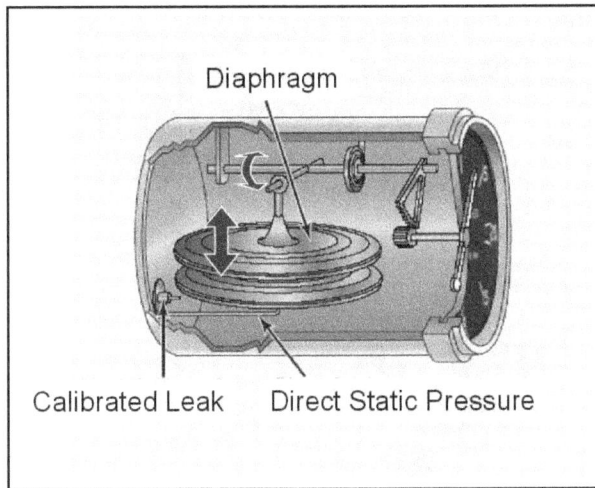

Figure 1-9. Vertical speed indicator

1-25. Inside of the instrument case is an aneroid (also called a diaphragm) much like the one in an airspeed indicator. Both the inside of this aneroid and the inside of the instrument case are vented to the static system. The case is vented through a calibrated orifice that causes pressure inside the case to change more slowly than pressure inside the aneroid. As the aircraft ascends, static pressure becomes lower and pressure inside the case compresses the aneroid, moving the pointer upward—showing a climb and indicating the number of feet per minute (FPM) that the aircraft is ascending.

1-26. When the aircraft levels off and static pressure is no longer changing, pressure inside the case becomes the same as that inside the aneroid and the pointer returns to the horizontal, or zero, position. When the aircraft descends, static pressure increases and the aneroids expand, moving the pointer downward, indicating a descent. The pointer indication in a VSI lags a few seconds behind the actual change in pressure. The VSI is more sensitive than an altimeter and useful in alerting the aviator of an upward or downward trend, thereby helping maintain a constant altitude.

INSTANTANEOUS VERTICAL SPEED INDICATOR

1-27. Instantaneous vertical speed indicators (IVSIs) (Figure 1-10, page 1-10) differ from VSI construction by having two accelerometer-actuated air pumps that sense an upward or downward pitch of the aircraft and instantaneously creating a pressure differential. By the time that pressure caused by the pitch acceleration dissipates, the altitude pressure change is effective.

1-28. Because accelerometers are not vertically stabilized, some error is generated in turns. If a zero indication is maintained on the IVSI when the aircraft is entering a turn, some loss in altitude will be encountered. A corresponding gain in altitude results when the aircraft is recovering from a turn. The IVSI should not be used for directly controlling vertical speed when the aircraft is rapidly banking in excess of 40 degrees. The indicator is not affected once the aircraft is in a steady turn.

1-29. The fade-out of acceleration in a steady turn happens when a turn has been started and the accompanying change in normal acceleration has been completed. Fade-out occurs because the accelerator masses settle to new balance points corresponding to the normal acceleration maintained in the turn. When a 30-degree bank is being established, altitude deviation should not exceed 90 feet while the IVSI is maintained at zero. In more steeply banked turns, turn error rapidly increases with bank angle.

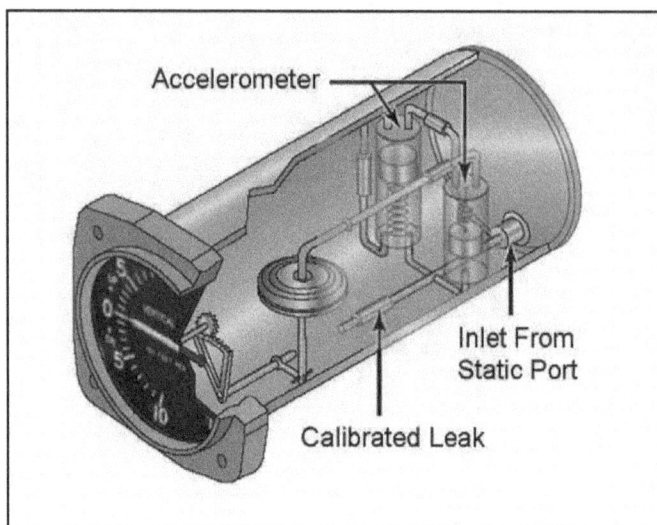

Figure 1-10. Instantaneous vertical speed indicator

SECTION II – COMPASS SYSTEMS

1-30. The Earth is a huge magnet surrounded by a magnetic field made up of invisible lines of flux. These lines leave the surface at the magnetic north pole and reenter at the magnetic South Pole. Lines of magnetic flux have two important characteristics: any magnet free to rotate aligns with them, and an electrical current is induced into any conductor that cuts across them. Most direction indicators installed in aircraft make use of one of these two characteristics.

MAGNETIC COMPASS

1-31. A magnet is a piece of material, usually a metal containing iron, which attracts and holds lines of magnetic flux. Every magnet, regardless of size, has two poles: north and south. When one magnet is placed in the field of another, the unlike poles attract each other and like poles repel.

1-32. The magnetic compass (Figure 1-11, page 1-11) is one of the oldest, simplest, and most basic instruments. AR 95-1 requires a magnetic compass for all flights. The compass bowl is the interior portion of the compass card that supports the dial and float. The bowl is filled with liquid that has minimum volume and viscosity changes with temperature variations. Some compasses have an expansion bellows to allow for fluid expansion. The bowl supports a metal float that has two small magnets attached to it. A graduated scale, called a card, is wrapped around the float and viewed through a glass window with a lubber line across the center of the glass. The float and card assembly has a hardened steel pivot in its center that rides inside a special, spring-loaded, hard-glass jewel cup. The buoyancy of the float takes most of the weight off the pivot, and the fluid dampens the oscillation of the float and card. This jewel-and-pivot type of mounting allows the float to freely rotate and tilt about 18 degrees. Compass indications are erratic and unreliable at steeper bank angles.

1-33. The compass card is marked with letters representing the cardinal directions—north, east, south, and west—and a number for each 30 degrees between these letters. The final "0" is omitted from these directions as in the following examples.

Examples of Compass Card Degree Equivalents		
3 equals 30 degrees	6 equals 60 degrees	33 equals 330 degrees

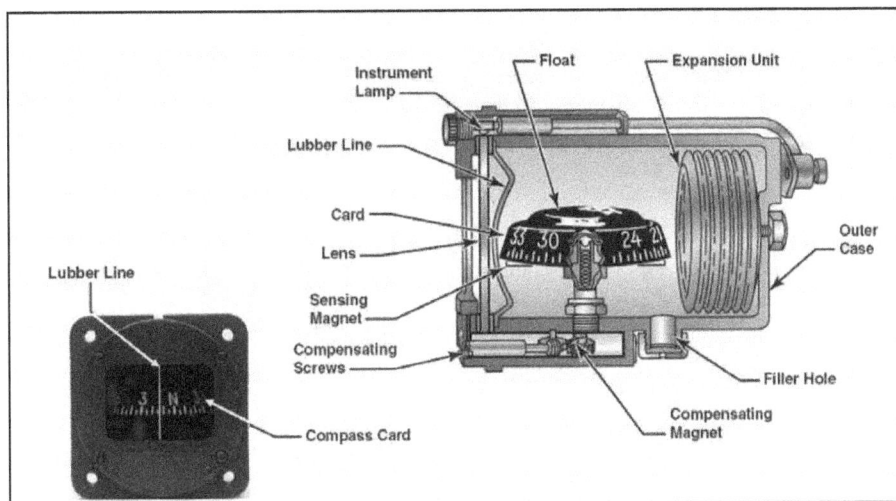

Figure 1-11. Magnetic compass

1-34. There are long and short graduation marks between the letters and numbers, with each long mark representing 10 degrees and each short mark representing 5 degrees. The numbers and letters on the graduated scale are marked to allow the aviator to view the direction being flown. The markings appear backward from conventional compasses that are viewed from above.

COMPASS ERROR

Variation

1-35. The Earth rotates about its geographic axis, and maps and charts are drawn using meridians of longitude that pass through the geographic poles. Directions measured from the geographic poles are called true directions. The north magnetic pole, to which the magnetic compass points, is not collocated with the north geographic pole but is some 1,300 miles away. Directions measured from the magnetic poles are called magnetic directions. In aerial navigation, the difference between true and magnetic directions is called variation. In surveying and land navigation, the difference is called declination.

1-36. Figure 1-12, page 1-12, shows the isogonic lines that identify the number of degrees of variation in their area. The line that passes near Chicago is called the agonic line, and anywhere along this agonic line, the two poles are aligned and there is no variation.

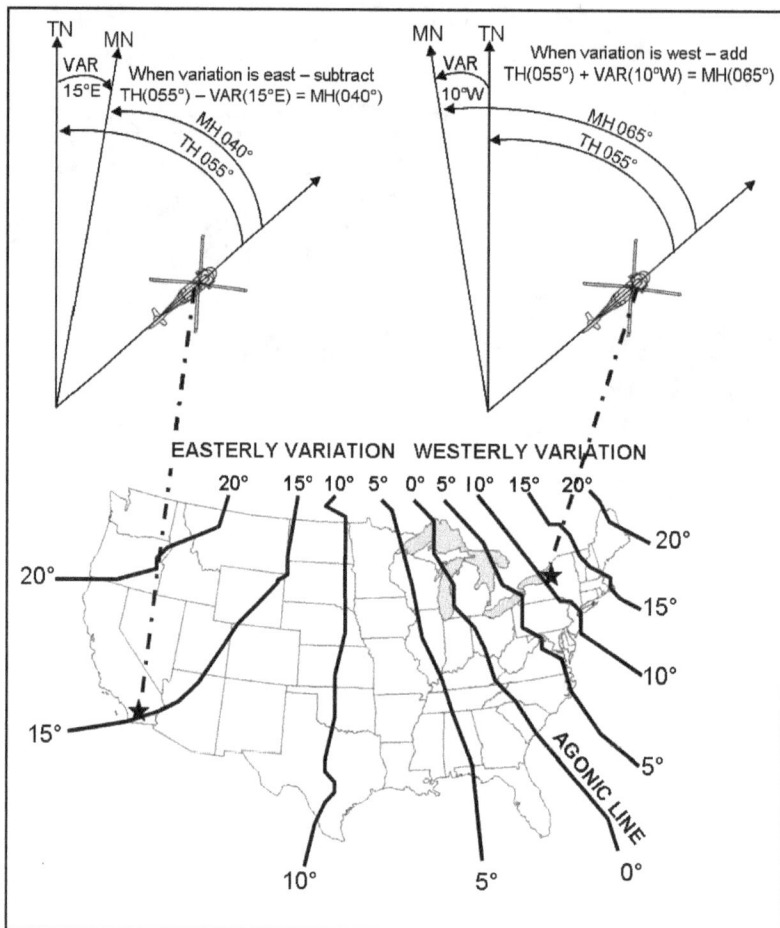

Figure 1-12. Lines of magnetic variation

1-37. Variation values to the east of the agonic line are called westerly variation; the magnetic north pole is west of true north (TN). Likewise, the variation values west of the agonic line are known as easterly variation; the magnetic north pole is east of true north. Variation error does not change with the aircraft's heading and is the same anywhere along that particular isogonic line.

1-38. Magnetic north (MN) changes in small amounts each year. Aeronautical charts are updated periodically to correct for this yearly change. On instrument flight rules (IFR) en route low- and high-altitude charts, all radials and bearings are displayed as magnetic and, therefore, do not require the use of the compass correction formula.

1-39. When aviators plot a course on an aeronautical chart, they measure the degrees of heading against latitude and longitude lines. This measure is called a true heading (TH) because it is being measured relative to the true north pole. Because the aviator relies on the magnetic compass for direction, the aviator will be steering the aircraft relative to the magnetic north pole. Therefore, the aviator must convert the TH, as plotted on the navigation chart, to a magnetic heading (MH) by which to steer, using the compass. A method for remembering magnetic variation is to add westerly variation and subtract easterly variation by using the phrase "west is best/east is least." The following example demonstrates how to convert the true heading to a magnetic heading.

Example of Compass Correction

To convert TH to MH, add westerly variation to TH to get MH (see right-hand example Figure 1-12). In other words, the aviator must steer 065 degrees magnetic to fly over a true heading of 055 degrees.

055 degrees (TH) + 10 degrees west (variation) = 065 degrees (MH).

Likewise, subtract easterly variation from TH to get MH (see left hand example Figure 1-12). In other words, the aviator must steer 040 degrees magnetic to fly over a true heading of 055 degrees.

055 degrees (TH) - 15 degrees east (variation) = 040 degrees (MH).

1-40. To find true heading when magnetic heading is known, the equation in the previous example is written in reverse. This procedure is shown in the following example.

Example of Reversing the Equation for Compass Correction

Convert MH to TH by adding easterly variation and subtracting westerly variation. This is the reverse of changing from TH to MH. The 10 degrees west is subtracted from the MH (065 degrees), and this figure (055 degrees) is the TH. Likewise, the 15 degrees east is added to the MH (040 degrees), and this figure (055 degrees) is the TH.

065 degrees (MH) - 10 degrees west (variation) = 055 degrees (TH).

040 degrees (MH) + 15 degrees east (variation) = 055 degrees (TH).

Deviation

1-41. Magnets in a compass align with any magnetic field. Local magnetic fields in an aircraft caused by electrical current flowing in the structure, in nearby wiring, or in any magnetized part of the structure will conflict with the Earth's magnetic field and cause a compass error called deviation. To reduce deviation, the compensating assembly is adjusted as much as possible. A Department of Defense (DD) Form 1613 (Pilot's Compass Correction Card) (Figure 1-13) is prepared and mounted near the compass. Figures from this card are applied to the indications of the compass so that a desired heading may be flown.

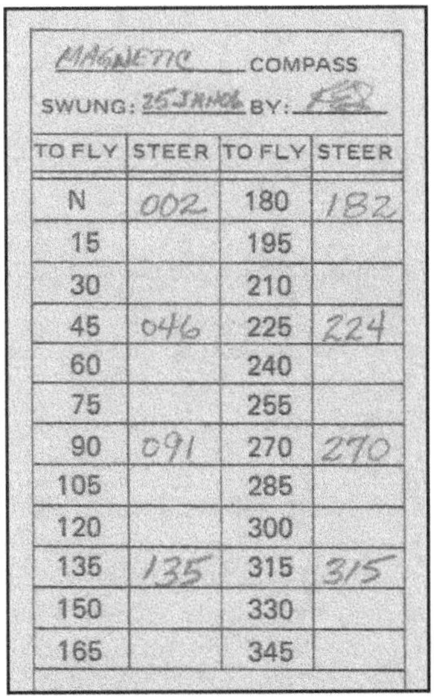

Figure 1-13. Pilot compass correction card

Dip Error

1-42. The lines of magnetic flux are considered to leave the Earth at the magnetic north pole and enter at the magnetic south pole. At both locations, the lines are perpendicular to the Earth's surface. At the magnetic equator, which is halfway between the poles, the lines are parallel with the surface. Magnets in the compass align with this field, and near the poles they dip, or tilt, the float and card. The float is balanced with a small dip-compensating weight and stays relatively level when operating in the middle latitudes of the northern hemisphere. The dip, along with this weight, causes two very noticeable errors: turning error and acceleration error.

Turning Error

1-43. Pull of the vertical component of the Earth's magnetic field causes northerly turning error, which is apparent on a heading of north or south. If an aircraft flying a heading of north makes a turn east, the aircraft banks to the right and the compass card tilts to the right. The vertical component of the Earth's magnetic field pulls the north-seeking end of the magnet to the right, and the float rotates, causing the card to rotate toward the west, the direction opposite the direction of the turn (Figure 1-14).

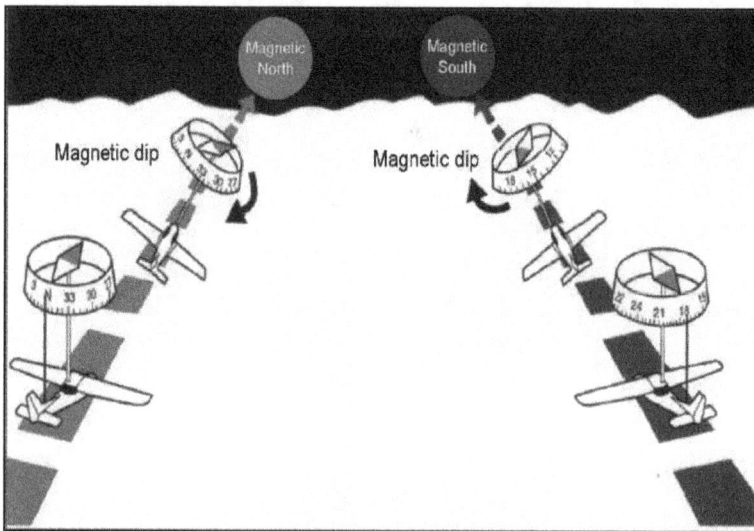

Figure 1-14. Turning error

1-44. If the turn is made from north to west, the aircraft banks to the left and the card tilts to the left. The magnetic field pulls on the end of the magnet, causing the card to rotate toward the east. This indication is, again, opposite to the direction in which the turn is being made. The rule for this error is the following: when the aircraft starts a turn from a northerly heading, compass indication lags behind the turn.

1-45. When an aircraft is flying on a heading of south and begins a turn east, the magnetic field of the earth pulls on the end of the magnet, rotating the card toward the east, the same direction in which the turn is being made. If the turn is made from the south toward the west, magnetic pull starts the card rotating toward the west, again; in the same direction in which the turn is being made. The rule for this error is the following: when the aircraft starts a turn from a southerly heading, compass indication leads the turn.

Acceleration Error

1-46. In acceleration error, dip-correction weight causes the end of the float and card marked "N" (this is the south-seeking end) to be heavier than the opposite end. When the aircraft is flying at a constant speed on a heading of either east or west, the float and card are level. Effects of magnetic dip and weight are about equal. If the aircraft accelerates on a heading of east (Figure 1-15), inertia of the weight holds its end of the float back and the card rotates toward north. The card swings back to its east indication as soon as the speed of the aircraft stabilizes.

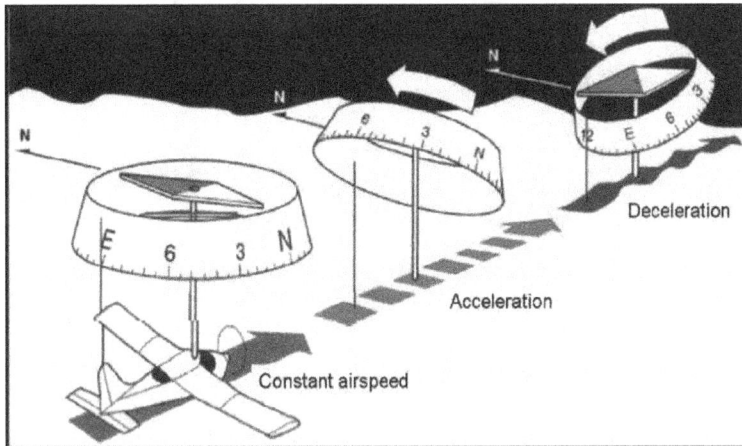

Figure 1-15. Acceleration error

1-47. If, while flying on this easterly heading, the aircraft decelerates, inertia causes the weight to move ahead and the card rotates toward the south until the speed again stabilizes. While the aircraft is flying on a heading of west, inertia from acceleration causes the weight to lag and the card rotates toward the north. When the aircraft decelerates on a heading of west, inertia causes the weight to move ahead and the card rotates toward the south. A helpful way to remember acceleration error is the acronym ANDS: acceleration-north/deceleration-south.

Oscillation Error

1-48. Oscillation is a combination of all other errors, including rough air or poor control technique, and results in the compass card swinging back and forth around the heading being flown. When setting the gyroscopic heading indicator to agree with the magnetic compass, use the average indication between the swings.

RADIO MAGNETIC INDICATOR

1-49. The radio magnetic indicator (RMI) (Figure 1-16, page 1-16) is a navigational aid providing aircraft magnetic or directional gyro heading and very (high frequency) omnidirectional range (VOR) or automatic direction finder (ADF) bearing information. Remote indicating compasses were developed to compensate for errors in and limitations of older types of heading indicators.

1-50. The slaving control and compensator unit has a push button, providing a means of selecting either the slaved gyro or free gyro mode. This unit also has a slaving meter and two manual heading-drive buttons. The slaving meter indicates the difference between displayed heading and magnetic heading. A right deflection indicates a clockwise error of the compass card; a left deflection indicates a counterclockwise error. When the aircraft is in a turn and the card rotates, the slaving meter shows a full deflection to one side or the other. When the system is in free gyro mode, the compass card may be adjusted by depressing the appropriate heading-drive button.

Figure 1-16. Radio magnetic indicator

1-51. The remote compass transmitter is a separate unit and is usually mounted in a wingtip to eliminate the possibility of magnetic interference. The remote compass transmitter contains the flux valve, which is the direction-sensing device of the system. A concentration of lines of magnetic force, after being amplified, becomes a signal relayed to the heading indicator unit, which is remotely mounted. This signal operates a torque motor in the heading indicator unit, which precesses the gyro unit until aligned with the transmitter signal. The remote compass transmitter is connected electrically to the RMI. The two pointers are driven by any two combinations of a global positioning system (GPS), an ADF, and/or a VOR.

SECTION III – GYROSCOPIC SYSTEMS

GYROSCOPE

1-52. A gyroscope is a wheel or rotor mounted to spin rapidly around an axis. The gyroscope is free to rotate about one axis or both axes that are perpendicular to each other and the axis of spin. A spinning gyroscope offers resistance (inertia) to any force that tends to change the direction of the axis of spin. The rotor has great weight (high density) for its size and is rotated at high speeds; therefore, it offers high resistance to any applied force.

PROPERTIES

Rigidity

1-53. When spinning, the rotor remains in its original plane of rotation regardless of how the base is moved and the aircraft rotates about the rotor. Attitude and heading instruments operate on the principle of rigidity.

Precession

1-54. Precession is the resultant action or deflection of a spinning rotor when a deflective force is applied to its rim. Precession causes a force applied to a spinning wheel to be felt 90 degrees from the point of application in the direction of rotation (Figure 1-17, page 1-17). Rate indicators, such as the turn-and-slip indicator and turn coordinator, operate on the principle of precession.

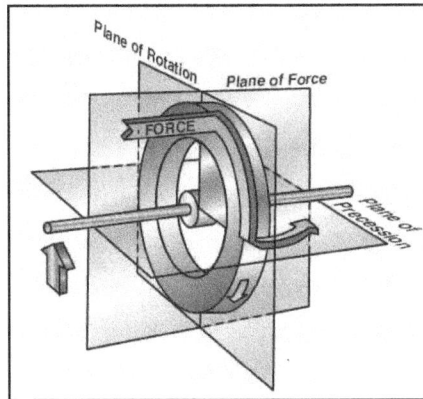

Figure 1-17. Precession diagram

Instrument Power Sources

1-55. Army aircraft use electrical power to keep rotors of gyroscopic instruments rotating continuously. At higher altitudes and lower temperatures, electrically-operated gyroscopes have proven more reliable than vacuum-driven gyroscopes. In electrically-driven gyroscopes, the rotor and stator of an electric motor are enclosed in a gyroscopic housing and become, in effect, the gyro. The gyro, or rotor, is operated on current supplied from the electrical system of the aircraft. An advantage of this system is that the instrument case can be hermetically sealed, eliminating the danger of moisture condensation while blocking foreign material. When the gyro reaches operating speed, enough heat is generated to ensure effective lubrication at altitudes where the outside air temperature is extremely low.

ATTITUDE INDICATOR

1-56. The attitude indicator was originally referred to as an artificial horizon and later as a gyro horizon. Its operating mechanism is a small brass wheel with a vertical spin axis, spun at a high speed by an electric motor (Figure 1-18, page 1-18). The gyro is mounted in a double gimbal, allowing the aircraft to pitch and roll about the gyro, which remains fixed in space.

1-57. A horizon disk is attached to the gimbals, which keeps the horizon disk in the same plane as the gyro while the aircraft pitches and rolls. On early instruments, a bar represented the horizon, but now a disc with a line represents the horizon, both pitch marks, and bank-angle lines. The top half of the instrument dial and horizon disc is blue or white, representing sky; the bottom half is brown or black, representing ground. A bank index at the top or bottom of the instrument shows the bank angle marked on the banking scale with any possible variation of lines representing 10, 20, 30, 45, 60, or 90 degrees based on manufacturer criteria.

1-58. Mounted in the instrument case is a small symbolic aircraft, which appears to fly relative to the horizon. A knob at the bottom center of the instrument case raises or lowers the aircraft to compensate for pitch trim changes as airspeed changes. The width of wings of the symbolic aircraft and the dot in the center of the wings represent a pitch change of about 1 to 2 degrees.

1-59. When an aircraft engine is first started and electric power is supplied to the instruments, the gyro is not erect. A self-erecting mechanism inside the instrument, actuated by the force of gravity, applies a precessive force, causing the gyro to rise to its vertical position. This erection can take as long as five minutes but is normally complete within two to three minutes.

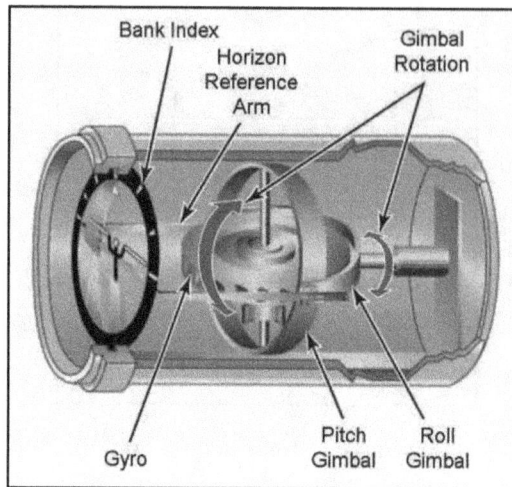

Figure 1-18. Attitude indicator

1-60. Attitude indicators are free from most errors, but depending upon the speed with which the erection system functions, there may be a slight nose-up indication during a rapid acceleration and a nose-down indication during a rapid deceleration. A small bank angle and pitch error may occur after a 180-degree turn. These inherent errors are small and correct themselves quickly after the aircraft returns to straight-and-level flight.

TURN-AND-SLIP INDICATOR/TURN COORDINATOR

TURN-AND-SLIP INDICATOR

1-61. The first gyroscopic aircraft instrument was the turn-and-bank indicator. More recently, it has been called a turn-and-slip indicator (Figure 1-19, page 1-19).

1-62. The inclinometer in the instrument is a black glass ball sealed inside a curved glass tube partially filled with a liquid, much like compass fluid. This ball measures relative strength of the force of gravity and force of inertia caused by a turn. When the aircraft is flying straight-and-level, no inertia is acting on the ball, and the ball remains in the center of the tube between two wires. In a turn made with too steep a bank angle, the force of gravity is greater than inertia and the ball rolls down to the inside of the turn. If the turn is made with too shallow a bank angle, inertia is greater than gravity and the ball rolls upward to the outside of the turn. The inclinometer only indicates the relationship between bank angle and rate of yaw.

1-63. A small gyro, located in either device, is spun either by air or by an electric motor (Figure 1-19). The gyro is mounted in a single gimbal with its spin axis parallel to the lateral axis of the aircraft and axis of the gimbal parallel with the longitudinal axis.

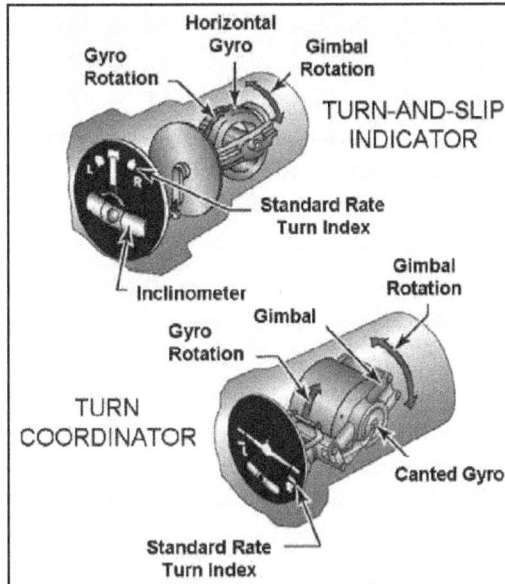

Figure 1-19. Turn indicator

1-64. When the aircraft yaws, or rotates about its vertical axis, a force is produced in the horizontal plane that, because of precession, causes the gyro and its gimbal to rotate about the gimbal axis. The gyro is restrained in this rotation plane by a calibration spring—rolling over just enough to cause the pointer to deflect until aligned with one of the doghouse-shaped marks on the dial when the aircraft is making a standard-rate turn.

1-65. The dial of these instruments is marked 2 MIN TURN. Some turn-and-slip indicators used in faster aircraft are marked 4 MIN TURN. In either instrument, a standard-rate turn is being made whenever the needle aligns with a doghouse-shaped mark.

TURN COORDINATOR

1-66. The major limitation of the older turn-and-slip indicator is the sensing of rotation only about the vertical axis of the aircraft, telling nothing of the rotation around the longitudinal axis, which in normal flight, occurs before the aircraft begins to turn.

1-67. A turn coordinator operates on precession, the same as the turn indicator, but its gimbal frame is angled upward about 30 degrees from the longitudinal axis of the aircraft, allowing a sense of roll and yaw. Some turn coordinator gyros are dual-powered and can be driven by air or electricity. Rather than using a needle as an indicator, the gimbal moves a dial in which the rear view is of a symbolic aircraft. The bezel of the instrument is marked to show wings-level flight and bank angles for a standard-rate turn (Figure 1-19).

1-68. The inclinometer, similar to the one in a turn-and-slip indicator, is called a coordination ball. It shows the relationship between bank angle and rate of yaw. The turn is coordinated when the ball is in the center between the marks. The aircraft is skidding when the ball rolls toward the outside of the turn and is slipping when it is moving toward the inside of the turn.

Note. A turn coordinator does not sense changing pitch attitudes of the aircraft. Some instruments are labeled NO PITCH INFORMATION.

SECTION IV – FLIGHT MANAGEMENT SYSTEM

1-69. Many newer aircraft are equipped with a flight management system (FMS) consisting of a flight management computer (FMC), one or more control display units (CDUs), an internal navigation database, and various displays and annunciators (electrically powered indicators). The FMS uses aircraft sensors and navigation database information to compute and display aircraft position, performance data, and navigation information during all phases of flight. The FMS may interface and provide data and signals to autopilot, flight director, and engine fuel control systems.

1-70. The FMC is a sophisticated computer system that gathers aircraft position information from multiple onboard sensors and navigation aids including VOR, distance measuring equipment (DME), tactical air navigation (TACAN), inertial navigation system (INS), GPS, and air data computers. From this sensor data, the FMC computes and continually updates the aircraft present position throughout the flight. Using this aircraft position information, navigation functions—such as course and distance to a waypoint, desired track, ground speed, and estimated time of arrival—are computed and displayed on the CDU and other aircraft instruments. Navigation information may also be provided in the form of steering commands to autopilot and flight director systems. In addition, fuel-flow information may be used by the FMC to calculate and update fuel consumption and specific range.

1-71. The CDU serves as the aircrew's interface to the FMC and associated navigation sensors. The CDU normally consists of a display screen, data-entry pad, and function and line select keys. The CDU allows menu-driven selection of various FMS modes such as initialization, fuel planning, performance, and navigation. The aviator may input a flight-plan route, vertical profile and speed information, aircraft weight and fuel parameters, and certain waypoint data into the FMC. Data from the navigation database may be displayed and reviewed by the aviator on the CDU.

1-72. An FMS normally contains an internal navigation database with either regional or worldwide coverage. The database typically includes information on navigation aids, airports, runways, waypoints, routes, airways, intersections, departures, arrivals, and instrument approaches. Aircrews may also store defined routes and waypoints in the database. Navigation databases require periodic updates, normally on a 28-day cycle, to ensure that data are current. Refer to the appropriate operator's manual for the specific capabilities of the system installed in the aircraft.

HORIZONTAL SITUATION INDICATOR

1-73. The horizontal situation indicator (HSI) is a direction indicator that uses the output from a flux valve to drive the dial, which acts as the compass card. This instrument (Figure 1-20) combines the magnetic compass with navigation signals and a glide slope. The HSI gives the aviator an indication of the location of the aircraft with relationship to the chosen course.

1-74. In Figure 1-20, page 1-21, the aircraft heading displayed on the rotating azimuth card under the upper lubber line is 184 degrees. The course-indicating arrowhead shown is set to 295 degrees; the tail indicates the reciprocal, 115 degrees. The course deviation bar operates with a VOR/Localizer (VOR/LOC) navigation receiver to indicate left or right deviations from the course selected with the course-indicating arrow; operating in the same manner, the angular movement of a conventional VOR/LOC needle indicates deviation from course.

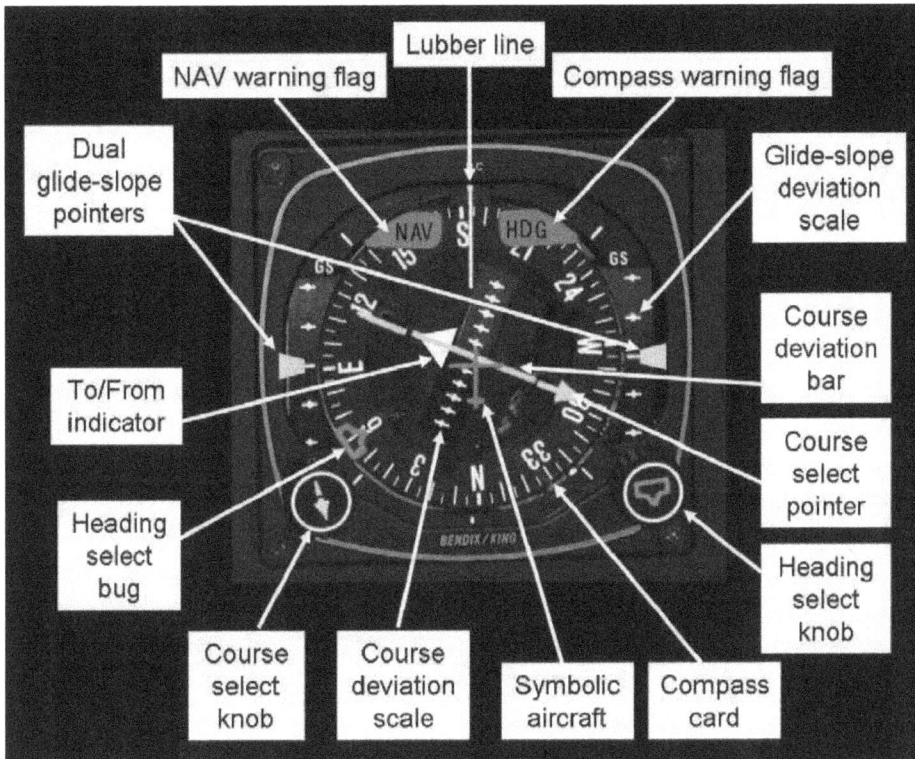

Figure 1-20. Horizontal situation indicator

1-75. The desired course is selected by rotating the course select pointer, in relation to the azimuth card, by means of the course select knob. The HSI shows the fixed aircraft symbol and course deviation bar to display relative position to the selected course. The TO/FROM indicator is a triangular-shaped pointer. When the indicator points to the head of the course, the arrow shows the course selected, if properly intercepted and flown, will take the aircraft to the chosen facility. When the indicator points to the tail of the course, the arrow shows that the course selected, if properly intercepted and flown, will take the aircraft directly away from the chosen facility.

1-76. The glide-slope pointer indicates the relation of the aircraft to the glide slope. When the pointer is below the center position, the aircraft is above the glide slope and an increased rate of descent is required. In some installations, the azimuth card is a remote indicating compass; however, in others the heading must be checked occasionally against the magnetic compass and reset.

VERTICAL SITUATION INDICATOR

1-77. The vertical situation indicator provides a cockpit display of the helicopter's pitch, roll attitude, turn rate, slip or skid, and certain navigational information. The vertical situation indicator accepts command instrument system processor signals and displays the flight command information needed to arrive at a predetermined point. The system also monitors and displays warnings when selected navigation instrument readings lack reliability.

1-78. The vertical situation indicator is typically composed of a miniature airplane, navigation warning indicator flags, trim knobs for pitch and roll, a bank angle scale and an index, a turn rate indicator, an inclinometer, and a course/glide slope deviation pointer. An example of a vertical situation indicator is the one installed in a UH-60 (Figure 1-21), which in addition to the typical items listed above, has pitch and roll command bars and a collective position pointer.

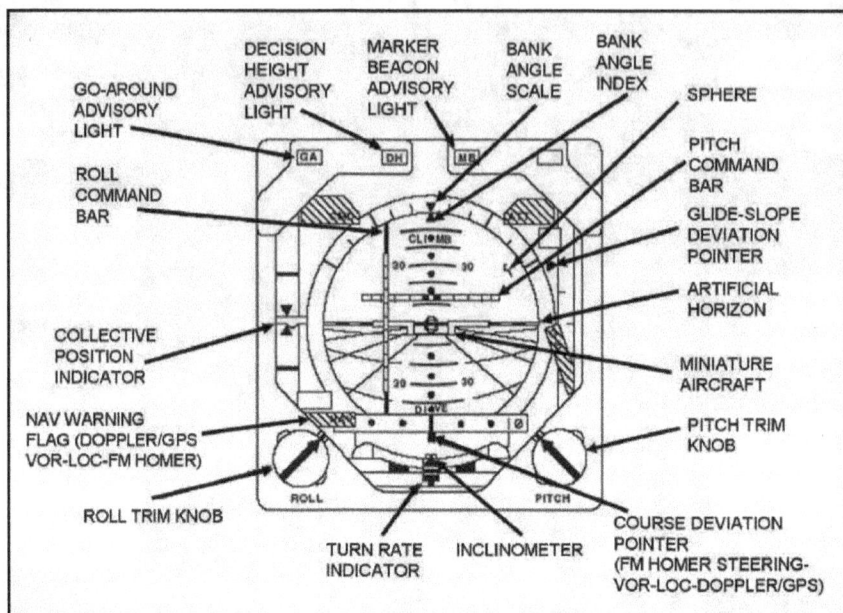

Figure 1-21. UH-60 vertical situation indicator

Chapter 2

Rotary Wing Instrument Flight Maneuvers

Instrument flying in helicopters is essentially visual flying with the flight instruments substituted for various reference points on the helicopter and natural horizon. Control changes, required to produce a given attitude by reference to instruments, are identical to those used in helicopter visual flight rules (VFR) flight; therefore, the thought processes remain the same.

SECTION I – MANEUVER PERFORMANCE

2-1. Proper instrument interpretation is the basis for aircraft control during instrument flying. Pilot skill, in part, depends on an understanding of how a particular instrument or system functions, including its indications and limitations. With this knowledge, an aviator can quickly scan an instrument and translate information into a control response.

2-2. Aircraft attitude is the relationship of its longitudinal and lateral axes to the horizon of the Earth. An aircraft is flown in instrument flight by controlling attitude and power, as necessary, to produce desired performance. All basic instrument maneuvers require correct attitude and power settings. Flight instruments used for instrument flight are categorized as control, performance, and/or navigation.

Contents

INSTRUMENTS

CONTROL

2-3. Control instruments display immediate attitude and power indications and are calibrated to permit attitude and power adjustments in precise amounts. Control is determined by reference to the power and attitude indicators (figure 2-1, page 2-2, bold dashed boxes). These power indicators vary with aircraft and may include tachometers and torque.

Figure 2-1. Control instruments of a UH-60

PERFORMANCE

2-4. Performance instruments indicate the aircraft's actual performance. Performance is determined by referencing the airspeed indicator, turn-and-slip indicator, heading indicator, altimeter, and VSI (Figure 2-2, bold dashed boxes).

Figure 2-2. Performance instruments of a UH-60

NAVIGATION

2-5.   Navigation instruments indicate aircraft position in relation to a selected navigation facility or fix. This group of instruments includes various types of course, range, and glide-slope indicators and bearing pointers usually found on the GPS, HSI, and/or RMI (figure 2-3, bold dashed boxes). Some aircraft have navigation instrument indications combined with the attitude indicator and other instruments.

Figure 2-3. Navigation instruments on a UH-60

PROCEDURAL STEPS

2-6.   Procedural steps are provided to guide the aviator to successfully react and apply the appropriate flight control inputs based on indications derived from control, performance, and navigation instruments. When following the procedural steps, aviators—

- Establish an attitude and power setting on the control instruments resulting in desired performance; known or computed attitude changes and approximate power settings reduce aviator workload.
- Maintain trim in rotary wing aircraft by cross-checking the instruments and using the cyclic centering button and/or pedals.
- Cross-check performance instruments to determine if the established attitude or power setting provides desired performance; cross-checking involves both seeing and interpreting. When noting a deviation, determine the magnitude and direction of adjustment required to achieve desired performance.
- Adjust the attitude or power setting on control instruments as necessary.

PRIMARY AND SUPPORTING METHODS

2-7.   Another basic method for presenting attitude instrument flying classifies instruments as they relate to control function and aircraft performance (table 2-1, page 2-4). All maneuvers involve some degree of motion about the lateral (pitch), longitudinal (bank/roll), and vertical (yaw) axes. Attitude control is stressed in terms of pitch (figure 2-4, page 2-4), bank (figure 2-5, page 2-4), power, and trim.

Table 2-1. Maneuver instruments

Pitch	Bank	Power
Airspeed indicator	Attitude indicator	Airspeed indicator
Attitude indicator	Heading indicator	Torque indicator
Altimeter	Magnetic compass	
Vertical speed indicator	Turn-and-slip indicator	

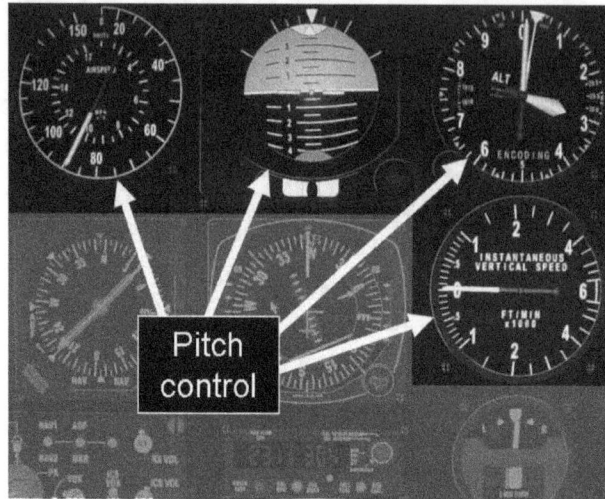

Figure 2-4. Pitch control instruments

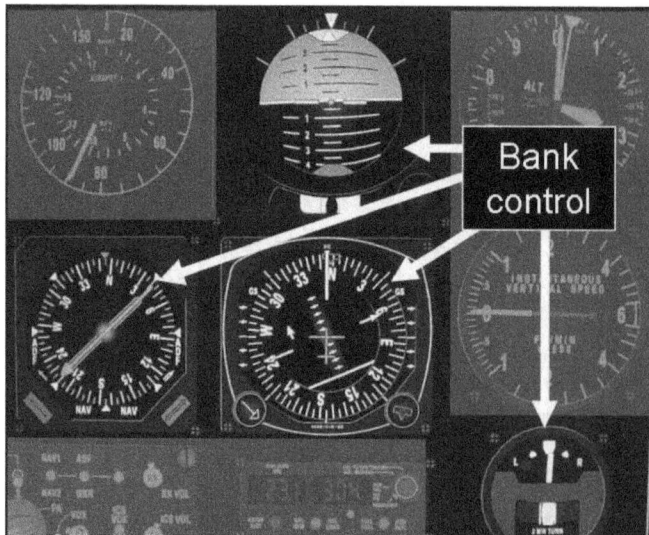

Figure 2-5. Bank control instruments

2-8.   For any maneuver or condition of flight, the pitch, bank, and power control requirements are most clearly indicated by specific maneuver instruments (table 2-1). The instruments that provide the most pertinent and essential information are referred to as primary instruments. Supporting instruments back up and supplement information shown on primary instruments. Straight-and-level flight at a constant airspeed, for example, means an exact altitude is to be maintained with no bank (constant heading). The pitch, bank, and power instruments that provide data related to maintaining this flight condition are the following:

- Altimeter, which supplies the most pertinent altitude information and is primary for pitch.
- Heading indicator, which supplies the most pertinent bank or heading information and is primary for bank.
- Airspeed indicator, which supplies the most pertinent information concerning performance in level flight in terms of power output and is primary for power.

2-9.   Although the attitude indicator is the basic attitude reference, this concept of primary and supporting instruments does not devalue any particular flight instrument. The attitude indicator is the only instrument that portrays instantly and directly the actual flight attitude. Always use the attitude indicator, when available, in establishing and maintaining pitch-and-bank attitudes. Instrument maneuvers presented, in detail, in later sections of this chapter identify the specific use of primary and supporting instruments.

SECTION II – FLIGHT MANAGEMENT SYSTEM

2-10.   Three fundamental skills needed to achieve smooth, positive control of the helicopter during instrument flight are instrument cross-check, instrument interpretation, and aircraft control.

CROSS-CHECK

2-11.   A major factor influencing a cross-check, or scanning technique, is the way in which instruments respond to attitude and power changes. The control instruments provide a direct and immediate indication of attitude and power changes, but indications on the performance instruments will lag. Lag will not appreciably affect the tolerances within which the aviator controls the aircraft; however, at times, a slight, unavoidable delay in knowing the results of attitude/power changes will occur.

2-12.   When the attitude and power are smoothly controlled, the lag factor is negligible and the indications on the performance instruments will stabilize or change smoothly. Do not make abrupt control movements in response to the lagging indications on the performance instruments without first checking the control instruments. Failure to do so leads to erratic aircraft maneuvers, which will cause additional fluctuations and lag in the performance instruments. Frequent scanning of the control instruments assists in maintaining smooth aircraft control.

2-13.   The attitude indicator is the instrument that should be used to develop all maneuvering attitudes and be scanned most frequently. A description of a typical scan is as follows: an aviator glances from the attitude indicator, taking only a brief glance at one of the flight instruments (for this discussion, the instruments surrounding the attitude indicator are called the flight instruments), back to the attitude indicator, then glancing at another flight instrument, back to the attitude indicator, and so on (Figure 2-6, page 2-6).

Figure 2-6. Cross-check pattern

COMMON ERRORS

2-14. New aviators will typically perform cross-checks by rapidly looking at each instrument without knowing exactly what to look for. With increasing experience and familiarity in basic instrument maneuvers and the indications associated with them, aviators learn what to look for, when to look, and what response to make. As proficiency increases, cross-checking occurs primarily from habit, with the aviator suiting scanning rate and sequence to the flight situation demands. If an aviator fails to maintain basic instrument proficiency through practice, many of the following common scanning errors are expected. An aid to remembering cross-check errors is the acronym FOE: fixation, omission, and emphasis.

Fixation

2-15. Fixation, staring at a single instrument, usually occurs for a good reason but has poor results. For instance, an aviator staring at an altimeter reading 200 feet below the assigned altitude may wonder how the needle came to rest there. While the aviator is gazing at the instrument, perhaps with increasing tension on the controls, a heading change occurs unnoticed and more errors accumulate. The following example describes how fixation can occur.

Example of Fixation

An aviator may establish a shallow bank for a 90° turn and stare at the heading indicator throughout the turn instead of maintaining a cross-check of other pertinent instruments. Although the aircraft is turning and the aviator does not need to recheck the heading indicator for about 25 seconds after turn entry, his eyes are fixated on the instrument.

2-16. This problem may not be entirely due to cross-check error but may relate to difficulties with the uncertainty of reading the heading indicator (interpretation) or inconsistency in rolling out of turns (control).

Omission

2-17. Omission of an instrument from a cross-check is caused by failure to anticipate significant instrument indications following attitude changes. The following example illustrates how this situation could occur.

Example of Omission

During a roll-out from a 180° steep turn, the aviator may establish straight-and-level flight with reference to the attitude indicator alone, neglecting to check the heading indicator for constant heading information.

2-18. Because of precession error, the attitude indicator temporarily shows a slight error, correctable by quick reference to the other flight instruments.

Emphasis

2-19. Emphasis on a single instrument, instead of all instruments necessary for attitude information, is an understandable fault during initial stages of training. An individual naturally tends to rely on the instrument most readily understood, even when that instrument provides erroneous or inadequate information. Reliance on a single instrument is poor technique. An aviator can maintain reasonably close altitude control with the attitude indicator but cannot hold altitude with precision without including the altimeter in the cross-check.

INSTRUMENT INTERPRETATION

2-20. Instrument interpretation requires aviators to learn and understand the purpose and use of all flight instruments. They must also understand the performance capabilities of the aircraft. The aviator's knowledge and the use of a cross-check enable him to perform maneuvers and apply techniques applicable to that aircraft across different flight conditions.

2-21. Figure 2-7 illustrates the difference between two different aircraft, both performing a five-minute climb, with the same attitude indicator setting and the same power setting. The TH-67 is climbing at 500 FPM, as shown on the VSI, and 90 knots, while the CH-47 is climbing at 2,000 FPM and 120 knots. The CH-47 is able to climb higher and faster and fly further in five minutes because it has better performance than the TH-67.

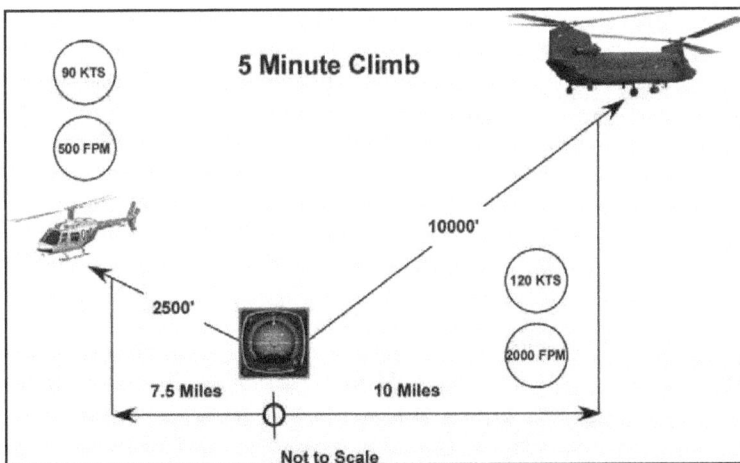

Figure 2-7. Instrument interpretation comparison

2-22. Aircraft attitude is the key to instrument interpretation as aviators learn the performance capabilities of the aircraft. When the aviator determines pitch attitude, the airspeed indicator, altimeter, VSI, and attitude indicator provide necessary information. When the aviator determines bank attitude, the heading indicator, turn-and-slip indicator, and attitude indicator are interpreted. For each maneuver, learn the performance expectations and the combination of instruments to be interpreted to control aircraft attitude.

AIRCRAFT CONTROL

2-23. Helicopter control is the result of accurately interpreting and translating flight instrument readings into correct control responses. Aircraft control involves adjustments to pitch, bank, power, and trim to achieve a desired flight path.

PITCH

2-24. Pitch attitude control is controlling movement of the helicopter about its lateral axis. After interpreting pitch attitude by reference to the pitch instruments (attitude indicator, altimeter, airspeed indicator, and vertical speed indicator), cyclic control adjustments are made to affect the desired pitch attitude.

BANK

2-25. Bank attitude control is controlling the angle made by the lateral tilt of the rotor and natural horizon, or movement of the helicopter about its longitudinal axis. Cyclic control adjustments are made to attain the desired attitude based on proper interpretation of bank instruments (attitude indicator, heading indicator, and turn indicator). Use a bank angle that approximates the degree to turn up to a standard rate turn (try not to exceed 30 degrees).

POWER

2-26. Power control is the application of collective pitch. In straight-and-level flight, changes of collective pitch are made to correct for altitude deviations if the error is more than 100 feet or the airspeed deviates by more than 10 knots. If the error is less than that amount, use a slight cyclic climb or descent. To fly a helicopter by instrument reference, knowledge of the approximate power settings is required for that particular helicopter in various load configurations and flight conditions.

TRIM

2-27. Trim refers to the use of the cyclic centering button, if the helicopter is so equipped, to relieve possible cyclic pressures. Trim also refers to the use of pedal adjustment to center the ball of the turn indicator. Pedal trim is required during all power changes.

FRICTION

2-28. Proper adjustment of collective pitch and cyclic friction assists an aviator in relaxing during instrument flight. Friction is adjusted to minimize overcontrolling and to prevent creeping but not applied to such a degree that control movement is limited. Many helicopters equipped for instrument flight contain stability augmentation systems or an autopilot to help relieve aviator workload.

SECTION III – INSTRUMENT TAKEOFF

2-29. Instrument takeoff (ITO) is accomplished by referring to outside visual references and flight instruments. The amount of attention given to each reference varies with the individual, aircraft type, and existing weather conditions. ITO is a composite visual and instrument takeoff when conditions permit and is not be confused with a hooded takeoff. ITO procedures and techniques are invaluable aids during takeoffs at night, toward and over water or desert areas and during reduced visibility. Immediate transition to instrument references is necessary any time that disorientation occurs or when outside visual references become unreliable. Procedures and techniques described here are modified, as necessary, to conform to the appropriate aircrew training manual (ATM).

PREPARING

2-30. Before performing an ITO, an aviator performs a before-takeoff check of flight and navigation instruments as well as flight publications. Select appropriate navigational aids (NAVAIDs) to be used for the departure, and set navigation instruments and switches as required; ATC clearance and departure procedures (DPs) must be thoroughly understood. Review of an emergency return approach should include frequencies; final approach course; DA/DH or MDA and minimum safe, sector, or emergency safe altitudes; and specific duties briefed to all crew members.

2-31. Adjust the attitude indicator, as appropriate. After aligning the helicopter with the runway or takeoff pad, prevent forward movement by setting the parking brake, if the aircraft is equipped with a wheel-type landing gear. Apply sufficient friction to the collective pitch control to minimize overcontrolling and prevent creeping. Avoid excessive friction because it limits collective pitch movement.

PERFORMING FROM HOVER/GROUND

2-32. An ITO may be accomplished from a hover or the ground as visibility restrictions permit. A composite takeoff is accomplished using normal visual meteorological conditions (VMC) procedures while combining reference to flight instruments with outside visual references, providing the aviator with a smooth transition to instrument meteorological conditions (IMC) flight. ITOs may be accomplished entirely on instruments because of visibility restrictions induced by rotor downwash on dust, sand, or snow. Helicopters often operate from unprepared or remote locations in the presence of loose dirt or snow; this debris within the downwash can affect pitot-static instrumentation. Aircrew manuals warn that airspeed indications should be considered unreliable when forward airspeed is less than 25 to 40 knots depending upon aircraft size and weight. In addition, altimeters and VSIs actually indicate a loss of altitude as power is applied for takeoff.

TAKEOFF

2-33. After rechecking instruments for proper operation, commence takeoff (Figure 2-8, page 2-10) by applying collective pitch of a predetermined power setting. Add power smoothly and steadily to gain airspeed and altitude simultaneously and prevent settling to the ground. Helicopters with wheel-type landing gear may elect to make running takeoffs if operating from smooth surfaces. As power is applied and the helicopter becomes airborne, maintain desired heading with the pedals and use cyclic to maintain desired ITO pitch attitude. When obtaining a positive climb indication, adjust the pitch attitude as specified in the ATM. When takeoff attitude is established, cross-check the VSI and altimeter to ensure that the helicopter is still climbing. While the aircraft is below airspeeds required for accurate altitude or VSI readings, predetermined power settings and pitch attitudes provide the most reliable source of climb information. A cross-check is started at the time that the aircraft leaves the ground and should include all available instruments to provide a smooth transition to coordinated flight.

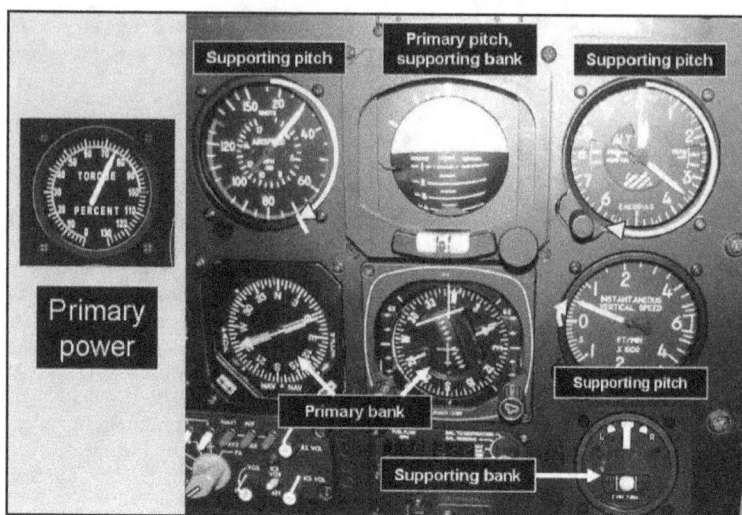

Figure 2-8. Instrument takeoff indications

COMMON ERRORS

2-34. Common errors during ITOs include the following:
- Failure to maintain heading.
- Overcontrolling pedals.
- Failure to use required power.
- Failure to adjust pitch attitude as climbing airspeed is reached.

SECTION IV – STRAIGHT-AND-LEVEL FLIGHT

2-35. Straight-and-level flight consists of maintaining the desired altitude, heading, airspeed, and pedal trim. Use pitch attitude to maintain or adjust airspeed, bank control to maintain or adjust heading, and power control to maintain or adjust altitude.

PITCH ATTITUDE CONTROL

2-36. Pitch attitude is the angular relation of the helicopter's longitudinal axis and natural horizon. If available, the attitude indicator establishes desired pitch attitude. In level flight, pitch attitude varies with airspeed and center of gravity. At a constant altitude and stabilized airspeed, pitch attitude is approximately level (Figure 2-4, page 2-4).

ATTITUDE INDICATOR

2-37. The attitude indicator provides a direct indication of the helicopter's pitch attitude. In visual flight, the cyclic is used to raise and lower the nose of the helicopter in relation to the natural horizon to attain desired pitch attitude. During instrument flight, follow the same procedure in raising or lowering the miniature aircraft in relation to the horizon bar.

2-38. The attitude indicator may show small misrepresentations of pitch attitude during maneuvers involving acceleration, deceleration, or turns. These misrepresentations are caused by delays following flight control inputs, known as control lag, and delays in instrument readings, known as instrument lag. Precession errors can be detected quickly by cross-checking other pitch instruments.

2-39. The miniature aircraft, properly adjusted on the attitude indicator while on the ground, does not generally require readjustment in flight. If the miniature aircraft is not located on the horizon bar after leveling off at cruising airspeed, adjust the miniature aircraft while maintaining level flight with other pitch instruments. Once the miniature aircraft is properly adjusted, the aviator is now provided with an accurate pitch attitude. When making initial pitch attitude corrections to maintain altitude, changes are small and smoothly applied. The initial movement of the horizon bar should not exceed one bar width high or low. If further change is required, an additional correction of one-half bar normally corrects any deviation from desired altitude. This one-and-one-half bar correction is normally the maximum pitch attitude correction from level flight attitude. Cross-check other pitch-related instruments to determine whether a correction to the pitch attitude is sufficient. If more correction is required or if the airspeed varies more than 10 knots from that desired, the pilot must make the appropriate power setting.

ALTIMETER

2-40. The altimeter indirectly indicates pitch attitude in straight-and-level flight. Because the altitude should remain constant, deviation from the desired altitude shows a need for a change in pitch attitude and, if necessary, power. When losing altitude, raise the pitch attitude and, if necessary, add power; conversely, when gaining altitude, lower the pitch attitude and, if necessary, reduce power.

2-41. The rate at which the altimeter moves helps in determining pitch attitude. A very slow movement indicates a small deviation from the desired pitch attitude, while fast movement indicates a large deviation. Make corrective action promptly with small control changes. Movement of the altimeter is always corrected by two distinct changes: a change of attitude to stop the altimeter and then a change of attitude to return smoothly to the desired altitude. If the altitude and airspeed are 100 feet and 10 knots below that desired, respectively, apply power along with an increase of pitch attitude. If the altitude and airspeed are 100 feet and 10 knots above that desired, reduce power and lower the pitch attitude. A small lag in the movement of the altimeter is customary; however, for practical purposes, consider the altimeter as providing an immediate indication of a change or a need for change in pitch attitude.

VERTICAL SPEED INDICATOR

2-42. The initial movement of the vertical speed needle is nearly instantaneous and indicates vertical movement of the helicopter. Use the VSI with the altimeter to maintain level flight. If a movement on the VSI is detected, use corrective measures to return to a zero indication. If corrections are made promptly, there is usually little or no change in altitude. If the pilot does not zero the needle of the VSI immediately, results on the altimeter reflect as a gain or loss of altitude. Reduce overcontrolling by neutralizing the controls to allow the pitch attitude to stabilize; readjust the pitch attitude by noting indications of other pitch instruments such as the attitude indicator.

2-43. Occasionally, the VSI may be slightly out of calibration, erroneously indicating a slight climb or descent when the helicopter is actually in level flight. The aviator should compensate for this error when the VSI for pitch control has not been properly adjusted by maintenance personnel such as in the following example: if the VSI shows a descent of 100 FPM when the helicopter is in level flight, use that indication as level flight; any deviation from that reading indicates a change in attitude.

AIRSPEED INDICATOR

2-44. In addition to indicating airspeed, the airspeed indicator indirectly indicates helicopter pitch attitude. With a given power setting and pitch attitude, airspeed remains constant. If airspeed increases, the nose is too low and should be raised; if airspeed decreases, the nose is too high and should be lowered. A rapid airspeed change indicates a large change in pitch attitude; a slow airspeed change indicates a small change in pitch attitude. Little lag accompanies indications of the airspeed indicator. If, while the aviator is making attitude changes, some lag exists between control application and change of airspeed, this most likely occurs because of cyclic control lag. Departure from desired airspeed because of an inadvertent pitch attitude change also results in altitude change. An airspeed increase because of a low pitch attitude results in a decrease in altitude. Correction in pitch attitude regains airspeed and altitude.

BANK CONTROL

2-45. A helicopter's bank attitude is the angular relation of its lateral axis and natural horizon. To maintain a straight course in visual flight, keep the helicopter's lateral axis level with the natural horizon. Assuming that the helicopter is in coordinated flight, any deviation from a laterally level attitude produces a turn (Figure 2-5, page 2-4).

ATTITUDE INDICATOR

2-46. The attitude indicator directly indicates the helicopter's bank attitude. For instrument flight, the miniature aircraft and horizon bar of the attitude indicator are substituted for the actual helicopter and natural horizon. Any change in the helicopter's bank attitude is indicated instantly by the miniature aircraft. If the helicopter is properly trimmed and the rotor tilts, a turn begins. The turn can be stopped by leveling the miniature aircraft with the horizon bar. The ball in the turn-and-slip indicator is always kept centered through proper pedal trim.

2-47. Bank angle is indicated by the pointer on the banking scale at the top of the instrument. Small bank angles, which may not be seen by observing the miniature aircraft, can easily be determined by referring to the banking scale pointer. Pitch-and-bank attitudes can be determined simultaneously on the attitude indicator. Even if the miniature aircraft is not level with the horizon bar, pitch attitude can be established by observing the relative position of the miniature aircraft and horizon bar.

2-48. The attitude indicator may show small misrepresentations of bank attitude during maneuvers involving turns. This precession error can be immediately detected by closely cross-checking other bank instruments. The aviator normally notices precession when the aircraft rolls out of a turn. If, on the completion of a turn, the miniature aircraft is level and helicopter is still turning, make a small change of bank attitude to center the turn needle and stop movement of the heading indicator.

HEADING INDICATOR

2-49. In coordinated flight, the heading indicator indirectly indicates the helicopter's bank attitude. A banked helicopter turns; however, when the lateral axis of the helicopter is level, the helicopter flies straight. Therefore, in coordinated flight, the heading indicator shows a constant heading when the helicopter is level laterally. A deviation from desired heading indicates a bank in the direction of the turn. A small bank angle is indicated by a slow change of heading; a large bank angle is indicated by a rapid change. When noticing a turn, apply opposite cyclic until the heading indicator indicates the desired heading while maintaining trim. When making correction to the desired heading, do not use a bank angle greater than that required to achieve a standard rate turn. In addition, if the number of degrees of change is small, limit the bank angle to the number of degrees to be turned. Bank angles greater than a standard rate turn require more skill and precision. During straight-and-level flight, the heading indicator is the primary reference for bank control.

TURN INDICATOR

2-50. During coordinated flight, the needle of the turn-and-slip indicator indirectly indicates helicopter bank attitude. When the needle is displaced from the vertical position, the helicopter is turning in the direction of displacement. Thus, if the needle is displaced to the left, the helicopter is turning left; bringing the needle back to vertical position with the cyclic produces straight flight. Close observation of the needle is necessary to accurately interpret small deviations from the desired position.

2-51. Cross-check the ball of the turn-and-slip indicator to determine if the helicopter is in coordinated flight. If the rotor is laterally level and torque is properly compensated for by pedal pressure, the ball remains in the center. To center the ball, level the helicopter laterally by reference to other bank instruments and then center the ball with pedal trim. Torque correction pressures vary as power changes are made. Always check the ball following such changes.

POWER CONTROL

2-52. Establishing specific power settings is accomplished through collective pitch adjustments and throttle control, where necessary. For turbine-powered helicopters, power is observed on the torque gauge. At a given airspeed, a specific power setting determines whether the helicopter is in level flight, a climb, or a descent (for example, cruising airspeed maintained with cruising power results in level flight). By increasing the power setting and holding airspeed constant, the helicopter climbs. Conversely, by decreasing power and holding airspeed constant, the helicopter descends. A turbine-powered helicopter requires a 10 to 15 percent change in torque to establish climbs or descents if airspeed and attitude remain the same.

2-53. When the aviator increases power in a helicopter with a counterclockwise main rotor blade rotation, the added power causes the nose to pitch up and yaw to the right. When power is reduced, the nose pitches down and yaws to the left. The yawing effect is most pronounced in single-rotor helicopters and is absent in counterrotating helicopters. The aviator applies pedal trim during power changes to compensate for unwanted yaw.

2-54. To maintain constant altitude and airspeed in level flight, coordinate pitch attitude and power control. The relationship between altitude and airspeed determines the need for a change in power/pitch attitude. If altitude is constant and airspeed is high or low, change power to obtain the desired airspeed. During changes in power, make an accurate interpretation of the altimeter and counteract deviation from the desired altitude by an appropriate change of pitch attitude. If altitude is low and airspeed is high, or vice versa, a change in pitch attitude alone may return the helicopter to proper altitude and airspeed. If airspeed and altitude are both low or high, a change in both power and pitch attitude is necessary.

2-55. Changes in airspeed can easily be made if the approximate power settings are known for various airspeeds flown. When airspeed changes any appreciable amount, adjust torque about 5 percent over or under the setting necessary to maintain the new airspeed. Include the torque meter in the cross-check to determine when proper adjustments have been accomplished. As the airspeed changes, adjust pitch attitude to sustain a constant altitude while maintaining a constant heading throughout the change. As desired airspeed is approached, adjust power to the new cruising power setting and further adjust pitch attitude to maintain altitude. Torque adjustments of about 5 percent result in a change of airspeed at a moderate rate, which allows time to adjust pitch and bank smoothly. Figures 2-9 and 2-10, page 2-14, illustrate instrument indications for straight-and-level flight at normal cruise and during the transition from normal cruise to slow cruise. After the aviator stabilizes airspeed at slow cruise, the attitude indicator shows an approximate level pitch attitude.

Figure 2-9. Straight-and-level flight at normal cruise speed

Figure 2-10. Straight-and-level flight with airspeed deceasing

2-56. The altimeter is the primary pitch instrument during level flight, whether the aircraft is flying at a constant airspeed or during a change in airspeed. Altitude should not change during airspeed transitions. The heading indicator remains the primary bank instrument. When airspeed changes any appreciable amount, the torque meter is momentarily the primary instrument for power control; when the aircraft approaches the desired airspeed, the airspeed indicator again becomes the primary instrument for power control.

2-57. Straight-and-level flight relies on a cross-check of pitch-and-bank instruments and power control instruments. With a constant power setting, a normal cross-check should be satisfactory. When changing power, increase the rate of the cross-check to cover pitch-and-bank instruments to counteract deviations.

COMMON ERRORS

2-58. Common errors made during straight-and-level flight include the following:

- Failure to maintain altitude.
- Failure to maintain heading.
- Overcontrolling pitch and bank during corrections.
- Improper use of power.
- Failure to maintain proper pedal trim.
- Failure to cross-check all available instruments.

SECTION V – STRAIGHT CLIMBS AND DESCENTS

2-59. Any power setting and load condition has only one airspeed that provides the most efficient rate of climb. Consult climb data for the helicopter to determine this setting. The technique varies according to airspeed on entry and whether the maneuver will be a constant-airspeed or constant-rate climb.

CLIMBS

ENTRY

2-60. To enter a constant-airspeed climb from cruise airspeed when climb speed is lower than cruise speed, simultaneously increase power to the climb power setting and adjust pitch attitude to the approximate climb attitude. An increase in power causes the helicopter to start climbing, and only slight back cyclic pressure is required to change from level to climb attitude. Use the attitude indicator to accomplish pitch change. If transition from level flight to a climb is smooth, the VSI shows an immediate upward trend and stops at a rate appropriate to the stabilized airspeed and attitude (Figure 2-11, page 2-16).

Figure 2-11. Climb entry

2-61. When the helicopter stabilizes on a constant airspeed and attitude, the airspeed indicator becomes primary for pitch. The torque meter continues to be primary for power and is monitored closely to determine if the proper climb power setting is being maintained (Figure 2-12).

Figure 2-12. Stabilized constant airspeed climb

2-62. The technique and procedures for entering a constant-rate climb are similar to a constant-airspeed climb. For training purposes, a constant-rate climb is entered from climb airspeed. In helicopters with low climb rates, 500 FPM is appropriate; in helicopters capable of high climb rates, use a rate of 1,000 FPM.

2-63. Entering a constant-rate climb means increasing power to the approximate setting for the desired rate. As power is applied, the airspeed indicator is primary for pitch until vertical speed approaches the desired rate. The VSI then becomes primary for pitch. Change pitch attitude accordingly with the attitude indicator to maintain the desired vertical speed. When the VSI becomes primary for pitch, the airspeed indicator becomes primary for power (Figure 2-13). Adjust power to maintain desired airspeed. Closely coordinate pitch attitude and power corrections. If vertical speed is correct but airspeed is low, add power. As power increases, lowering the pitch attitude slightly may become necessary to avoid increasing the vertical rate. Adjust pitch attitude smoothly to avoid overcontrolling. Small power corrections are usually sufficient to return airspeed to the desired indication.

Figure 2-13. Stabilized constant-rate climb

LEVEL-OFF

2-64. Level-off from a constant-airspeed climb is started before reaching the desired altitude. Although the amount of lead varies with the helicopter being flown and piloting technique, the most important factor is vertical speed. Use 10 percent of vertical velocity as the lead point as in the following example.

Example of Using Lead to Level Off

If the climb rate is 500 FPM, initiate level-off at about 50 feet before the aircraft reaches the desired altitude. When proper lead altitude is reached, the altimeter becomes primary for pitch. Adjust pitch attitude to level flight attitude for that airspeed, and cross-check the altimeter and vertical speed indicator to determine when level flight has been attained at the desired altitude.

2-65. To level-off at cruise airspeed if this speed is higher than climb airspeed, leave power at the climb power setting until airspeed approaches cruise airspeed and then reduce to cruise power setting. Level-off from a constant-rate climb is accomplished in the same manner as level-off from a constant-airspeed climb.

DESCENTS

ENTRY

2-66. If airspeed is higher than descending airspeed and a constant-airspeed descent at the descending airspeed is required, reduce power to the descending power setting and maintain a constant altitude using cyclic pitch control. When the aircraft is approaching the descending airspeed, the airspeed indicator becomes primary for pitch and the torque meter is primary for power. As airspeed is held constant, the helicopter begins to descend. For a constant-rate descent, reduce power to the approximate setting for the desired rate. If descent begins at the descending airspeed, the airspeed indicator is primary for pitch until the VSI approaches the desired rate. At this time, the VSI becomes primary for pitch and the airspeed indicator becomes primary for power. Coordinate power and pitch attitude control as for constant-rate climbs.

LEVEL-OFF

2-67. Level-off from a constant-airspeed descent may be made at descending airspeed or cruise airspeed (if this is higher than descending airspeed). As in a climb level-off, the amount of lead depends on descent rate and control technique. For a level-off at descending airspeed, lead should be about 10 percent of vertical speed. At lead altitude, increase power to the setting necessary to maintain descending airspeed in level flight. At this point, the altimeter becomes primary for pitch and the airspeed indicator becomes primary for power.

2-68. To level-off at a higher airspeed than descending airspeed, increase power about 100 to 150 feet before reaching the desired altitude. The power setting should be what is necessary to maintain desired airspeed in level flight. Hold vertical speed constant until about 50 feet above desired altitude. At this point, the altimeter becomes primary for pitch and the airspeed indicator becomes primary for power. Level-off from a constant-rate descent should be accomplished in the same manner as level-off from a constant-airspeed descent.

COMMON ERRORS

2-69. Common errors made during straight climbs and descents include the following:

- Failure to maintain heading.
- Improper use of power.
- Poor control of pitch attitude.
- Failure to maintain proper pedal trim.
- Failure to level-off on desired altitude.

SECTION VI – TURNS

2-70. Pitch, bank, and power principles related to straight-and-level flight apply while performing level turns. This maneuver requires an understanding of how to enter; maintain bank, altitude, and airspeed during; and recover from the turn. Turns are classified as normal (standard rate or less) or steep. Most aviators practice steep turns using 30 degrees of bank, which is the maximum bank angle recommended under instrument conditions.

2-71. Helicopters normally operate under instrument conditions between 80 and 120 knots. TAS determines the bank angle necessary to maintain a standard-rate turn. To determine the approximate bank angle, divide airspeed by 10 and add one-half of the result as shown in the following example.

Example of Determining Bank Angle
At 80 knots (kt), about 12 degrees of bank is required (80 ÷ 10 = 8 + 4 = 12); at 120 kt, about 18 degrees of bank is required.

2-72. Enter a turn by applying lateral cyclic in the desired turn direction. Enter using the attitude indicator to establish approximate bank angle. When the turn indicator indicates a standard-rate turn, the turn indicator becomes primary for bank. The attitude indicator is now a supporting instrument. During level turns, the altimeter is primary for pitch and the airspeed indicator is primary for power (Figure 2-14, page 2-19). If an increase in power is required to maintain airspeed, slight forward cyclic pressure may be required because the helicopter tends to pitch up as collective pitch angle is increased. Apply pedal trim, as required, to keep the ball centered.

Figure 2-14. Standard rate turn to the left

2-73. Return to straight-and-level flight by applying cyclic in the direction opposite the turn. The rate of rollout is the same used when rolling into the turn. The attitude indicator becomes the primary reference for bank during turn recovery. When the helicopter is about level, the heading indicator is primary for bank as in straight-and-level flight. Cross-check the airspeed indicator and ball to sustain airspeed and pedal trim.

PREDETERMINED HEADING

2-74. A helicopter turns as long as its lateral axis is tilted; therefore, recovery starts before the desired heading is reached. The amount of lead varies with the turn rate and piloting technique. As a guide, when making a standard rate turn, use a lead of one-half the bank angle as shown in the following example.

Example of Using Lead Point
If using a 12° bank angle, use half, or 6°, as the lead point for rolling out on the desired heading.

2-75. The bank angle should never exceed the number of degrees to be turned. As in any standard rate turn, the recovery rate should be the same as the rate for entry. During turns to predetermined headings, cross-check primary and supporting pitch, bank, and power instruments closely.

TIMED

2-76. A timed turn is when the clock and turn-and-slip indicator are used to change a heading a definite number of degrees in a given time. Using a standard-rate turn, a helicopter turns 45 degrees in 15 seconds. Using a half-standard-rate turn, a helicopter turns 45 degrees in 30 seconds. Timed turns can be used if the heading indicator becomes inoperative.

2-77. Before performing timed turns, the turn coordinator must be calibrated to determine the accuracy of its indications. To accomplish calibration, establish a standard-rate turn by referring to the turn-and-slip indicator. As the sweep second hand of the clock passes a cardinal point (12, 3, 6, or 9), check the heading on the heading indicator. While holding the indicated rate of turn constant, note heading changes at 10-second intervals. If the helicopter turns more or less than 30 degrees in that interval, a smaller or larger deflection of the needle is necessary to produce a standard-rate turn. When calibrating the turn-and-slip indicator during turns in each direction, note corrected deflections. If any deflections are noted, apply them during all timed turns.

2-78. The same cross-check and control technique used to make turns to a predetermined heading is used in making timed turns, except substitute the clock for the heading indicator. The needle of the turn-and-slip indicator is primary for bank control, the altimeter is primary for pitch control, and the airspeed indicator is primary for power control. Begin the roll in when the clock's second hand passes a cardinal point, hold the turn at the calibrated standard-rate indication (or half standard rate for small changes in heading), and begin roll-out when the computed number of seconds has elapsed. If roll-in and rollout rates are the same, the time taken during entry and recovery need not be considered in the time computation. Check the heading indicator for the accuracy of turns when practicing timed turns with a full instrument panel. Use the magnetic compass at the completion of the turn to check accuracy, taking compass deviation errors into consideration when executing turns without the heading indicator.

CHANGING AIRSPEED

2-79. Changing airspeed in turns is an effective maneuver for increasing proficiency in all three basic instrument skills. Because the maneuver involves simultaneous changes in all components of control, proper execution requires a rapid cross-check and interpretation as well as smooth control. Proficiency also contributes to confidence in instruments during attitude and power changes involved in more complex maneuvers.

2-80. Pitch and power control techniques are the same as those used during airspeed changes in straight-and-level flight. As discussed previously, the bank angle necessary for a given turn rate is proportional to the TAS. Turns are executed at standard rate; therefore, the bank angle must be varied in direct proportion to airspeed change to maintain a constant turn rate. During a reduction of airspeed, decrease the bank angle and increase the pitch attitude to maintain altitude and a standard-rate turn.

2-81. The altimeter and needle on the turn indicator should remain constant throughout the turn. The altimeter is primary for pitch control, and the turn needle is primary for bank control. The torque meter is primary for power control while airspeed is changing. As airspeed approaches the new indication, the airspeed indicator becomes primary for power control.

2-82. Methods of changing airspeed in turns include changing airspeed after the turn is established and initiating an airspeed change simultaneously with turn entry. Regardless of the method, the rate of cross-check must be increased as power is reduced. As the helicopter decelerates, check the altimeter and VSI for pitch changes and bank instruments for bank changes. If the needle of the turn-and-slip indicator shows a deviation from the desired deflection, change the bank. Adjust the pitch attitude to maintain altitude. When approaching the desired airspeed, the airspeed indicator becomes primary for power control. Adjust the torque meter to maintain desired airspeed. Use pedal trim to ensure the maneuver is coordinated. Until the control technique is smooth, frequently cross-check the attitude indicator to keep from overcontrolling and provide approximate bank angles appropriate for changing airspeeds.

COMPASS

2-83. Use of gyroscopic heading indicators makes heading control easy; however, if the heading indicator fails, use the magnetic compass for heading reference. When making compass-only turns, adjust for lead or lag created by acceleration and deceleration errors (refer to Chapter 1) so that rollout occurs on the desired heading. When the aviator turns to a heading of north, lead for the rollout must include the number of degrees of latitude plus the lead normally used in turn recovery as described in the following example.

Example of Using the Magnetic Compass During Turn to the North
When turning from an easterly direction to north, where the latitude is 30 degrees, start rollout when the compass reads 037 degrees (30 degrees plus 1/2 the 15 degrees bank angle, or an amount appropriate for the rollout rate).

2-84. During a turn to a south heading, maintain the turn until the compass passes south the number of degrees of latitude minus normal rollout lead. This procedure is described in the following example.

Example of Using the Magnetic Compass During Turn to the South

When turning from an easterly direction to the south, start rollout when the magnetic compass reads 203° (180 degrees plus 30 degrees minus 1/2 of the 15 degrees bank angle). When making similar turns from a westerly direction, begin rollout at 323 degrees for a turn north and 157 degrees for a turn south.

2-85. A quick reference diagram is provided to help visualize the correction Figure 2-15 is a compass turn correction diagram.

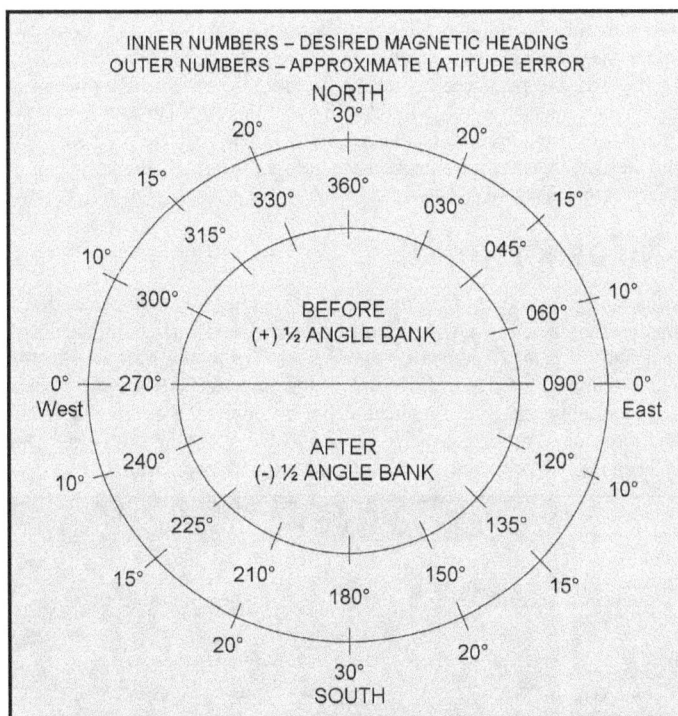

INNER NUMBERS – DESIRED MAGNETIC HEADING
OUTER NUMBERS – APPROXIMATE LATITUDE ERROR

BEFORE (+) ½ ANGLE BANK

AFTER (-) ½ ANGLE BANK

Figure 2-15. Compass turn correction diagram

2-86. A simple method of calculating compass turns is to use timed turns. Take the difference between current heading and desired heading, and divide by three (standard rate turn of 3 degrees per second). The product is the number of seconds to enter into a standard-rate turn to arrive at the desired heading (table 2-2, page 2-22). This procedure works in any hemisphere/latitude, regardless of turning direction, and eliminates the need to memorize a chart or more complicated mathematical formula partly based on latitude. This procedure also limits distraction caused by direct and frequent viewing of the magnetic compass in the turn.

Table 2-2. Compass turn computation

Current heading	Desired heading	Headings difference divided by 3	Seconds in turn
120°	030°	90° ÷ 3	30
180°	280°	100° ÷ 3	33
320°	020°	60° ÷ 3	20
225°	140°	85° ÷ 3	28
Enter standard rate turn for the computed seconds, stop the turn, and arrive at the desired heading.			

THIRTY-DEGREE BANK

2-87. A 30-degree bank turn is seldom necessary, or advisable, in IMC and is considered a steep turn in a helicopter. Although entry and recovery techniques are the same as for other turns, it is more difficult in a 30-degree bank turn to control pitch because of the decrease in vertical lift as bank increases. Because of this decrease, there is a tendency to lose altitude/airspeed; therefore, to maintain a constant altitude and airspeed, additional power is required. The altimeter and VSI will indicate necessary corrections. Check the indications on the attitude indicator, and make necessary adjustments. Recheck the altimeter and VSI to determine whether the correction was adequate.

CLIMBING AND DESCENDING

2-88. The climbing and descending turn techniques for straight climbs and descents and those for standard-rate turns are combined. Start the climb or descent and turn simultaneously. The primary and supporting instruments for a stabilized constant airspeed left climbing turn are illustrated in Figure 2-16. Leveling-off from a climbing or descending turn is the same as leveling-off from a straight climb or descent. Returning to straight-and-level flight can occur by stopping the turn and leveling-off, leveling-off and stopping the turn, or simultaneously leveling-off and stopping the turn. During climbing and descending turns, keep the ball of the turn indicator centered with pedal trim.

Figure 2-16. Stabilized left climbing turn, constant airspeed

COMMON ERRORS

2-89. Common errors made during turns include the following:

- Failure to maintain desired turn rate and airspeed.
- Failure to maintain altitude in level turns.
- Variation in the rate of entry and recovery.
- Failure to use proper lead in turns to a heading.
- Failure to properly compute time during timed turns.
- Failure to use proper leads and lags during compass turns.
- Improper use of power.
- Failure to use proper pedal trim.

SECTION VII – OTHER MANEUVERS

UNUSUAL ATTITUDES

2-90. Any maneuver not required for normal helicopter instrument flight is an unusual attitude and may be caused by any one or a combination of factors such as turbulence, disorientation, instrument failure, confusion, preoccupation with cockpit duties, carelessness in cross-checking, errors in instrument interpretation, or lack of proficiency in aircraft control. Because of the instability characteristics of the helicopter, unusual attitudes can be extremely critical. When experiencing an unusual attitude, make quick attitude corrections to straight-and-level flight then return to desired airspeed and altitude as soon as possible.

2-91. To recover from an unusual attitude, correct bank-and-pitch attitude and adjust power as necessary. All components are changed almost simultaneously with little lead of one over the other. Aviators must perform this task with and without the attitude indicator. If the helicopter is in a climbing or descending turn, correct bank, pitch, and power. The bank attitude is corrected by referring to the turn-and-slip indicator and attitude indicator. Pitch attitude is corrected by reference to the altimeter, airspeed indicator, VSI, and attitude indicator. Adjust power by referring to the airspeed indicator and torque meter. Because displacement of the controls used in recoveries from unusual attitudes may be greater than those for normal flight, make careful adjustments as straight-and-level flight is approached. Cross-check other instruments closely to avoid overcontrolling.

COMMON ERRORS

2-92. Common errors made during unusual attitude recoveries include the following:

- Failure to make proper pitch, bank, and power corrections.
- Overcontrolling pitch/bank attitude and power.
- Excessive loss of altitude.

AUTOROTATIONS

2-93. A straight-ahead or turning autorotation is practiced by reference to instruments ensuring that an aviator can take prompt corrective action to maintain positive aircraft control in case of engine failure. To enter autorotation, reduce collective pitch, smoothly maintaining safe rotor revolutions per minute (RPM), and apply pedal trim to keep the ball of the turn-and-slip indicator centered. The pitch attitude of the helicopter should be approximately level as shown by the attitude indicator. The airspeed indicator is the primary pitch instrument and is adjusted to recommended autorotation speed. The heading indicator is primary for bank in a straight-ahead autorotation. In a turning autorotation, a standard-rate turn is maintained by reference to the needle of the turn-and-slip indicator.

COMMON ERRORS

2-94. Common errors made during autorotation include the following:

- Uncoordinated entry because of improper pedal trim.
- Poor airspeed control because of improper pitch attitude.
- Poor heading control in straight-ahead autorotation.
- Failure to maintain proper rotor RPM and a standard-rate turn during turning autorotation.

Chapter 3

Fixed Wing Instrument Flight Maneuvers

Instrument flying techniques differ according to aircraft type, class, performance capability, and instrumentation. Therefore, this chapter augments Chapter 2 and covers only the differences for fixed wing aircraft. Recommended procedures, performance data, operating limitations, and flight characteristics of a particular aircraft are available in the appropriate operator's manual and ATM.

SECTION I – INSTRUMENT TAKEOFF

3-1. Aviator competency in ITO will provide the proficiency and confidence necessary for use of flight instruments during departures under conditions of low visibility, rain, low ceilings, or disorientation at night. A sudden rapid transition from visual to instrument flight can result in serious disorientation and control problems. ITO techniques vary with different types of airplanes, but the following method applies to most and should be accomplished according to the appropriate ATM and operator's manual.

Contents

TAKEOFF

3-2. Align the airplane with the centerline of the runway with the nose wheel straight. Lock or hold the brakes firmly to avoid creeping while preparing for takeoff. Slight changes in heading can be detected by setting the heading indicator with the nose index on the mark nearest the published runway heading. Make certain that the instrument is uncaged (if a caging feature is available) by rotating the knob after uncaging, and check for constant heading indication. Advance the power levers to an RPM that provides partial rudder control. Release the brakes, advancing the power smoothly to takeoff setting.

3-3. During the takeoff roll, hold the heading constant on the heading indicator by using the rudder. Multiengine propeller-driven airplanes also use differential power to maintain direction. The use of brakes to control heading usually results in overcontrolling and extending the takeoff roll and should be avoided. Any deviation in heading should be quickly corrected.

3-4. Heading and airspeed indicators must be cross-checked rapidly as the aircraft accelerates. The attitude indicator may falsely indicate a slight nose-up attitude. As flying speed is approached (about 15 to 25 knots below takeoff speed), smoothly apply elevator control for the desired takeoff attitude on the attitude indicator (about a two-bar-width climb indication for most airplanes). Continue with a quick cross-check of the heading indicator and attitude indicator as the airplane leaves the ground. Do not pull the aircraft off; fly the aircraft off while holding the attitude constant. Maintain pitch-and-bank control by referencing the attitude indicator, and make coordinated corrections in heading when indicated on the heading indicator. Cross-check the altimeter and VSI for a positive rate of climb (steady clockwise rotation of the altimeter needle at a rate that can be interpreted with experience and the VSI showing an appropriate stable rate of climb).

3-5. Raise the landing gear and flaps when the altimeter shows a safe altitude (about 100 feet), maintaining attitude by referencing the attitude indicator. Because of control pressure changes during gear and flap operation, overcontrolling is likely unless the aviator notes pitch indications accurately and quickly. Trim off control pressures necessary to hold the stable climb attitude. Check the altimeter, VSI, and airspeed for a smooth acceleration to the predetermined climb speed (altimeter and airspeed increasing, vertical speed stable). At climb speed, reduce power to the climb setting if required. Throughout the ITO, perform rapid cross-check and interpretation, along with positive and smooth control. During liftoff, the changing control reactions of gear and flap retraction and power reduction demand rapid cross-check, adjustment of control pressures, and accurate trim changes.

COMMON TAKEOFF ERRORS AND RESOLUTIONS

3-6. Common takeoff errors and resolutions include the following:

- Failure to perform an adequate cockpit check before takeoff; do not attempt instrument takeoffs with inoperative airspeed indicators (pitot tube obstructed), gyros caged, or controls locked.
- Improper alignment on the runway. Improper brake application may allow the airplane to creep after alignment; alignment with the nose wheel or tail wheel cocked may cause improper alignment on the runway.
- Improper application of power. Abrupt application of power complicates directional control; add power with a smooth, uninterrupted motion.
- Improper use of brakes. Incorrect seat or rudder pedal adjustment, with feet in an uncomfortable position, often causes inadvertent application of brakes and excessive heading changes.
- Overcontrolling rudder pedals. This fault may be due to late recognition of heading changes, tension on the controls, misinterpretation of the heading indicator (and correcting in the wrong direction), and failure to appreciate changing effectiveness of rudder control as the aircraft accelerates; heading changes observed and corrected instantly with small movement of the rudder pedals reduce swerving tendencies.
- Failure to maintain attitude after becoming airborne. If the aviator is reacting to proprioceptive sensations when the airplane lifts off, pitch control is guesswork; do not allow excessive pitch or apply excessive forward-elevator pressure, depending on reaction to trim changes.
- Inadequate cross-check. Fixations are likely during trim changes, attitude changes, gear and flap retractions, and power changes; after checking an instrument or applying a control, continue the cross-check and note the effect of the control during the next cross-check sequence.
- Inadequate interpretation of instruments; failure to immediately understand instrument indications indicates that further study of the maneuver is necessary.

SECTION II – STRAIGHT-AND-LEVEL FLIGHT

PITCH CONTROL

3-7. The pitch attitude of an airplane is the angle between the longitudinal axis of the airplane and the actual horizon. In level flight, the pitch attitude varies with airspeed and load. For training purposes, the latter factor can normally be disregarded. At a constant airspeed, there is only one specific pitch attitude for level flight. At slow cruise speeds, the level-flight attitude is nose-high; at fast cruise speeds, the level-flight attitude is nose-low. Figure 3-1, page 3-3 shows the attitude at normal cruise speeds. The pitch instruments are the attitude indicator, altimeter, VSI, and airspeed indicator.

Figure 3-1. Pitch attitude and airspeed in level flight

ATTITUDE INDICATOR

3-8.   The attitude indicator is the same as in a helicopter. Desired pitch attitude is obtained by using the elevator control (control wheel, not cyclic) to raise or lower the miniature aircraft in relation to the horizon bar. Properly adjusting the miniature aircraft on the attitude indicator on the ground before takeoff should indicate approximately level flight at normal cruise speed after the aviator completes level-off from a climb. If further adjustment of the miniature aircraft is necessary, the other pitch instruments must be used to maintain level flight while the adjustment is made.

3-9.   In practicing pitch control for level flight using only the attitude indicator, restrict the displacement of the horizon bar initially to a bar width up or down, then a half-bar width, and finally, a one and-one-half bar width.

3-10. Pitch attitude changes for corrections to level flight by reference to instruments are much smaller than those commonly used for visual flight. When the airplane is correctly trimmed for level flight, the elevator displacement and the control pressures necessary to effect these standard pitch changes are usually very slight. The following hints help determine how much elevator control pressure is required:

- Relax, and learn to control using the senses rather than muscle; considerable conscious effort is needed to perfect this technique during the early stages of instrument training. A tight grip on the controls makes feeling control pressure changes difficult.
- Make smooth and small pitch changes with a positive pressure; practice these small corrections until becoming proficient in making pitch corrections up or down, freezing (holding constant) the one-half, full, and one-and-one-half bar widths on the attitude indicator.
- Avoid unnecessary inputs to the flight controls. With the airplane properly trimmed for level flight, momentarily release all pressure on the elevator control; the airplane should remain stable and will maintain level flight if left alone when properly trimmed. Some aviators may find it difficult to resist the impulse to move the controls even when their eyes provide data that no control change is called for.

ALTIMETER

3-11. At constant power, any deviation from level flight (except in turbulent air) must be the result of a pitch change. Therefore, the altimeter indirectly indicates the pitch attitude in level flight (assuming constant power). Because the altitude should remain constant when the airplane is in level flight, any deviation from the desired altitude signals the need for a pitch change. When the aircraft gains the desired altitude, the nose must be adjusted accordingly.

3-12. The rate of movement of the altimeter needle is as important as its direction of movement for maintaining level flight without the use of the attitude indicator. An excessive pitch deviation from level flight results in a relatively rapid change of altitude; a slight pitch deviation causes a slow change. Thus, if the altimeter needle moves rapidly clockwise, assume a considerable nose-high deviation from level-flight attitude. Conversely, if the needle moves slowly counterclockwise to indicate a slightly nose-low attitude, assume the pitch correction necessary to regain the desired altitude is small. The addition of the altimeter to the attitude indicator in cross-check assists in recognizing rate of movement of the altimeter needle.

3-13. When a pitch error is detected, corrective action should be taken promptly but with light control pressures and two distinct changes of attitude: a change of attitude to stop the needle movement and a change of attitude to return to the desired altitude.

3-14. Apply just enough elevator pressure to slow down the rate of needle movement when the needle movement indicates an altitude deviation. If needle movement slows down abruptly, ease off some of the pressure until the needle continues to move, but slowly. Slow needle movement means airplane attitude is close to level flight. Add a little more corrective pressure to stop the direction of needle movement. At this point, level flight has been attained; a reversal of needle movement means that the aircraft has passed through level flight. Relax the control pressures carefully, continuing to cross-check, because changing airspeed will cause changes in the effectiveness of a given control pressure. Adjust the pitch attitude with elevator pressure for the rate of change of altimeter needle movement that has been correlated with normal pitch corrections, and return to the desired altitude. For errors of less than 100 feet, use a half-bar-width correction. For errors in excess of 100 feet, use an initial full-bar-width correction.

VERTICAL SPEED INDICATOR

3-15. The VSI indirectly indicates pitch attitude and is both a trend and a rate instrument. As a trend instrument, the initial vertical movement of the airplane is shown immediately that, disregarding turbulence, can be considered a reflection of pitch change. To maintain level flight, use the VSI with the altimeter and attitude indicator. Note any up or down trend of the needle from zero and apply a very light corrective elevator pressure. As the needle returns to zero, relax the corrective pressure. If control pressures have been smooth and light, the needle reacts immediately and deliberately and the altimeter shows little or no change of altitude.

3-16. Lag refers to the delay involved before the needle attains a stable indication following a pitch change. Used as a rate instrument, lag characteristics of the VSI must be considered. Lag is directly proportional to the speed and magnitude of a pitch change. If a slow, smooth pitch change is initiated, the needle moves with minimum lag to a point of deflection corresponding to the extent of the pitch change and then stabilizes as the aerodynamic forces are balanced in the climb or descent. A large and abrupt pitch change produces erratic needle movement and a reverse indication and introduces greater time delay before the needle stabilizes. Aviators should not chase the needle when flight through turbulent conditions produces erratic needle movements.

3-17. When using the VSI as a rate instrument and cross-checking with the altimeter and attitude indicator to maintain level flight, keep in mind that the amount that the altimeter has moved from the desired altitude governs the rate necessary to return to that altitude. Make an attitude change resulting in a vertical-speed rate approximately double the error in altitude. If the altitude is off by 100 feet, for example, the rate of return should be about 200 FPM.

3-18. If altitude is off by more than 100 feet, the correction should be correspondingly greater but should never exceed the optimum rate of climb or descent for the airplane at a given airspeed and configuration. A deviation of more than 200 FPM from the desired rate of return is considered overcontrolling as described in the following example.

Example of How to Avoid Overcontrolling
If a pilot is attempting to return to an altitude at a rate of 300 FPM, he should avoid overcontrolling by not exceeding a rate of 500 FPM.

3-19. The VSI is the primary pitch instrument that the aviator uses to reestablish altitude. Occasionally, the VSI is slightly out of calibration and may indicate a climb or descent when the airplane is in level flight. If the instrument cannot be adjusted, consider the error when using the VSI for pitch control; for example, if the needle indicates a descent of 200 FPM while in level flight, use this indication as the zero position. Therefore, a 300 FPM rate of descent would be indicated on the VSI as a 500 FPM rate of descent.

AIRSPEED INDICATOR

3-20. The airspeed indicator presents an indirect indication of the pitch attitude. At a constant power setting and pitch attitude, airspeed remains constant. As the pitch attitude lowers, airspeed increases, and the nose should be raised. As the pitch attitude rises, airspeed decreases and the nose should be lowered. A rapid change in airspeed indicates a large pitch change, and a slow change of airspeed indicates a small pitch change.

3-21. The apparent lag in airspeed indications with pitch changes varies greatly among different airplanes and is due to the time required for the airplane to accelerate or decelerate when the pitch attitude is changed. There is no appreciable lag because of the construction or operation of the instrument. Small pitch changes, smoothly executed, result in an immediate change of airspeed.

3-22. Pitch control in level flight is a question of cross-check and interpretation of the instrument panel for the instrument information that will enable visualization and control of pitch attitude. Regardless of individual differences in cross-check technique, all aviators should use the instruments giving the best information for controlling the airplane in any given maneuver. Aviators should also check other instruments to aid in maintaining the important, or primary, instruments at the desired indication.

3-23. The primary instrument is one that gives the most pertinent information for a particular maneuver and is usually held at a constant indication. Which instrument is primary for a particular maneuver should be considered in the context of the specific airplane, weather conditions, aviator experience, operational conditions, and other factors. Attitude changes must be detected and interpreted instantly for immediate control action in high-performance airplanes. On the other hand, a reasonably proficient instrument aviator in a slower aircraft may rely more on the altimeter for primary pitch information, especially if the aviator determines that too much reliance on the attitude indicator fails to provide necessary precise attitude information. Whether the aviator decides to regard the altimeter or the attitude indicator as primary depends on which approach will best help control the attitude. In this manual, the altimeter is normally considered as the primary pitch instrument during level flight.

COMMON PITCH ERRORS AND RESOLUTIONS

3-24. Pitch errors and their resolutions include the following:
- Improper adjustment of the attitude indicator's miniature aircraft to the wings-level attitude; following initial level-off from a climb, check the attitude indicator and make any necessary adjustment in the miniature aircraft for level flight indication at normal cruise airspeed.
- Insufficient cross-check and interpretation of pitch instruments; for example, the airspeed indication is low. Believing that the aircraft is in a nose-high attitude, the aviator reacts with forward pressure without noting that a low power setting is the cause of the airspeed discrepancy; increase cross-check speed to include all relevant instrument indications before making a control response.

- Uncage the attitude indicator when the airplane is not in level flight. The altimeter and heading indicator must be stabilized with airspeed indication at normal cruise when the aviator pulls out the caging knob; this adjustment will cause the instrument to read straight-and-level at normal cruise airspeed.
- Failure to interpret the attitude indicator in terms of existing airspeed.
- Late pitch corrections. When the altimeter shows a 20-foot error, there is a reluctance to correct such an error, perhaps because of fear of overcontrolling. If overcontrolling is the error, the more that an aviator practices small corrections and determines the cause of overcontrolling, the closer the aviator is to holding the altitude. By tolerating a deviation, errors increase.
- Chasing the vertical-speed indications; this tendency can be corrected by proper cross-check of other pitch instruments as well as by increasing the understanding of the instrument characteristics.
- Using excessive pitch corrections for the altimeter evaluation; rushing a pitch correction by making a large pitch change usually compounds the existing error.
- Failure to maintain established pitch corrections. This is a common error associated with cross-check and trim errors; for example, having established a pitch change to correct an altitude error, an aviator tends to slow down the cross-check, waiting for the airplane to stabilize in the new pitch attitude. To maintain the attitude, continue to cross-check and trim off the pressures being held.
- Fixations during cross-check. After initiating a heading correction, aviators tend to become preoccupied with bank control and fail to notice a pitch error; likewise, during an airspeed change, unnecessary gazing at the power instrument is common. A small error in power setting is of less consequence than large altitude and heading errors.

BANK CONTROL

3-25. The bank attitude of an airplane is the angle between the lateral axis of the airplane and the natural horizon. To maintain a straight-and-level flight path, keep the wings of the airplane level with the horizon (assuming that the airplane is in coordinated flight). Any deviation from straight flight resulting from bank error should be corrected by coordinated aileron and rudder pressure.

3-26. The instruments used for bank control are the attitude indicator, heading indicator, and turn coordinator/turn-and-slip indicator. Control inputs affect each control instrument differently.

ATTITUDE INDICATOR

3-27. The attitude indicator is the same as the attitude indicator in a helicopter, but the desired bank is set by the aileron control (control wheel, not cyclic).

HEADING INDICATOR

3-28. The bank attitude of an aircraft in coordinated flight is shown on the heading indicator. A rapid movement of the heading indicator needle (or azimuth card in a directional gyro) indicates a large angle of bank, whereas a slow movement of the needle or card reflects a small angle of bank. By noting the rate of movement of the heading indicator and comparing that movement to the attitude indicator's degrees of bank, aviators will learn to look for important bank information on the heading indicator. This experience is especially useful when the attitude indicator's precession error makes a precise check of heading information necessary to maintain straight flight.

3-29. Make a correction to the desired heading using a bank angle no greater than the number of degrees to be turned when noting deviations from straight flight on the heading indicator. Limit bank corrections to a bank angle no greater than that required for a standard-rate turn. Use of larger bank angles, which normally results in overcontrolling and erratic bank control, requires a very high level of proficiency.

TURN COORDINATOR

3-30. A turn coordinator is not installed in most Army aircraft. However, this instrument is used in the single-engine phase of fixed wing qualification.

3-31. The miniature aircraft on the turn coordinator indirectly indicates bank attitude. When the miniature aircraft is level, the airplane is in straight flight. If the ball is centered, a left deflection of the miniature aircraft means that the left wing is low and the airplane is in a left turn. Thus, when the miniature aircraft is in a stabilized deflection, the airplane is turning in the direction indicated. Return to straight flight is accomplished by coordinated aileron and rudder pressure to level the miniature aircraft. Include the miniature aircraft in the cross-check, and correct for even the smallest deviations from the desired position. When used to maintain straight flight, control pressures must be applied very lightly and smoothly.

3-32. The ball of the turn coordinator is a separate instrument located under the miniature aircraft because the two instruments are used together. The ball instrument indicates the quality of the turn. If the ball is off center, the airplane is slipping or skidding and the miniature aircraft under these conditions shows an error in bank attitude. Instrument indications are shown in Figure 3-2 (slips) and Figure 3-3 (skids). If the wings are level and the airplane is properly trimmed, the ball will remain in the center and the airplane will be in straight flight. If the ball is not centered, the airplane is improperly trimmed (or the aviator is holding rudder pressure against proper trim).

Figure 3-2. Slip indication

Figure 3-3. Skid indication

3-33. To maintain straight-and-level flight with proper trim, note the direction of ball displacement. If the ball is to the left of center and the left wing is low, apply left rudder pressure (or release right rudder pressure) to center the ball and correct the slip. At the same time, apply right aileron pressure, as necessary, to level the wings, cross-checking the heading indicator and attitude indicator when centering the ball. If the wings are level and the ball is displaced from the center, the airplane is skidding. Note the direction of ball displacement, and use the same corrective technique as for an indicated slip. Center the ball (left ball/left rudder, right ball/right rudder), use aileron as necessary for bank control, and retrim.

3-34. To trim the airplane using only the turn coordinator, use aileron pressure to level the miniature aircraft and rudder pressure to center the ball. Hold these indications with control pressures, gradually releasing them when applying rudder trim sufficient to relieve all rudder pressure. Apply aileron trim, if available, to relieve aileron pressure. With a full instrument panel, maintain a wings-level attitude by reference to all available instruments while trimming the airplane.

COMMON HEADING ERRORS

3-35. Heading errors usually result from the following:

- Failure to cross-check the heading indicator, especially during changes in power or pitch attitude.
- Misinterpreting changes in heading with resulting corrections in the wrong direction.
- Failure to note and remember a preselected heading.
- Failure to observe the rate of heading change and its relation to bank attitude.
- Overcontrolling in response to heading changes especially during changes in power settings.
- Anticipating heading changes with premature application of rudder control.
- Failure to correct small heading deviations. Unless zero error in heading is the goal, an aviator will find himself tolerating larger deviations; correction of a 1-degree error takes less time than a 20-degree error.
- Correcting with improper bank attitude. By correcting a 10-degree heading error with a 20-degree bank correction, an aviator can roll past the desired heading before having bank established, which requires another correction in the opposite direction; do not multiply existing errors with errors in corrective technique.
- Failure to note the cause of a previous heading error and, thus, repeating the same error; for example, the airplane is out of trim with a left wing low tendency. An aviator repeatedly corrects for a slight left turn yet does nothing about trim.
- Failure to set the heading indicator properly or failure to uncage.

POWER CONTROL

3-36. Power produces thrust, which with the appropriate angle of attack of the wing, overcomes the forces of gravity, drag, and inertia to determine airplane performance. Power control must be related to its effect on altitude and airspeed because any change in power setting results in a change in the airspeed or the altitude of the airplane. At any given airspeed, the power setting determines whether the airplane is in level flight, a climb, or a descent. An increase in power while holding airspeed constant during straight-and-level flight causes the aircraft to climb. A decrease in power, while the aviator holds airspeed constant during straight-and-level flight, causes the aircraft to descend. When altitude is held constant, the power applied will determine airspeed.

3-37. The relationship between altitude and airspeed determines the need for a change in pitch or power. If the airspeed is off the desired value, always check the altimeter before deciding that a power change is necessary. Aviators can think of altitude and airspeed as interchangeable. Therefore, aviators can trade altitude for airspeed by lowering the nose or convert airspeed to altitude by raising the nose. If the altitude is higher than desired and airspeed is low (or vice versa), a change in pitch alone may return the airplane to the desired altitude and airspeed. If both airspeed and altitude are high or if both are low, then a change in both pitch and power is necessary to return to the desired airspeed and altitude.

3-38. For changes in airspeed in straight-and-level flight, pitch, bank, and power must be coordinated to maintain a constant altitude and heading. When power is changed to vary airspeed in straight-and-level flight, a single-engine, propeller-driven airplane tends to change attitude around all axes of movement. Therefore, to maintain constant altitude and heading, apply various control pressures in proportion to the changes in power. When the aviator adds power to increase airspeed, the pitch instruments will show a climb unless forward-elevator control pressure is applied as the airspeed changes. When the aviator increases power, the airplane tends to yaw and roll to the left unless counteracting aileron and rudder pressures are applied. Keeping ahead of these changes requires an increase in cross-check speed, which varies with the type of airplane and its torque characteristics, the extent of power and speed change involved, and the technique used in making the power change.

POWER SETTINGS

3-39. Power control and airspeed changes are much easier when the aviator already knows the approximate power settings necessary to maintain various airspeeds in straight-and-level flight. However, to change airspeed any appreciable amount, the common procedure is to underpower or overpower on initial power changes to accelerate the rate of airspeed change. (For small speed changes or in airplanes that decelerate or accelerate rapidly, overpowering or underpowering is not necessary.)

3-40. Figures 3-4, 3-5, and 3-6 illustrate a method to reduce airspeed from 200 knots to 160 knots while the aviator maintains straight-and-level flight.

Figure 3-4. Straight-and-level flight

3-41. Instrument indications, prior to the power reduction, are shown in Figure 3-4. The basic attitude is established and maintained on the attitude indicator, and the specific pitch, bank, and power control requirements are detected on these primary instruments:

- Altimeter—primary pitch.
- HSI, RMI, or compass—primary bank.
- Airspeed indicator—primary power.

3-42. Supporting pitch-and-bank instruments are shown in the illustrations. The supporting power instrument is the torque gauge. The torque gauge becomes the primary power instrument when the aviator makes a smooth power reduction (underpower) (Figure 3-5, page 3-10). With practice, an aviator will be able to change a power setting, with only a brief glance at the power instrument, by sensing the movement of the power levers, the change in sound, and the changes in the feel of control pressures.

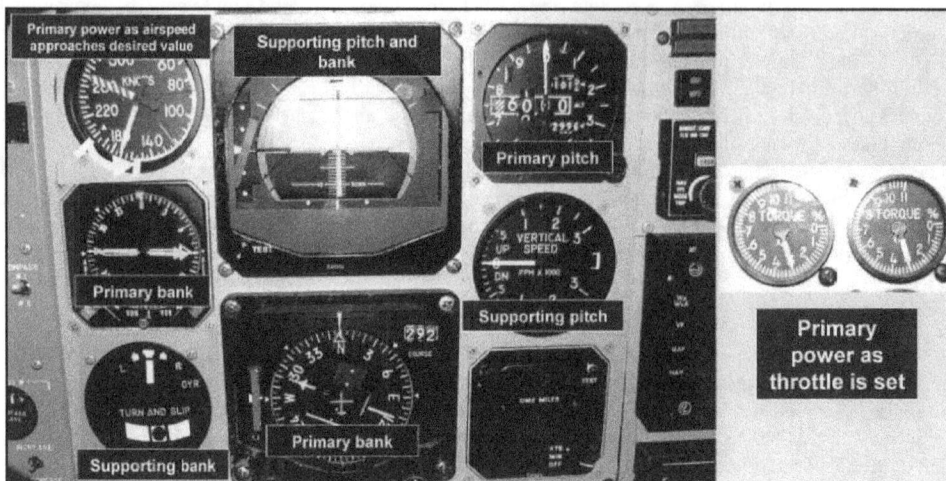

Figure 3-5. Airspeed deceasing

3-43. As the thrust decreases, increase the speed of the cross-check and be ready to apply left rudder, back-elevator, and aileron control pressure the instant that the pitch-and-bank instruments show a deviation from altitude and heading. When proficient, an aviator will cross-check, interpret, and control the changes with no deviation of heading and altitude. Assuming smooth air and ideal control technique, as airspeed decreases, a proportionate increase in airplane pitch attitude is required to maintain altitude. Similarly, effective torque control means counteracting yaw with rudder pressure.

3-44. As power is reduced, the altimeter is primary for pitch, the heading indicator is primary for bank, and the torque gauge is temporarily primary for power. Control pressures should be trimmed off as the airplane decelerates. As airspeed approaches 160 knots (the desired airspeed), torque is adjusted and becomes the supporting power instrument. The airspeed indicator again becomes primary for power (Figure 3-6).

Figure 3-6. Reduced airspeed stabilized

AIRSPEED CHANGES

3-45. Practice of airspeed changes in straight-and-level flight provides an excellent means of developing increased proficiency in all three basic instrument skills and brings out some common errors to be expected during training. Having learned to control the airplane in a clean configuration (minimum drag conditions), aviators can increase proficiency in cross-check and control by practicing speed changes while extending or retracting the flaps and landing gear. While practicing, be sure to comply with the airspeed limitations specified in the appropriate aircraft operator's manual for gear and flap operation.

3-46. Sudden and exaggerated attitude changes may be necessary to maintain straight-and-level flight as the landing gear is extended and the flaps are lowered in some airplanes. The nose tends to pitch down with gear extension, and when flaps are lowered, lift increases momentarily (at partial flap settings), followed by a marked increase in drag as the flaps near maximum extension.

3-47. Control technique varies according to the lift and drag characteristics of each airplane. Accordingly, knowledge of the power settings and trim changes associated with different combinations of airspeed, gear, and flap configurations, such as in the following example, will reduce instrument cross-check and interpretation problems.

Example of Control Technique

Assume that in straight-and-level flight an airplane indicates 145 knots with power at 95 percent torque, gear and flaps up. After reduction in airspeed, with gear and flaps fully extended, straight-and-level flight at the same altitude requires 98 percent torque. Maximum gear extension speed is 125 knots; maximum flap extension speed is 105 knots.

3-48. Airspeed reduction to 95 knots, gear and flaps down, can be made in the following manner:
- Increase RPM to high, because a high power setting will be used in full drag configuration.
- Reduce torque to 50 percent; as the airspeed decreases, increase cross-check speed.
- Make trim adjustments for an increased angle of attack and decrease in torque.

3-49. By lowering the gear at 125 knots, the nose may tend to pitch down while the rate of deceleration increases. Increase pitch attitude to maintain constant altitude, and trim off some of the back-elevator pressures. By lowering full flaps at this point, cross-check, interpretation, and control must be very quick. A less difficult technique is to stabilize the airspeed and attitude with gear down before lowering the flaps.

3-50. Because 75 percent torque will hold level flight at 95 knots with the gear down, increase power smoothly to that setting as the airspeed indicator shows about 100 knots and retrim. The attitude indicator now shows about two-and-a-half bar width nose-high in straight-and-level flight. Actuate the flap control and simultaneously increase power to the predetermined setting (98 percent) for the desired airspeed, and trim off the pressures necessary to hold constant altitude and heading. The attitude indicator now shows a bar-width nose low in straight-and-level flight at 95 knots. A high level of proficiency in the basic skills involved in straight-and-level flight is developed when an aviator can consistently maintain constant altitude and heading with smooth pitch, bank, power, and trim control during these pronounced changes in trim.

COMMON POWER ERRORS

3-51. Power errors usually result from the following:
- Failure to know the power settings and pitch attitudes appropriate to various airspeeds and airplane configurations.
- Abrupt use of power levers.
- Failure to lead the airspeed during power changes. For example, during airspeed reduction in level flight, especially with gear and flaps extended, adjust the power levers to maintain the slower speed before reaching the desired airspeed; otherwise, the airplane will decelerate to a

speed lower than desired, resulting in further power adjustments. How much to lead the airspeed depends upon how fast the airplane responds to power changes.

- Fixation on airspeed or torque instruments during airspeed changes, resulting in erratic control of both airspeed and power.

TRIM TECHNIQUE

3-52. Proper trim technique is essential for smooth and precise aircraft control during all phases of flight. By relieving all control pressures, holding a given attitude constant is mush easier and an aviator can devote more attention to other cockpit duties.

3-53. An aircraft is trimmed by applying control pressures to establish a desired attitude and then adjusting the trim so that the aircraft will maintain that attitude when flight controls are released. Trim the aircraft for coordinated flight by centering the ball of the turn-and-slip indicator. Center the ball of the turn-and-slip indicator by using rudder trim in the direction that the ball is displaced from the center. Differential power control on multiengine aircraft is an additional factor affecting coordinated flight. Use balanced power or thrust, when possible, to aid in maintaining coordinated flight.

3-54. Changes in attitude, power, or configuration require a trim adjustment in most cases. Using trim alone to establish a change in aircraft attitude invariably leads to erratic aircraft control. Smooth and precise attitude changes are attained by a combination of control pressures and trim adjustments. Therefore, when used correctly, trim adjustment is an aid to smooth aircraft control.

3-55. Some aircraft have a yaw damper system. The yaw damper may have to be turned off while trimming the aircraft.

3-56. Common trim errors usually result from the following:

- Improper adjustment of seat or rudder pedals for comfort; tension in the legs and ankles makes relaxing rudder pressure difficult.
- Confusion as to the operation of trim devices, which differ among various airplane types. Some trim wheels are aligned appropriately with the airplane's axes; others are not; some rotate in a direction contrary to what is expected.
- Faulty sequence in trim technique. Trim should be used, not as a substitute for control with the wheel (stick) and rudders, but to relieve pressures already held to stabilize attitude; by gaining proficiency, an aviator becomes familiar with trim settings—just as with power settings—and will be able, with little conscious effort, to trim off pressures continually as they occur.
- Excessive trim control. Excessive trim control induces control pressures that must be held until retrim is properly completed; use trim frequently and in small amounts.
- Failure to understand the cause of trim changes; by not understanding the basic aerodynamics related to the basic instrument skills, an aviator will continually lag behind the airplane.

SECTION III – STRAIGHT CLIMBS AND DESCENTS

CLIMBS

3-57. For a given power setting and load condition, there is only one attitude that will give the most efficient rate of climb. The airspeed and the climb power setting that will determine this climb attitude are given in the performance data found in the appropriate aircraft operator's manual. Details of the technique for entering a climb vary according to airspeed on entry and the type of climb (constant airspeed or constant rate) desired. (Heading and trim control are maintained as discussed under straight-and-level flight.)

CONSTANT-AIRSPEED CLIMB

3-58. To enter a constant-airspeed climb from cruising airspeed, raise the miniature aircraft to the approximate nose-high indication for the predetermined climb speed. The attitude will vary according to the type of airplane flown. Apply light back-elevator pressure to initiate and maintain the climb attitude. The pressures will vary as the airplane decelerates. Power may be advanced to the climb power setting simultaneously with the pitch change or after the pitch change is established and the airspeed approaches climb speed. If the transition from level flight to climb is smooth, the VSI will show an immediate upward trend. Continue to move slowly, and then stop at a rate appropriate to the stabilized airspeed and attitude. Primary and supporting instruments for the climb entry are shown in Figure 3-7.

Figure 3-7. Climb entry

3-59. Once the airplane stabilizes at a constant airspeed and attitude, the airspeed indicator is primary for pitch and the heading indicator remains primary for bank (Figure 3-8, page 3-14). Monitor the torque gauge as the primary power instrument to ensure the proper climb power setting is being maintained. If the climb attitude is correct for the power setting selected, the airspeed will stabilize at the desired speed. If the airspeed is low or high, make an appropriate small pitch correction.

Figure 3-8. Stabilized constant airspeed climb

CONSTANT-RATE CLIMB

3-60. The technique for entering a constant-rate climb is very similar to that used for entry to a constant-airspeed climb from climb airspeed. As the power is increased to the approximate setting for the desired rate, simultaneously raise the miniature aircraft to the climbing attitude for the desired airspeed and rate of climb. As the power is increased, the airspeed indicator is primary for pitch control until the vertical speed approaches the desired value. As the vertical-speed needle stabilizes, the vertical speed becomes primary for pitch control and the airspeed indicator becomes primary for power control (Figure 3-9, page 3-15).

Figure 3-9. Stabilized constant rate climb

3-61. Pitch and power corrections must be prompt and closely coordinated. For example, if vertical speed is correct but airspeed is low, add power. As power is increased, the miniature aircraft must be lowered slightly to maintain constant vertical speed. If vertical speed is high and airspeed is low, lower the miniature aircraft slightly and note the increase in airspeed to determine whether a power change is necessary. Familiarity with power settings helps to keep pitch and power corrections at a minimum.

LEVEL-OFF

3-62. To level-off from a climb and maintain an altitude, start the level-off before reaching the desired altitude. The amount of lead varies with rate of climb and aviator technique. If the airplane is climbing at 1,000 FPM, the airplane will continue to climb at a decreasing rate throughout the transition to level flight. An effective practice is to lead the altitude by 10 percent of the vertical speed shown (500 FPM/50-foot lead, 1,000 FPM/100-foot lead).

3-63. To level-off at cruising airspeed, apply smooth, steady forward-elevator pressure toward level-flight attitude for the speed desired. As the attitude indicator shows the pitch change, the vertical-speed needle will move slowly toward zero, the altimeter needle will move more slowly, and the airspeed will show acceleration (Figure 3-10, page 3-16). Constant changes in pitch and torque control will have to be made as the airspeed increases when the altimeter, attitude indicator, and VSI show level flight. As the airspeed approaches cruising speed, reduce power to the cruise setting. The amount of lead depends on the rate of acceleration of the airplane.

3-64. To level-off at climbing airspeed, lower the nose to the pitch attitude appropriate to that airspeed in level flight. Power is simultaneously reduced to the setting for that airspeed as the pitch attitude is lowered. If the power reduction is at a rate proportionate to the pitch change, airspeed will remain constant.

Figure 3-10. Level-off

DESCENTS

3-65. A descent can be made at a variety of airspeeds and attitudes by reducing power, adding drag, and lowering the nose to a predetermined attitude. Sooner or later, the airspeed will stabilize at a constant value. Meanwhile, the only flight instrument providing a positive attitude reference, by itself, is the attitude indicator. Without the attitude indicator (such as during a partial-panel descent), the airspeed indicator, the altimeter, and the VSI will show varying rates of change until the airplane decelerates to a constant airspeed at a constant attitude. Maintain cruise airspeed during descent by reducing power and decreasing pitch. Adjust pitch for rate of descent and power to maintain correct airspeed. During the transition, changes in control pressure and trim, as well as cross-check and interpretation, must be very accurate to maintain positive control.

AIRSPEED DESCENT

3-66. The following method for entering descents is effective either with or without an attitude indicator. First, reduce airspeed to the selected descent airspeed while maintaining straight-and-level flight, and then make a further reduction in power (to a predetermined setting). As the power is adjusted, simultaneously lower the nose to maintain constant airspeed and trim off control pressures.

3-67. During a constant-airspeed descent, any deviation from the desired airspeed calls for a pitch adjustment. For a constant-rate descent, the entry is the same but the vertical-speed indicator is primary for pitch control (after the aircraft stabilizes near the desired rate) and the airspeed indicator is primary for power control. Pitch and power must be closely coordinated when the aviator makes corrections (Figure 3-11, page 3-17).

Figure 3-11. Constant airspeed descent, airspeed high—reduce power

LEVEL-OFF

3-68. Level-off from a descent must be started before reaching the desired altitude. The amount of lead depends on the descent rate and control technique. With too little lead, an aviator tends to overshoot the selected altitude unless the technique is quick. Lead the altitude by 100 to 150 feet for a level-off at airspeed higher than descending speed (assuming a 500-FPM rate of descent). At the lead point, add power to the appropriate level-flight cruise setting (Figure 3-12). Because the nose tends to rise as airspeed increases, hold forward-elevator pressure to maintain vertical speed at the descending rate until about 50 feet above altitude and smoothly adjust the pitch attitude to the level-flight attitude for the airspeed selected.

3-69. To level-off from a descent at descent airspeed, lead the desired altitude by about 50 feet, simultaneously adjusting the pitch attitude to level flight and adding power to a setting that will hold the airspeed constant (Figure 3-12, page 3-18). Trim off the control pressures and continue with the normal straight-and-level flight cross-check.

Figure 3-12. Level-off at descent airspeed

COMMON CLIMB AND DESCENT ERRORS AND RESOLUTIONS

3-70. Common errors and their resolutions include the following:

- Overcontrolling pitch on climb entry. An inexperienced aviator has a tendency to make larger than necessary pitch adjustments; overcome the inclination to make large control movements by applying small control pressures smoothly. Cross-check quickly for results of the change, and continue with the pressures as the instruments show the desired results at a rate that can be interpreted; small pitch changes are more easily controlled, stopped, and corrected.
- Failure to vary the rate of cross-check during speed, power, or attitude changes for climb and descent entries.
- Failure to maintain a new pitch attitude. For example, an aviator raises the nose to the correct climb attitude; as airspeed decreases, the aviator may continue to lead the input, which can cause overcontrol, further increasing the pitch attitude. Another error is if the aviator does not maintain the proper pitch attitude, which could allow the nose to lower; this undercontrol may not provide the desired climb rate. Control pressures change with airspeed changes; therefore, the aviator must increase cross-checks and readjust control pressures as necessary for desired pitch attitude.
- Failure to trim off pressures; unless the aviator trims, there will be difficulty in determining whether control pressure changes are induced by aerodynamic changes or aviator movements.
- Failure to learn and use proper power settings.
- Failure to cross-check airspeed and vertical speed before making pitch or power adjustments.
- Improper pitch and power coordination on slow-speed level-offs because of slow cross-check of airspeed and altimeter indications.
- Failure to cross-check the VSI against other pitch control instruments.
- Failure to note the rate of climb or descent to determine the lead for level-offs.
- Failure to maintain descending attitude with forward-elevator pressure as power is increased to level flight cruise setting causes ballooning (allowing the nose to pitch up).
- Failure to recognize the approaching straight-and-level flight indications when leveling-off.

STANDARD-RATE TURNS

3-71. To enter a standard-rate level turn, apply coordinated aileron and rudder pressures in the desired direction of turn. Aviators commonly roll into turns at a much too rapid rate. During initial training in turns, base control pressures on the rate of cross-check and interpretation. There is nothing to be gained by maneuvering an airplane faster than the capacity to keep up with the changes in instrument indications.

3-72. On the roll in, use the attitude indicator to establish the approximate angle of bank and then check the turn coordinator's miniature aircraft for a standard-rate turn indication. Maintain the bank for this rate of turn, using the turn coordinator's miniature aircraft as the primary bank reference and the attitude indicator as the supporting bank instrument (Figure 3-13). Note the exact angle of bank shown on the banking scale of the attitude indicator when the turn coordinator indicates a standard-rate turn.

Figure 3-13. Standard rate turn

3-73. During roll-in, check the altimeter, VSI, and attitude indicator for the necessary pitch adjustments as the vertical lift component decreases with an increase in bank. If constant airspeed is to be maintained, the airspeed indicator becomes primary for power and the power levers must be adjusted as drag increases. As the bank is established, trim off the pressures applied during pitch and power changes.

3-74. To recover to straight-and-level flight, apply coordinated aileron and rudder pressures opposite the direction of turn. If an aviator strives for the same rate of roll-out used to roll into the turn, he will encounter fewer problems in estimating the lead necessary for roll-out on exact headings, especially on partial-panel maneuvers. The attitude indicator becomes the primary bank instrument when the aviator initiates the turn recovery. When the airplane is approximately level, the heading indicator is the primary bank instrument. Pitch, power, and trim adjustments are made as changes in vertical lift component and airspeed occur. The ball should be checked throughout the turn, especially if control pressures are held rather than trimmed off.

3-75. Some airplanes are very stable during turns, and slight trim adjustments permit hands-off flight while the airplane remains in the established attitude. Other airplanes require constant, quick cross-check and control during turns to correct overbanking tendencies. Because of the interrelationship of pitch, bank, and airspeed deviations during turns, the cross-check must be fast to prevent an accumulation of errors.

STEEP TURNS

3-76. For purposes of instrument flight training in conventional aircraft, any turn with a 45-to 60-degree bank angle or greater is considered steep (Figure 3-14). The exact angle of bank at which a normal turn becomes steep is unimportant. What is important is to learn to control the airplane with bank attitudes in excess of those normally used on instruments. Practice in steep turns will not only increase proficiency in basic instrument flying skills but also enable smooth, quick, and confident reaction to unexpected abnormal flight attitudes under instrument flight conditions.

Figure 3-14. Steep right turn

3-77. Aerodynamic forces inhibit aircraft control at progressively steeper bank attitudes. Skill in cross-check, interpretation, and control is increasingly necessary in proportion to the amount of these changes. The techniques for entering, maintaining, and recovering from the turn are the same in principle for steep turns as for shallow turns.

3-78. Enter a steep turn exactly as a shallow turn, but prepare to cross-check quickly as the turn becomes steeper. Because of the reduced vertical lift component, pitch control is usually the most difficult aspect of this maneuver. Unless immediately noted and corrected with a pitch increase, the loss of vertical lift results in rapid movement of the altimeter, vertical speed, and airspeed needles. The faster the rate of bank change, the more suddenly the lift changes occur. If the cross-check is fast enough to note the immediate need for pitch changes, smooth, steady back-elevator pressure will maintain constant altitude. However, if an aviator overbanks to excessively steep angles without adjusting pitch as bank changes occur, pitch corrections require increasingly stronger elevator pressure. The loss of vertical lift and increase in wing loading finally reach a point where further application of back-elevator pressure tightens the turn without raising the nose.

3-79. Despite the application of back-elevator pressure, the aircraft is in a diving spiral when the aviator observes a rapid downward movement of the altimeter needle or vertical-speed needle, along with an increase in airspeed. Immediately shallow the bank with smooth and coordinated aileron and rudder pressures, hold or slightly relax elevator pressure, and increase the cross-check of the attitude indicator, altimeter, and VSI. Reduce power if the airspeed increase is rapid. The altimeter needle moves slower as the vertical lift increases and the vertical speed trends upward. When noting the elevator is effective in raising the nose, hold the bank attitude shown on the attitude indicator and adjust elevator control pressures smoothly for the nose-high attitude appropriate to the bank maintained. If pitch control is consistently late on entries to steep turns, roll-out immediately to straight-and-level flight and analyze any errors. Practice shallower turns until able to keep up with the attitude changes and control responses required, and then proceed to steeper banks as quicker and more accurate control techniques are developed.

3-80. The power necessary to maintain a constant airspeed increases as the bank and drag increase. With practice, an aviator quickly learns the power settings appropriate to specific bank attitudes and can make adjustments without undue attention to airspeed and power instruments. When the aviator keeps the pitch attitude relatively constant, there is more time to cross-check, interpret, and control for accurate airspeed and bank control.

3-81. During recovery from steep turns to straight-and-level flight, elevator and power control must be coordinated with bank control in proportion to the changes in aerodynamic forces. Back-elevator pressures must be released and power decreased. Errors are more exaggerated and more difficult to correct and analyze unless the rates of entry and recovery are consistent with the level of proficiency in the basic instrument flying skills.

CLIMBING AND DESCENDING TURNS

3-82. To execute climbing and descending turns, combine the technique used in straight climbs and descents with various turn techniques. The aerodynamic factors affecting lift and power control must be considered in determining power settings, and the rate of cross-check and interpretation must be increased to enable an aviator to control bank as well as pitch changes.

CHANGE OF AIRSPEED DURING TURNS

3-83. Changing airspeed during turns (Figure 3-15) is an effective maneuver for increasing proficiency in all three basic instrument skills. Because the maneuver involves simultaneous changes in all components of control, proper execution requires a quick cross-check and interpretation as well as smooth control. Proficiency in the maneuver will also contribute to aviator confidence in the instruments during attitude and power changes involved in more complex maneuvers. Pitch and power control techniques are the same as those used during changes in airspeed during straight-and-level flight.

Figure 3-15.Change of airspeed in turn

3-84. The angle of bank necessary for a given rate of turn is proportional to the TAS. Because turns are executed at a standard rate, the angle of bank must be varied in direct proportion to the airspeed change to maintain a constant rate of turn. During a reduction of airspeed, an aviator must decrease the angle of bank and increase the pitch attitude to maintain altitude and a standard-rate turn.

3-85. The altimeter and turn coordinator indications should remain constant throughout the turn. The altimeter is primary for pitch control, and the miniature aircraft of the turn coordinator is primary for bank control. The torque gauge is primary for power control while the airspeed is changing. As the airspeed approaches the new indication, the airspeed indicator becomes primary for power control.

3-86. Two methods of changing airspeed in turns may be used. In the first method, airspeed is changed after the turn is established; in the second method, the airspeed change is initiated simultaneously with the turn entry. Regardless of the method used, the rate of cross-check must be increased as power is reduced. As the airplane decelerates, check the altimeter and VSI for needed pitch changes and the bank instruments for needed bank changes. If the miniature aircraft of the turn coordinator shows a deviation from the desired deflection, change the bank. Adjust pitch attitude to maintain altitude. When the aircraft approaches the desired airspeed, the airspeed indicator becomes primary for power control and the torque gauge is adjusted to maintain the desired airspeed. Trim is important throughout the maneuver to relieve control pressures. Until an aviator's control technique is smooth, frequent cross-check of the attitude indicator is essential to keep from overcontrolling and to provide approximate bank angles appropriate to the changing airspeeds.

COMMON TURN ERRORS

PITCH

3-87. Pitch errors and their resolutions include the following:
- Preoccupation with bank control during turn entry and recovery. Check pitch instruments when initiating bank pressures. If bank control pressure and rate of bank change are consistent, an aviator soon develops a sense of timing regarding attitude change. Control the total attitude instead of one factor at a time.
- Failure to understand the need for changing pitch attitude as the vertical lift component changes, causing consistent loss of altitude during entries.
- Changing the pitch attitude before necessary (because of a slow cross-check and a rapid rate of entry); the error occurs during the turn entry because of a mechanical and premature application of back-elevator control pressure.
- Overcontrolling pitch changes.
- Failure to properly adjust the pitch attitude as the vertical lift component increases during the rollout causing consistent gain in altitude on recovery to headings.
- Failure to trim during turn entry and following turn recovery (if the turn is prolonged).
- Failure to maintain straight-and-level cross-check after rollout (commonly follows a perfectly executed turn).
- Erratic rates of bank change on entry and recovery resulting from failure to cross-check pitch instruments with changes in lift.

BANK

3-88. Bank and heading errors and their resolutions include the following:
- Overcontrolling resulting in overbanking upon turn entry and overshooting and undershooting headings as well as aggravated pitch, airspeed, and trim errors.
- Fixation on a single bank instrument; be selective during the cross-check and avoid fixating on a single instrument as described in the following example.

An Example of Using Other Cues During Turns

On a 90 degrees change of heading, leave the heading indicator out of the cross-check for about 20 seconds after establishing a standard-rate turn because, at 3 degrees per second, the aircraft will not approach the lead point until that time has elapsed.

- Failure to check for precession of the horizon bar following recovery from a turn. If the heading indicator shows a change in heading when the attitude indicator shows level flight, the airplane is turning. If the ball is centered, the attitude gyro has precessed; conversely if the ball is not centered, the airplane may be in a slipping or skidding turn. Center the ball with rudder pressure, check the attitude indicator and heading indicator, stop a continued heading change, and retrim.

- Failure to use the proper degree of bank for the amount of heading change desired; rolling into a 20-degree bank for a heading change of 10 degrees will normally overshoot the heading. Use the bank attitude appropriate to the amount of heading change desired.

- Failure to remember the new heading; this fault is likely when the aviator rushes the maneuver.

- Turning in the wrong direction because of misreading or misinterpreting the heading indicator or confusion as to the location of points on the compass; turn in the shortest direction to reach a given heading, unless there is a specific reason to turn the long way around. To avoid turning in the wrong direction—

  - The aviator should be familiar enough with the compass rose to be able to visualize the positions of the eight major points around the azimuth and quickly determine the correct direction to be flown; for example, to turn from a heading of 305 degrees to a heading of 110 degrees, the shortest way around is to the right.

  - The aviator should be able to quickly determine reciprocal headings as in the following example.

Example of Determining a Reciprocal Heading

Subtracting 200 from 305 and adding 20, the answer is 125 degrees (as the reciprocal of 305 degrees); thus, execute a turn to the right. Likewise, to figure the reciprocal of a heading less than 180 degrees, add 200 and subtract 20. Compute quickly by using multiples of 100s and 10s, and then add or subtract 180 degrees from the actual heading.

- Failure to check the ball of the turn coordinator when the aviator interprets the instrument for bank information. If the roll rate is reduced to zero, the miniature aircraft of the turn coordinator indicates only direction and rate of turn. Unless the ball is centered, do not assume that the turn results from a banked attitude.

POWER

3-89. Power and airspeed errors result from the following:

- Failure to cross-check the airspeed indicator when the aviator makes pitch changes.

- Erratic use of power control; these type of errors may be due to improper friction control, inaccurate power lever settings, the tendency to chase the airspeed readings, abrupt or overcontrolled pitch-and-bank changes, or failure to recheck the airspeed to note the effect of a power adjustment.

- Poor coordination of power lever controls. Errors occur when poor coordination of power lever controls is combined with pitch-and-bank changes associated with slow cross-check and can be caused by a failure to understand the aerodynamic factors related to turns.

TRIM

3-90. Trim errors result from the following mistakes:

- Failure to recognize the need for a trim change because of slow cross-check and interpretation; for example, a turn entry at a rate too rapid for the cross-check leads to confusion in cross-check and interpretation with resulting tension on the controls.
- Failure to understand the relationship between trim and attitude/power changes.
- Tendency to chase the vertical-speed needle. Overcontrolling leads to tension and prevents the aviator from sensing the pressures to be trimmed off.
- Failure to trim following power changes.

SECTION V – OTHER MANEUVERS

APPROACH TO STALL

3-91. Practicing approach to stall recoveries in various airplane configurations builds confidence in an aviator's ability to recognize and recover the airplane in unexpected situations such as stalls. Approach to stall should be practiced from straight-and-level flight and from shallow banks. Prior to stall recovery practice, select a safe altitude above the terrain, free of conflicting air traffic, verifying that adequate weather conditions are present and appropriate radar traffic advisory services are available. During approaches to stalls, power is applied while smoothly and simultaneously increasing the angle of attack to induce an indication of a stall. The approaches to stalls are accomplished in the following configurations:

- **Takeoff.** Begin from level flight near liftoff speed.
- **Clean.** Begin from a reduced airspeed, such as pattern airspeed, in level flight.
- **Approach or landing.** Initiate at the appropriate approach or landing airspeed.

3-92. Promptly respond to a stall warning device or an aerodynamic indication by smoothly reducing the angle of attack and applying maximum power or as recommended by the appropriate aircraft operator's manual. The recovery should be completed without an excessive loss of altitude and on a predetermined heading, altitude, and airspeed.

UNUSUAL ATTITUDES AND RECOVERIES

3-93. An unusual attitude is an airplane attitude not normally required for instrument flight. Unusual attitudes may result from a number of conditions such as turbulence, disorientation, instrument failure, confusion, preoccupation with cockpit duties and carelessness in cross-checking, errors in instrument interpretation, or lack of proficiency in aircraft control. Unusual attitudes are often unexpected during instrument flight (except in training), and the reaction of an inexperienced aviator to an unexpected abnormal flight attitude is usually instinctive rather than deliberate. Avoid responding with abrupt muscular effort, which is hazardous in turbulent conditions, at excessive speeds, or at low altitudes; however, techniques for rapid and safe recovery from unusual attitudes can be learned. When noting an unusual attitude on the cross-check, focus on returning the aircraft to straight-and-level flight as quickly as possible.

RECOGNIZING UNUSUAL ATTITUDES

3-94. When an abnormal instrument rate of movement or indication is noted, assume an unusual attitude and perform a rapid cross-check to confirm the attitude, instrument error, or instrument malfunction. Nose-high attitudes are shown by the rate and direction of movement of the altimeter needle, vertical-speed needle, airspeed needle, and the attitude indicator (except in extreme attitudes) (Figure 3-16, page 3-25).

Figure 3-16. Unusual attitude—nose high

3-95. Nose-low attitudes are shown by the same instruments but in the opposite direction (Figure 3-17).

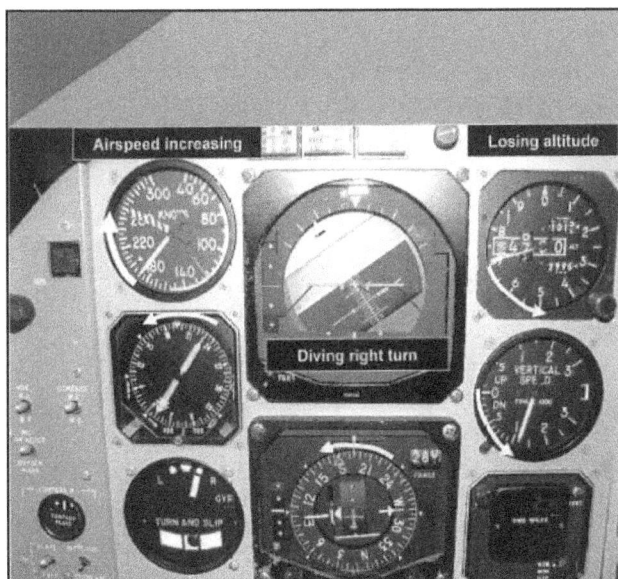

Figure 3-17. Unusual attitude—nose low

RECOVERY FROM UNUSUAL ATTITUDES

3-96. In moderate unusual attitudes, the aviator can normally be reoriented by establishing a level flight indication on the attitude indicator. However, the aviator should not depend on this instrument if the attitude indicator is the spillable type because upset limits may have been exceeded, making the unit inoperative because of mechanical malfunction. Even if the instrument is operating properly, errors up to 5 degrees of pitch-and-bank may result. Its indications are difficult to interpret in extreme attitudes. When the unusual attitude is detected, recommended recovery procedures in the appropriate aircraft operator's manual are initiated. If there are no recommended procedures, the recovery is initiated by reference to the airspeed indicator, altimeter, VSI, and turn coordinator.

Note. Refer to the airplane operator's manual to determine if the attitude indicator is a spillable type.

Nose-High Attitudes

3-97. When airspeed is decreasing or below the desired airspeed—
- Increase power (in proportion to the observed deceleration).
- As the nose pitches to the horizon, decrease bank to wings level.
- Adjust pitch to reverse the airspeed trend and return to a level flight attitude.
- Adjust power to cruise setting.
- Cross-check the slip indicator.
- Trim the aircraft.

3-98. Corrective control applications are made almost simultaneously but in the sequence given above. A level pitch attitude is indicated by reversal and stabilization of the airspeed indicator and altimeter needles. Straight coordinated flight is indicated by a level miniature aircraft and centered ball of the turn coordinator.

Nose-Low Attitudes

3-99. When airspeed is increasing or is above the desired airspeed—
- Smoothly reduce power as required.
- Level wings.
- Adjust pitch up to the horizon.
- Adjust power to maintain desired airspeed and altitude.
- Cross-check the slip indicator.
- Trim the aircraft.

3-100. All components of control are changed simultaneously for a smooth recovery. However, during initial training, a positive recovery is made in the sequence provided above. The instinctive reaction to a nose-down attitude is to pull back on the elevator control.

3-101. After initial control has been applied, continue with a rapid cross-check for possible overcontrolling because the necessary initial control pressures may be excessive. As the rate of movement of the altimeter and airspeed indicator needles decreases, the attitude is approaching level flight. When the needles stop and reverse direction, the aircraft is passing through level flight. As the indications of the airspeed indicator, altimeter, and turn coordinator stabilize, incorporate the attitude indicator into the cross-check.

3-102. The attitude indicator and turn coordinator are checked to determine bank attitude. Then corrective aileron and rudder pressures are applied. The ball should be centered. If not centered, skidding and slipping sensations can easily aggravate disorientation and retard recovery. When entering the unusual attitude from an assigned altitude (either by the instructor or by ATC if operating under IFR), return to the original altitude after stabilizing in straight-and-level flight.

COMMON RECOVERY ERRORS

3-103. Errors noted in connection with basic instrument skills are aggravated during unusual attitude recoveries. Common errors include the following:

- Failure to keep the airplane properly trimmed. A cockpit interruption when an aviator is holding pressures can lead into unusual attitudes.
- Disorganized cockpit. Hunting for charts and logs detracts attention from the instruments.
- Slow cross-check and fixations. The impulse is to stare when an instrument discrepancy is noted.
- Attempting to recover by senses other than sight (see FM 3-04.301 for more information).
- Failure to practice basic instrument skills.

This page intentionally left blank.

Chapter 4

Air Navigation Charts

All aviators must be able to navigate. By understanding and using air navigational charts, aviators are able to maintain situational awareness and accomplish missions during VFR and IFR conditions. The following chapter explains DOD-approved charts used by aviators to navigate while instrument flying. The chapter also covers basic plotting and measuring techniques used to plan instrument flights.

SECTION I – AIR NAVIGATION

MEASURING A POSITION USING LATITUDE AND LONGITUDE

EQUATOR

4-1.   The equator is an imaginary circle equidistant from the poles of the earth. Circles parallel to the equator (lines running east and west) are parallels of latitude. They measure degrees of latitude north or south of the equator. The angular distance from the equator to the pole is one-fourth of a circle, or 90

Contents

degrees. Thus, latitude runs from 90 degrees north to 90 degrees south of the equator. Fort Rucker, Alabama lies approximately at the 30 degrees north latitude. The following example shows a distance conversion.

Example of a Distance Conversion
1 degree of latitude is 60 nautical miles (NM), 69 statute miles (SM), or 111 kilometers (KM).
1 minute of latitude is 1 NM, 1.15 SM, or 1.85 KM.

MERIDIAN

4-2.   Meridians of longitude are drawn from North Pole to South Pole and at right angles to the equator. The prime meridian, which passes through Greenwich, England, is used as the zero-degree line from which measurements are made in degrees east and west to 180 degrees. Fort Rucker, Alabama, lies about at the 90 degrees west longitude. Any specific geographical point can be located by reference to its latitude and longitude.

DEGREES, MINUTES, AND SECONDS

4-3.   Degrees, minutes, and seconds are the most universal format used to mark maps and the most cumbersome:
- There are 60 seconds in a minute (60 inches equal 1 foot).
- There are 60 minutes in a degree (60 feet equal 1 degree).

Degrees, Minutes, Seconds Example

DDD° MM' SS.S"

32° 18' 23.1" N 122° 36' 52.5" W

4-4. A few easy conversions between seconds and decimal minutes help when the aviator works with maps that use degrees, minutes, and seconds:

- Fifteen seconds is one quarter of a minute, or 0.25 minutes.
- Thirty seconds is one half of a minute, or 0.5 minutes.
- Forty-five seconds is three quarters of a minute, or 0.75 minutes.

DEGREES AND DECIMAL MINUTES

4-5. This format is found in the IFR supplement and is most commonly used when working with electronic navigation equipment. To convert decimal minutes (MM.MMM) to degrees, minutes, and seconds, multiply decimal point numbers by 60.

Degrees and Decimal Minutes Example

For latitude 32° 18.385' N, multiply .385 by 60, and the coordinate converts to 32° 18' 23.1" N; longitude 122° 36.875' W converts to 122° 36' 52.5"

W.DDD° MM.MMM' = 32° 18.385' N 122° 36.875' W

DECIMAL DEGREES

4-6. This is the format that most computer-based mapping systems display. The coordinates are stored internally in a floating point data type; no additional work is required to print them as a floating point number. Positive values of latitude are north of the equator, negative values to the south. Watch the sign on the longitude; most programs use negative values for west longitude, but a few are opposite (Figure 4-1, page 4-3).

Decimal Degrees Example

DDD.DDDDD°

32.30642° N 122.61458° W

or +32.30642, -122.61458

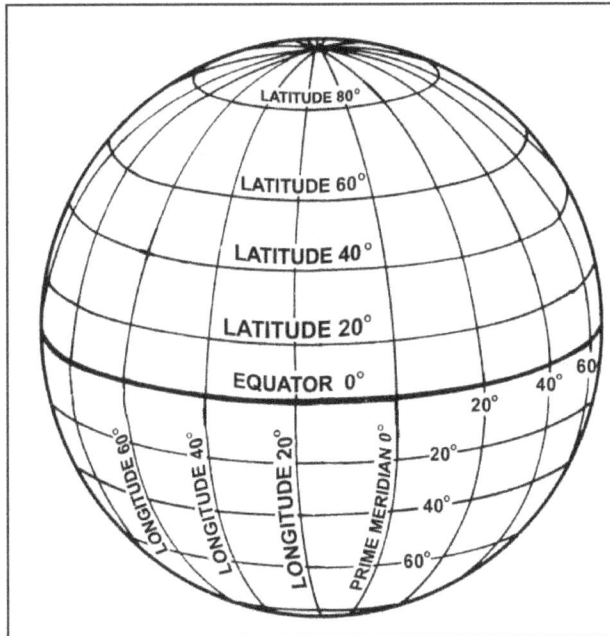

Figure 4-1. Longitude and latitude

MEASURING DIRECTION

EARTH CIRCUMFERENCE

4-7. The circumference of the earth is divided into 360 degrees; each degree is further divided into 60 minutes. Moving one minute east or west on the equator is equal to 1 nautical mile. Thus, a nautical mile is the circumference of the earth divided by 360, giving the distance in 1 degree, which is further divided by 60 for the distance in one minute of arc.

DISTANCE

4-8. The circumference of the earth is 24,857 statute miles, or 40,003.2 kilometers. The statute mile has been standardized at 5,280 feet. The nautical mile has been standardized at 6,076 feet. Therefore, 1 statute mile is equal to 0.87 nautical mile, or 1.609 kilometers, for the purposes of measuring distance (table 4-1).

Table 4-1. Distance conversions

	1 SM	1 NM	1 KM
Feet	5,280	6,076.1	3280.8
SM	1.0	1.15	0.621
NM	0.87	1.0	0.539
KM	1.609	1.852	1.0

SPEED

4-9. A nautical knot is a measure of speed equal to 1 nautical mile per hour. To determine this speed, sailors would throw lines over the sides of the ships. Each line was divided into 47 feet, 3 inch, sections called knots. The line was run over the ship's side while a 28-second glass was emptying itself. The length of the knot was derived from the proportion that one hour (3,600 seconds) is to 28 seconds as 1 nautical mile (6,080 feet) is to the length of 1 knot (47 feet, 3 inches). Therefore, a knot is equal to 1 nautical mile per hour, or 1.15 statute miles per hour (see Chapter 1 for a discussion on the different types of airspeed).

Example of Knots to Statute Mile Conversion
120 knots on the airspeed indicator is equal to 138 (statute) miles per hour (120 X 1.15 = 138).

NAVIGATION CHARTS

4-10. An air navigation chart is a diagram representing the earth's surface. In this manual, aeronautical chart discussion is limited to charts used for instrument navigation. Both the National Geospatial-Intelligence Agency (NGA) charts and FAA National Aeronautical Charting Office (NACO) charts are approved Department of Defense (DOD)/United States (U.S.) Government Flight Information Publications (FLIPs), and aviators may fly procedures in both sets. FAA NACO charts may contain more civil procedures than NGA charts. Generally, only one of each type of procedure is included in NGA charts. NGA does not normally include multiple instrument landing system (ILS) procedures to the same airfield; the NGA chooses one to include. Mission needs must be considered when the aviator determines which FLIP to use; aviators can choose, depending on the flight destination. All DOD approaches are now included in the NACO publications. If a procedure is not in either set of charts, then the procedure is a non-DOD/U.S. Government procedure and must have United States Army Aeronautical Services Agency (USAASA) approval before use.

CHARACTERISTICS

4-11. Each chart has a different purpose, and no one chart is best for every use. A chart cannot be both equal in angles and equal in area. Secondary charts assist aviators in finding and plotting coordinates and finding cardinal directions parallel throughout the chart. They also assist when it is necessary to join two or more charts together, promoting easier assembly.

INSTRUMENT FLIGHT RULES EN ROUTE CHARTS

4-12. En route charts show civil and military airports with an approved instrument approach procedure (IAP) and many non-IFR airports. En route charts do not show terrain or cultural landmarks (such as roads and cities); only large bodies of water are depicted. Low-altitude en route charts are for use up to, but not including, 18,000 feet MSL.

4-13. The objective of an IFR en route flight is to navigate within the lateral limits of a designated airway at an altitude consistent with ATC clearance. The ability to fly instruments in the system safely and competently is enhanced by understanding the vast array of data available to the aviator within instrument charts. NACO maintains the database and produces the charts for the U.S. Government.

4-14. En route high-altitude charts provide aeronautical information for en route IFR navigation at or above 18,000 feet MSL. Information includes the portrayal of jet routes, identification and frequencies of radio aids, selected airports, distances, time zones, special-use airspace, and related information. From altitudes of 18,000 feet MSL to FL450, aviators should establish routes using NAVAIDs not more than 260 nautical miles apart. Scales vary from 1 inch equals 45 nautical miles to 1 inch equals 18 nautical miles. The charts are revised every 56 days.

4-15. Appropriate IFR en route low-altitude charts are required to effectively depart from one airport and navigate en route under instrument conditions. The IFR en route low-altitude chart is the instrument equivalent of the sectional chart. When folded, the cover of the NACO en route chart displays a map of the United States, showing coverage areas. Cities near congested airspace are shown in black type, and their associated area chart is listed in the box in the lower left-hand corner of the map coverage box. Also noted is the highest off-route obstruction clearance altitude. The effective date of the chart is printed on the other side of the folded chart. Information concerning military training routes (MTRs) is also included on the chart cover. Scales vary from 1 inch equals 5 nautical miles to 1 inch equals 20 nautical miles. The en route charts are revised every 56 days. When the NACO en route chart is unfolded, the legend is displayed and provides information concerning airports, NAVAIDs, air traffic services (ATS), and airspace.

4-16. Area navigation (RNAV) routes, including routes that use GPS for navigation, are normally not depicted on IFR en route charts; however, a number of RNAV routes have been established in the high-altitude structure and are depicted on the RNAV en route high-altitude charts. RNAV instrument DPs and standard terminal arrival routes (STARs) are contained in the U.S. Terminal Procedures booklets. Graphic notices and supplemental data also contain a tabulation of RNAV routes.

4-17. In addition to published routes, aviators may fly a random RNAV route under IFR if approved by ATC. Random RNAV routes are direct routes (based on area navigation capability) between waypoints defined in terms of latitude/longitude coordinates, degree-distance fixes, or offsets from established routes/airways at a specified distance and direction.

4-18. Radar monitoring by ATC is required on all random RNAV routes. These routes can only be approved in a radar environment. Factors considered by ATC in approving random RNAV routes include the capability to provide radar monitoring and compatibility with traffic volume and flow. ATC radar monitors each flight; however, navigation on the random RNAV route is the responsibility of the aviator.

4-19. Reliance on RNAV systems for instrument approach operations is becoming more commonplace as new systems, such as GPS and wide area augmentation system (WAAS), are developed and deployed. To foster and support full integration of RNAV into the National Airspace System (NAS), the FAA has developed a charting format for RNAV approach charts.

AIRPORT INFORMATION

4-20. Airport information is provided in the legend, and the symbols used for the airport name, elevation, and runway length are similar to the sectional chart presentation. Instrument approaches are found at airports with blue or green symbols, while a brown airport symbol denotes airports that do not have published instrument approach procedures. Asterisks indicate the part-time nature of tower operations, lighting facilities, and airspace classifications (consult the communications panel on the chart for primary radio frequencies and hours of operation). The asterisk also indicates filing that airport as an alternate is not approved during specified hours. A box after an airport name with a C inside indicates Class C airspace while a box with a D inside indicates Class D airspace (Figure 4-2, page 4-6).

CHARTED INSTRUMENT FLIGHT RULES ALTITUDES

Minimum En Route Altitude

4-21. The minimum en route altitude (MEA) is the lowest published altitude between radio fixes that ensures acceptable navigational signal coverage and meets obstacle clearance requirements between those fixes. The MEA ensures a navigation signal strong enough for adequate reception by the aircraft navigation (NAV) receiver and adequate obstacle clearance along the airway. Verbal ATC communication is not necessarily guaranteed with MEA compliance. The obstacle clearance, within the limits of the airway, is typically 1,000 feet in nonmountainous areas and 2,000 feet in designated mountainous areas. MEAs can be authorized with breaks in signal coverage; if this is the case, the NACO en route chart notes the MEA gap parallel to the affected airway. MEAs are usually bidirectional; however, they can be unidirectional. Arrows are used to indicate the direction to which the MEA applies.

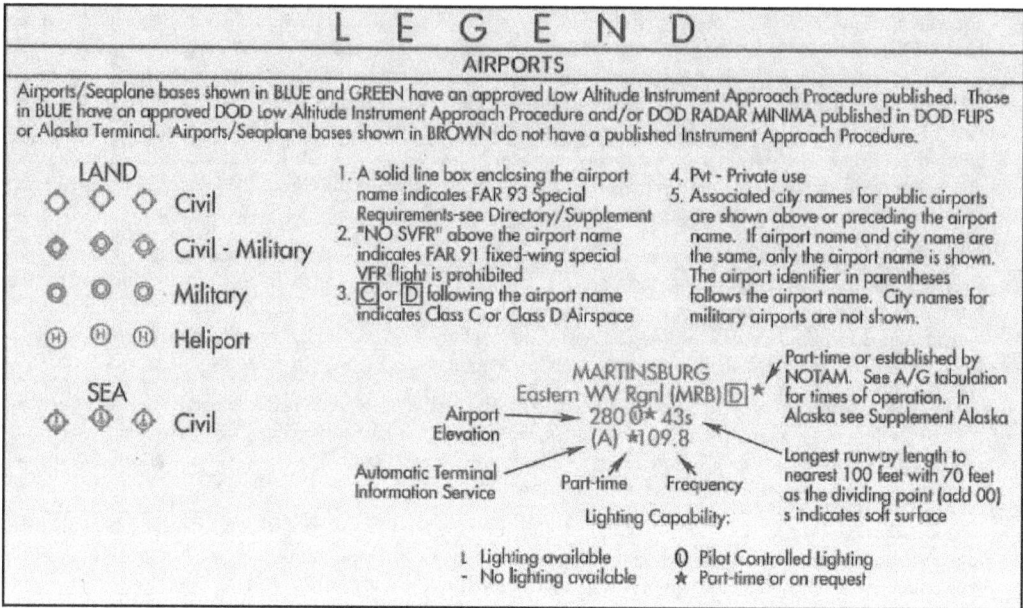

Figure 4-2. En route airport legend

Minimum Obstruction Clearance Altitude

4-22. The minimum obstruction clearance altitude (MOCA) is the lowest published altitude in effect between radio fixes on VOR airways, off-airway routes, or route segments that meets obstacle clearance requirements for the entire route segment and ensures acceptable navigational signal coverage only within 25 statute (22 nautical) miles of a VOR. The MOCA provides the same obstruction clearance as an MEA; however, the NAV signal reception is only ensured within 22 nautical miles of the closest NAVAID defining the route. The MOCA is listed below the MEA and indicated on NACO charts by a leading asterisk (*3400).

Minimum Reception Altitude

4-23. The minimum reception altitude (MRA) is the lowest altitude at which an airway intersection can be determined. The MRA identifies an intersection from an off-course NAVAID. If reception is line-of-sight based, signal coverage extends to the MRA or above. However, if the aircraft is equipped with DME and the chart indicates the intersection can be identified with such equipment, the aviator could define the fix without attaining the MRA. On NACO charts, the MRA is indicated by the symbol, and the altitude is preceded by MRA (MRA 9300).

Minimum Crossing Altitude

4-24. The minimum crossing altitude (MCA) is the lowest altitude at certain fixes at which an aircraft must cross when it is proceeding in the direction of a higher MEA. The MCA is depicted along an MEA route segment where altitude increases. The MCA is usually indicated when the route approaches steeply rising terrain and obstacle clearance and/or signal reception is compromised. In this case, the pilot is required to initiate a climb so that the MCA is reached by the time that the intersection is crossed. On NACO charts, the MCA is indicated by the symbol, Victor airway number, and applied direction.

Maximum Authorized Altitude

4-25. The maximum authorized altitude (MAA) is a published altitude representing the maximum usable altitude or FL for an airspace structure or route segment. The MAA is the highest altitude at which the airway can be flown without aircraft navigation systems receiving conflicting navigation signals from NAVAIDs operating on the same frequency. Chart depictions appear as MAA-15000.

4-26. A sideways T ⌐ is depicted on the chart when an MEA, MOCA, and/or MAA changes on a segment other than a NAVAID,. If there is an airway break without the symbol, assume that the altitudes have not changed. When a change of MEA to a higher MEA is required, the climb may commence at the break, ensuring obstacle clearance.

Off Route Obstruction Clearance Altitude

4-27. The off route obstruction clearance altitude (OROCA) is an off-route altitude that provides obstruction clearance with a 1,000-foot buffer in nonmountainous terrain areas and a 2,000-foot buffer in designated mountainous areas within the United States. This altitude may not provide signal coverage from ground-based NAVAIDs, ATC radar, or communications coverage.

Navigation Symbology

Types of Navigational Aids

4-28. VOR is the principal NAVAID that supports Victor airways. Many other navigation tools are also available to the aviator. Nondirectional beacons (NDBs) broadcast signals accurate enough to provide stand-alone approaches, and DME allows the aviator to pinpoint a reporting point on the airway. Though primarily navigation tools, these NAVAIDs can also transmit voice broadcasts.

4-29. TACAN channels are represented as the two- or three-digit numbers following the three-letter identifier in the NAVAID boxes. The NACO terminal procedures provide a frequency-pairing table for TACAN-only sites. On NACO charts, very high frequency (VHF) and ultra high frequency (UHF) NAVAIDs (VORs) are depicted in black, while low frequencies (LFs) and medium frequencies (MFs) are depicted as brown (Figure 4-3, page 4-8).

Identifying Intersections

4-30. Intersections along the airway route are established by a variety of NAVAIDs. An open triangle △ indicates the location of an ATC reporting point at an intersection; a solid triangle ▲ means that a report is compulsory (Figure 4-4, page 4-9). NDBs, localizers, and off-route VORs are used to establish intersections. NDBs are sometimes collocated with intersections; if so, the passage of the NDB marks the intersection. A bearing to an off-route NDB also can provide intersection identification. The presence of a localizer course can be determined from a feathered arrowhead symbol on the en route chart ═══════◄. If crosshatched markings appear on the left-hand side of the arrowhead, ═══════◄ a back course (BC) signal is transmitted. On NACO charts, the localizer symbol is depicted to identify an intersection.

4-31. When an aircraft is traveling on an airway, off-route VORs remain the most common means of identifying intersections. Arrows depicted next to the intersection, ⇢⌐, indicate the NAVAID being used for identification. Another means of identifying an intersection is with the use of DME. A hollow arrowhead ◁ indicates that DME is authorized for intersection identification. If DME mileage at the intersection is a cumulative distance of the route segments, the mileage is totaled and indicated by a D-shaped symbol with a number inside ◄⌐00⌐. Typically, distance numbers do not appear on the initial segment. Approved IFR GPS units are also used to report intersections if the intersection name resides in a current database.

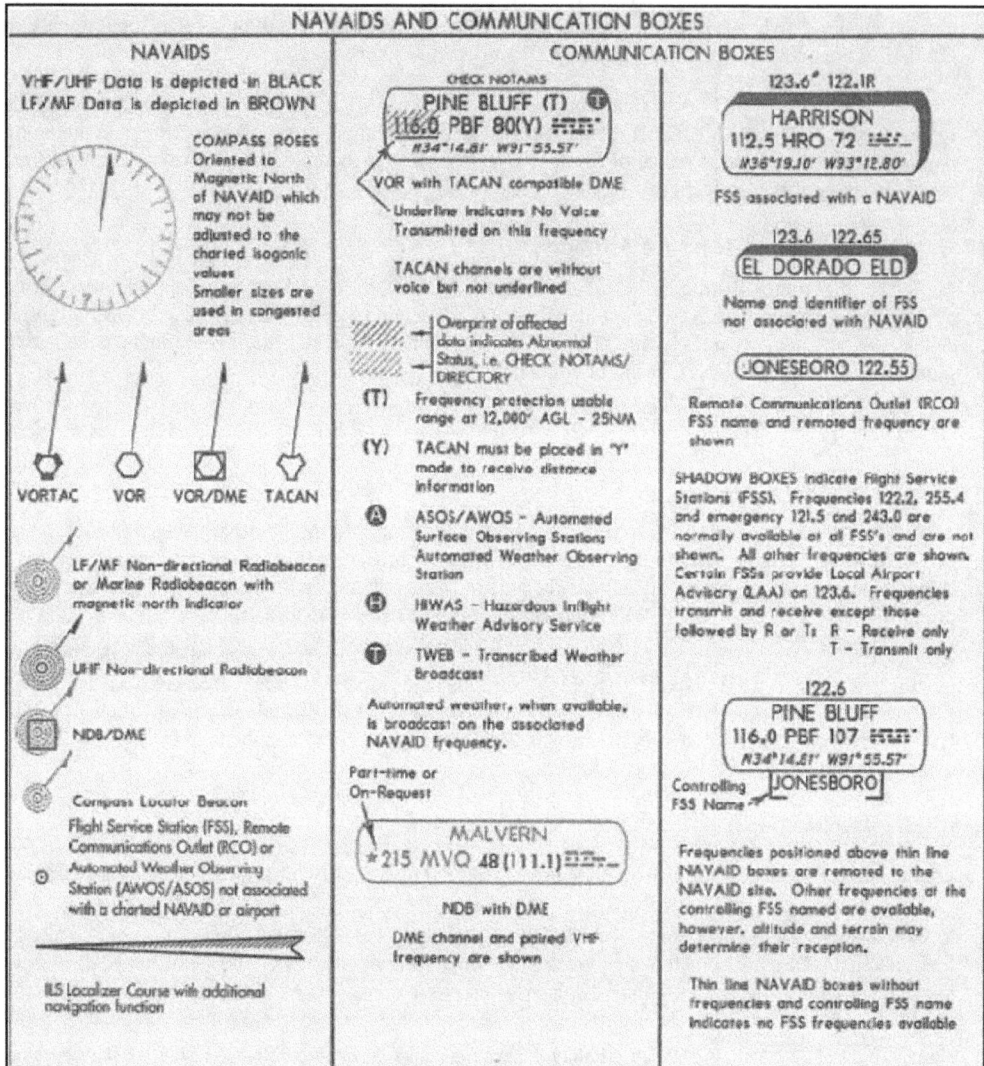

Figure 4-3. Navigational aid and communication boxes

AIR TRAFFIC SERVICES AND AIRSPACE INFORMATION

ROUTE DATA

VHF/UHF Data is depicted in BLACK
LF/MF Data is depicted in BROWN

- V4 — VOR Airway
- A0 — LF/MF Airway
- A0 — Uncontrolled LF/MF Airway
- A0 — Oceanic Route
- A0 — ATS Route
- T000 — Low Altitude RNAV Route, GNSS required
- Substitute Route See NOTAMs
- Unusable Route Segment
- V193 — Preferred Single Direction Route
- 000.0 NAME 00 / 000 NAME — Facility Locators used in formation of reporting points
- 000 — Radial outbound from a UHF/VHF NAVAID
- 000 — Bearing inbound to a LF/MF NAVAID
- 000 000 — Total Mileage between Compulsory Reporting Points and/or NAVAIDs
- 00 00 — Mileage between other Reporting Points, NAVAIDs and/or Mileage Breakdown
- Denotes DME fix (distance same as airway mileage)
- 00 — Denotes DME fix (encircled mileage shown when not otherwise obvious)
- x x — Mileage Breakdown or Computer Nav Fix (CNF) (no ATC functions)
- 00 — Overall Mileage (Flight Planning and Military IFR Routes)
- EVEN — Direction of Flight Indicator (Canada only)
- 00 / 00 — VOR Changeover Point giving mileage to NAVAIDs (Not shown at midpoint locations)

- ♦0000 / •0000 — Minimum Obstruction Clearance Altitude (MOCA)
- 0000 0000 — Minimum Enroute Altitude (MEA)
- 0000G — MEA for GNSS RNAV aircraft
- MAA - 00000 — Maximum Authorized Altitude (MAA)
- MEA, MOCA and/or MAA change at other than NAVAIDs
- Minimum Reception Altitude (MRA)
- Minimum Crossing Altitude (MCA)

FIXES/ATC REPORTING REQUIREMENTS

- Fix-Compulsory and Non-Compulsory Position Report
- RNAV Waypoint-Compulsory and Non-Compulsory Position Report
- Offset arrows indicate facility forming a fix (away from VHF/UHF, toward LF/MF NAVAID)
- Holding Pattern with max. restricted airspeed 210K applies to altitudes above 6000' to and including 14000' 175K applies to all altitudes

TACAN FIX DATA

Ident — NAME 00 000°/00 — Chan
Radial from TACAN
Distance from TACAN

AIRSPACE INFORMATION

Open area (white) indicates controlled airspace (Class E) unless otherwise indicated. All airspace 14,500' and above is controlled (Class E)
Shaded area (brown) indicates uncontrolled airspace below 14,500' (Class G)
In Canada – Indicates Class B Airspace above 12,500'
Oceanic Control Area (CTA)
Additional Control Area Limit

Class B Airspace | Class C Airspace | Mode C Area See FAR 91.215

BOUNDARIES

- Air Route Traffic Control Center (ARTCC)
- NAME / 000.0 000.0 — ARTCC Remoted Sites with discrete VHF and UHF frequencies
- Flight Information Region (FIR)
- CTA/FIR MIAMI OCEANIC KZMA / FL 180 — Ceiling / GND — Floor / NY RADIO — Call Sign / 129.9 — Frequency / Type of Area Traffic Service
- Air Defense Identification Zone (ADIZ)
- 125 — Off Route Obstruction Clearance Altitudes (OROCA) Example: 12,500 feet
- International Boundary (omitted when coincident with ARTCC or FIR)
- US/Russia Maritime Boundary
- Area of Enlargement (contains only data for through flights) See Area Charts for complete data
- Official Time Zone
- International Date Line

SPECIAL USE AIRSPACE

P-00 / R-000 / A-000 / W-000 | WALL 1 MOA | WALL 2 MOA
Line delimits internal separation of same Special Use Area

P - Prohibited Area   A - Alert Area
R - Restricted Area   W - Warning Area
MOA - Military Operations Area
In Canada: CYA - Advisory Area
CYD - Danger Area
CYR - Restricted Area
SEE AIRSPACE TABULATION FOR COMPLETE INFORMATION.

MISCELLANEOUS

ALTIMETER — Altimeter Setting Change
8°W — 2000 Isogonic Line and Value
ALL MILEAGES ARE NAUTICAL EXCEPT AS NOTED
ALL RADIALS AND BEARINGS ARE MAGNETIC
ALL ALTITUDES ARE MSL UNLESS OTHERWISE STATED
ALL TIME IS COORDINATED UNIVERSAL TIME (UTC)
During periods of Daylight Saving Time (DT) effective hours will be one hour earlier than shown. All states observe DT except Arizona and that portion of Indiana in the Eastern Time Zone.
North American Datum of 1983 (NAD 83), for charting purposes is considered equivalent to World Geodetic System 1984 (WGS 84).
FOR ADDITIONAL SYMBOL INFORMATION REFER TO THE CHART USER'S GUIDE

EXAMPLE OF GROUPING

Reporting Points (coordinates are shown for offshore and holding fixes)
Airway Restriction (airway penetrates Prohibited & Restricted Airspace)
ARCEY N00°00.00' W00°00.00'
MAA-14000 4000 2000G 2000
R-72
A4 14 53
54 / V30 18 / 90 / R
3500 V30 36 MEA GAP
Holding Pattern
MEA is established with a gap in navigation signal coverage
000.0 NAME 00
NAME MRA 4000
EVEN 4200 3000
A4 32
Shoreline Vignette

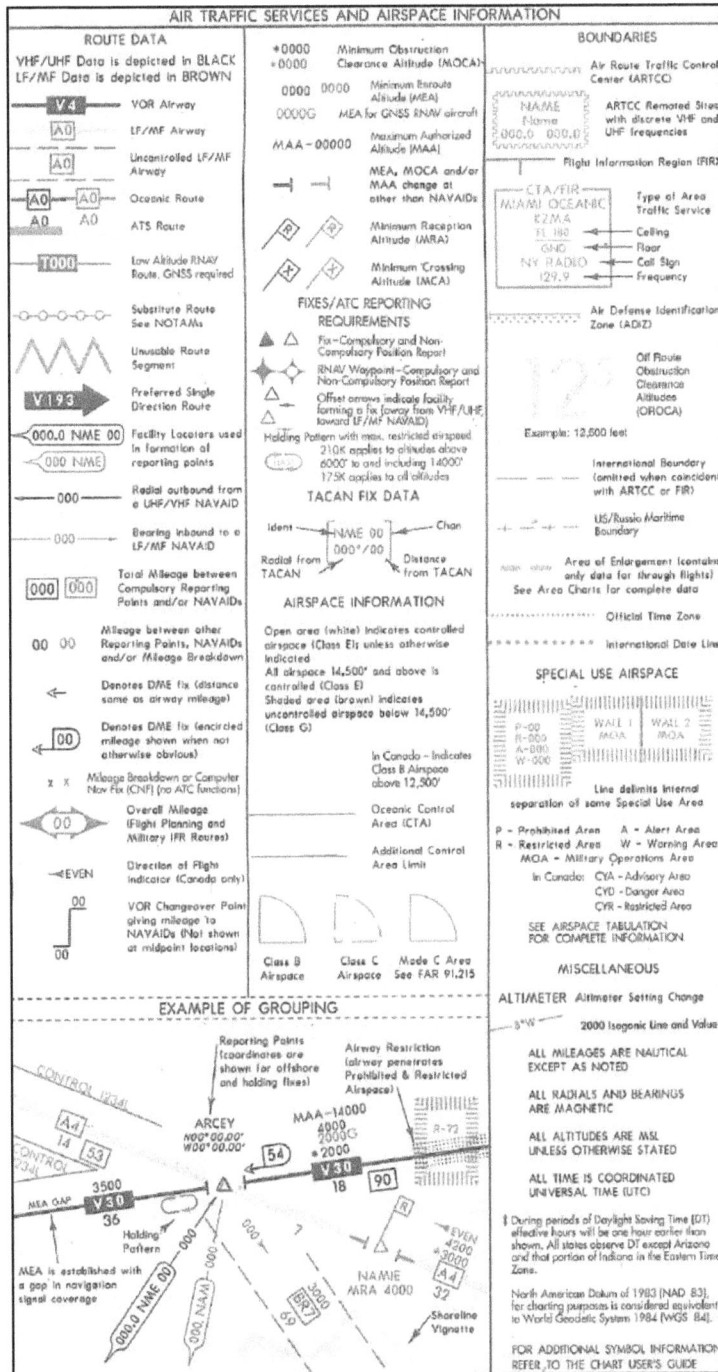

Figure 4-4. Air traffic services and airspace information

Other Route Information

4-32. DME and GPS provide valuable route information such as mileage, position, and ground speed. Even without this equipment, information provided on the charts makes the necessary calculations, using time and distance. The en route chart depicts point-to-point distances on the airway system in nautical miles. Distances from VOR to VOR are charted with a number inside of a box 000 . To differentiate distances when two airways cross, TO with the three-letter VOR identifier appears next to the distance box TO PDX 97 .

4-33. A VOR changeover point (COP) is depicted on charts by this symbol: 85 . The numbers indicate the distance at which to change the VOR frequency. The frequency change might be required because of signal reception or conflicting frequencies. If a COP does not appear on an airway, the frequency should be changed midway between the facilities. A COP at an intersection often indicates a course change.

4-34. Occasionally an "x" will appear at a separated segment of an airway that is not an intersection. The "x" is a mileage breakdown or computer navigation fix and indicates a course change.

4-35. The ATC computerized system has reduced the need for holding en route. However, published holding patterns are still found on charts at junctures where ATC has deemed a holding pattern necessary to enable traffic flow. When a holding pattern is charted, the controller may provide the holding direction and the statement as published (Figure 4-4, page 4-10).

4-36. Boundaries separating the jurisdiction of Air Route Traffic Control Centers (ARTCCs) are depicted on charts with blue serrations: ⊐⎍⎍⎍⎍⎍⎍⎍⎍⎍⎍⎍⎍⌐. The name of the controlling facility is printed on the corresponding side of the division line. ARTCC remote sites are depicted as blue serrated boxes and contain the center name, sector name, and sector frequency.

Weather Information and Communication Features

Automated Flight Service Station

4-37. En route NAVAIDs also provide weather information and serve communication functions. When a NAVAID is shown as a shadowed box, an automated flight service station (AFSS) of the same name is directly associated with the facility. If an AFSS is located without an associated NAVAID, the shadowed box is smaller and contains only the name and identifier. The AFSS frequencies are provided on top of the box (frequencies 121.5, 122.2, 255.4, and 243.0 are normally available at all flight service stations [FSSs] and are not shown above the boxes).

Remote Communications Outlet

4-38. A remote communications outlet (RCO) associated with a NAVAID is designated by a box with the controlling AFSS frequency on the top and the name under the box. Without an associated facility, the RCO box contains the AFSS name and remote frequency.

```
        122.6
   ⌐ PINE BLUFF ¬
   116.0 PBF 107 ⋮⋮⋮⋮
    N34°14.81' W91°55.57'
      ⌊JONESBORO⌋
```
```
( JONESBORO 122.55 )
```

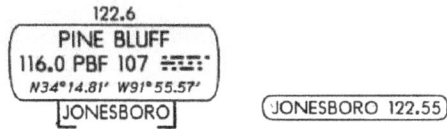

Hazardous In-Flight Weather Advisory Service and Transcribed Weather Broadcast

4-39. The Hazardous In-flight Weather Advisory Service (HIWAS) and the Transcribed Weather Broadcast (TWEB) are continuously transmitted over selected NAVAIDs and depicted in the NAVAID box. HIWAS is depicted by a white H in a black circle in the upper left corner of the box; TWEB broadcasts show as a white T in a black circle in the upper right corner.

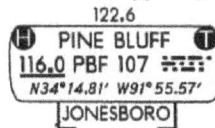

```
            122.6
   Ⓗ  PINE BLUFF  Ⓣ
   116.0 PBF 107 ⋮⋮⋮⋮
    N34°14.81' W91°55.57'
       ⌊JONESBORO⌋
```

DEPARTURE PROCEDURE CHART

4-40. Departure Procedure (DP) charts are ATC-coded departure procedures established at certain airports to simplify clearance delivery procedures. DPs provide obstacle clearance protection to aircraft in IMC while reducing communications and departure delays. DPs are published in text/charted graphic form. Regardless of format, all DPs provide a way to depart the airport and make the transition to the en route structure safely. When available, aviators are strongly encouraged to file and fly a DP at night during marginal VMC and IMC.

4-41. DPs provide obstacle clearance given that the aircraft crosses the end of the runway at least 35 feet AGL, climbs to 400 feet above airport elevation before turning, and climbs at least 200 feet per nautical mile (FPNM), unless a higher climb gradient is specified to the assigned altitude. ATC may vector an aircraft off a previously assigned DP; however, the 200 FPNM or the FPNM specified in the DP is required. Textual DPs are listed by airport in the DOD FLIP (Terminal) volumes. Graphic DPs are depicted in the DOD FLIP (Terminal) volumes following the approach procedures for the airport.

STANDARD TERMINAL ARRIVAL ROUTE CHARTS

4-42. Standard Terminal Arrival Route (STAR) charts are ATC-coded IFR arrival routes established for certain airports to simplify clearance delivery procedures. STARs depict prescribed routes so that the instrument pilot can make the transition from the en route structure to a fix in the terminal area from which an instrument approach can be conducted. If the appropriate STAR is not available, the aviator can write No STAR in the flight plan. However, if the controller is busy, the aviator might be cleared along the same route. If necessary, the controller has the aviator copy the entire text of the procedure.

INSTRUMENT APPROACH PROCEDURE CHART

4-43. Instrument approach procedure (IAP) charts provide an IFR descent from the en route environment to a point where a safe landing can be made. The instrument approach chart is divided into five main sections: the margin identification, pilot briefing information, plan view, profile view, landing minimums (and notes), and airport diagram (Figure 4-5, page 4-12).

MARGIN IDENTIFICATION

4-44. The margin identification, found at the top and bottom of the chart, depicts airport location and procedure identification. The approach plates are organized by city first, then airport name and state.

Military airfields are organized by airfield name first, then city and state. For example, Cairns Army Airfield (AAF) at Fort Rucker, Alabama, is alphabetically listed under C for Cairns.

4-45. In the center of the top margin is the FAA chart reference number and approving authority and, at the bottom center, the airport's latitude and longitude coordinates. The chart's amendment status appears below the city and state on the left side in the bottom margin, along with the amendment's effective date. The five-digit date format in the amendment (06050) is read, the fiftieth day of 2006.

4-46. The procedure identification (top and bottom margin area of Figure 4-5) is derived from the type of navigational facility providing final-approach course guidance. A runway number is listed when the approach course is aligned within 30 degrees of the runway centerline (ILS runway [RWY] 6 or VOR or GPS RWY 24); this type of approach allows a straight-in landing under the right conditions. Some airports have parallel runways and simultaneous approach procedures. To distinguish between the left, right, and center runways, an L, R, or C follows the runway number (ILS RWY 16R). If the approach course diverges more than 30 degrees from the runway centerline, a letter from the beginning of the alphabet is assigned (VOR-A). Letter designation signifies the expectation for the procedure to culminate in a circling approach to land. In some cases, an airport might have more than one circling approach.

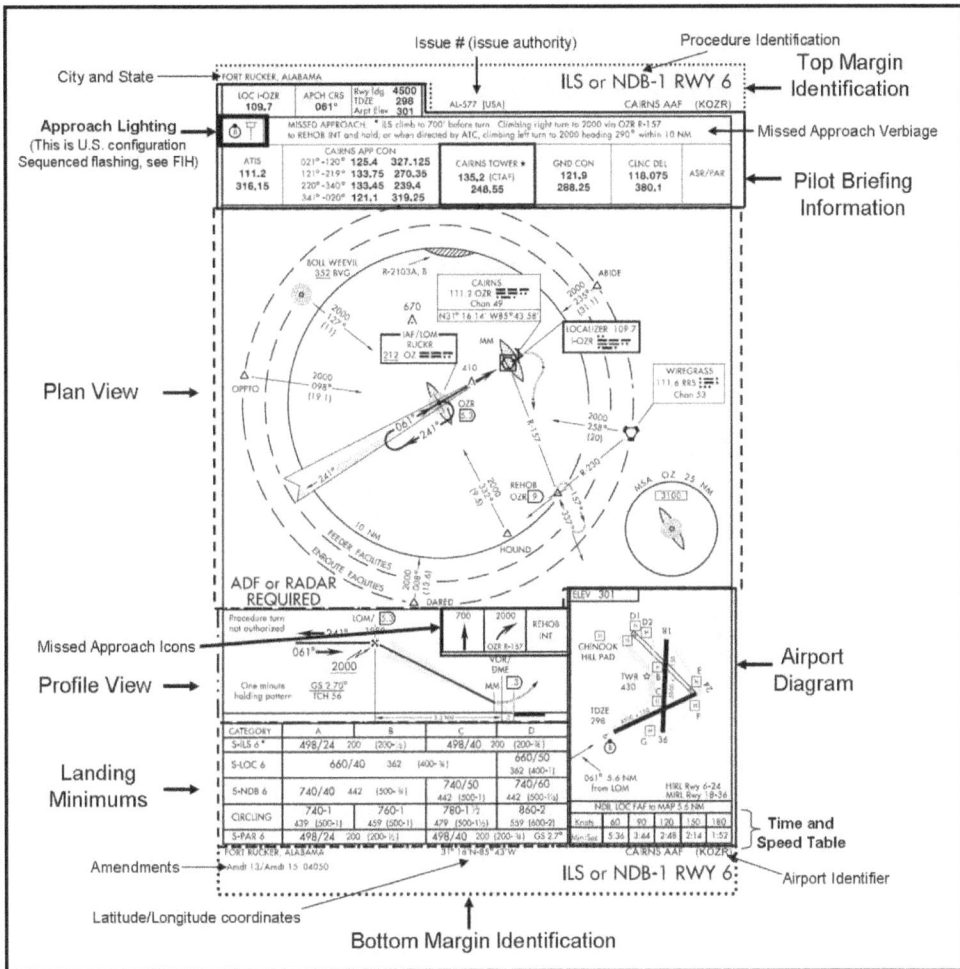

Figure 4-5. Instrument approach chart

4-47. More than one navigational system, separated by a slash, indicates that more than one type of equipment is required to execute the final approach (VOR/DME RWY 31). More than one navigational system separated by "or" indicates either type of equipment may be used to execute final approach (VOR or GPS RWY 6). Multiple approaches of the same type to the same runway using the same guidance have an additional letter from the end of the alphabet, number, or term in the title (ILS Z RWY 28, Silver ILS RWY 28, or ILS 2 RWY 28). VOR/DME RNAV approaches are identified as VOR/DME RNAV RWY (runway number). Helicopters have special IAPs designated with COPTER in the procedure identification (COPTER LOC/DME 25L). Other types of navigation systems may be required to execute other portions of the approach before intercepting the final-approach segment or during a missed approach.

PILOT BRIEFING INFORMATION

4-48. Pilot briefing information format consists of three horizontal rows of boxed procedure-specific information along the top edge of the chart. Altitudes, frequency, and course and elevation values (except HATs and HAAs) are charted in bold type. The top row contains the primary procedure navigation information, final approach course, landing distance available, touchdown zone, and airport elevations. The middle row contains procedure notes and limitations, icons indicating if nonstandard alternate and/or takeoff minimums apply, approach lighting symbology, and a full-text description of the missed approach procedure. The bottom row contains air-to-ground communication facilities and frequencies in the order used during an approach.

4-49. When an alternate airport is required, standard IFR alternate minimums apply according to AR 95-1.

A black triangle with a white A, ▲ , appearing in the middle row (Figure 4-6) indicates nonstandard IFR alternate minimums exist for the airport. If an NA appears after the A, ▲ NA , alternate minimums are not authorized. This information is found on the Roman numeral pages in the beginning of the DOD FLIP (Terminal) charts.

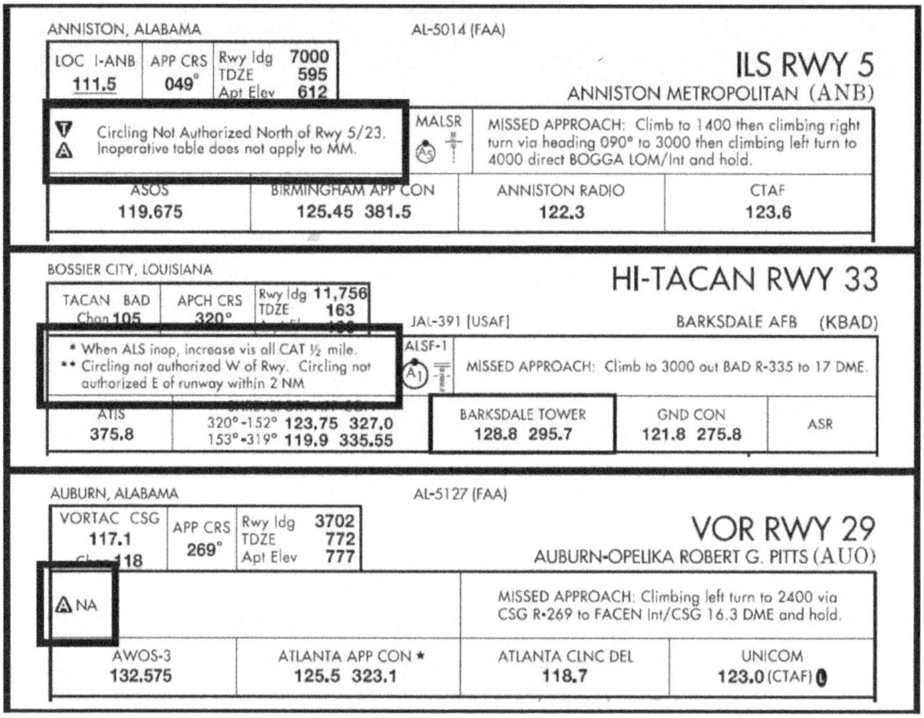

Figure 4-6. Procedures and notes

4-50. Procedural notes are included in a box located on the middle row. A procedural note might indicate, "Circling not authorized west of RWY." Other notes might concern a local altimeter setting and the resulting change in the minimums. The use of radar may also be noted in this section. Additional notes may be found in the plan view.

4-51. A black triangle with a white T, ▼ , (appears in the notes area), signifies that the airport has nonstandard IFR takeoff minimums. The appropriate section in the front of the DOD FLIP (Terminal) charts is consulted in this case.

PLAN VIEW

4-52. The plan view provides a graphical overhead view of the procedure and depicts the routes that guide the aviator from the en route segments to the initial approach fix (IAF) (Figure 4-5, page 4-12). During initial approach, the aircraft has departed the en route phase of flight and is maneuvering to enter an intermediate or final segment of the instrument approach. An initial approach can be made within the terminal area along prescribed routes such as an arc, a radial, or a course; a heading or a radar vector; or a combination thereof. Procedure turns and high-altitude teardrop penetrations are initial approach segments. Features of the plan view include the procedure turn, obstacle elevation, minimum safe altitude (MSA), and procedure track (Figure 4-5, page 4-12).

4-53. Most NACO/DOD FLIP (Terminal) charts contain a reference or distance circle with a 10 nautical mile radius. Normally, approach features within the plan view are shown to scale; however, only data within the reference circle are always drawn to scale. The circle is centered on an approach fix and has a radius of 10 nautical miles unless otherwise indicated. When a route segment outside of the circle is drawn to scale, the symbol interrupts the segment.

4-54. Dashed circles or concentric rings around the distance circle are used when the information necessary to the procedure will not fit to scale within the limits of the plan view area. They serve as a means to systematically arrange this information in its relative position outside and beyond the reference circle. These concentric rings are labeled en route and feeder facilities. The en route facilities ring depicts NAVAIDs, fixes, and intersections that are part of the en route low-altitude airway structure used in the approach procedure. The feeder facilities ring includes radio aids to navigation, fixes and intersections used by ATC to direct aircraft to intervening facilities/fixes between the en route structure, and the IAF. Feeder routes are not part of the en route structure.

4-55. The primary airport depicted in the plan view is drawn with enough detail to show the runway orientation and final approach course alignment. Airports other than the primary approach airport are not depicted in the plan view.

4-56. Known spot elevations and obstacles are indicated on the plan view in MSL altitudes. The largest dot and number combination indicates the highest elevation. An inverted V with a dot in the center depicts an obstacle. The highest obstacle is indicated with a bolder, larger version of the same symbol. Two interlocking inverted "Vs" signify a group of obstacles.

4-57. The MSA circle appears in the plan view (Figure 4-5, page 4-12), except in approaches for which appropriate NAVAIDs (VOR or NDB) are unavailable. The MSA is provided for emergency purposes only and guarantees 1,000 feet obstruction clearance in the sector indicated with reference to the bearing in the circle. For conventional navigation systems, the MSA is normally based on the primary omnidirectional facility on which the IAP is predicated. The MSA depiction on the approach chart contains the facility identifier of the NAVAID used to determine the MSA altitudes. For RNAV approaches, the MSA is based on the runway waypoint for straight-in approaches or the airport waypoint for circling approaches. For GPS approaches, the MSA center is the missed approach waypoint. The MSL altitudes appear in boxes within the circle, which is typically a 25-nautical mile radius unless otherwise indicated. The MSA circle refers to the letter identifier of the NAVAID or waypoint that describes the center of the circle. MSAs are not depicted on terminal arrival area (TAA) approach charts.

4-58. NAVAIDs in the plan view are necessary for completion of the instrument procedure and include the facility name, frequency, letter identifier, and Morse code sequence. A heavy-lined NAVAID box depicts the primary NAVAID used for the approach. An "I" in front of the NAVAID identifier (Figure 4-5, page 4-12, I-OZR) listed in the NAVAID box indicates a localizer and a TACAN channel (Chan 49), which signifies DME availability. The requirement for an ADF, DME, or RADAR in the approach is noted in the plan view.

4-59. Intersections, fixes, radials, and course lines describe route and approach sequencing information. The main procedure or final approach course is a thick, solid line. A DME arc, which is part of the main procedure course, is also represented as a thick, solid line. A feeder route is depicted with a medium line and provides heading, altitude, and distance information. All three components must be designated on the chart to provide a navigable course. Radials, such as lead radials, are shown by thin lines. The missed approach track is drawn using a thin-dashed line with a directional arrow. A visual flight path segment appears as a thick, dashed line with a directional arrow. IAFs are charted when associated with a NAVAID or when freestanding.

4-60. The missed approach holding pattern track is represented with a thin, dashed line. When collocated, the missed approach holding pattern and procedure turn holding pattern are indicated as a solid-black line. Arrival holding patterns are depicted as thin, solid lines.

Course Reversal Elements in Plan View and Profile View

4-61. Course reversals are included in an IAP and depicted in one of three ways: a 45/180-degree procedure, holding pattern, or teardrop procedure. The maneuvers are required when it is necessary to reverse direction to establish the aircraft inbound on an intermediate or final approach course. Components of the required procedure are depicted in the plan view and profile view. The maneuver must be completed within the distance and at the minimum altitude specified in the profile view. Aviators should coordinate with the appropriate ATC facility relating to course reversal during the IAP.

Procedure Turns

4-62. A procedure turn barbed arrow indicates the direction or side of the outbound course on which the procedure turn is made. Headings are provided for course reversal using the 45-degree procedure turn. However, the point at which the turn may be commenced and type and rate of turn are at the discretion of the aviator. Some options are the standard 45-degree procedure turn (45/180), holding/racetrack pattern, teardrop procedure turn, or 80/260-degree course reversal. Absence of the procedure turn barbed arrow in the plan view indicates that a procedure turn is not authorized. A maximum procedure turn speed of not greater than 200 knots indicated airspeed (KIAS) should be observed when the aircraft turns outbound over the IAF and throughout the procedure turn maneuver to ensure staying within the obstruction clearance area. The normal procedure turn distance is 10 nautical miles but may be reduced to a minimum of 5 nautical miles where only Category A or helicopter aircraft are operated or increased to as much as 15 nautical miles to accommodate high-performance aircraft. Descent below the procedure turn altitude begins after the aircraft is established on the inbound course. The procedure turn is not required when "No PT" appears or radar vectoring to final approach is provided and when conducting a timed approach or the procedure turn is not authorized. Aviators contact the appropriate ATC facility when in doubt if a procedure turn is required.

Holding in Lieu of Procedure Turn

4-63. A holding in lieu of procedure turn may be specified for course reversal in some procedures. In such cases, the holding pattern is established over an intermediate fix (IF) or a FAF. The holding pattern distance or time specified in the profile view must be observed. Maximum holding airspeed limitations set forth for all holding patterns apply. The holding pattern maneuver is completed when the aircraft is established on the inbound course after executing the appropriate entry. If cleared for the approach before returning to the holding fix and the aircraft is at the prescribed altitude, additional circuits of the holding pattern are not necessary nor expected by ATC. It is the aviator's responsibility to advise ATC, upon receipt of the approach clearance, if electing to make additional circuits to lose excessive altitude or become better established on course. When holding in lieu of a procedure turn is conducted, the holding pattern must be followed except when radar vectors to the final-approach course are provided or when "No PT" is shown on the approach course.

Teardrop Procedure

4-64. When a teardrop procedure turn is depicted and a course reversal is required (unless otherwise authorized by ATC), this type of procedure must be executed. The teardrop procedure consists of departure from an IAF on the published outbound course, followed by a turn toward and intercepting the inbound course at or before the intermediate fix or point. Its purpose is to permit an aircraft to reverse direction and lose considerable altitude within reasonably limited airspace. Where no fix is available to mark the beginning of the intermediate segment, assume that the segment commences at a point 10 nautical miles before the FAF. When the facility is located on the airport, an aircraft is considered to be on final approach upon completing the penetration turn; however, the final approach segment begins on the final approach course 10 nautical miles from the facility.

Terminal Arrival Area

4-65. Terminal arrival area (TAA) procedures provide a transition method for arriving aircraft with GPS/RNAV equipment. TAAs also eliminate or reduce the need for feeder routes, departure extensions, and procedure turns or course reversal. The TAA is controlled airspace established with standard or modified RNAV approach configurations. Three areas in a standard TAA are straight-in, left base, and right base. Arc boundaries of the three TAA areas are published portions of the approach and allow aircraft to make the transition from the en route structure directly to the nearest IAF. When crossing the boundary of these areas or when released by ATC within the area, the aviator proceeds directly to the appropriate waypoint IAF for the approach area being flown. An aviator has the option, in all areas, of proceeding directly to the holding pattern.

4-66. The TAA has a T structure normally providing a "No PT" for aircraft using the approach (Figure 4-7, page 4-17). The TAA provides the aviator and air traffic controller with an efficient method for routing traffic from the en route to the terminal structure. The basic T contained in the TAA normally aligns the procedure on the runway centerline with the missed approach point (MAP) located at the threshold, the FAF 5 nautical miles from the threshold, and the IF 5 nautical miles from the FAF.

4-67. To descend from a high en route altitude to the initial segment altitude, a hold in lieu of a procedure turn provides the aircraft with an extended distance for the necessary descent gradient. The holding pattern constructed for this purpose is always established on the center IAF waypoint. Other modifications may be required for parallel runways or because of operational requirements. When published, the RNAV chart depicts the TAA through icons representing each TAA associated with the RNAV procedure. These icons are depicted in the plan view of the approach plate and are generally arranged on the chart according to their position relative to the aircraft's arrival from the en route structure.

PROFILE VIEW

4-68. The profile view is a side-view drawing of the procedure illustrating the vertical approach path altitudes, headings, distances, and fixes (Figure 4-8, page 4-17). The view includes minimum altitude and maximum distance for the procedure turn, altitudes over prescribed fixes, distances between fixes, and the missed approach procedure. The profile view aids in the aviator's interpretation of the IAP; however, the profile view is not drawn to scale.

4-69. The precision approach glide-slope intercept altitude (Figure 4-8, page 4-18) is a minimum altitude for glide-slope interception after completion of the procedure turn illustrated by an altitude number and zigzag line with an arrow pointer. It applies to precision approaches and, except where otherwise prescribed, applies as a minimum altitude for crossing the FAF when the glide slope is inoperative or not used. Precision approach profiles also depict the glide-slope angle of descent, threshold crossing height (TCH), and glide-slope altitude at the outer marker (OM).

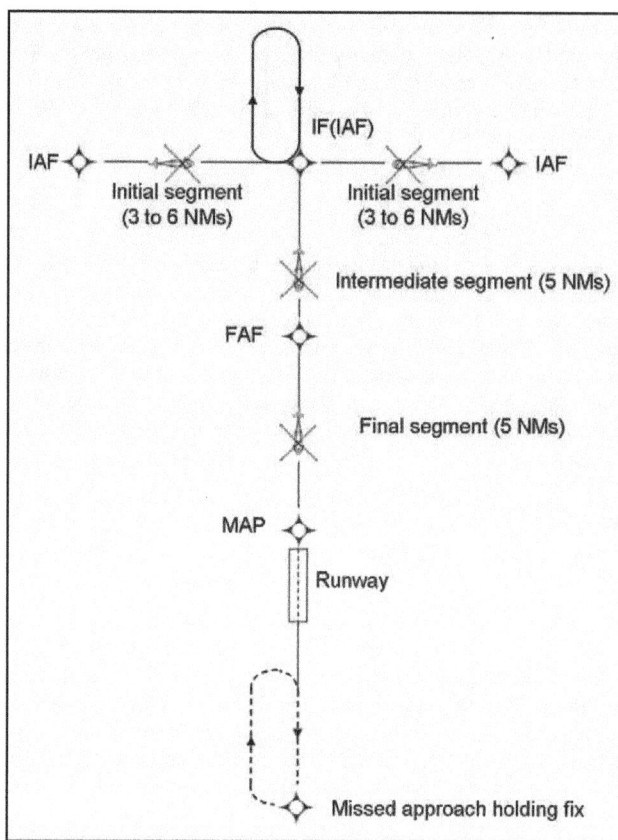

Figure 4-7. Basic T design of terminal arrival area

4-70. In nonprecision approaches, a final descent is initiated at the FAF or after completing the procedure turn and established inbound on the procedure course. The FAF is clearly identified by use of the Maltese cross symbol in the profile view. If the FAF is not indicated in the profile view, the MAP is based on station passage when the facility is on the airport or at a specified distance (VOR/DME or GPS procedures).

4-71. Step-down fixes in nonprecision procedures are provided between the FAF and airport for authorizing a lower MDA after passing an obstruction. Step-down fixes are identified by NAVAID, NAVAID fix, waypoint, and radar and are depicted by a vertical dashed line. Normally, there is only one step-down fix between the FAF and MAP, but there can be several. If the step-down fix cannot be identified for any reason, the minimum altitude at the step-down fix becomes the MDA for the approach. However, circling minimums apply if they are higher than the step-down fix minimum altitude and a circling approach is required.

4-72. The visual descent point (VDP) is a defined point on the final approach course of a nonprecision straight-in approach procedure. A normal descent from the MDA to the runway touchdown point may be commenced, provided visual reference is established. The VDP is identified on the profile view of the approach chart by the symbol "V" (Figure 4-8, page 4-18).

4-73. The MAP varies, depending upon the approach flown. For the ILS, the MAP is at the DA/DH. In nonprecision procedures, the aviator determines the MAP by timing from the FAF when the approach aid is well away from the airport, a fix or NAVAID when the navigation facility is located on the field, or waypoints as defined by GPS or VOR/DME RNAV. The aviator may execute the MAP early, but aviators should, unless otherwise cleared by ATC, fly the IAP as specified on the approach plate to the MAP at or above the MDA or DA/DH before executing a turning maneuver.

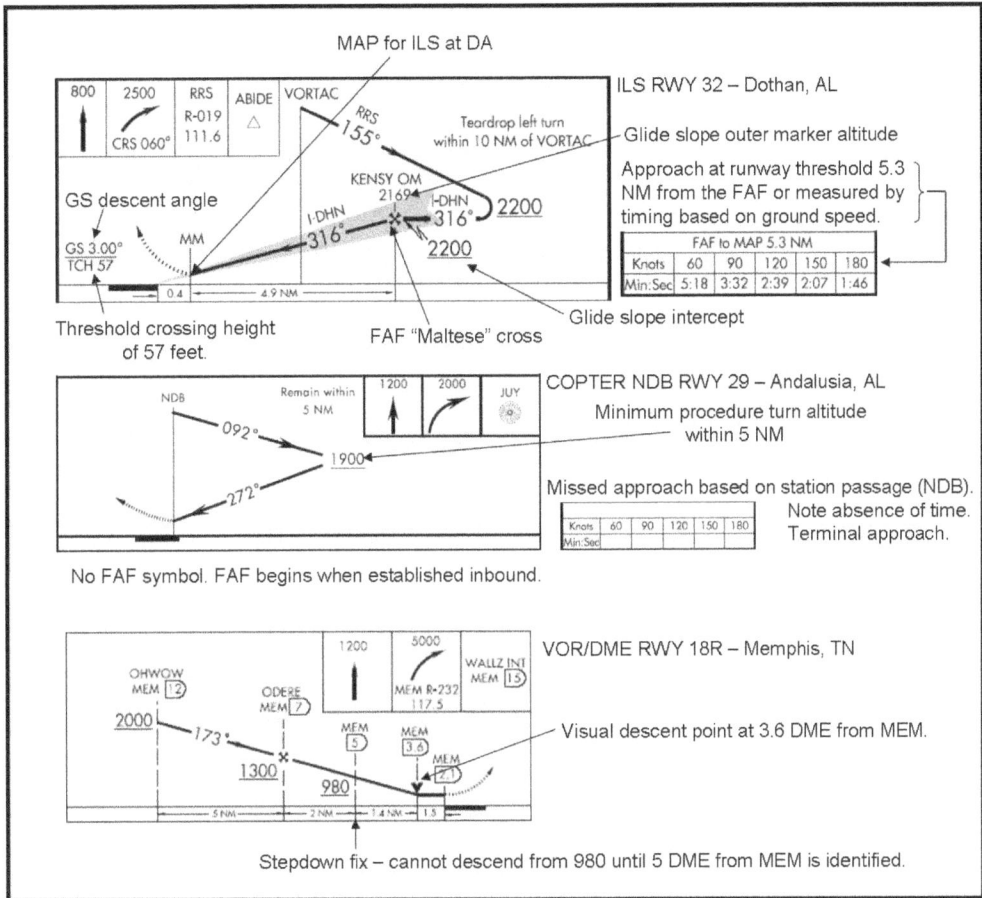

Figure 4-8. Profile view features

4-74. A complete description of the missed approach procedure appears in the pilot briefing information section (Figure 4-5, page 4-12), and missed approach icons appear in the profile view. When initiating a missed approach, the aviator will be directed to climb straight ahead (climb to 2,500) or commence a turning climb to a specified altitude (climbing left turn to 2,500). In some cases, the procedure will direct the aviator to climb straight ahead to an initial altitude, then turn or enter a climbing turn to the holding altitude (climb to 900, then continue a climbing right turn to 2,500 direct ABC VOR and hold).

4-75. When the missed approach procedure specifies holding at a facility or fix, the aviator proceeds according to the missed approach track and pattern depicted on the plan view. An alternate missed approach procedure may also be issued by ATC. The textual description specifies the NAVAIDs or radials that identify the holding fix.

4-76. The profile view also depicts minimum, maximum, recommended, and mandatory block altitudes used in approaches. Minimum altitude is depicted with the altitude underscored $\dfrac{2500}{}$. On final approach, aircraft are required to maintain an altitude at or above the depicted altitude until reaching the subsequent fix. Maximum altitude is depicted with the altitude overscored $\overline{4300}$, and aircraft must remain at or below the depicted altitude. Mandatory altitude is depicted with the altitude both underscored and overscored $\overline{\underline{5500}}$, and altitude is to be maintained at the depicted value. Recommended altitudes are advisory altitudes and are neither overscored nor underscored. When an overscore or underscore spans two numbers, a mandatory block altitude is indicated and aircraft are required to maintain altitude within the range of the two numbers (Figure 4-7, page 4-17).

LANDING MINIMUMS

4-77. The landing minimums section sets forth the lowest altitude and visibility requirements for the approach, whether precision or nonprecision, straight-in or circling, or radar vectored. When a fix is incorporated in a nonprecision final segment, two sets of minimums may be published, depending on whether the fix can be identified. Two sets of minimums may also be published when a second altimeter source is used in the procedure. The minimums ensure that final approach obstacle clearance is provided from the start of the final segment to the runway or MAP, whichever occurs last. The same minimums apply to day and night operations unless different minimums are specified. Published circling minimums provide obstacle clearance when aviators remain within the appropriate area of protection (Figure 4-9, page 4-20).

4-78. Minimums for straight-in and circling appear directly under each aircraft category (Figure 4-9, page 4-20). When there is no solid division line between minimums for each category on the straight-in or circling rows, minimums apply to the two or more undivided categories.

INSTRUMENT APPROACH MINIMA
LOW ALTITUDE

CATEGORY	A	B	C	D
S-ILS 27		362/24 200 (200-½)		
S-LOC 27	440/24 278 (300-½)		440/40 278 (300-¾)	
CIRCLING	520-1 350 (400-1)	620-1 450 (500-1)	620-1½ 450 (500-1½)	720-2 550 (600-2)
S-PAR 27		262/16 100 (100-¼) GS 2.50°		

Precision Straight in to Runway 27

Non-Precision (Localizer) Straight in to Runway 27

Precision Approach Radar Straight in to Runway 27

Aircraft Category

Decision Altitude (DA) MSL

* Prevailing Visibility/RVR (RVR in 100s of feet)

Height of DH above touchdown zone (HAT)

Ceiling in feet & Prevailing Visibility in SM

Minimum Descent Altitude (MDA)

Height of MDA above airport (HAA)

Glide Slope Angle

Height of MDA above touchdown zone (HAT)

* Slash(/) denotes RVR Values and a dash(-) denotes Prevailing Visibility

COPTER MINIMA ONLY

CATEGORY	COPTER
H-176°	680-½ 363 (400-½)

Copter Approach Direction

Height of MDA/DH Above Landing Area (HAL)

No circling minimums are provided

EXAMPLE OF A SPECIFIC RADAR APPROACH

CAIRNS AAF (KOZR), AL (Fort Rucker) (04050 USA)   **ELEV 301**
RADAR - (E) (125.4 327.125 021°-120°) (133.75 270.35 121°-219°) (133.45 239.4 220°-340°) (121.1 319.25 341°-020°) ⚠ NA

	RWY	GS/TCH/RPI	CAT	DA/ MDA-VIS	HAT/ HAA	CEIL-VIS
PAR	6	2.7°/45/	AB	498/24	200	(200-½)
			CD	498/40	200	(200-¾)
	36	2.9°/13/	ABCD	496-¾	200	(200-¾)
ASR	6		ABC	680/40	382	(400-¾)
			D	680/50	382	(400-1)
	36		ABC	680-1	384	(400-1)
			D	680-1¼	384	(400-1¼)
CIR	All Rwy		A	740-1	439	(500-1)
			B	760-1	459	(500-1)
			C	780-1½	479	(500-1½)
			D	860-2	559	(600-2)

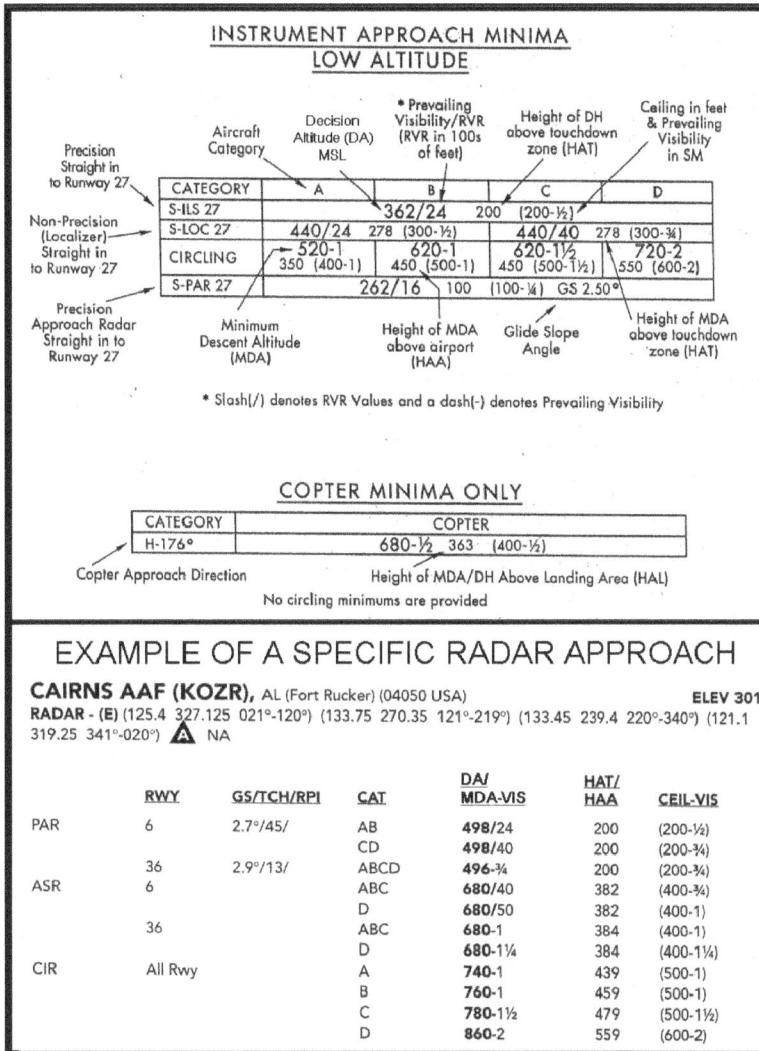

Figure 4-9. Landing minimums

Altitudes

4-79. Terms used to describe minimum approach altitudes differ between precision and nonprecision approaches (Figure 4-9). Precision approaches use DA, charted in feet MSL and measured with a barometric altimeter, followed by DH, which is referenced to the HAT. DA will replace DH for Category I precision IAP. Category II and III approach DHs are referenced to AGL and measured with a radar altimeter. Category II and III approaches require special ground and airborne equipment to be installed and operational, as well as special aircrew training and authorization (see AR 95-1).

4-80. Nonprecision approaches use MDA referenced to feet MSL and measured with a barometric altimeter. Minimums are also referenced to HAT for straight-in approaches or HAA for circling approaches. Height above landing (HAL) is a term specific to helicopters, which means height above a designated helicopter landing area used for helicopter IAPs. On NACO charts, figures listed parenthetically are for military operations, not civil aviation.

4-81. Minimums are specified for various aircraft approach categories based on a value 1.3 times the stalling speed of the aircraft in the landing configuration at maximum certified gross landing weight. If necessary to maneuver the aircraft at speeds in excess of the upper limit of a speed range for a category, the minimums for the next higher category should be used. For example, an aircraft falling into Category A but circling to land at a speed in excess of 91 knots should use approach Category B minimums (table 4-2).

Table 4-2. Aircraft approach categories and circling limits

Category	A	B	C	D	E
Maneuvering Speed (knots)	0-90	91-120	121-140	141-165	166 & higher
Circling Approach Area Radii (miles)	1.3	1.5	1.7	2.3	4.5

Note. All U.S. military helicopters may use the aircraft approach Category A minima published in authorized FLIP. Because aircraft speeds are used in determining turning radii and obstacle clearance areas for circling and turning missed approaches, helicopters operating at speeds greater than Category A use the higher category minima. Procedures containing the word COPTER in the procedure title (COPTER VOR 190) are approved under terminal instrument procedures (TERPS) helicopter criteria for helicopter use only and are restricted to 90 KIAS, unless a lesser speed is annotated on the approach plate.

Visibility

4-82. Visibility figures are provided in statute miles or runway visual range (RVR), which is reported in hundreds of feet. RVR is measured by a transmissometer, which represents the horizontal distance measured at points along the runway and is based on sighting of either high-intensity runway lights or on the visual contrast of other targets, whichever yields greater visual range. RVR is horizontal visual range, not slant visual range, and is used in lieu of prevailing visibility when the aviator determines minima for a particular runway (table 4-3).

4-83. Visibility figures are depicted after the DA/DH or MDA in the minima section. If visibility in statute miles is indicated, an altitude number, hyphen, and a whole or fractional number appear (for example, 530-1, which indicates 530 feet MSL and 1 statute mile visibility). This is the descent minimum for the approach. The RVR value is separated from the minimum altitude with a slash (1065/24, which indicates 1,065 feet MSL and a RVR of 2,400 feet). If RVR was prescribed for the procedure but not available, a conversion table would be used to provide the equivalent visibility, in this case, of 1/2 statute mile visibility (table 4-3). The conversion table is also available in the DOD FLIP (Terminal) chart.

Table 4-3. Runway visual range conversion table

RVR (ft)	Visibility (SM)	RVR (ft)	Visibility (SM)
1,200	1/4*	4,000	3/4
1,600	1/4	4,500	7/8
2,400	1/2	5,000	1
3,200	5/8	6,000	1 1/4
* copter only			

4-84. In addition to COPTER approaches, instrument-equipped helicopters may fly standard approach procedures. The required visibility minimum may be reduced to one-half of the published visibility minimum for Category A aircraft, but in no case may the reduction be less than 1/4 mile, or 1,200 feet RVR. Reduction of visibility for approaches labeled "copter only" is not authorized.

4-85. Point in space approach refers to a helicopter IAP to a MAP more than 2,600 feet from an associated helicopter landing area. For example, the COPTER RNAV (GPS) 028 degrees displays a helicopter IAP with a portion of the approach that is conducted VFR to three helicopter landing points (Figure 4-10, page 4-23).

AIRPORT DIAGRAM

4-86. Airport diagrams are specifically designed to assist in the movement of ground traffic at locations with complex runway/taxiway configurations and provide information for updating geodetic position navigational systems aboard aircraft. The airport diagram, located on the bottom right side of the chart, includes helpful features. IAPs for some larger airports devote an entire page to an airport diagram. Information concerning runway orientation, lighting, final approach bearings, airport beacon, and obstacles all serve to guide the pilot in the final phases of flight. See Figure 4-5, page 4-12, for an example of an airport diagram.

4-87. The diagram shows the runway configuration in solid black, while taxiways and aprons are shaded gray. Other runway environment features shown are runway identification, dimensions, magnetic heading, displaced threshold, arresting gear, usable length, and slope. Airport elevation is indicated in a separate box at the top of the airport diagram box. The touchdown zone elevation (TDZE), the highest elevation within the first 3,000 feet of the runway, is designated at the approach end of the procedure's runway. Beneath the airport diagram is the time and speed table providing distance and the amount of time required to transit the distance from the FAF to the MAP for selected ground speeds.

4-88. Approach lighting systems and visual glide-slope indicators are depicted on the approach chart. White on black symbols, , are used for identifying pilot-controlled lighting (PCL). Runway lighting aids are noted (runway end identifier lights [REIL], high intensity runway lights [HIRL]) as well as the runway centerline lighting (RCL). Refer to FIH, section B, for a current description and information.

Remote Altimeter Settings

4-89. Weather planning minimums are computed when the aviator identifies that an MDA or a DA/DH has been raised because of the need to use a remote altimeter setting. In some cases, new minimums are shown in the minimum box. When not shown, the method illustrated in Figure 4-11, page 4-24, is used to compute new weather planning minimums.

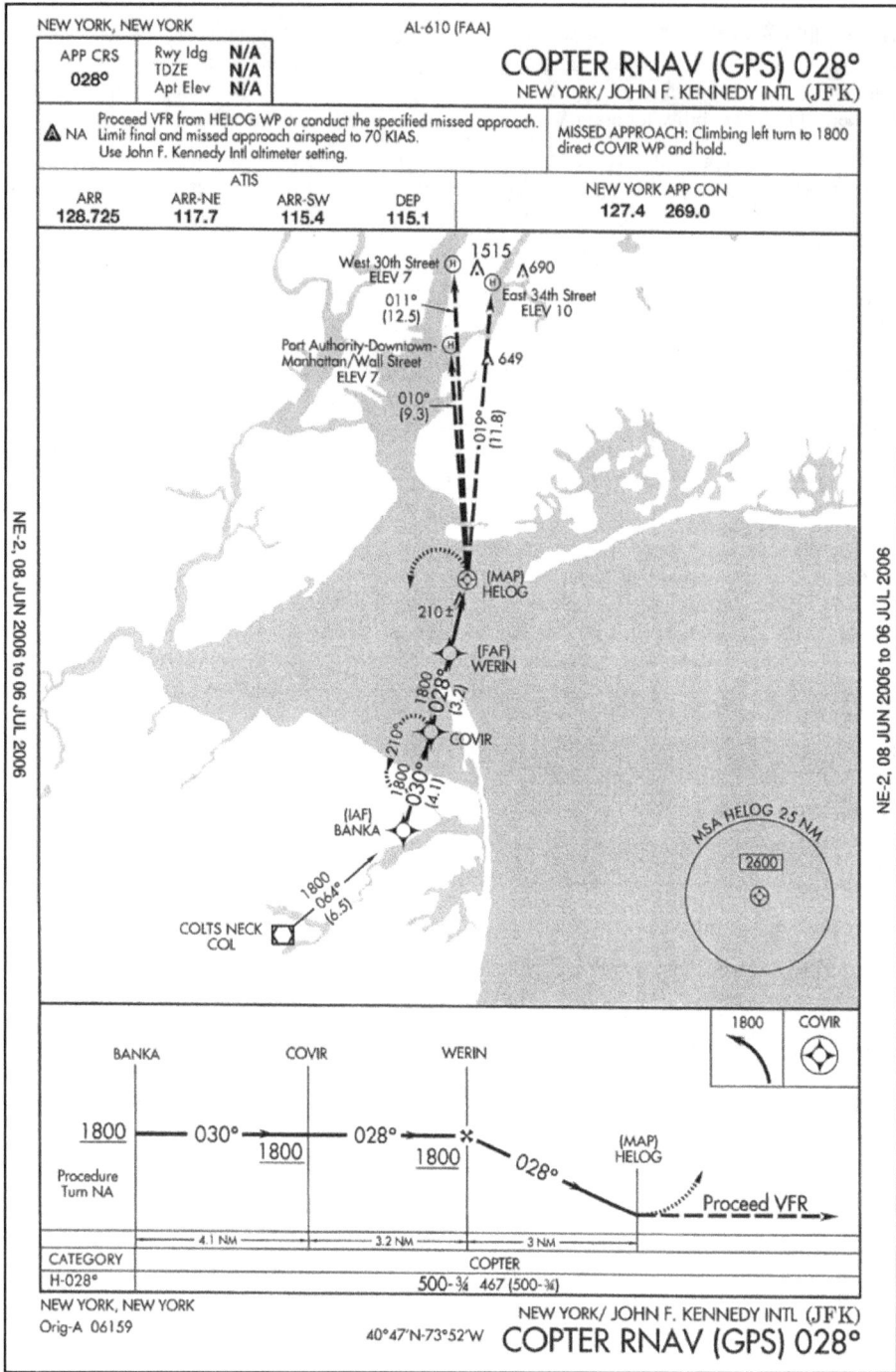

NEW YORK, NEW YORK   AL-610 (FAA)

APP CRS	Rwy ldg	N/A
028°	TDZE	N/A
	Apt Elev	N/A

COPTER RNAV (GPS) 028°
NEW YORK/ JOHN F. KENNEDY INTL (JFK)

⚠ NA   Proceed VFR from HELOG WP or conduct the specified missed approach.
       Limit final and missed approach airspeed to 70 KIAS.
       Use John F. Kennedy Intl altimeter setting.

MISSED APPROACH: Climbing left turn to 1800
direct COVIR WP and hold.

ATIS				NEW YORK APP CON	
ARR	ARR-NE	ARR-SW	DEP	127.4	269.0
128.725	117.7	115.4	115.1		

Figure 4-10. Point in space approach

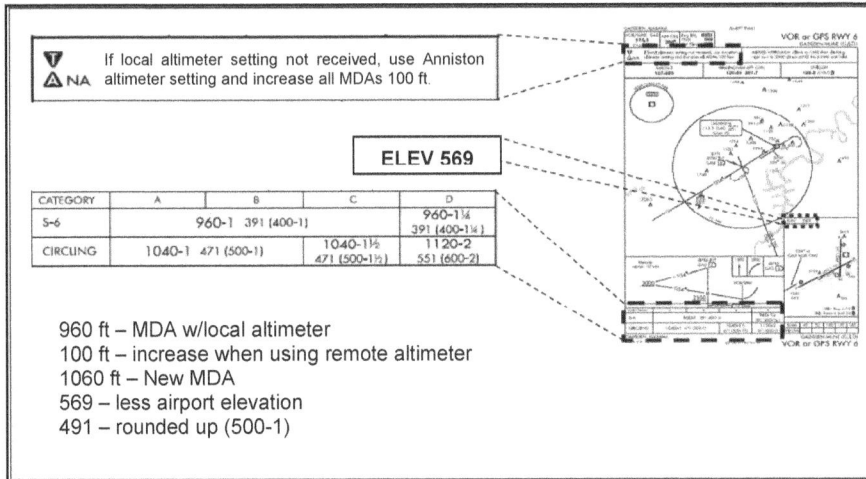

Figure 4-11. Remote altimeter settings

INOPERATIVE COMPONENTS

4-90. Certain procedures can be flown with inoperative components. According to the Inoperative Components Table (Figure 4-12, page 4-25), an ILS approach with a malfunctioning medium-intensity approach lighting system (MALS) with runway alignment indicator lights (MALSR = MALS with RAIL) can be flown if the minimum visibility is increased by 1/4 mile (figure 4-12). A note in this section might read as follows: "Inoperative Table does not apply to ALS or HIRL Runway 13L."

4-91. For helicopter operations, add the visibility requirement for the inoperative components chart to the visibility requirement for the approach to be flown. This increased visibility may be reduced by one-half for Category A aircraft but in no case may it be reduced to less than 1/4 mile, or 1,200 feet RVR. For approaches labeled "copter only," do not reduce the visibility; increase for inoperative components.

SECTION II – PLOTTING AND MEASURING

4-92. Plotting is establishing points and lines on a chart with reference to meridians and parallels. Measuring refers to distance and direction on a chart. The chart serves as a record and provides necessary information for a successful flight. Accurate chart work is a fundamental navigational skill.

PLOTTER

4-93. A plotter (Figure 4-13, page 4-26)—an instrument that primarily aids in drawing lines and in measuring distances on an aeronautical chart—is made of transparent plastic, and has lines and scales printed in black. The rectangular part of the plotter has a straight edge for drawing lines and scales for measuring distances. The semicircular part of the plotter has three circular scales for measuring direction.

RECTANGULAR PART

4-94. All scales on the rectangular part are for measuring distances in nautical miles. The two upper scales read outward from the center in both directions. The three lower scales read from left to right. Scales of 1:500,000 (Sectional Aeronautical Charts), 1:1,000,000 (Operational Navigation Charts and World Aeronautical Charts), and 1:2,000,000 (charts such as Jet Navigation Charts) are provided. No scale is provided for the IFR en route chart measurement/ratio (1 inch equals 12 nautical miles).

INOP COMPONENTS
02276

INOPERATIVE COMPONENTS OR VISUAL AIDS TABLE

Landing minimums published on instrument approach procedure charts are based upon full operation of all components and visual aids associated with the particular instrument approach chart being used. Higher minimums are required with inoperative components or visual aids as indicated below. If more than one component is inoperative, each minimum is raised to the highest minimum required by any single component that is inoperative. ILS glide slope inoperative minimums are published on the instrument approach charts as localizer minimums. This table may be amended by notes on the approach chart. Such notes apply only to the particular approach category(ies) as stated. See legend page for description of components indicated below.

(1) ILS, MLS, and PAR

Inoperative Component or Aid	Approach Category	Increase Visibility
ALSF 1 & 2, MALSR, & SSALR	ABCD	1/4 mile

(2) ILS with visibility minimum of 1,800 RVR

	Approach	Increase
ALSF 1 & 2, MALSR, & SSALR	ABCD	To 4000 RVR
TDZL RCLS	ABCD	To 2400 RVR
RVR	ABCD	To 1/2 mile

(3) VOR, VOR/DME, VORTAC, VOR (TAC), VOR/DME (TAC), LOC, LOC/DME, LDA, LDA/DME, SDF, SDF/DME, GPS, RNAV, and ASR

Inoperative Visual Aid	Approach Category	Increase Visibility
ALSF 1 & 2, MALSR, & SSALR	ABCD	1/2 mile
SSALS, MALS, & ODALS	ABC	1/4 mile

(4) NDB

ALSF 1 & 2, MALSR, & SSALR	C	1/2 mile
	ABD	1/4 mile
MALS, SSALS, ODALS	ABC	1/4 mile

CORRECTIONS, COMMENTS AND/OR PROCUREMENT

FOR CHARTING ERRORS CONTACT:	FOR CHANGES, ADDITIONS, OR RECOMMENDATIONS ON PROCEDURAL ASPECTS:	TO PURCHASE CHARTS CONTACT:
National Aeronautical Charting Office, FAA N/ACC1, SSMC-4, Sta. #2335 1305 East-West Highway Silver Spring, MD 20910-3281 Telephone Toll-Free (800) 626-3677 Internet/E-Mail: 9-AMC-Aerochart@FAA.gov	Contact Federal Aviation Administration, ATA 110 800 Independence Avenue, SW Washington, DC 20591 Telephone Toll Free 1-(866) 295-8236	FAA, National Aeronautical Charting Office, Distribution Division, AVN-530 6303 Ivy Lane, Suite 400 Greenbelt, Maryland 20770 Telephone Toll Free (800) 638-8972 9-AMC-NACOWebmaster@FAA.gov

Requests for the creation or revisions to Airport Diagrams should be in accordance with FAA Order 7910.4B.

INOP COMPONENTS
02276

Figure 4-12. Inoperative components

CIRCULAR SCALES

4-95. The circular scales are calibrated in degrees. The outer scale, reading from 0 degrees to 180 degrees (right to left), is for direction in the first and second chart quadrants (north through east to south, Figure 4-13). Because these directions are to the right on the chart, the outer scale has an arrow pointing to the right. The inner scale, reading from 180 degrees to 360 degrees (right to left), is for directions in the third and fourth quadrants (Figure 4-13). The center of curvature of both scales is marked by a small hole.

SIXTY-DEGREE CENTER SCALE

4-96. This scale is an aid for aviators to measure courses that are nearly north or south. The outer scale reads from 150 degrees to 210 degrees, while the inner scale reads from 030 degrees to 330 degrees.

MEASUREMENTS AND COURSE LINES

4-97. To measure a course, the aviator places the center hole on a meridian about midway along the plotted course line, with the straight edge parallel to the course line. If the chart meridians do not intersect the course line, the line is extended and the straight edge of the plotter is moved parallel to the course line until the center hole lies over a meridian. The small arrows on the circular scale determine correct direction. The scale on which the small black arrow points in the direction of the course should be noted. The scale should be read up from the smaller values toward the larger values.

4-98. To determine the direction of a course line, place the straight edge of the plotter along the course line and, while keeping them aligned, slide the plotter over to the nearest meridian of longitude so that the center hole in the plotter lies over the meridian (Figure 4-13). Reading off the outer protractor scale, determine what number of degrees matches the meridian. This is the true course. There will actually be two numbers on the plotter, the course heading and the reciprocal. Use the one that makes sense. If the course was almost due east and the true heading choices are 100 degrees and 280 degrees, the heading would be 100 degrees, for example.

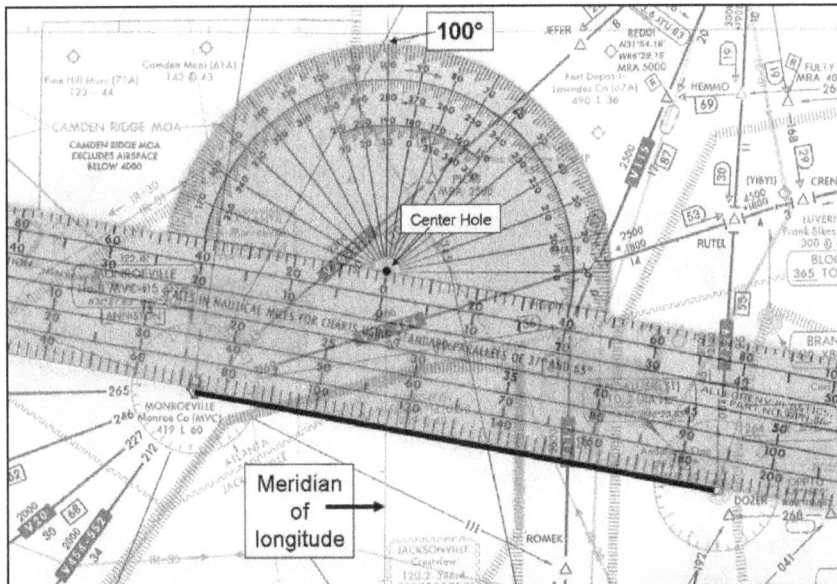

Figure 4-13. East/west course reading, using outer/inner scale

4-99. For some courses approaching vertical angles on the chart, it may become difficult or impossible for the aviator to line up the course line at the meridian. In these instances, use a parallel of latitude and read the course off the inner scale printed on the protractor. The following example is depicted in Figure 4-14.

Example of Using the Inner Scale on the Protractor

A course drawn from the Blood NDB direct to the Montgomery very (high frequency) omnidirectional radio range tactical air navigation aid (VORTAC) has a true heading of 335 degrees (Figure 4-14) with a reciprocal heading of 155 degrees .

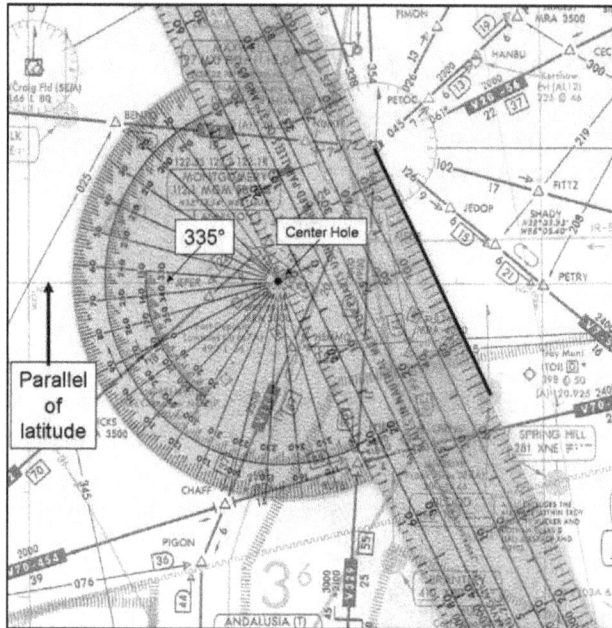

Figure 4-14. North course reading, using inner scale

4-100. To draw a given course line from a known point, the aviator places the point end of a pencil at the known point. While the plotter is being pushed and pivoted against the pencil, the straight edge remains on the known point while the center hole and desired heading (number of degrees on the protractor) are being aligned with a meridian. The pencil is in place for drawing the course line when the plotter has been properly aligned with a meridian. In drawing a course line that is nearly north or south, 0 to 180 degrees, the center scale may be used. The following example of plotting a course line is depicted in Figure 4-15, page 4-28.

Example of Plotting a Course Line

If a 040 degrees course line is desired from the Summerdale NDB, the course line is drawn as depicted in Figure 4-15.

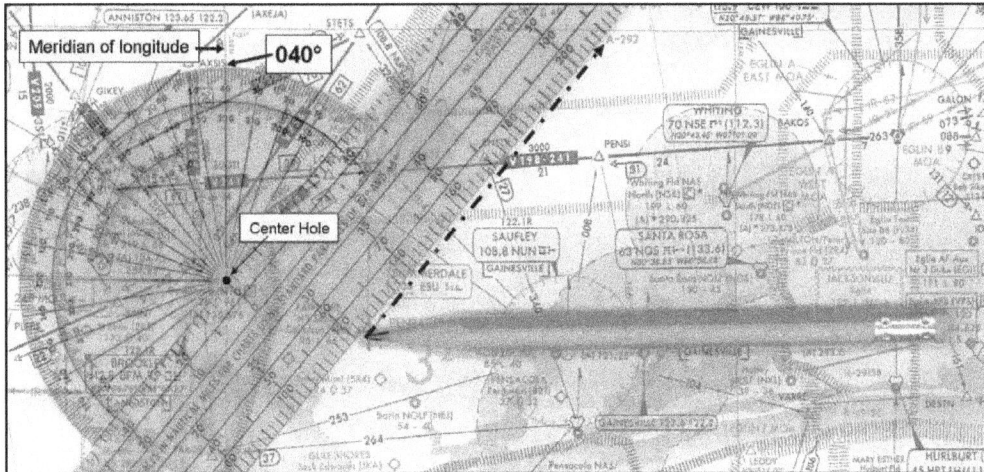

Figure 4-15. Drawing a course line from a known point

This page intentionally left blank.

Chapter 5

Air Navigation Handheld Computer

A dead reckoning (DR) computer is a combination of two devices: a specially designed instrument for solving wind triangles and a circular slide rule for solving mathematical problems. Many different types of DR navigational computers exist, but construction and design features of major types are similar. Electronic versions of the DR, also known as the CPU-26A/P computer, are available for download.

SECTION I – CALCULATOR SIDE

5-1. The slide rule side of the handheld computer consists of two circular scales. The miles scale (outer scale) is stationary while the minutes scale (inner scale) rotates.

Contents

VALUES

5-2. Numbers on the computer scale (Figure 5-1) represent multiples of 1, 2, 5, or 10; care must be used to determine the value of the numbers shown. For example, the number 12 on either scale (outer or inner) may represent 0.12, 1.2, 12, 120, or 1,200. On the inner scale, minutes may be converted to hours by reference to the adjacent hour scale; for example, two hours is adjacent to 12 (meaning 120 minutes) as found in Figure 5-1.

5-3. The higher the scale values, the fewer the graduations between numbers. There are only 5 graduations, for example, between 15 and 16, compared to 10 graduations between 14 and 15. When the aviator uses numbers between 15 and 16, each graduation equals .2; when used as 150 and 160, each unit represents 2, and so on. The same application applies to the 10 graduations between 10 and 11, which equal .1; these .1 graduations can also indicate one-minute marks between 1:40 and 1:50.

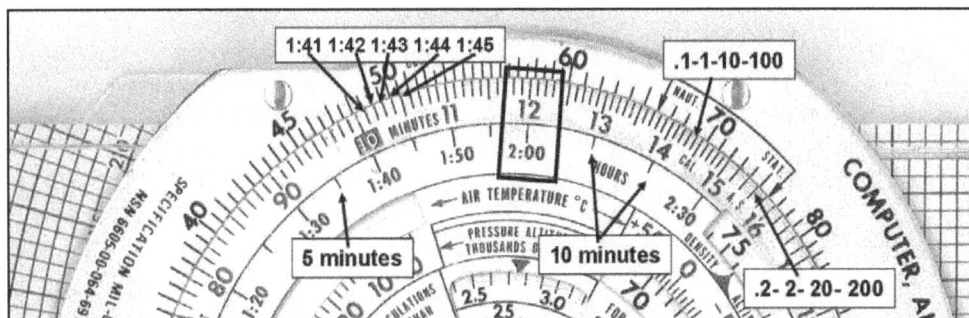

Figure 5-1. CPU-26A/P calculator side

INDEXES

5-4. Three of the indexes on the outer stationary scale are used for converting statute miles, nautical miles, and kilometers. These indexes are appropriately labeled NAUT (nautical) at 66, STAT (statue) at 76, and KM at 122. On the inner rotating scale are two rate indexes. The large black arrow at 60 (speed index or 60 index) is the hour index. The small arrow at 36 is the second (SEC) index (3,600 seconds equal 1 hour). The STAT index on the inner scale is used in mileage conversion. Each scale has a 10 index used as a reference mark for multiplication and division (Figure 5-2).

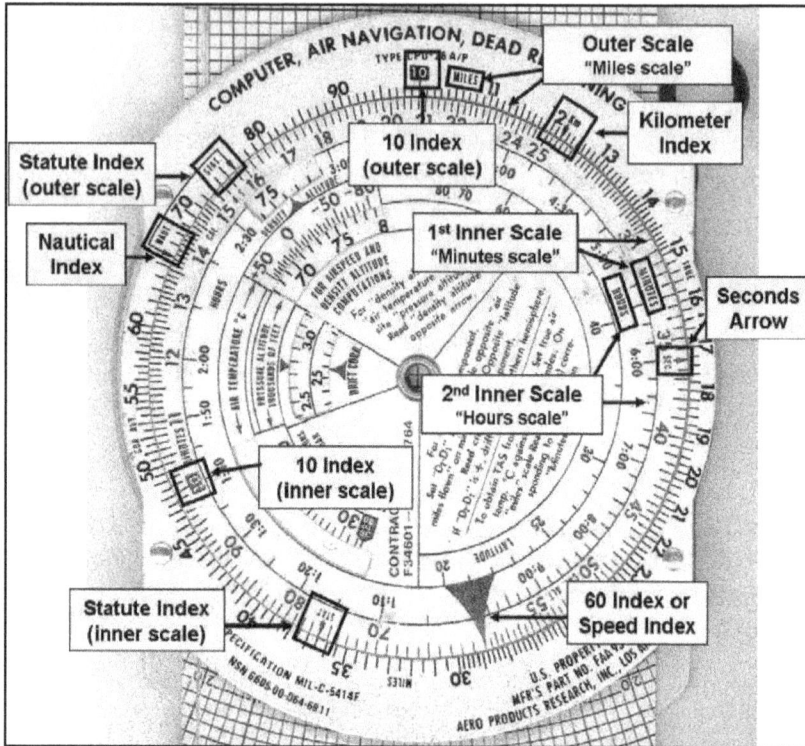

Figure 5-2. Calculator side of CPU-26A/P computer

TIME AND DISTANCE

5-5.   Time and distance problems (Figure 5-3, page 5-3) use three items: time, distance, and speed. Two of three items must be known. Figure 5-3 depicts the following examples of computing time and distance. Figure 5-4, page 5-3, depicts the following example of computing speed.

Example of Computing Time
How much time is required to fly 329 NM at a ground speed of 170 kt (Figure 5-3)? 1:56 hours.
Set 60 index under 17 (outer scale) for 170 kt.
Under 32.9 (outer scale) for 329 NM, read 116 minutes (inner scale) or 1:56 (hours scale).

Example of Computing Distance

If an aircraft has a ground speed of 170 kt & flies for 1 hour & 35 minutes, how many NM will the aircraft have flown (Figure 5-3)? 269 miles.

Set 60 index under 17 for 170 (outer scale).

Above 1:35 (hour scale), read just left of 27 for 269 miles (outer scale).

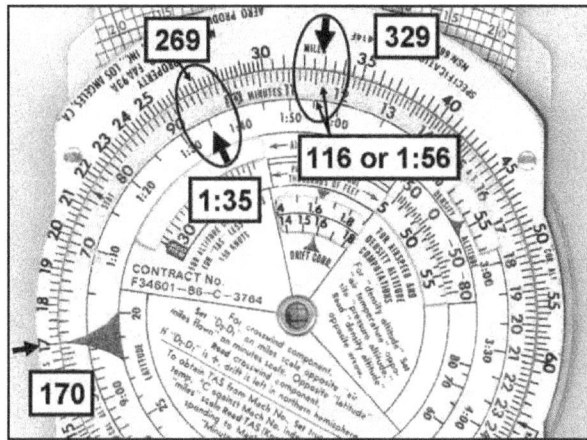

Figure 5-3. Computing time and distance

Computing Speed Example

An aircraft flies 250 NM in 1:40; what is the speed of the aircraft (Figure 5-4)? 150 kt.
Set 1:40 (hour scale) under 25 (outer scale) for 250 NM.

Directly over the speed index is 15; therefore, the answer is 150 kt (outer scale).

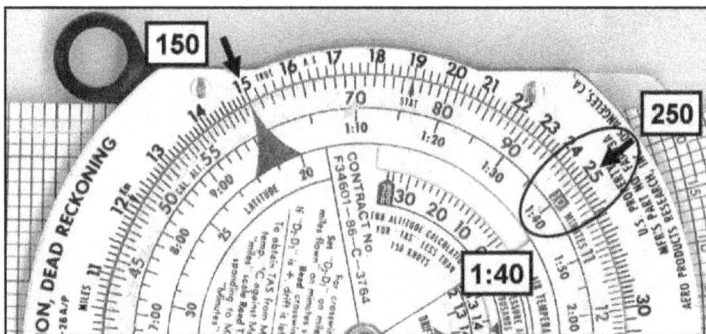

Figure 5-4. Computing speed

SHORT TIME AND DISTANCE (USE OF THE 36 INDEX)

5-6. The 36 index (Figure 5-5, page 5-4) is used to solve for short distances, usually less than 10 nautical miles, and when time calculations are in seconds and minutes instead of minutes and hours. When the aviator uses the 36 (seconds) index, the minutes scale reads as seconds (first example) and the hour scale reads as minutes and seconds (second example). Figure 5-5 depicts the following examples.

---

36 Index Scale Examples

Example 1

If an aircraft has a ground speed of 90 kt & flies for 1.3 NM, how much time is required to fly the distance (Figure 5-5)? 52 sec.

Set the 36 index under 90 (outer scale) for 90 kt.

Below 13 (outer scale) for 1.3 NM, read 52 sec (minutes scale).

Note. Read left, or counterclockwise, from the 60 (speed) index; the correct time is taken from the minutes scale and read as seconds.

Example 2

If an aircraft has a ground speed of 90 kt and flies for 4.5 NM, how much time is required to fly the distance (Figure 5-5)? 3:00 minutes.

Set the 36 index under 90 (outer scale) for 90 kt.

Below 45 (outer scale) for 4.5 NM read 3:00 minutes (hour scale).

Note. Read right, or clockwise, from the 60 (speed) index; the correct time is taken from the hours scale and read as minutes and seconds.

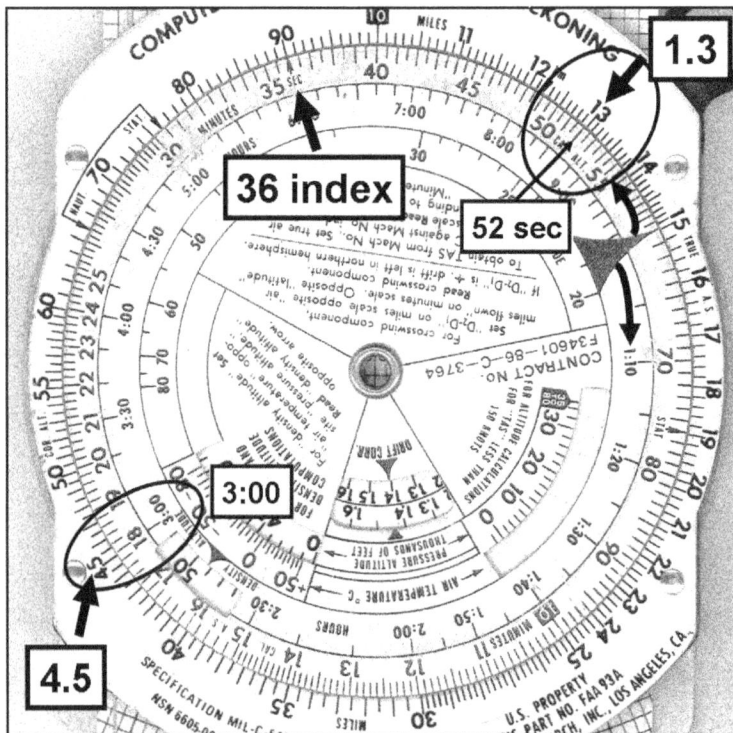

Figure 5-5. Short time and distance

COMPUTING TIME FOR OUTBOUND LEG DURING HOLDING

5-7. Because holding is concerned with inbound time and not distance inbound, knowing wind velocity and direction is not necessary. By using the computer side of the dead-reckoning computer, the aviator can determine the time outbound that will result in one minute inbound. Place the initial 60-second outbound time on the outer scale over the inbound time on the inner scale, and the number above the speed index is the number of seconds to subsequently fly outbound to achieve a one-minute inbound time. The following examples show how to compute estimated outbound times depicted in Figures 5-6 and 5-7.

Estimated Outbound Time More Than 1 Minute Example

If an outbound time of 1 minute results in an inbound time of 45 sec, how much time on the subsequent outbound leg must the aircraft fly to achieve an inbound time of 1 minute (Figure 5-6)? 80 sec.

Set 45 for actual inbound time of 45 sec (inner scale) under 60 for time flown outbound of 1 minute or 60 sec (outer scale).

Above speed index, read 80 (outer scale) for 80 sec subsequent outbound time to be flown.

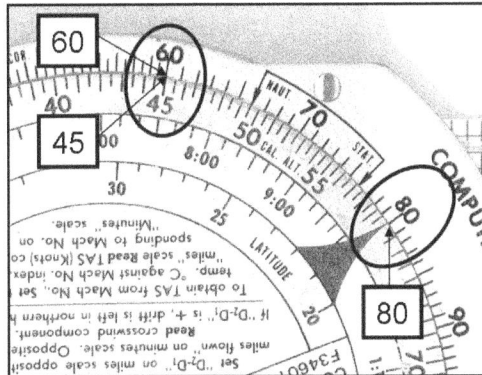

Figure 5-6. Estimated outbound time more than one minute

Estimated Outbound Time Less Than 1 Minute Example

If an outbound time of 1 minute results in an inbound time of 82 sec, how much time on the subsequent outbound leg must the aircraft fly to achieve an inbound time of 1 minute (Figure 5-7)? 44 sec.

Set 82 for actual inbound time of 82 sec (inner scale) under 60 for time flown outbound of 1 minute or 60 sec (outer scale).

Above the speed index, read 44 (outer scale) for 44 sec subsequent outbound time to be flown.

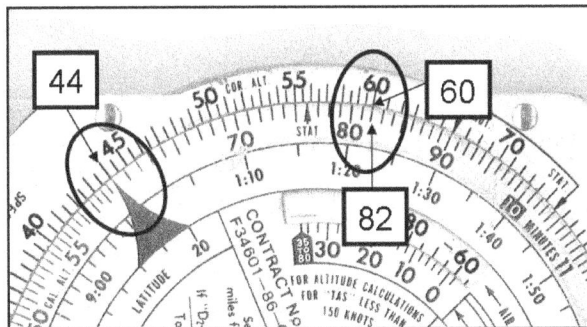

Figure 5-7. Estimated outbound time less than one minute

FUEL CONSUMPTION

5-8.   Fuel consumption problems are solved in the same manner as time and distance problems, except gallons per hour and gallons are used in place of miles per hour and miles.

GALLONS AND POUNDS CONVERSION

5-9.   The CPU-26A/P is useful for determining weights of fuel and gallon-pound conversions. table 5-1 shows gallons-to-pounds or pounds-to-gallons conversion ratios. Figure 5-8 provides an example of gallons-to-pounds conversion based on the following example.

Table 5-1. Gallons and pounds conversion

Fuel	Conversion
JP-4	6.5:1
JP-5/JET-A	6.8:1
JP-8/JET A-1	6.7:1
JP = Jet propulsion	

Gallons and Pounds Conversion Example

If 172 gallons of JP-8 are added to the aircraft, how many pounds does that fuel weigh (Figure 5-8)? 1,150 pounds of JP-8.

Using JP-8 as onboard fuel, set the 10 index (inner scale) under 67 (outer scale) for 6.7:1. The inner scale now represents gallons, & the outer scale represents pounds.

Find 17 on the inner scale, move right (clockwise) to the next mark (17.2), & read above to see 11.5. The answer is 1,150 pounds.

The black boxed 10 index is a representation of 1.0 gallons, which is set in this equation under 67 (outer scale) for 6.7 pounds (weight of 1 gallon of JP-8, Table 5-1). Therefore, reading from the 10 index clockwise; 11 is equal to 1.1 gallons, 12 is equal to 1.2 gallons, & so on. Continue clockwise to the next mark after 17 (1.7 gallons), which is equal to 1.72; the decimal point must be moved two places to the right to achieve 172.0 gallons. Consequently, the same number of decimal point places must be moved for the correct fuel weight so that 11.5 (outer scale) reads as 1,150.0 pounds.

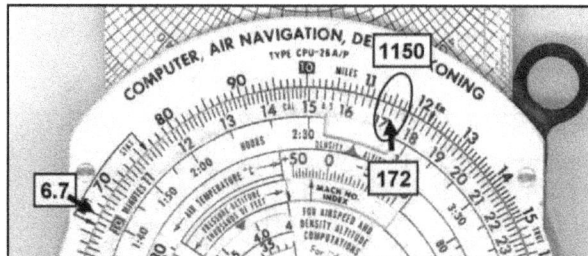

Figure 5-8. Gallons and pounds conversion

COMPUTING ENDURANCE TIME

5-10.   The CPU-26A/P can be used for determining endurance time based on fuel burn rate and gallons of useable fuel onboard. Figure 5-9, page 5-7, shows an endurance time based on the example depicted.

Computing Endurance Time Example

If an aircraft has a fuel burn rate of 130 gallons per hour & 230 gallons of useable fuel onboard, how long until aircraft fuel burnout (Figure 5-9) occurs? 1 hour & 46 minutes.
Set the 60 index under 13 (outer scale) for 130 gallons per hour.

Below 23 (outer scale) for 230 gallons, read 106 minutes (minutes scale), or 1 hour & 46 minutes (hours scale).

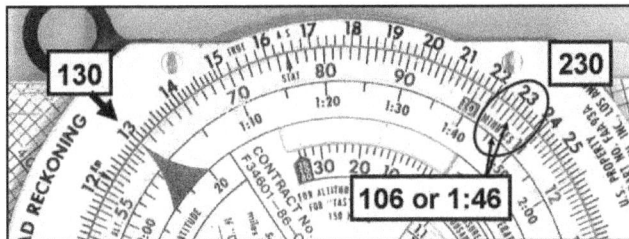

Figure 5-9. Computing time for fuel consumption

COMPUTING FUEL REQUIRED

5-11. The CPU-26A/P can be used during premission planning to determine fuel requirements. Figure 5-10 shows calculations based on the following example.

Fuel Required Example

If an aircraft has an estimated burn rate of 280 pounds per hour and time of flight of 2 hours & 5 minutes, how many pounds of fuel are required for the mission (Figure 5-10)? 585 pounds of fuel required.
Set the 60 index (inner scale) under 28 (outer scale) for 280 pounds per hour.

Above 2:05 (hours scale), read 58.5 (outer scale) for 585 pounds of fuel required.

Note. This computation does not include VFR and IFR reserves.

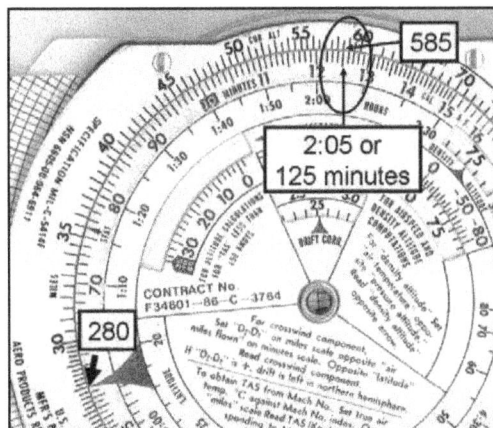

Figure 5-10. Fuel required

Computing Rate of Fuel Consumption

5-12. The CPU-26A/P can be used to compute fuel consumption rate. Figure 5-11 shows computations for the following example.

Rate of Fuel Consumption Example

If an aircraft burns 410 pounds of fuel in 30 minutes, how many pounds is the aircraft burning per hour (Figure 5-11)? 820 pounds per hour.

Set 30 (minutes/inner scale) under 41 (outer scale) for 410 pounds burned.

Above the 60 index (inner scale), read 82 (outer scale) for 820 pounds per hour.

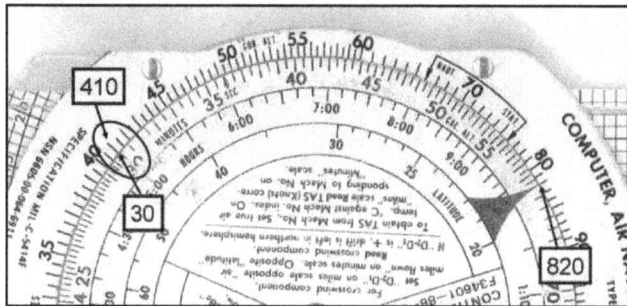

Figure 5-11. Rate of fuel consumption

TRUE AIRSPEED

5-13. The window marked FOR AIRSPEED AND DENSITY ALTITUDE COMPUTATIONS (figure 5-12, page 5-9, provides a means for computing TAS when CAS, temperature, and altitude are known or vice versa. To change from one to the other, correct for altitude and temperature differences existing from those standard at sea level. Free air temperature (FAT) is read from a free air thermometer, and pressure altitude is found by setting the altimeter at 29.92 inches Hg and reading the altimeter directly.

True Airspeed Computation Example

The CAS is 120 kt, FAT is –15 degrees Celsius (C), & pressure altitude is 8,000 ft. What is the TAS (Figure 5-12)? 132 kt.

Set –15 degrees C for air temperature above the 8 position mark in the "pressure altitude thousands of ft" window for 8,000 ft.

Over 12 (inner scale) for 120 kt, read 13.2 (outer scale) for a TAS of 132 kt.

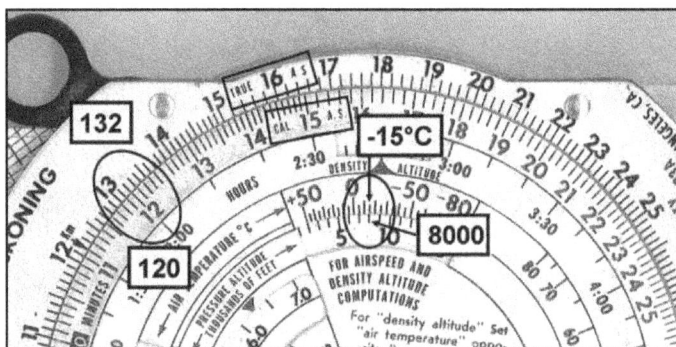

Figure 5-12. True airspeed computation

Note. The outer scale is marked TRUE A.S. between 15 and 17. The inner scale is marked CAL. A.S. between 14 and 16.

Note. To solve CAS when TAS is known, locate TAS on the outer scale and read answer (CAS) in the inner scale.

DISTANCE CONVERSION

5-14. This problem is made simple by a small conversion scale, consisting of three arrows, labeled NAUT, STAT, and Km. These arrows are located on the outer scale at 66, 76, and 12.2 respectively and point toward the inner scale.

OUTER SCALE COMPUTATIONS

5-15. The following example shows distance conversions using the outer scale of the CPU-26A/P. Figure 5-13, page 5-10, illustrates the calculations in the following example.

Distance Conversion (Outer Scale) Example
To change 20 NM to SMs or Km (Figure 5-13):
Set 20 (inner scale) under the NAUT arrow at 66 (outer scale).
Under STAT arrow head (outer scale), read 23 (inner scale); the answer is 20 NM = 23 SM.
Under Km arrowhead (outer scale), read 37 (inner scale); the answer is 20 NM or 23 SM = 37 KM.

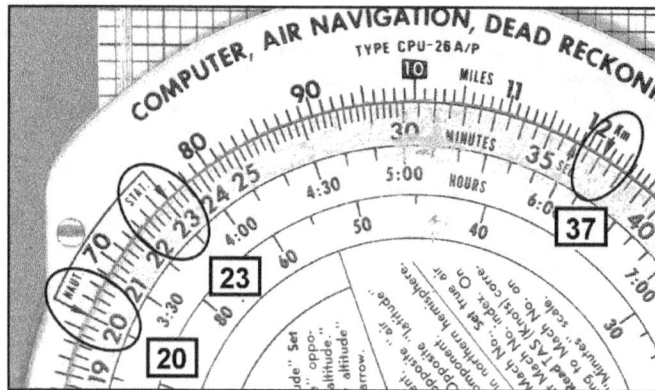

Figure 5-13. Nautical, statute, and kilometer correlation

INNER SCALE COMPUTATIONS

5-16. The following example shows distance conversions using the inner scale of the CPU-26A/P. Figure 5-14 illustrates the calculations in the following example.

Distance Conversion (Inner Scale) Example

Another statute index arrow is located on the inner scale at 76. The index arrow allows for the conversion of SM (inner scale) to NM or KM on the outer scale.

Align the statute index (inner scale) directly below the NAUT on the outer scale.

Select any value, and the corresponding value will be above or below the selected value. For example, 90 SM equals 78 NM (Figure 5-14).

Align the statute index (inner scale) directly below the Km on the outer scale to read selected/corresponding value as in the above example.

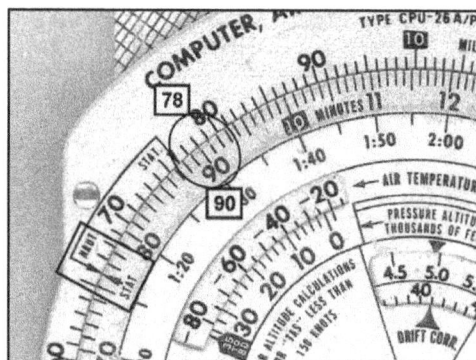

Figure 5-14. Inner scale computation

TRUE ALTITUDE CALCULATION

5-17. The window marked FOR ALTITUDE CALCULATIONS provides a means for computing corrected altitude by applying any variations from standard temperature to indicated or calibrated altitude. Figure 5-15, page 5-11, illustrates the calculations in the following example.

Altitude Calculation Example

Pressure altitude is 9,000 feet, indicated altitude is 9,100 feet, and the FAT is −15 degrees C. What is the corrected altitude (Figure 5-15)? 8,700 feet.

Set −15 degrees C for the air temperature above the 9 position mark in the "pressure altitude thousands of feet" window for 9,000 feet.

Above 91 for 9,100 feet indicated altitude (inner scale), read 87 for 8,700 feet corrected altitude (outer scale).

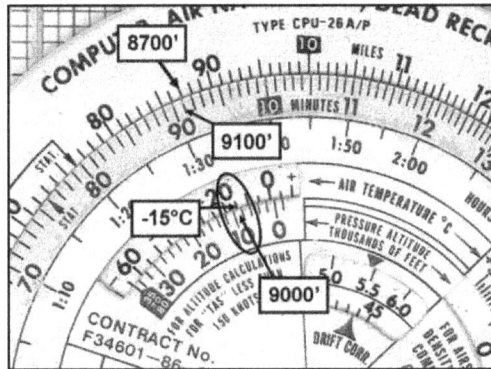

Figure 5-15. True altitude calculation

MULTIPLICATION AND DIVISION CALCULATIONS

5-18. The computer can be used for multiplication and division. The index for these problems is the 10 index.

MULTIPLICATION

5-19. CG-26A/P can be used for simple multiplication calculations. Figure 5-16, page 5-12, illustrates calculations for the following example.

Altitude Calculation Example

If the aircraft is climbing at 450 fpm for 8 minutes, how much altitude would be gained (Figure 5-16)? 3,600 feet.

Set 10 index (inner scale) under 45 (outer scale) for 450.

Above 80 (inner scale) for 8 minutes, read 36 (outer scale) for 3,600 feet.

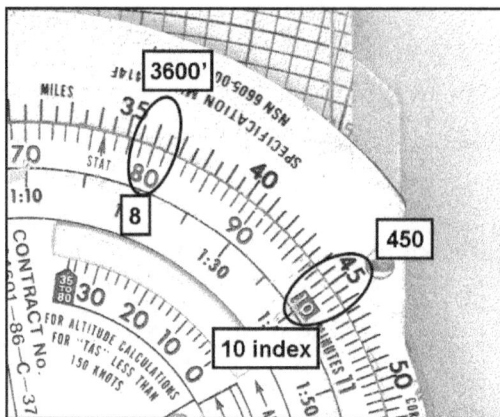

Figure 5-16. Multiplication

DIVISION

5-20. CG-26A/P can be used for simple division calculations. Figure 5-17 illustrates calculations for the following example.

Rate of Descent Calculation Example

An aircraft must lose 9,000 feet in 20 minutes; what is the rate-of-descent (Figure 5-17)? 450 FPM.

Set 90 (outer scale) for 9,000 feet over 20 (inner/minutes scale).

Find 10 index (inner scale), and read 45 (outer scale) for 450 FPM.

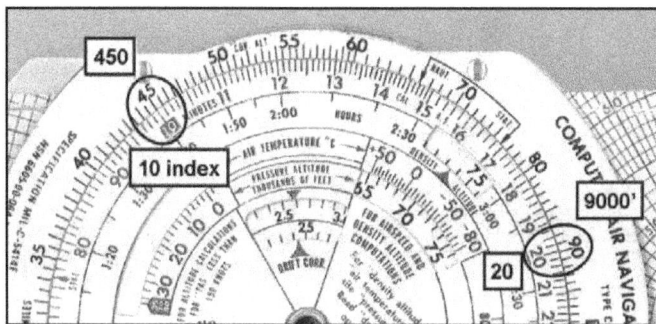

Figure 5-17. Division

CONVERTING DISTANCE TO TIME

5-21. Certain IFR DPs require a minimum climb rate to assure proper obstruction clearance. However, the minimum climb requirement is stated in terms of feet to be gained per nautical mile. The aviator can easily convert FPNM to a number representative of FPM. Figure 5-18, page 5-13, illustrates the following example.

> **Converting Distance to Time Example**
>
> With a ground speed of 90 knots and a climb requirement of 400 FPNM, what is the rate of climb in FPM (Figure 5-18)? 600 FPM.
>
> Set 60 (speed) index to 90 (outer scale) for 90 knots.
>
> Above 40 (inner scale) for 400 feet, read 60 (outer scale) for 600 FPM.

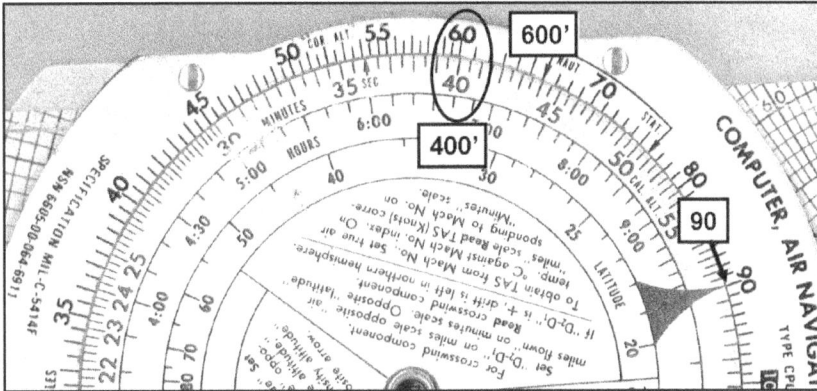

Figure 5-18. Converting feet per nautical mile to feet per minute

SECTION II – WIND SIDE

DISK AND CORRECTION SCALES

5-22. Solve wind problems by the grid side of the DR computer (Figure 5-19, page 5-14), which consists of a transparent, rotational plotting disk mounted in a frame on the reverse side of the circular slide rule. A compass rose is located around the plotting disk. The correction scale on the top frame of the circular grid is graduated in degrees right and left of the true index (labeled TRUE INDEX). This scale is used for calculating drift or drift correction (labeled DRIFT RIGHT and DRIFT LEFT). A small reference circle, called a grommet, is located at the center of the plotting disk.

REVERSIBLE GRID

5-23. A reversible sliding grid (Figure 5-19), inserted between the circular slide-rule and plotting disk, is used for wind computations. The slide has converging lines, spaced 2 degrees apart, between the concentric arcs marked 0 to 150 and 1 degree apart above the 150 arc. Concentric arcs are used to calculate speed and spaced 2 units (usually knots or miles per hour) apart. The direction of the centerline coincides with the index. The common center of the concentric arcs and point at which all converging lines meet is located at the lower end of the slide. On one side of the sliding grid, the speed arcs are scaled from 0 to 270. The low range of speeds on the sliding grid helps solve navigation problems for aircraft with slow flight-speed characteristics. On the reverse side, which is not shown in Figure 5-19, the scale ranges from 70 to 800 knots; this side is normally used by aircraft that can exceed speeds of 270 knots.

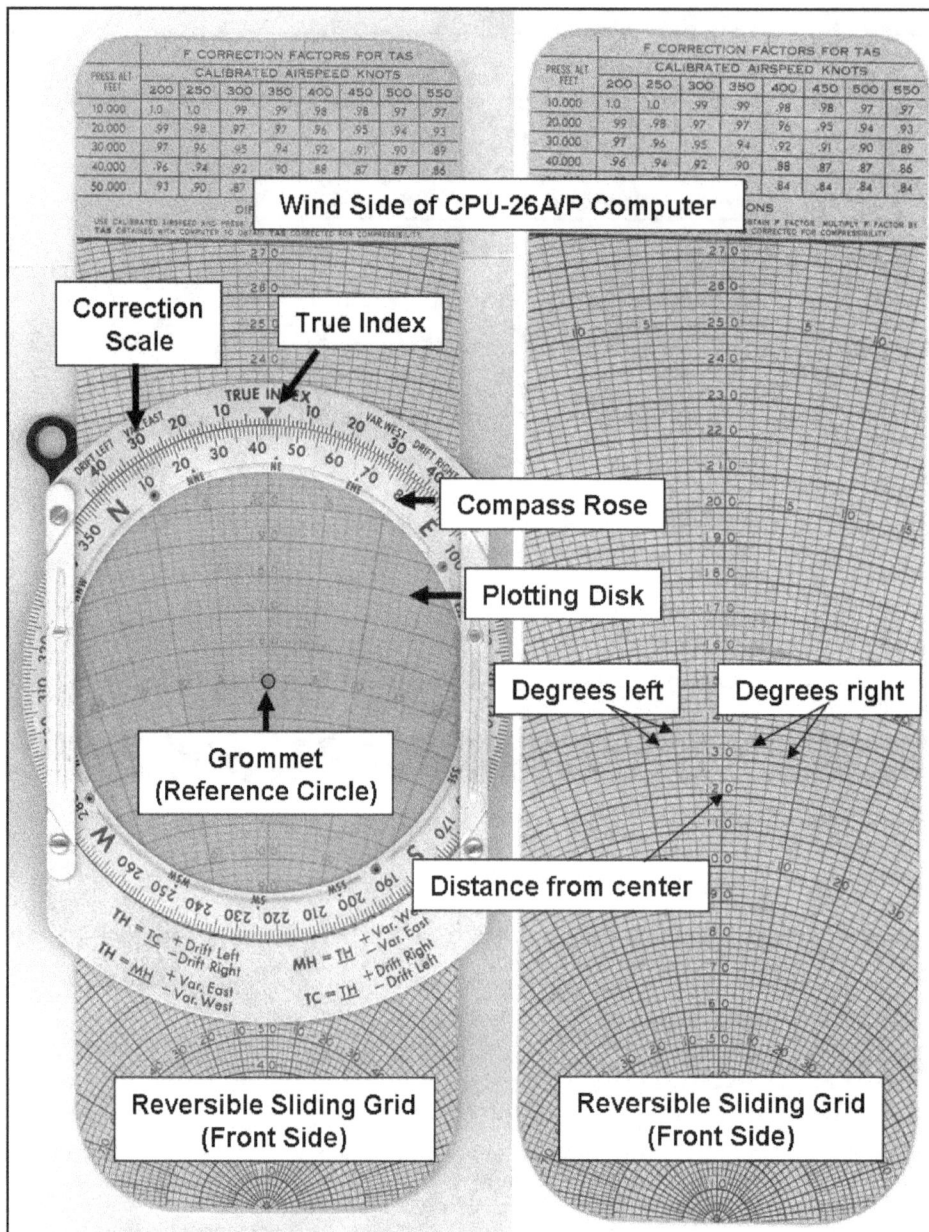

Figure 5-19. Wind side of CPU-26A/P computer

DETERMINING HEADING AND GROUND SPEED

5-24. To determine the total effect of wind on a flight, wind direction and velocity, TAS, and true course (track) must be known. Figure 5-20, page 5-15, illustrates the following example.

Heading and Ground Speed Example

The wind is from 160 degrees at 30 knots; TAS is 120 knots; and the course (track) is 090 degrees. What are the heading and ground speed? 104 degrees and 106 knots.

Set 160 (direction from which the wind is blowing) under the TRUE INDEX (Figure 5-20, left side).

Plot the wind vector above the grommet 30 units (wind speed), and place a wind dot within a circle at this point (Figure 5-20, left side).

Set 90 (course/track) at the TRUE INDEX (Figure 5-20, right side).

Adjust the sliding grid so that the TAS arc (120 knots) is at the wind dot (Figure 5-20, right side). Note that the wind dot is at the 14 degrees converging line to the right of centerline.

Under the 14 degrees correction scale (DRIFT RIGHT) to the right of center at the top of the computer, read the heading (104 degrees).

Under the grommet, read the ground speed (106 knots) (Figure 5-20, right side).

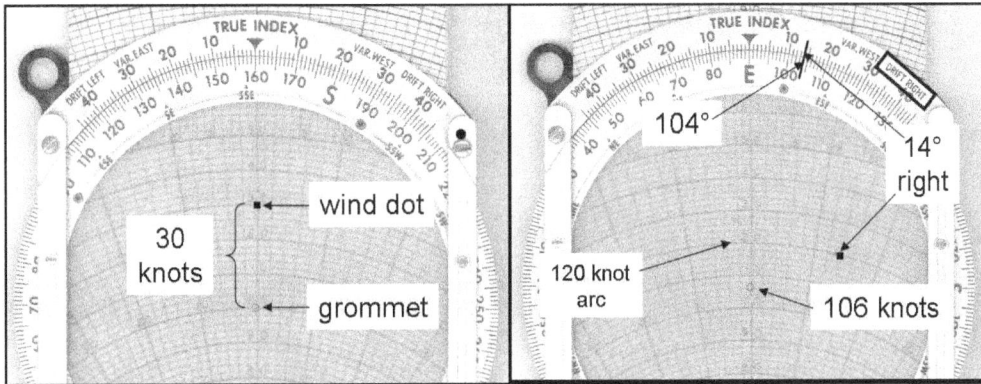

Figure 5-20. Heading and ground speed

DETERMINING UNKNOWN WIND

5-25. To solve for an unknown wind condition, four factors are required: true course (track), ground speed, true heading, and TAS. Figure 5-21, page 5-16, illustrates the following example.

Determining Unknown Wind Example

True course (track) is 090 degrees, ground speed is 106 knots, true heading 085 degrees, and TAS is 116 knots; what are the wind direction and speed? The unknown wind is 045 degrees at 14 knots.

Place the true course under the index (Figure 5-21, left side).

Place the line representing the ground speed under the grommet (Figure 5-21, left side).

Subtract true heading from true course (track), and find the true heading is 5 degrees less than the true course, which means the 5 degrees is a left wind correction angle.

With the center on 106, the ground speed, move up the grid to the TAS line of 116 knots. Then move left 5 degrees and use a pencil to make a wind dot on the 116 knots arc (Figure 5-21, left side).

Rotate the compass rose/plotting disk until the wind dot is resting directly on the centerline (Figure 5-21, right side).

By checking the lines between the grommet & wind dot, find the wind speed is 14 knots (Figure 5-21, right side).

Find wind direction by looking under the true index; the wind direction is 045 degrees (Figure 5-21, right side).

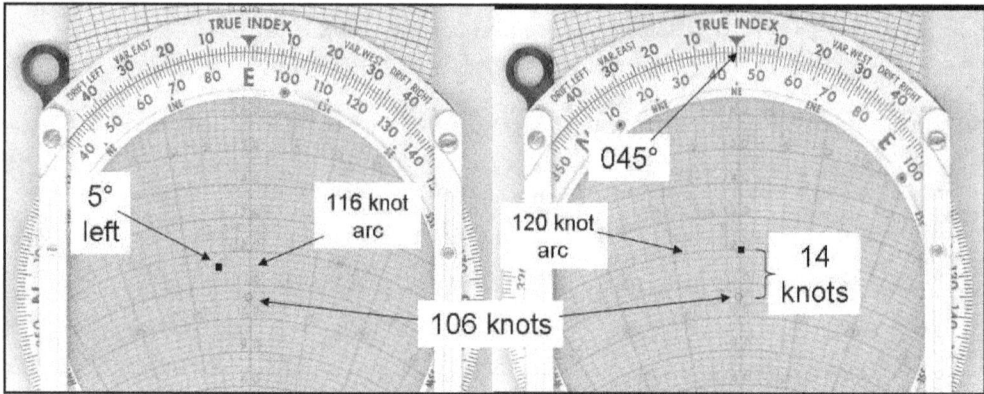

Figure 5-21. Determining unknown wind

DETERMINING ALTITUDE FOR MOST FAVORABLE WIND

5-26. By comparing winds aloft, the aviator can determine the best altitude to obtain the highest ground speed. Figure 5-22 illustrates the following example.

Determining Altitude for Most Favorable Wind

Winds aloft are 3,000 feet – 210 degrees at 20 knots, 6,000 feet – 240 degrees at 12 knots, and 9,000 feet – 290 degrees at 08 knots.

The true course/track is 160degrees and a ground speed of 100 knots.

Plot the winds aloft on the plotting disk, ensuring that the compass rose and arc are properly aligned for each entry (Figure 5-22, left side). Left side is positioned for last entry of 290 at 08 knots for 9,000 feet.

Place the true course/track (160 degrees) under the index (Figure 5-22, right side).

Place the line representing the ground speed under the grommet (Figure 5-22, right side).

The most favorable altitude is 9,000 feet; with a tailwind, the ground speed is 105 knots. The winds at 3,000 feet and 6,000 feet are headwinds.

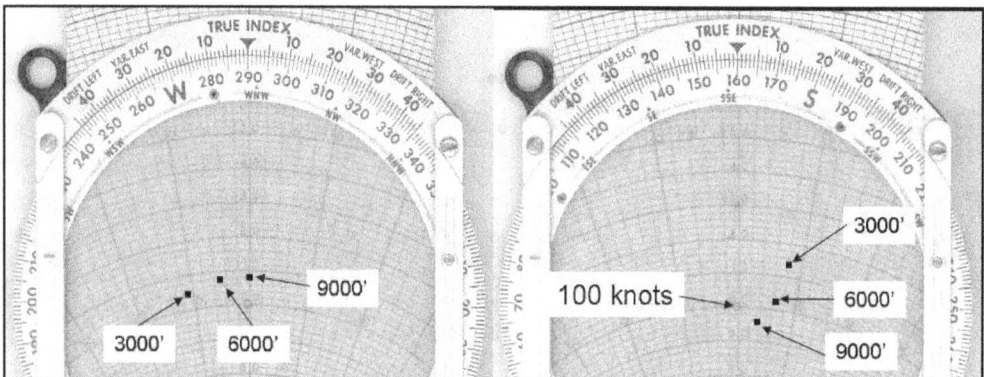

Figure 5-22. Determining altitude for most favorable wind

DETERMINING RADIUS OF ACTION

5-27. Radius of action means the time or distance that an aircraft can fly out on a given course, turn around, and have enough fuel to return to the departure point. Figure 5-23 and figures 5-24 and 5-25, page 5-18, illustrate the following three examples.

Determining Radius of Action Example (Part I)

The true course/track is 060 degree, TAS is 120 knots, wind is 050 degrees at 20 knots, and useable fuel is 110 gallons/740 pounds (JP-8) at a fuel consumption of 42 gallons/280 pounds an hour. How long can the aircraft fly outbound before having to return to the departure point? 1 hour and 15 minutes.

Place the wind direction of 050 degrees under the true index; use the 100 arc as the base point by placing the grommet centered on the 100 arc; then move up to the 120 arc for a wind speed of 20 knots, and place a small pencil mark in the center (Figure 5-23, left side).

Rotate the compass rose until the true course/track of 060 degrees is under the true index (Figure 5-23, center).

To find the ground speed, slide the grid until the wind dot is on the 120 arc, representing the TAS of 120 knots. Then look at the grommet to find the ground speed, which is 100 knots (Figure 5-23, center). Record values for use later.

Now, reverse the compass rose to the reciprocal of 060 degrees, which is 240 degrees, the true course back to the departure point (Figure 5-23, right side).

To find ground speed, slide the grid until the wind dot is on the 120 knots arc, which is the TAS. Look at the grommet to find ground speed, which is 140 knots (Figure 5-23, right side).

Add ground speed outbound to ground speed back to departure point (100 + 140 = 240); the total is 240 knots.

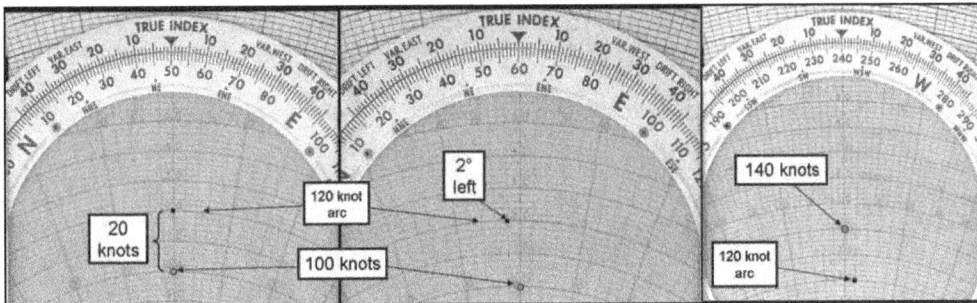

Figure 5-23. Determining radius of action, part I

Determining Radius of Action (Part II)

Now, change fuel in pounds/gallons to fuel in hours on the calculator side. Set 60 index under 28 (outer scale) for 280 pounds of fuel consumption (Figure 5-24, page 5-18, left side).

Look directly under 74 (outer scale) for 740 pounds of useable fuel, and find 2 hours and 39 minutes (hours scale) (Figure 5-24, left scale). The density altitude index obscures the hours scale, so note that 15 (minute scale) aligns with 2 hours and 30 minutes. Count over 4½ graduations; each graduation equals 2 minutes, to be directly under 74. Now add the 9 minutes to the 2 hours and 30 minutes for a total of 2 hours and 39 minutes (Figure 5-24, left side).

AR 95-1 requires a 30-minute reserve for rotary wing and 45-minute reserve for fixed wing on an IFR flight, so deduct 30 minutes (rotary-wing) or 45 minutes (fixed wing) from the total hours & minutes. The total is now 2 hours and 9 minutes (rotary wing) or 1 hour and 54 minutes (fixed wing). The remainder of the calculations will continue to use the rotary wing information.

Now place 24 (outer scale) for 240 knots, total of out and back ground speeds, directly over 2 hours and 9 minutes (hours scale) (Figure 5-24, right side).

Visually move along the outer scale counterclockwise to the ground speed back to departure point of 14 for 140 knots. Look directly under 14, and read 75 minutes, or 1 hour and 15 minutes, on the hours scale. The aircraft should turn back to the departure point at 1 hour and 15 minutes to have enough fuel to make the return trip and arrive at the departure point with a 30-minute reserve.

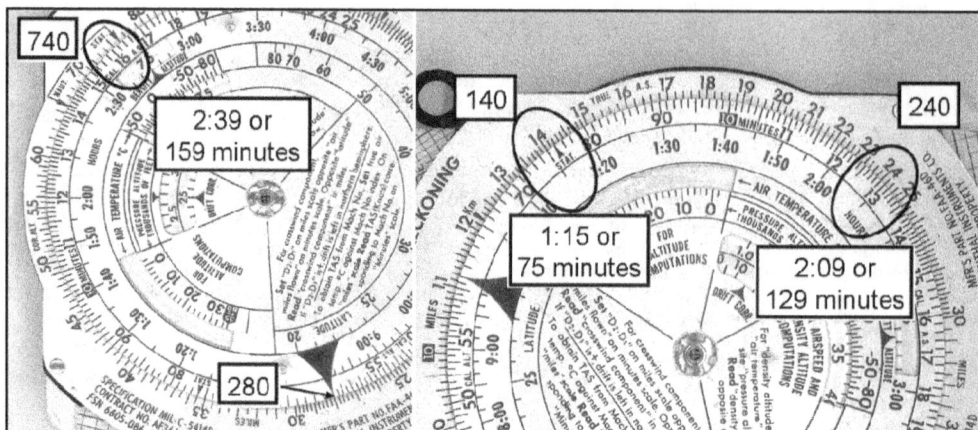

Figure 5-24. Determining radius of action, part II

Determining Radius of Action (Part III)

To convert the times calculated above to distance, perform the following actions:

Set 60 index under 10 (outer scale) for 100 knots ground speed outbound (Figure 5-25, left side).

Look directly over 75 minutes, or 1 hour and 15 minutes (hours scale), and find that the aircraft will fly 125 NM in this time (Figure 5-25, left side).

The radius of action is 125 NM. The radius of action in time is 1 hour and 15 minutes.

To check the problem, find the time required to fly back over the 125-mile course with a ground speed back to departure point of 140 knots as follows:

Set 60 index under 14 (outer scale) for 140 knots ground speed back to departure point (Figure 5-25, right side).

Under 12.5 (outer scale) for 125 NM, find the aircraft will take 53.5 minutes, round up to 54 minutes, (minutes scale) to make the return trip (Figurer 5-25, right side).

This is the final check. By adding the time out of 1 hour and 15 minutes to the time back of 54 minutes, the total time equals 2 hours and 9 minutes. The calculations are confirmed and accurate.

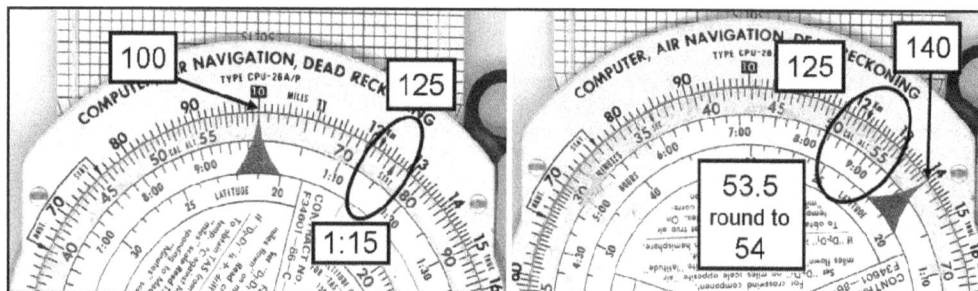

Figure 5-25. Determining radius of action, part III

Chapter 6

Instrument Weather

After more than a century of flight, weather is still the most likely factor to result in fatal accidents. From the hangar, second guessing an aviator's decisions is easy. Many aviators have had the experience of hearing about a weather-related accident and thinking themselves immune from a similar experience because they believe that they would never attempt to fly in adverse conditions. Aviators escaping aviation weather accidents indicate that they found themselves in weather conditions they did not expect and could not safely handle. Although the focus of this manual is instruments, the principles in this chapter apply to all flight. More detailed weather information is found in FM 1-230.

EFFECTS OF WIND

6-1.   Wind is a mass of air moving over the surface of the Earth in a definite direction. When the wind is blowing from the north at 25 knots, it simply means that air is moving southward over the Earth's surface at the rate of 25 nautical miles in one hour.

Contents

6-2.   Under these conditions, any inert object free from contact with the Earth is carried 25 nautical miles southward in one hour. This effect becomes apparent when clouds, dust, and toy balloons are observed being blown along by the wind. An aircraft flying within the moving mass of air is similarly affected. Therefore, at the end of one hour of flight, the aircraft is in a position that results from a combination of these two motions:

- The movement of the air mass in reference to the ground.
- The forward movement of the aircraft through the air mass.

6-3.   These two motions are independent. As far as the aircraft's flight through the air is concerned, there is no difference, whether the air mass is moving or stationary. An aviator flying in a 70-knot gale is unaware of any wind (except for possible turbulence) unless the ground is observed. In reference to the ground, however, the aircraft would appear to fly faster with a tailwind, slower with a headwind, or to drift right or left with a crosswind.

6-4.   In addition, wind has an effect on ground speed and drift. An aircraft flying eastward at an airspeed of 120 knots in still air has a ground speed of 120 knots (Figure 6-1, page 6-2). If the air mass is moving eastward at 20 knots, airspeed of the aircraft is not affected, but progress of the aircraft over the ground is 120 knots plus 20 knots, or a ground speed of 140 knots. Conversely, if the air mass is moving westward at 20 knots, the airspeed of the aircraft still remains the same, but ground speed becomes 120 knots minus 20 knots, or 100 knots.

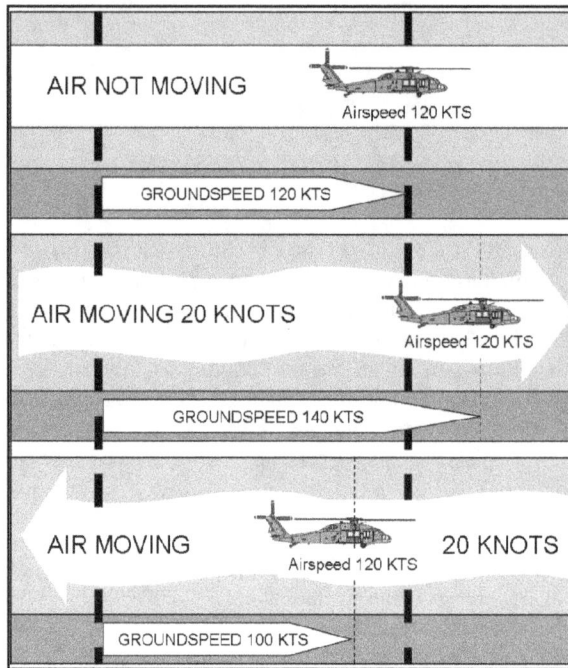

Figure 6-1. Wind effect and ground speed

6-5.   Assuming that no correction is made for wind effect, if an aircraft is heading eastward at 120 knots through an air mass moving southward at 20 knots, at the end of one hour, the aircraft is almost 120 miles east of its point of departure because of its progress through the air. It is also 20 miles south because of the motion of the air. Under these circumstances, airspeed remains 120 knots, but ground speed is determined by combining the movement of the aircraft with that of the air mass. Ground speed can be measured as the distance from the point of departure to the position of the aircraft at the end of one hour. The ground speed can be computed by the time required to fly between two points a known distance apart and can be determined before flight by constructing a wind triangle (Figure 6-2).

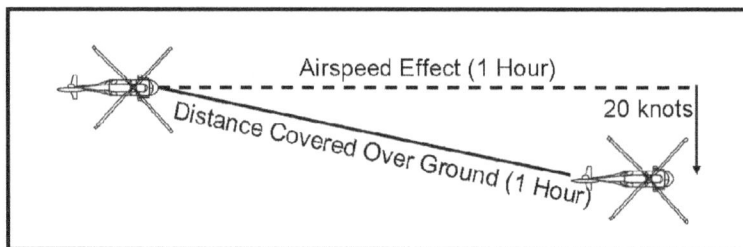

Figure 6-2. Wind drift

6-6.   Heading is the direction in which the aircraft is flying. Track is its actual path over the ground, which is a combination of the motion of the aircraft and motion of the air. The angle between the heading and track is drift angle. If the aircraft's heading coincides with the true course and the wind is blowing from the left, the track will not coincide with the true course. The wind will drift the aircraft to the right so that the track will fall to the right of the desired course or true course (Figure 6-3). Standard wind drift correction procedures are depicted in table 7-1, page 7-21.

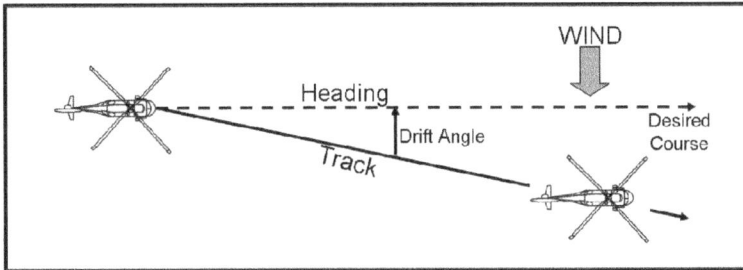

Figure 6-3. Wind drift angle

6-7. By determining the amount of drift, the aviator can counteract the effect of wind and make the track of the aircraft coincide with the desired course. If the air mass is moving across the course from the left, the aircraft will drift to the right and a correction must be made by heading the aircraft sufficiently to the left to offset this drift. Therefore, if the wind is from the left, correction is made by pointing the aircraft to the left a certain number of degrees to correct for wind drift. This wind correction angle is expressed in terms of degrees right or left of the true course (Figure 6-4).

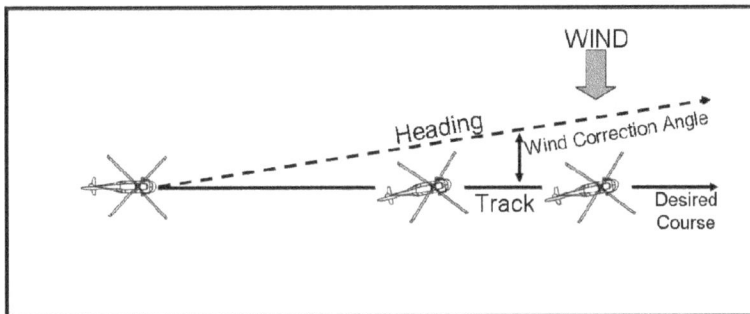

Figure 6-4. Wind correction angle

TURBULENCE

6-8. Turbulence is caused by winds, thermals, and other movement of air. Turbulence effects on aircraft can range from occasional bumps to extreme airspeed and altitude variations in which aircraft control is difficult. To reduce the risk factors associated with turbulence, aviators must learn methods of avoidance as well as piloting techniques.

6-9. Turbulence avoidance begins with a thorough preflight weather briefing. Many reports and forecasts are available to assist the aviator in determining areas of potential turbulence to include the severe weather warning (WW), significant meteorological information (SIGMET) (WS), convective SIGMET (WST), airman's meteorological information (AIRMET) (WA), severe weather outlook (advisory circular [AC]), center weather advisory (CWA), area forecast (FA), and pilot reports (pilot weather reports [PIREPs]). Because thunderstorms always indicate turbulence, areas of known and forecast thunderstorm activity are always of interest to the aviator. In addition, clear air turbulence (CAT) associated with jet streams, strong winds over rough terrain, and fast-moving cold fronts are also good indicators of turbulence.

6-10. Aviators are alert while in flight for the signposts of turbulence. Clouds with vertical development—such as cumulus, towering cumulus, and cumulonimbus—are indicators of atmospheric instability and possible turbulence. Standing lenticular clouds lack vertical development but indicate strong mountain wave turbulence. (For more information on cloud types, see FM 1-230. While en route, aviators can monitor the HIWAS broadcast for updated weather advisories or contact the nearest AFSS or en route flight advisory service (EFAS) for the latest turbulence-related PIREPs.

6-11.   Avoid turbulence associated with strong thunderstorms. Circumnavigate cells by at least 20 miles. Turbulence may also be present in the clear air above a thunderstorm. Fly at least 1,000 feet above the cloud tops for every 10 knots of wind at that level, or fly around the storm. Do not underestimate turbulence underneath a thunderstorm. Never attempt to fly under a thunderstorm even if the other side is visible. The possible results of turbulence and wind shear under the storm could be disastrous.

6-12.   Aircraft control is difficult for the aviator to maintain while flying in moderate to severe turbulence The aviator may not be able to maintain a proper scan of the instruments because of the higher workload associated with turbulence (Figure 6-5). Aviators should immediately reduce power and slow the aircraft to the recommended turbulence penetration speed as described in the appropriate aircraft operator's manual. To minimize the load factor imposed on the aircraft, the wings should be kept level and the aircraft's pitch attitude should be held constant, while the altitude of the aircraft is allowed to fluctuate up and down. Maneuvering to maintain a constant altitude only increases stress on the aircraft. If necessary, the aviator should advise ATC of the fluctuations and request a block altitude clearance. In addition, the power should remain constant at a setting to maintain the recommended turbulence penetration airspeed.

Figure 6-5. Instrument scan in severe turbulence (blurry instrument panel)

6-13.   PIREPs are the best source of information on the location and intensity of turbulence. Therefore, aviators are encouraged to familiarize themselves with the turbulence reporting criteria found in the AIM. The AIM also describes the procedure for volunteering turbulence-related PIREPs.

STRUCTURAL ICING

6-14.   The very nature of IFR requires flight in visible moisture such as clouds. At the right temperatures, this moisture can freeze on the aircraft, causing increased weight, degraded performance, and unpredictable aerodynamic characteristics. Understanding, avoiding, and early recognition, followed by prompt action, are the keys to avoiding this potentially hazardous situation.

6-15.   Structural icing refers to the accumulation of ice on the exterior of the aircraft and is broken down into three classifications: rime ice, clear ice, and mixed ice. For ice to form, moisture must be present in the air, and the air must be cooled to a temperature of 0 degrees Celsius (32 degrees Fahrenheit [F]) or lower.

Aerodynamic cooling can lower the surface temperature of an airfoil, causing ice to form on the airframe even when the ambient temperature is slightly above freezing.

6-16.   Rime ice forms if droplets are small and freeze immediately when contacting the aircraft surface. This type of ice usually forms on areas such as the leading edges of wings or struts. Rime ice has a somewhat rough-looking appearance and a milky-white color. Clear ice forms from larger water droplets or freezing rain that can spread over a surface. This is the most dangerous type of ice because it is clear, hard to see, and can change the shape of the airfoil. Freezing rain and drizzle occur during inversion levels and are extremely hazardous. Mixed ice is a mixture of clear ice and rime ice. It has the characteristics of both types and can form rapidly. Ice particles become imbedded in clear ice, building a very rough accumulation. Table 6-1 lists the temperatures at which various types of ice form.

Table 6-1. Temperature ranges for ice formation

Outside Air Temperature Ranges	Icing Type
0°C to -10°C	Clear
-10°C to -15°C	Mixed clear & rime
-15°C to -20°C	Rime

6-17.   Structural icing is a condition that can only worsen; therefore, during an inadvertent icing encounter, the aviator must act to prevent additional ice accumulation. Regardless of the level of anti-ice or deice protection offered by the aircraft, the first course of action should be to avoid the area of visible moisture with icing conditions. Therefore, the aviator should descend to an altitude below the cloud bases, climb to an altitude above the cloud tops, climb to an altitude of minus 20 degrees Celsius or below, or turn to a different course. If one of these courses of action is not possible, the aviator should move to an altitude free of icing. Report icing conditions to ATC, and request new routing or altitude if icing will be a hazard. Refer to the AIM for information on reporting icing intensities, and comply with AR 95-1 and the aircraft operator's manual for flight into icing. Commanders will assess the risk management considerations for flight into icing conditions based on severity of icing, duration of time in icing conditions, criticality of mission, and availability of deice and anti-ice systems.

FOG

6-18.   Instrument aviators must anticipate conditions leading to the formation of fog and take appropriate action early in flight. Before a flight, close examination of current and forecast weather should alert the aviator to possible fog formation. When fog is a consideration, aviators should plan adequate fuel reserves and alternate landing sites. En route, the aviator must stay alert for fog formation through weather updates from EFAS, the automatic terminal information service (ATIS), and the automated surface observation system (ASOS)/automated weather observing system (AWOS) sites.

6-19.   Two conditions lead to the formation of fog: air is cooled to saturation, or sufficient moisture is added to the air until saturation occurs. In either case, fog can form when the temperature/dew-point spread is 5 degrees or lower. Aviators planning to arrive at their destination near dusk with decreasing temperatures should be particularly concerned about possible fog formation.

VOLCANIC ASH

6-20.   Volcanic eruptions create volcanic ash clouds containing an abrasive dust that poses a serious safety threat to flight operations. Ash clouds are not easily discernible from ordinary clouds when aviators encounter clouds at some distance from a volcanic eruption.

6-21.   When an aircraft enters a volcanic ash cloud, dust particles and smoke may become evident in the cabin often along with the odor of an electrical fire. Inside the volcanic ash cloud, the aircraft may also experience lightning and St. Elmo's fire on the windscreen. The abrasive nature of volcanic ash can pit the windscreens, thus reducing or eliminating forward visibility. The pitot-static system may become clogged, causing instrument failure. Severe engine damage is probable in both piston and turbine-powered aircraft.

6-22.　Every effort is made to avoid volcanic ash. Because volcanic ash clouds are carried by the wind, aviators should plan their flights to remain upwind of ash-producing volcanoes. Visual detection and airborne radar are not considered reliable means of avoiding volcanic ash clouds. Aviators witnessing volcanic eruptions or encountering volcanic ash should immediately pass this information along in a PIREP (if in flight, immediately inform the nearest agency). As with other hazards to flight, the best source of volcanic information comes from PIREPs. The National Weather Service monitors volcanic eruptions, estimates ash trajectories, and passes this information along to aviators in a SIGMET. Volcanic ash forecast transport and dispersion (VAFTAD) charts are also available. These charts depict volcanic ash cloud locations in the atmosphere following an eruption and forecast dispersion of the ash concentrations over 6- and 12-hour time intervals (see AC 00-45).

THUNDERSTORMS

6-23.　A thunderstorm contains nearly every weather hazard known to aviation. Turbulence, hail, rain, snow, lightning, sustained updrafts and downdrafts, and icing conditions are all present in thunderstorms. Do not take off in the face of an approaching thunderstorm or fly an aircraft not equipped with thunderstorm detection in clouds. Likewise, do not fly at night in areas of suspected thunderstorm activity.

6-24.　Unlike VMC, in which thunderstorms can be easily detected and avoided, in IMC flight there is greater difficulty in determining where thunderstorms are located or where they are likely to develop. Aviators should obtain a weather update immediately before departure to determine thunderstorm location, approximate direction, and speed of movement, as well as suspected areas of instability along the planned route where thunderstorms might develop. Because of the dynamic nature of thunderstorms, aircrews should seek frequent updates while en route.

6-25.　There is no useful correlation between the external visual appearance of thunderstorms and the severity or amount of turbulence or hail within them. All thunderstorms are considered hazardous, and thunderstorms with tops above 35,000 feet are considered extremely hazardous.

6-26.　Weather radar, airborne or ground-based, normally reflects areas of moderate to heavy precipitation (radar does not detect turbulence). The frequency and severity of turbulence generally increases with radar reflectivity closely associated with the areas of highest liquid water content of the storm. A flight path through an area of strong or very strong radar echoes separated by 20 to 30 miles, or less, may not be considered free of severe turbulence.

6-27.　The probability of lightning strikes occurring to aircraft is greatest when operating at altitudes where temperatures are between -5 degrees Celsius and +5 degrees Celsius. In addition, an aircraft flying in the clear air near a thunderstorm is also susceptible to lightning strikes. Thunderstorm avoidance is always the best policy.

WIND SHEAR

6-28.　Wind shear is defined as a change in wind speed and/or wind direction in a short distance. Wind shear can exist in a horizontal or vertical direction and, occasionally, in both. Wind shear can occur at any and all atmospheric levels and is typically associated with thunderstorms and low-level temperature inversions; however, the jet stream and weather fronts are also sources of wind shear. Wind shear is of greatest concern during takeoffs and landings.

6-29.　As Figure 6-6, page 6-7, illustrates, while an aircraft is on an instrument approach, a shear from a tailwind to a headwind causes the airspeed to increase and the nose to pitch up with a corresponding balloon above the glide path. A shear from a headwind to a tailwind has the opposite effect, and the aircraft sinks below the glide path.

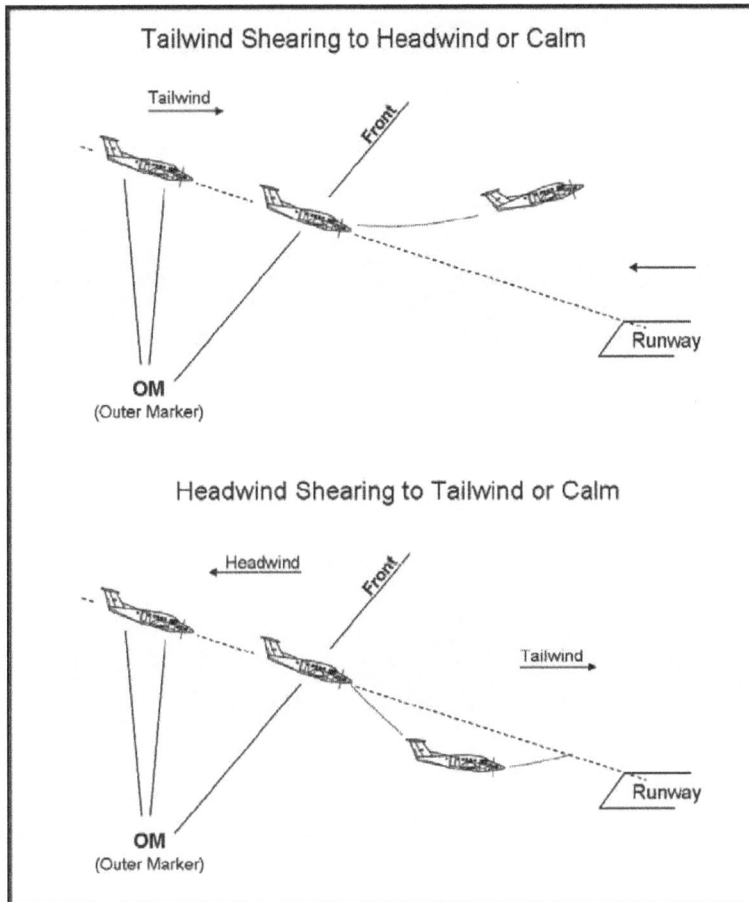

Figure 6-6. Glide-slope deviations in wind shear

6-30.   A headwind shear followed by a tailwind/downdraft shear is particularly dangerous because the aviator has reduced power and lowered the nose in response to the headwind shear. The aircraft is, therefore, in a nose-low, power-low configuration when the tailwind shear occurs. This situation makes recovery more difficult, particularly near the ground. This type of wind-shear scenario is likely to occur during an approach into an oncoming thunderstorm. Aviators should be alert for early indications of wind shear during the approach phase and be ready to initiate a missed approach. An aviator may not be able to recover an aircraft from a wind-shear encounter at low altitude.

6-31.   To inform aviators of hazardous wind shear activity, some airports have installed a low-level wind shear alert system (LLWAS) consisting of a centerfield wind indicator and several surrounding boundary-wind indicators. With this system, controllers are alerted of wind discrepancies (an indicator of wind-shear possibility) and provide this information to aviators. Aviators encountering wind shear are encouraged to pass along a PIREP. Refer to the AIM for additional information on wind-shear PIREPs. A typical wind-shear alert issued to an aviator is, "Wind-shear alert, centerfield wind 230 at 8, south boundary wind 170 at 20."

This page intentionally left blank.

Chapter 7

Navigation Aids

This chapter provides basic radio principles applicable to navigation equipment as well as an operational knowledge of how to use these systems in instrument flight. This information provides the framework for all instrument procedures including DPs, holding patterns, and approaches. Each of these maneuvers consists mainly of accurate attitude instrument flying and accurate tracking using navigation systems. Chapter 10 contains more information on DPs, holding patterns, and approaches.

SECTION I – BASIC RADIO PRINCIPLES

7-1. A radio wave is an electromagnetic (EM) wave with frequency characteristics that are useful in radio. The wave travels long distances through space (in or out of the atmosphere) without losing much strength. The antenna is used to convert the electric current into a radio wave, allowing for travel through space to the receiving antenna, which converts the radio wave back into an electric current.

Contents

RADIO WAVE PROPAGATION

7-2. All matter has a varying degree of conductivity or resistance to radio waves. The Earth itself acts as the greatest resistor to radio waves. Radiated energy traveling near the surface induces a voltage in the ground that subtracts energy from the wave, decreasing its strength as the distance from the antenna increases. Trees, buildings, and mineral deposits affect wave strength to varying degrees. Radiated energy in the upper atmosphere is likewise affected as the energy is absorbed by molecules of air, water, and dust. The characteristics of radio-wave propagation vary according to signal frequency, design, use, and limitations of equipment.

TYPES OF WAVES

SURFACE WAVE

7-3. Surface waves travel across the surface of the Earth. The surface wave's path is like being in a tunnel or alley, bound by the surface of the Earth and ionosphere, which prohibit the surface wave from vectoring into space. Generally, the lower the frequency, the farther the signal travels.

7-4. Surface waves are usable for navigation purposes because they reliably and predictably travel the same route daily and are not influenced by many outside factors. The surface-wave frequency range is generally from the lowest frequencies in the radio range (perhaps as low as 100 Hertz) up to about 1,000 kilohertz (1 megahertz). Although there is a surface-wave component to frequencies between 1 and 30 megahertz, the surface wave at these higher frequencies loses strength over very short distances.

SKY WAVE

7-5. The sky wave, at frequencies of 1 to 30 megahertz, is good for long distances because these frequencies are refracted, or bent, by the ionosphere causing the signal to be sent back to Earth from high in the sky (Figure 7-1). Used by high frequency (HF) radios in aircraft, messages are sent across oceans using only 50 to 100 watts of power. Frequencies producing a sky wave are not used for navigation because the signal pathway from transmitter to receiver is highly variable. The wave bounces off the ionosphere, which is always changing because of varying amounts of the sun's radiation (night/day, seasonal variations, and sunspot activity). The sky wave is not reliable for navigation purposes. For aeronautical communication purposes, the sky wave (HF) is about 80 to 90 percent reliable.

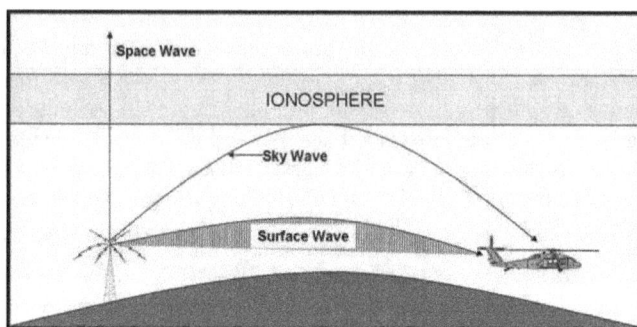

Figure 7-1. Surface, space, and sky wave propagation

SPACE WAVE

7-6.   Radio waves of 15 megahertz and above (up to many gigahertz), when able to pass through the ionosphere, are considered space waves. Most navigation systems operate with their signals propagating as space waves. Frequencies above 100 megahertz have nearly no surface or sky-wave components. They are space waves, except for GPS; the navigation signal is used before reaching the ionosphere. This signal usage makes the effect of the ionosphere, which can cause some propagation errors, minimal. GPS errors caused by passage through the ionosphere are significant and corrected for by the GPS receiver system.

7-7.   Space waves also reflect off hard objects and may be blocked if the object is between the transmitter and receiver. Site and terrain error, as well as propeller/rotor modulation error in VOR systems, is caused by this bounce. ILS course distortion is also the result of this phenomenon, which led to the need for ILS critical areas.

7-8.   Space waves are line-of-sight receivable, but those of lower frequencies bend over the horizon somewhat. Because the VOR signal at 108 to 118 megahertz is a lower frequency than DME at 962 to 1213 megahertz, when aircraft fly over the horizon from a VOR/DME station, the DME is normally the first to stop functioning.

RADIO WAVE RECEPTION DISTURBANCES

7-9.   Static distorts the radio wave and interferes with normal reception of both communications and navigation signals. Low-frequency airborne equipment is particularly subject to static disturbance. Signals in the higher frequency bands are static free.

7-10. Precipitation static (P-static) occurs when static electricity is generated on various aircraft surfaces in flight and is discharged onto other surfaces or into the air. An aircraft generally accumulates little or no static charge when flying in a clear atmosphere. An aircraft flying in particle-laden air may encounter P-static because charged particles adhere to the aircraft, create a charge through frictional contact, or divide into charged fragments on impact with the aircraft surfaces. Some problems caused by P-static are the following:

- Complete loss of VHF communications.
- Erroneous magnetic compass readings.

- High-pitched squeal on audio.
- Motorboat sound on audio.
- Loss of all avionics.
- Very low frequency (VLF) navigation system inoperative.
- Erratic instrument readouts.
- Weak transmissions and poor radio reception.
- St. Elmo's Fire.

PRECAUTIONS

7-11. Various types of navigation aids serve a special purpose; although operating principles and cockpit displays vary among navigation systems, several precautionary actions must be taken to prevent erroneous navigation signals:

- **Identification**. Check identification of any navigation aid and monitor during flight according to the navigation procedures in Section III.
- **Navigation information**. Use all suitable navigation equipment aboard the aircraft, and cross-check heading and bearing information; most aircraft navigation systems have fail flags or warnings that appear when reestablished criteria are not met.
- **Estimated time of arrival (ETA)**. Never overfly an ETA without a careful cross-check of navigation aids and ground checkpoints.
- **Notice to airmen (NOTAM)**. Check NOTAMs and FLIP for possible malfunctions or limitations to navigation aids.
- **Navigation aids**. Discontinue use of any navigation aids that may be malfunctioning or erroneous; if necessary, confirm aircraft position with radar or other equipment. Advise ATC of any problems receiving NAVAIDs; the problem may stem from the ground station, not aircraft equipment.

SECTION II – NAVIGATION SYSTEMS

NONDIRECTIONAL RADIO BEACON

7-12. The ground station portion of the nondirectional radio beacon is the NDB that transmits radio energy in all directions. The airborne receiver is the ADF.

FREQUENCY

7-13. The NDB is a low, medium, or UHF ground-based radio beacon that transmits nondirectional signals whereby a properly equipped aircraft can automatically determine and display bearing to any radio station within its frequency and sensitivity range. These facilities normally operate on frequencies between 190 and 1750 kilohertz or 275 to 287 megahertz and transmit a continuous carrier keyed to provide identification except during voice transmission. The 190 to 1750 kilohertz band is displayed on navigation charts as a brown-colored symbol, and the frequency range NDB used by Army aircraft. The 275- to 287-megahertz band is displayed on navigation charts as a black symbol, not currently received and used by most Army aircraft.

AUTOMATIC DIRECTION FINDER

Components

7-14. The purpose of the ADF is to point to an NDB. The ADF equipment includes two antennas, a receiver, and the indicator instrument. The sense antenna (nondirectional) receives signals with nearly equal efficiency from all directions. The loop antenna receives signals from two directions (bidirectional). The ADF can tell from loop antenna signals that the NDB is one of two possible directions, 180 degrees apart; the sense antenna helps the ADF determine which of the two is correct. When the loop and sense antenna inputs are processed together in the ADF radio, the aircraft is able to receive a radio signal in all directions.

7-15. The radio waves from an NDB consist of an electric field, called the E-field, and magnetic field, called the H-field. These fields are perpendicular in space, and their amplitudes vary sinusoidally with time. NDBs transmit a vertically polarized wave, meaning that the E-field is vertical and the H-field is horizontal. The H-field induces a voltage into the windings of the ADF loop antenna. The loop antenna consists of two perpendicular windings on a square ferrite core. By measuring the phase difference between these two windings, the ADF is able to determine the direction of the beacon.

7-16. All ADF systems have loop and sense antennas. With older ADFs, they are two separate antennas (UH-60A/L Black Hawk). The loop antenna is a flat antenna, usually located on the bottom of the aircraft, while the sense antenna may also be located there. More recent ADFs have a combined loop/sense antenna (UH-60Q/HH-60L Black Hawk and CH-47D Chinook), which works far better than older systems, has less drag, and is much less vulnerable to icing.

Operation

7-17. Most ADF receivers have several modes. If the antenna (ANT) mode is selected, the loop antenna is disabled, and receiving is done through the sense antenna. This mode provides the clearest audio reception, and is normally used to identify a station. On some ADFs, the needle should park in the 90-degree position when the receiver is in ANT mode; other models may work differently:

- In the ADF mode, the pointer is activated and the ADF tries to point to the station. Some ADF systems have a beat frequency oscillator (BFO) position that generates an audio tone for beacons identifying themselves using interrupted-carrier keying; this feature is seldom used in the United States except for a few marine beacons but can be useful in other parts of the world.
- If the ADF has a TEST button, this should cause the needle to slew to the 90-degree position whenever the button is pressed and held; if not, then this function is usually activated by switching to ANT mode.
- The ADF indicator consists of a needle and compass card. The needle points to the stations when the receiver is in ADF mode; the compass card is slaved automatically to the aircraft heading.

COMPASS LOCATOR

7-18. A radio beacon, used with ILS markers, is a compass locator. Compass locators are low-powered NDBs, operating between 200 and 415 kilohertz with a reliable reception range of at least 15 nautical miles, which is received and indicated by the ADF receiver. Higher powered low-frequency NDBs may be collocated with the marker beacons and used as compass locators. These generally carry transcribed weather broadcast information. When used with an ILS front course, the compass locator facilities are collocated with the OM and/or middle marker (MM) facilities. The coding identification of the outer locator consists of the first two letters of the three-letter identifier of the associated LOC. For example, with an ILS localizer identified by the letters "I-DAL" (Dallas/Love Field), the outer locator is identified as "DA." The middle locator at DAL is identified by the last two letters "AL." On the profile view of the approach chart, the locators are depicted by the letters LOM or LMM (locator outer marker or locator middle marker).

VOICE TRANSMISSION

7-19. NDB stations are capable of voice transmission—unless the letter W (without voice) is included in the class designator—and are often used for transmitting the prerecorded AWOS data. The aircraft must be in operational range of the NDB. Coverage depends on the strength of the transmitting station. Before relying on ADF indications, identify the station by listening to the Morse code identifier.

IDENTIFICATION

7-20. Most radio beacons within the United States transmit a continuous three-letter identifier. A two-letter identifier is normally used with an ILS. Some NDBs have only a one-letter identifier. Outside the contiguous U.S., one-, two-, or three-letter identifiers are transmitted.

ACCURACY

7-21. Course accuracy of the VOR is generally plus or minus 1 degree but no more than 2.5 degrees. When the aircraft nears the station, slight deviations from the desired track result in large deflections of the needle. Therefore, establish the correct drift correction angle as soon as possible. Make small heading corrections (not over 5 degrees) as soon as the needle shows a deviation from course, until the needle begins to rotate steadily toward a wingtip position or shows erratic left/right oscillations. Aviators are abeam a station when the needle points to the 90- or 270-degree position. Hold last corrected heading constant and time station passage when the needle shows either wingtip position or settles at or near the 180-degree position. The time interval from the first indications of station proximity to positive station passage varies with altitude (a few seconds at low levels to three minutes at high altitude).

7-22. When the aviator uses ADF equipment, the loop antenna is automatically positioned to the null position. However, the antenna can only rotate about the vertical axis (in relation to the aircraft) and cannot tilt. When the aircraft is banked, the antenna becomes tilted. This tilting moves the loop away from the null, and the motor is not capable of correcting for this error. This error is called dip error and is present anytime the aircraft is not in level flight. The magnitude of this error depends on the position of the aircraft from the station, altitude, range from the station, and angle of bank used. Dip error is most noticeable when the aircraft is banked and the station is on the nose or tail. The ADF bearings should be considered accurate only when the aircraft is in level flight.

DISTURBANCES

7-23. Radio beacons are subject to disturbances that may result in erroneous bearing information. Such disturbances result from intermittent or unpredictable signal propagation because of such factors as lightning and precipitation static. At night, radio beacons are vulnerable to interference from distant stations. Nearly all disturbances affecting the ADF bearing also affect the facility's identification. Noisy identification usually occurs when the ADF needle is erratic. Voice, music, or erroneous identification will usually be heard when a steady false bearing is being displayed.

Note. Because ADF receivers do not have a flag to warn the aviator when erroneous bearing information is being displayed, the aviator must continuously monitor the NDB's identification.

VERY HIGH FREQUENCY OMNIDIRECTIONAL RANGE

FREQUENCY

7-24. VOR operates within the 108.0 to 117.95 megahertz VHF frequency band and has a power output necessary to provide coverage within the assigned operational service volume. The equipment is subject to line-of-sight restriction, and its range varies proportionally to the altitude of the receiving equipment.

VOICE TRANSMISSION

7-25. Most VORs are equipped for voice transmission. VORs without voice capability are indicated on en route and sectional charts by underlining the VOR frequency and by the designation VORW in the IFR supplement. Because a large portion of the frequencies available on the VOR control panel may overlap the VHF communication frequency band, aviators may use the VOR receiver as a VHF communications receiver. For example, the AN/ARC-186 VHF-amplitude modulation (AM)/FM radio has frequencies 116.0 through 151.975 megahertz range and 108.0 through 115.975 megahertz receive only.

IDENTIFICATION

7-26. The only method of identifying a VOR is by its Morse code identification or the recorded automatic voice identification. Voice identification consists of a voice announcement (CAIRNS VOR), alternating with the usual Morse code identification. During periods of maintenance, the facility may radiate T-E-S-T in Morse code or the code may be removed.

RADIALS

7-27. The courses oriented from the station are called radials. The VOR information received by an aircraft is not influenced by aircraft attitude or heading (Figure 7-2). The following example shows VOR information.

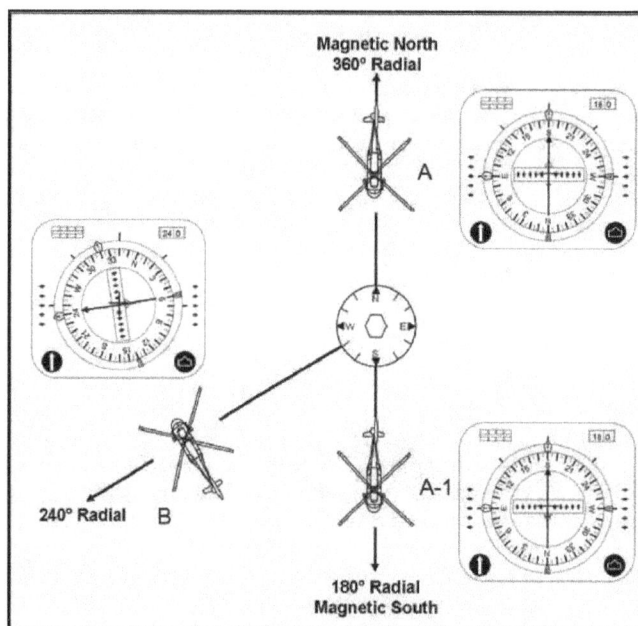

Figure 7-2. Very (high frequency) omnidirectional range radials

---

Example of VOR Information

For example, aircraft A (heading 180 degrees) is inbound on the 360 degrees radial, and the omnibearing selector (OBS) was used to select 180 degrees, thereby displaying a TO indication. If the OBS was used to select the 360 degrees radial, the instrument will display a reverse sensing. Reverse sensing is when the VOR needle indicates the reverse of normal operation. This reversal occurs when the aircraft is heading toward the station with a FROM (FR) indication or when the aircraft is headed away from the station with a TO indication.

After crossing the station, the aircraft is outbound on the 180 degrees radial at A-1 and displaying a FR indication. Aircraft B is shown crossing the 240 degrees radial while flying a heading of 340 degrees. The OBS was used to select 240 degrees, thereby displaying an FR indication. Similarly, at any point around the station, an aircraft can be located somewhere on a VOR radial. The heading selected on the OBS determines the sensitivity of the instrument.

TRACKING TO AND FROM THE STATION

7-28. To track to the station, rotate the OBS until TO appears and then center the course deviation indicator (CDI). Fly the course indicated by the index. If the CDI moves off center to the left, follow the needle by correcting course to the left, beginning with a 20-degree correction.

7-29. When an aviator flies the course indicated on the index, a left deflection of the needle indicates a crosswind component from the left. If the amount of correction brings the needle back to center, decrease the left course correction by half. If the CDI moves left or right now, the movement should be much slower and the aviator can make a smaller heading correction for the next iteration.

7-30. Keeping the CDI centered will take the aircraft to the station. To track to the station, the OBS value at the index is not changed. To home to the station, the CDI needle is periodically centered and the new course, under the index, is used for the aircraft heading. Homing will follow a circuitous route to the station, just as with ADF homing.

7-31. To track from the station on a VOR radial, first orient the aircraft's location, with respect to the station and the desired outbound track, by centering the CDI needle with a from indication, shown as FR. The track is intercepted by either flying over the station or establishing an intercept heading. The magnetic course of the desired radial is entered under the index, using the OBS, and the intercept heading is held until the CDI centers. Then the procedure for tracking to the station is used to fly outbound on the specified radial.

ACCURACY

7-32. The accuracy of course alignment of the VOR is excellent, generally ± 1 degree, but no more than 2.5 degrees. The effectiveness of the VOR depends on proper use and adjustment of both ground and airborne equipment.

7-33. On some VORs, minor course roughness may be observed, evidenced by course needle or brief flag alarm. At a few stations, usually in mountainous terrain, the aviator may occasionally observe a brief course needle oscillation, similar to the indication of approaching station. Aviators flying over unfamiliar routes are cautioned to be on the alert for these course needle oscillations and, in particular, to use the TO/FR indicator to determine positive station passage.

RECEIVER ACCURACY CHECK

7-34. Title 14 of the Code of Federal Regulations (14 CFR), part 91.171, provides certain VOR equipment accuracy checks and an appropriate endorsement within 30 days before flight under IFR for civil aircraft. This requirement does not apply to military aircraft because they are defined as public aircraft. Army aircraft operator manuals and checklists require avionics to be tested before each flight and any malfunction to be written on the appropriate forms in the aircraft logbook.

7-35. VOR system course sensitivity may be checked by noting the number of degrees of change when the aviator rotates the OBS to move the CDI from center to the last dot on either side. The course selected should not exceed 10 or 12 degrees either side. To ensure satisfactory operation of the airborne system, use the following means for checking VOR receiver accuracy:

- VOR test facility (VOT) or a radiated test signal from an appropriately rated radio repair station.
- Certified checkpoints on the airport surface.
- Certified airborne checkpoints.

Test Facility

7-36. The FAA VOT transmits a test signal that provides users with a convenient means to determine the operational status and accuracy of a VOR receiver while on the ground where a VOT is located. Locations of VOTs are published in the Airport/Facility Directory (A/FD). Two means of identification are used. One is a series of dots, and the other is a continuous tone. Information concerning an individual test signal can be obtained from the local FSS. The airborne use of VOT is permitted; however, its use is strictly limited to those areas/altitudes specifically authorized in the A/FD or appropriate supplement.

7-37. To use the VOT service, tune in the VOT frequency 108.0 megahertz on the VOR receiver. With the CDI centered, the OBS should read 0 degrees with the TO/FR indication showing FROM, or the OBS should read 180 degrees, with the TO/FR indication showing TO. Should the VOR receiver operate an RMI, the indication will be 180 degrees on any OBS setting.

7-38. A radiated VOT from an appropriately rated radio repair station serves the same purpose as an FAA VOT signal. The check is made in much the same manner as a VOT with some differences.

Certified Checkpoints

7-39. Airborne and ground checkpoints consist of certified radials received at specific points on the airport surface or over specific landmarks while the aircraft is airborne in the immediate vicinity of the airport. Locations of these checkpoints are published in the A/FD.

7-40. Should an error in excess of ± 4 degrees be indicated through use of a ground check, or ± 6 degrees using the airborne check, IFR flight will not be attempted without first correcting the source of the error. No correction other than the correction card figures supplied on the DD Form 1613 (Pilot's Compass Correction Card) should be applied in making these VOR receiver checks.

7-41. If a dual system VOR (units independent of each other except for the antenna) is installed in the aircraft, one system may be checked against the other. Turn both systems to the same VOR ground facility, and note the indicated bearing to that station. If the receivers are within 4 degrees of each other, both may be considered reliable.

TACTICAL AIR NAVIGATION

PRINCIPLES OF OPERATION

7-42. The theoretical and technical principles of operation of TACAN equipment are different from those of VOR; however, the result is the same. In addition to the displayed bearing information, TACAN adds a continuous display of range information. DME, an integral part of TACAN, provides continuous slant-range distance information.

GROUND EQUIPMENT

7-43. TACAN ground equipment consists of either a fixed or mobile transmitting unit. The airborne unit, with the ground unit, reduces the transmitted signal to a visual presentation of both azimuth and distance information. TACAN operates in the UHF band of frequencies. The system presently has a total of 252 channels available and is identified by two sets of channel numbers, from 1 to 126, with suffixes X or Y for discrimination between the sets.

7-44. TACAN ground equipment consists of a rotating type of antenna for transmitting bearing information and a receiver-transmitter (transponder) for transmitting distance information. The TACAN station is identified by an international Morse code tone modulated at 1,350 hertz with a reception interval of about 30 seconds. Permanent TACAN ground stations are usually dual transmitter equipped (one operating and one on standby) or full monitored installations, which automatically switch to the standby transmitter when a malfunction occurs. The ground monitor, set to alarm at any radial shift of ± 1 degree, is usually located in the base control tower or approach control and sets off a light and buzzer to warn the ground crew when an out-of-tolerance condition exists. Sometimes TACAN reception might be suspected of being in error, or bearing/distance unlock conditions might be encountered in flight. When errors occur, the aviator can check the status of the ground equipment by calling ATC. When ground equipment is undergoing tests or repairs, the identification is silenced to prevent transmission of erroneous signals.

MALFUNCTIONS

7-45. Several forms of TACAN malfunctions can give false or erroneous information to the navigation display equipment.

Bearing/Distance Unlock

7-46. TACAN bearing and distance signals are subject to line-of-sight restrictions because of utilization of UHF frequencies. Because of the transmission/reception principles, unlock (indicated by rotating of bearing pointer and/or range indicator) will occur if these signals are obstructed. Temporary obstruction of TACAN signals can occur in flight when aircraft fuselage, wing, gear, external stores, or wingmen get between the ground and aircraft antenna. Aircraft receiver memory circuits prevent unlock for short periods (about 10 seconds for DME and 2 seconds for azimuth). Beyond this, unlock occurs and will persist until the obstruction is removed and search cycles are completed. Unlock may occur during maneuvers, such as procedure turns, which cause the aircraft antenna to be obstructed for longer than 2 to 10 seconds.

Azimuth Cone of Confusion

7-47. The structure of the azimuth cone of confusion over a TACAN station is considerably different from other NAVAIDs. The azimuth cone can be up to 100 degrees or more in width (about 15 nautical miles wide at 40,000 feet). Indications on the aircraft instruments make the cone appear even wider. Approaching the TACAN station, usable azimuth information is lost before the actual cone is reached. This is correct although actual azimuth unlock is prevented by the memory circuit until after the aircraft has entered the cone. After the cone is crossed and usable signals are regained, the search cycle extends the unusable area beyond the actual cone. Only azimuth information is unusable in the cone of confusion; slant-range distance information continues to be displayed on the range indicator.

40-Degree Azimuth Error Lock-On

7-48. Because of the nature of the TACAN signal, the TACAN azimuth can lock on in multiples of 40 degrees from the true bearing, with no warning flag appearing. The aviator should cross-check other navigation aids available to verify TACAN azimuth. Rechanneling the airborne receiver to deliberately cause unlock may correct the problem. Although some TACAN sets are designed to eliminate 40-degree lock-on error, the aviator should cross-check the bearing with other available navigation aids.

Co-Channel Interference

7-49. Co-channel interference occurs when the aircraft is in a position to receive TACAN signals from more than one ground station on the same channel, normally at high altitude. DME, azimuth, or identification from either ground station may be received.

False or Incorrect Lock-on

7-50. False or incorrect lock-on is caused by misalignment or excessive wear of the airborne equipment channel selection mechanism. Rechanneling from the selected channel number and back, preferably from the direction opposite the original setting, sometimes corrects this problem.

VERY HIGH FREQUENCY OMNIDIRECTIONAL RANGE/TACTICAL AIR NAVIGATION

7-51. A VORTAC is a facility consisting of two components, VOR and TACAN, which provide three individual services: VOR azimuth, TACAN azimuth, and TACAN distance (DME) at one site. Although consisting of more than one component—incorporating more than one operational frequency and using more than one antenna system—a VORTAC is considered to be a unified navigation aid. Both components of a VORTAC operate simultaneously and provide the three services at all times.

7-52. Transmitted signals of VOR and TACAN are each identified by a three-letter code transmission and interlocked so that aviators using VOR azimuth with TACAN distance can be assured of both signals being received are from the same ground station. The frequencies of the VOR, TACAN, and DME at each VORTAC facility are paired according to a national plan to simplify airborne operation. Frequency pairing information is published in the FIH.

DISTANCE MEASURING EQUIPMENT

OPERATION

7-53. In the operation of DME, paired pulses at a specific spacing are sent out from the aircraft and received at the ground station. The ground station then transmits paired pulses back to the aircraft at the same pulse spacing but on a different frequency. The time required for the round trip of this signal exchange is measured in the airborne DME unit and translated into distance in nautical miles from the aircraft to the ground station.

LINE-OF-SIGHT PRINCIPLE

7-54. Operating on the line-of-sight principle, DME furnishes distance information with a very high degree of accuracy. Reliable signals may be received at distances up to 199 nautical miles at line-of-sight altitude with an accuracy of better than a half mile or 3 percent of the distance, whichever is greater. Distance information received from DME equipment is slant-range distance and not actual horizontal distance.

FREQUENCIES

7-55. DME operates on frequencies in the UHF spectrum between 962 megahertz and 1213 megahertz. Aircraft equipped with TACAN equipment will receive distance information from a VORTAC automatically, while aircraft equipped with only a VOR receiver must have a separate DME airborne unit.

FACILITIES

7-56. VOR/DME, VORTAC, ILS/DME, and LOC/DME navigation facilities provide course and distance information from collocated components under a frequency-pairing plan. Aircraft receivers equipped to provide automatic DME selection ensure reception of azimuth and distance information from these common sources when selected by the pilot.

IDENTIFICATION

7-57. VOR/DME, VORTAC, ILS/DME, and LOC/DME facilities are identified by synchronized identifications, which are transmitted on a time-sharing basis. The DME or TACAN coded identification is transmitted one time for each three or four times that the VOR or localizer coded identification is transmitted. When either the VOR or DME is inoperative, the aviator needs to recognize which identifier is retained for the operative facility. A single coded identification with a repetition interval of about 30 seconds indicates that the DME is operative.

Note. DME unlocks can occur periodically because of ground station overload when more than 100 aircraft interrogations are received at the same time. This problem is most likely to occur at locations of heavy traffic (such as Chicago [Illinois] O'Hare International Airport).

GLOBAL POSITIONING SYSTEM

7-58. The GPS is a space-based navigation system that provides highly accurate three-dimensional navigation information to an infinite number of equipped users anywhere on or near the Earth. The typical GPS integrated system provides position, velocity, time, altitude, steering information, ground speed, ground track error, heading, and variation.

SYSTEM OVERVIEW

Signal Accuracy

7-59. GPS measures distance by timing a radio signal that starts at the satellite and ends at the GPS receiver. The signal carries data that disclose satellite position and time of transmission and synchronize the aircraft GPS system with satellite clocks. There are two levels of accuracy available: standard positioning service (SPS) and precise positioning service (PPS). Course acquisition (C/A) data will provide position accurate to within 100 meters and can be received by anyone with a GPS receiver.

7-60. Current accuracy for SPS users is better than 7 meters horizontal with a probability of 95 percent. Precision data can be received only by authorized users (PPS) in possession of the proper codes. The data is accurate to within 16 meters.

Segments

7-61. GPS is composed of the three following major segments:
- **Space segment**. The GPS constellation is composed of multiple satellites whose orbits and spacing are arranged to optimize the GPS coverage area.
- **Control segment**. The control segment includes a number of monitor stations and ground antennas located throughout the world. Monitor stations use GPS receivers to track all satellites in view and accumulate ranging data from satellite signals; information is processed at the master control station (MCS) and used to manage the satellite system.
- **User segment**. The user segment consists of GPS equipment (such as aircraft avionics, surveying equipment, and handheld GPS receivers) used in a variety of ways; GPS equipment uses data transmitted by the satellites to provide instantaneous position information.

Navigation Database

7-62. Navigation databases supporting GPS equipment certified for en route and terminal operations contain, as a minimum, all airports, VORs, VORTACs, NDBs, and named waypoints (WPs) and intersections shown on en route and terminal area charts, SIDs, and STARs. In the terminal area, the database includes WPs for SIDs and STARs, as well as other flight operations from the beginning of a departure to the en route structure or from an en route fix to the beginning of an approach procedure. All named WPs are identified with a five-letter designation provided by the National Flight Data Center (NFDC). WPs unnamed by the NFDC, such as a DME fix, are assigned a five-letter alphanumeric coded name in the database. For example, D234T is a coded WP, representing a point located on the 234-degree radial of XYZ VORTAC at 20 nautical miles. The letter T is the twentieth letter of the alphabet and indicates a distance of 20 nautical miles.

USE OUTSIDE UNITED STATES NATIONAL AIRSPACE SYSTEM

7-63. GPS use may be further restricted depending on the area of operation. Flight using GPS is not authorized in some countries. If planning to use GPS outside the NAS, check for additional restrictions in the FLIP GP and area planning (AP) documents in areas of intended operation.

RECEIVER AUTONOMOUS INTEGRITY MONITORING

7-64. GPS equipment certified for IFR use must have the capability of verifying the integrity of the signals received from the GPS constellation. Loss of satellite reception and receiver autonomous integrity monitoring (RAIM) warnings may occur because of aircraft dynamics (changes in pitch or bank angle). Antenna location on the aircraft, satellite position relative to the horizon, and aircraft attitude may also affect reception of one or more satellites. Because the relative positions of the satellites are constantly changing, prior experience with the airport does not guarantee reception at all times and RAIM availability should always be checked. The integrity of the GPS signal is verified by determining if the integrity solution is out of limits for the particular phase of flight, if a satellite is providing corrupted information, or there are an insufficient number of satellites in view. When the integrity of the GPS information does not meet the integrity requirements for the operation being performed, the GPS avionics of the aircraft provide a warning in the cockpit. A GPS integrity warning in the cockpit is equivalent to an off flag on the HSI; the GPS navigation information may no longer be reliable. Refer to the aircraft operator's manual for specific information regarding GPS avionics.

DATABASE REQUIREMENTS

7-65. To use GPS for IFR navigation in the terminal area or for GPS nonprecision approaches, the aircraft's GPS equipment must include an updatable navigation database. GPS airborne navigation databases may come from the NGA via the mission planning system or from an approved commercial source.

MANUAL DATABASE MANIPULATION

7-66. Manual entry/update of the validated data in the navigation database is not possible. However, this requirement does not prevent the storage of user-defined data within the equipment.

EMBEDDED GLOBAL POSITIONING SYSTEM/INERTIAL NAVIGATION SYSTEM

7-67. Although GPS is meant to replace some navigation equipment, the embedding into the navigation system depends on the mission of the aircraft. The combination of GPS and INS is referred to as embedded global positioning system/inertial navigation system (EGI). GPS can greatly enhance the performance of an INS, and the INS, in turn, increases the usefulness of GPS equipment. INS can accurately measure changes in position and velocity over short periods using no external signal; however, errors are cumulative and increase with time. GPS can provide a continual position update that allows the INS to calculate error trends and improve its accuracy as time increases. The INS aids the GPS receiver by improving GPS antijam performance. When GPS is not available, (because of mountain shadowing of satellites, jamming, or high dynamic maneuvers), this improved INS provides the integrated navigation system with accurate position information until the satellites are in view or the jamming is over. GPS provides an in-flight alignment capability for the INS as an added advantage.

COURSE SENSITIVITY

7-68. The course deviation bar or indicator sensitivity related to GPS equipment varies with the mode of operation and type of equipment. Refer to the appropriate aircraft operator's manual for specific information. Unlike traditional ground-based NAVAIDs, GPS course sensitivity is normally linear, regardless of the distance from the WP.

WIDE-AREA AUGMENTATION SYSTEM

7-69. The Wide-Area Augmentation System (WAAS) augments the basic GPS signal for IFR use from takeoff through Category I precision approach. This system improves the accuracy, availability, and integrity currently provided by GPS, thereby improving capacity and safety.

System Description

7-70. Unlike traditional ground-based navigation aids, the WAAS covers a more extensive service area. Wide-area ground reference stations (WRSs) are linked to form a United States WAAS network. These precisely surveyed ground reference stations receive signals from GPS satellites, and any errors in the signals are then determined. Each station in the network relays the data to a wide-area master station (WMS) where correction information for specific geographical areas is computed. A correction message is prepared and uplinked to a geostationary satellite via a ground uplink station (GUS). The current WAAS site installation consists of 25 WRSs, two WMSs, four GUSs, and the required terrestrial communications to support the WAAS network. The message is then broadcast on the same frequency as GPS (L1, 1575.42 megahertz) to WAAS receivers within the broadcast coverage area of the WAAS. The WAAS broadcast message improves the GPS 95 percent signal accuracy from 100 meters to about 7 meters.

Planned Expansion

7-71. Planned expansion of the U.S. ground-station network will include Canada, Iceland, Mexico, and Panama and may expand to other countries. In addition, Japan and Europe are building similar systems, planned to be interoperable with the United States WAAS. The merging of these systems will create a worldwide seamless navigation capability, similar to GPS but with greater accuracy and availability.

Operations

7-72. The FAA is moving directly to a lateral navigation (LNAV)/vertical navigation (VNAV) capability using WAAS. This capability will facilitate improved instrument approaches to include vertical (glide path) guidance to an expanded number of airports. Concurrently, the FAA will evaluate the approach to achieve global navigation satellite system (GNSS) landing system (GLS) capability in later years.

LOCAL AREA AUGMENTATION SYSTEM

7-73. The local area augmentation system (LAAS) augments the GPS to provide an all-weather approach, landing, and surface navigation capability. LAAS focuses its service on a local area (about a 20- to 30-mile radius), such as an airport, and broadcasts its correction message via a VHF radio data link from a ground-based transmitter. LAAS has a profound effect on aviation navigation; LAAS yields the extreme high accuracy, availability, and integrity necessary for Category I, II, and III precision approaches. The end-state configuration pinpoints the aircraft's position to within 1 meter or less with a significant improvement in service flexibility and user operating costs. Curved approach paths, not possible using the current instrument landing systems, are possible for Category I, II, and III precision approaches. Approaches are designed to avoid obstacles, restricted airspace, noise-sensitive areas, or congested airspace. Unlike current landing systems, LAAS provides multiple precision approach capabilities to runways within the LAAS coverage area. Duplication of equipment solely for the purpose of serving multiple runways can be eliminated. Also, airports with the need for precise surface area navigation may use the accuracy of LAAS for the position determination of aircraft. Using this capability, controllers know the location of all airport service vehicles and taxiing aircraft to assist in the prevention of runway incursions in low-visibility conditions. Furthermore, aircraft operators benefit from the reduction of expenses associated with purchasing a variety of radio navigation equipment. Potentially, WAAS and LAAS could use the same aircraft avionics to accomplish both types of missions, reduce avionics maintenance costs, and realize savings in aircrew training.

INERTIAL NAVIGATION SYSTEM

DESCRIPTION

7-74. The INS is a primary source of ground speed, attitude, heading, and navigation information. A basic system consists of acceleration sensors mounted on a gyro-stabilized, gimbaled platform, a computer unit to process raw data and maintain present position, and a CDU for data input and monitoring. The aircrew can selectively monitor a wide range of data, define a series of courses, and update present position. The INS operates by sensing the movement of the aircraft. Its accuracy is theoretically unlimited and affected only by technology and manufacturing precision. Because neither transmitting nor receiving any signal, the INS is unaffected by electronic countermeasures or weather conditions.

OPERATION

7-75. Before use, the INS must be aligned. During alignment, present position coordinates are inserted manually while the INS derives local level and true north. This operation must be completed before the aircraft is moved. If alignment is lost in flight, navigation data may be lost; however, in some cases, attitude and heading information may still be used. Coordinate or radial and distance information describing points that define the route of flight are inserted as needed through the CDU. For complete operation procedures of any specific INS, consult the appropriate aircraft operator's manual.

SECTION III – NAVIGATION PROCEDURES

APPLICATION

7-76. Instrument procedures are flown using a combination of the techniques described in this chapter. Aircraft operator manuals should provide proper procedures for using the navigation equipment installed. The following discussions apply to ground-based radio aids to navigation only. A discussion on RNAV and GPS procedures is provided at the end of this section.

7-77. Unless otherwise authorized by ATC, no person may operate an aircraft within controlled airspace under IFR except as follows:

- On a Federal airway, along the centerline of that airway.
- On any other route, along the direct course between the navigational aids or fixes defining that route; however, this section does not prohibit maneuvering the aircraft to pass well clear of other air traffic or maneuvering of the aircraft in VFR conditions to clear the intended flight path both before and during climb or descent.

7-78. Where procedures depict a ground track, the aviator is expected to correct for known wind conditions. In general, the only time that wind correction should not be applied is during radar vectors. The following general procedures apply to all aircraft.

TUNE

7-79. Tune to or select the desired frequency or channel.

IDENTIFY

7-80. Positively identify the selected station via an aural or visual signal. Through human error or equipment malfunction, the intended station may not be the one being received. These problems may occur as the result of failure to select the correct frequency or the receiver to channelize to the new frequency.

7-81. For aircraft with the capability to translate Morse code station identification into an alphanumeric visual display, the visual display may be used as the sole means of identifying the station identification provided—

- The alphanumeric visual display must always be in view of the aviator.
- Loss of the Morse code station identification will cause the alphanumeric visual display to disappear or a warning to be displayed.

Note. Be cognizant of station identification being displayed. If from the DME portion of a VOR/DME station, only the DME alphanumeric display may be used; VOR azimuth station identification must still be identified aurally. Voice communication is possible on VOR, ILS, and ADF frequencies. The only positive method of identifying a station is by its Morse code identifier (aurally or alphanumeric display) or recorded automatic voice identification, indicated by VOR following the station name. Listening to other voice transmissions by an FSS or other facility (TWEB) is not a reliable method of station identification and is not used. Consult FLIP documents to determine availability of specific stations.

MONITOR STATION IDENTIFICATION

7-82. Monitor station identification to ensure that a reliable signal is being transmitted. Removal of identification serves as a warning to aviators that the facility is officially off the air for tune-up or repairs and may be unreliable although intermittent or constant signals are received. The navigation signal is considered unreliable when the station identifier is not being received. Three methods for monitoring station identification are the following:

- The first method is the traditional aural Morse code identifier; this is transmitted by all VOR, TACAN, VORTAC, NDB, and ILS transmitters. If this method is selected to monitor the station, aviators should monitor the station continuously during navigation.
- The second method applies to aircraft with the capability to translate Morse code station identification into an alphanumeric visual display.
- The third method of monitoring a station involves monitoring the visual warning, or off, flags; this method is acceptable as the sole means of monitoring the station identification if—
  - Initial station identification is accomplished via an aural Morse code identifier, alphanumeric display, or recorded automatic voice identification.
  - The off flag, or equivalent, is displayed immediately upon losing station identification.
  - The off flag, or equivalent, is displayed directly in the aviator's view immediately upon activation.

SELECT

7-83. Select the proper position for the navigation system switches.

SET

7-84. Set the selector switches to display the desired information on the navigation instruments.

MONITOR FOR WARNING FLAGS

7-85. Monitor the course warning flag (if installed) or aural or alphanumeric display continuously to ensure adequate signal reception strength.

CHECK

7-86. Check the appropriate instrument indicators for proper operation.

HOMING TO A STATION

7-87. Tune and identify the station. Turn the aircraft in the shorter direction to place the head of the bearing pointer under the top index of the RMI or upper lubber line of the HSI. Adjust aircraft heading, as necessary, to keep the bearing pointer under the top index or upper lubber line. Because homing does not incorporate wind-drift correction, in a crosswind, the aircraft follows a curved path to the station (Figure 7-3). Therefore, homing should be used only when maintaining course is not required.

Note. The online version of this manual contains a video clip of the procedure in Figure 7-3.

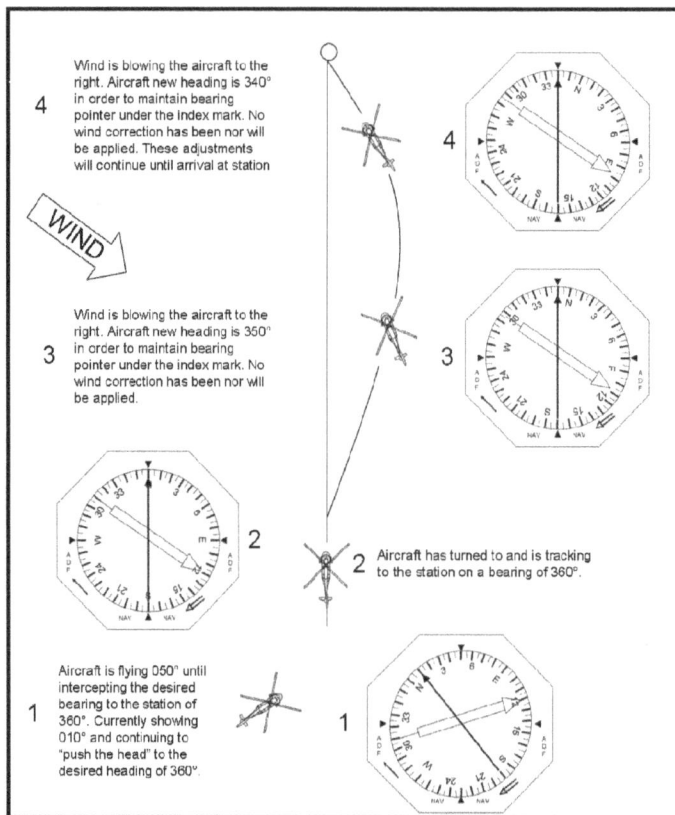

Figure 7-3. Homing to a station

TRACKING TO A STATION

PUSH THE HEAD, PULL THE TAIL

7-88. This is one of several techniques that may be used to achieve a desired track to a selected bearing/radial. Push the head towards the desired bearing/radial, and pull the tail towards the desired bearing/radial. This phrase states the method to obtain the intercept of a desired bearing or radial of a navigation aid. The application is shown below.

Push the Head

7-89. Figure 7-4 illustrates tracking to a station using the ADF/VOR needle. If the aircraft is flying toward the navigation aid, look at the heading. Then look at the head of the ADF/VOR needle. If the head of the needle is right of the desired heading, turn right until past the head of the needle. The aviator should continue flying on a course that is slightly right of the needle. The needle will be pushed to the left, back toward the desired on-course bearing. When the ADF/VOR needle is pointing toward the desired heading, the pilot can resume the desired heading.

Note. The online version of this manual contains a video clip of the procedure in Figure 7-4.

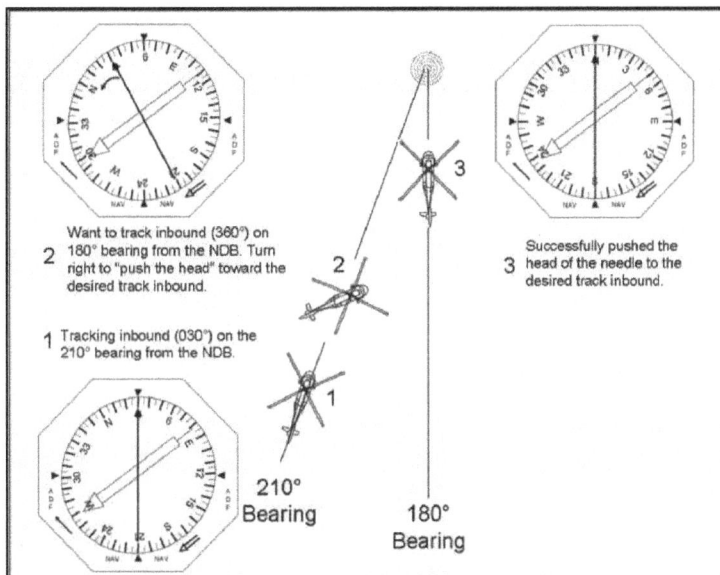

2 Want to track inbound (360°) on 180° bearing from the NDB. Turn right to "push the head" toward the desired track inbound.

1 Tracking inbound (030°) on the 210° bearing from the NDB.

3 Successfully pushed the head of the needle to the desired track inbound.

210° Bearing

180° Bearing

Figure 7-4. Push the head

Pull the Tail

7-90. Figure 7-5, page 7-18, illustrates tracking from a station using the ADF/VOR needle. If the aircraft is flying away from the navigation aid, look at the heading. Then look at the tail of the ADF/VOR needle. If the tail of the needle is left of the desired heading, turn right to pull the tail right. When the tail of the ADF/VOR needle is pointing toward the desired bearing from the station, the pilot can resume the desired heading.

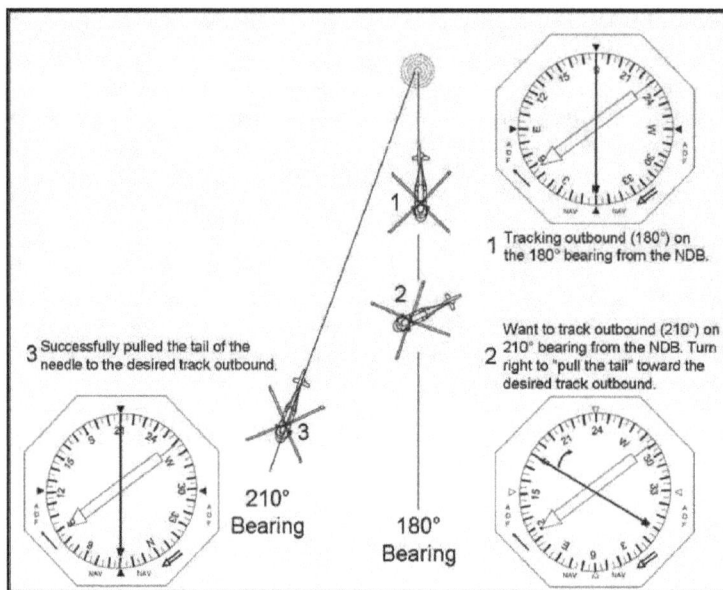

Note. The online version of this manual contains a video clip of the procedure in Figure 7-5.

Figure 7-5. Pull the tail

TRACKING INBOUND

7-91. Tracking inbound (Figure 7-6, page 7-19), NDB or VOR, uses a heading to maintain the desired track to or from the station, regardless of crosswind conditions. Interpretation of the heading indicator and needle is done to maintain a constant magnetic bearing to or from the station. Magnetic bearing is the direction to or from a radio transmitting station measured relative to magnetic north.

7-92. To track inbound, turn the aircraft in the shorter direction to place the head of the bearing pointer under the top index of the RMI or upper lubber line of the HSI. Maintain this heading until off-course drift is indicated by displacement of the needle, which occurs if during a crosswind (needle moving left equals wind from the left; needle moving right equals wind from the right). When a definite (2 to 5 degrees) change in needle reading occurs, turn the aircraft to push the head of the needle back to the desired bearing/radial. The angle of interception must be greater than the number of degrees of drift. The intercept angle depends on the rate of drift, aircraft speed, and station proximity (see table 7-1, page 7-21).

Note. The online version of this manual contains a video clip of the procedure in Figure 7-6.

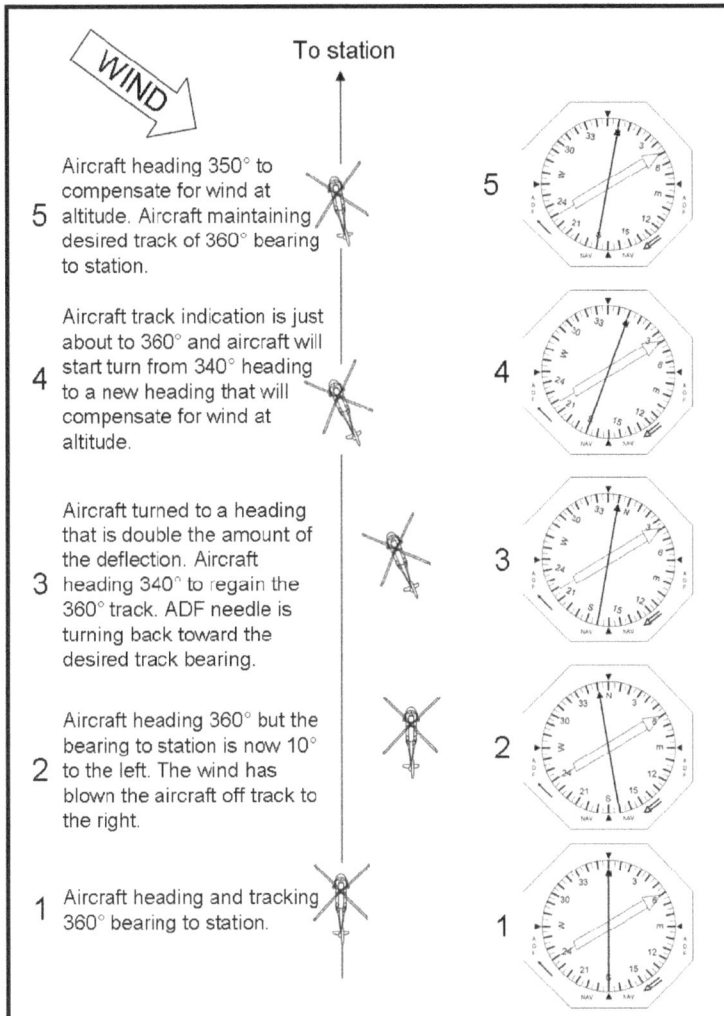

Figure 7-6. Tracking inbound

TRACKING OUTBOUND

7-93. To track outbound, the same bracketing principles apply, except that the tail of the needle moving left equals wind from the right and the tail of the needle moving right equals wind from the left. Wind correction is made away from the tail of the needle deflection. This action is displayed as pulling the tail of the needle to the desired heading, bearing, or radial. Note the example of outbound tracking in Figure 7-7, page 7-20.

Note. The online version of this manual contains a video clip of the procedure in Figure 7-7.

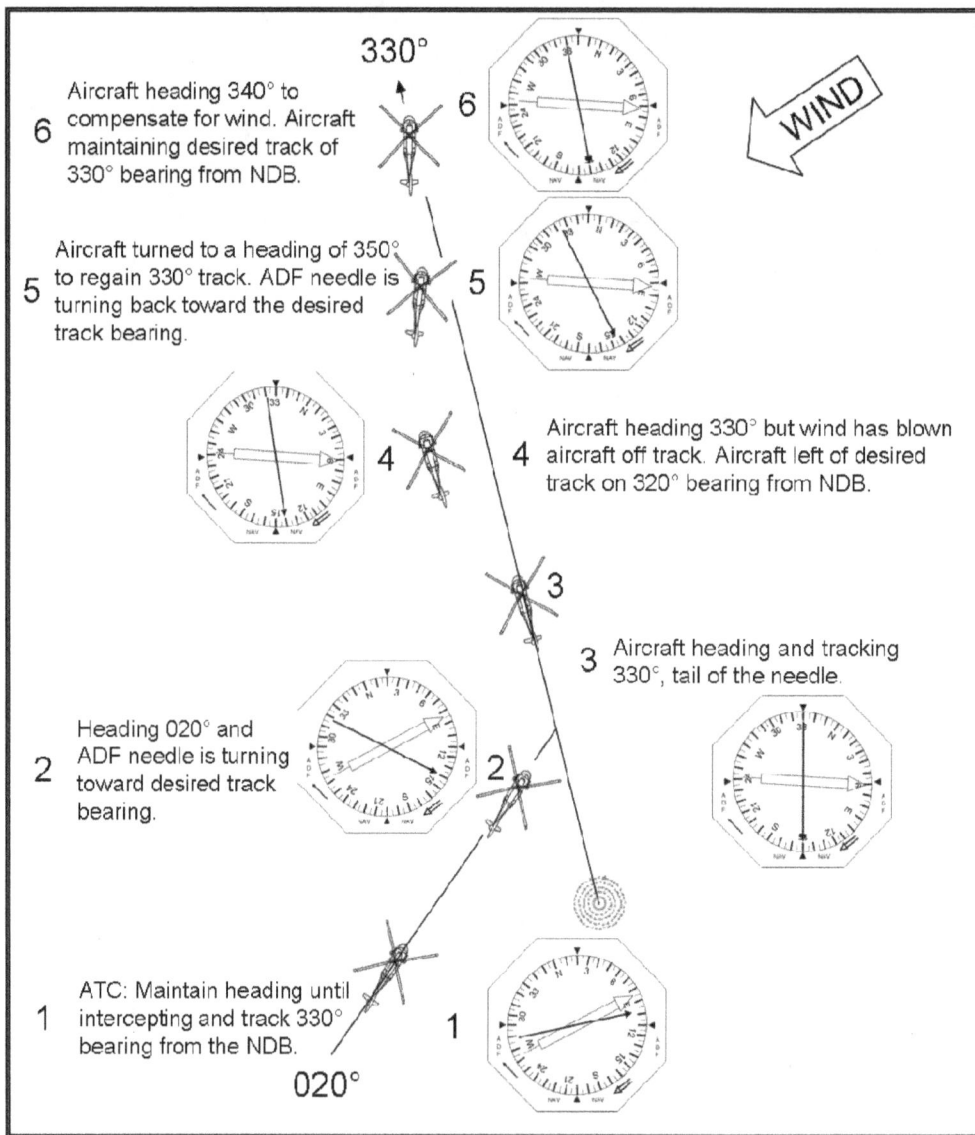

Figure 7-7. Tracking outbound

STANDARD WIND DRIFT CORRECTION

7-94. Wind-drift correction is a continuous process because of the varying nature of winds in speed and direction. Table 7-1 depicts standard wind drift correction procedures. When applying wind drift corrections, continually monitor the desired course to be flown.

Table 7-1. Standard wind drift correction

Condition	*Correction*
Initial correction	Used to return to course (reintercept).
	30° at airspeeds < 90 knots
	20° at airspeeds =/> 90 knots
First trial	Apply half the initial correction after course reinterception.
	15° at airspeeds < 90 knots
	10° at airspeeds =/> 90 knots
Too little wind correction	Repeat initial correction to return to course.
Second trial	Increase correction by applying ½ of the first trial correction (Example: ½ of 15° is 7.5° [rounded to 7]; 15° + 7° = 22°).
Too much wind correction	If trial drift correction is too large, turn to parallel course & allow wind to drift aircraft back on course; then decrease correction on next trial correction.
Bracketing process	Continue until a heading is determined that maintains aircraft course.
Corrections for unusually strong winds	After applying standard initial corrections and course is not reintercepted, correction of 40° or more may be required to return to course.

Note. All course corrections are applied to the tracked (maintained) course.

COURSE INTERCEPT

7-95. Course interceptions are performed in most phases of instrument navigation. The equipment used varies, but an intercept heading must be flown that results in an angle or rate of intercept sufficient to solve a particular problem.

RATE OF INTERCEPT

7-96. Rate of intercept, seen by the aviator as bearing pointer or HSI movement, is a result of the following factors:

- The angle at which the aircraft is flown toward a desired course (angle of intercept).
- True airspeed and wind (ground speed).
- Distance from the station.

ANGLE OF INTERCEPT

7-97. The angle of intercept is the angle between the heading of the aircraft (intercept heading) and desired course. Controlling this angle by selection/adjustment of the intercept heading is the easiest and most effective way to control course interceptions. Angle of intercept must be greater than the degrees from course but should not exceed 90 degrees. Within this limit, adjust to achieve the most desirable rate of intercept.

7-98. When selecting an intercept heading, the key factor is the relationship between distance from the station and degrees from the course. Each degree, or radial, is 1 nautical mile wide at a distance of 60 nautical miles from the station. Width increases or decreases in proportion to the 60 nautical mile distance. For example, 1 degree is 2 nautical miles wide at 120 nautical miles—and 1/2 nautical mile wide at 30 nautical miles. For a given ground speed and angle of intercept, the resultant rate of intercept varies according to the distance from the station. When selecting an intercept heading to form an angle of intercept, consider the following factors:

- Degrees from course.
- Distance from the station.
- True airspeed and wind (ground speed).

COMPLETING THE INTERCEPT

Lead Point

7-99. A lead point to roll out on the course must be determined because of turn radius of the aircraft. The lead point is determined by comparing bearing pointer or HSI movement with the time required to turn to course. Remember that the HSI deviation scale remains fully deflected until the aircraft is within 10 degrees of course for a VOR. Because deviation scale movement can be accurately compared with angle of intercept displayed by the heading pointer, use the deviation scale for completing intercepts whenever possible.

Rate of Intercept

7-100. To determine the rate of intercept, monitor the bearing pointer or HSI movement. If the movement of the bearing pointer or the HSI is quick, the rate of intercept should also be quick.

Turn

7-101. The time required to make the turn to course is determined by the intercept angle and the aircraft turn rate. Greater intercept angles and slower aircraft turn rates require more time.

Complete the Intercept

7-102. Use the HSI, when available, for completing the course intercept. The HSI deviation scale is more sensitive than a bearing pointer.

Undershoot or Overshoot

7-103. If the selected lead point will result in undershooting the desired course, either reduce the angle of bank or roll out of the turn and resume the intercept. If the selected lead point results in an overshoot, continue the turn and roll out with a correction back to the course.

Maintain Course

7-104. The aircraft is considered to be maintaining course centerline when the HSI is centered or the bearing pointer points to the desired course. A correction for known winds should be applied when completing the turn to a course, as shown in Figure 7-6, page 7-19, and figure 7-7, page 7-20.

7-105. Aviators should always attempt to fly as close to the course centerline as possible. TERPS design criteria provide maximum obstacle clearance protection when the course centerline is maintained.

INBOUND PROCEDURES

7-106. An aviator may use various methods to intercept a radial while flying to a station. Generally, setting up a 45-degree angle of intercept is recommended (Figure 7-9, page 7-25); a 30-degree angle of intercept (Figure 7-8, page 7-24) is also correct, as is double the angle off the nose method if the number of radials to be crossed is not in excess of 45 degrees. The double the angle off the nose method (Figure 7-12, page 7-28) and timed distance method for radial changes in excess of 45 degrees (Figure 7-10, page 7-26) are described in detail below.

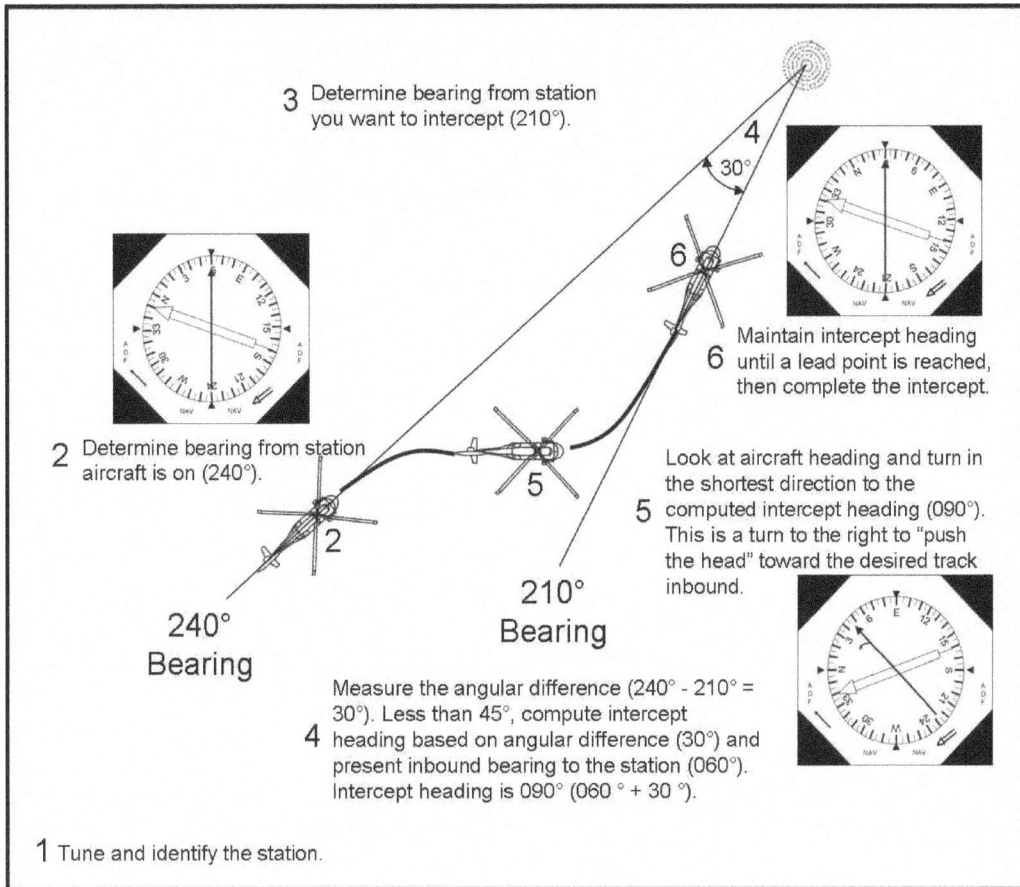

3 Determine bearing from station you want to intercept (210°).

30°

4

6

6 Maintain intercept heading until a lead point is reached, then complete the intercept.

2 Determine bearing from station aircraft is on (240°).

5

5 Look at aircraft heading and turn in the shortest direction to the computed intercept heading (090°). This is a turn to the right to "push the head" toward the desired track inbound.

240°
Bearing

210°
Bearing

Measure the angular difference (240° - 210° = 30°). Less than 45°, compute intercept
4 heading based on angular difference (30°) and present inbound bearing to the station (060°). Intercept heading is 090° (060 ° + 30 °).

1 Tune and identify the station.

Figure 7-8. Inbound course intercept of less than 45 degrees

Horizontal Situation Indicator

7-107. The HSI used in the following figures is a generic representation and has the following features/functions:

- Needle 1, representing an NDB signal.
- Needle 2, representing a VOR signal or GPS WP.
- Upper left indicator, representing distance to go in kilometers.
- Upper right indicator, the course set display.
- Lower left knob, the course selector.
- Lower right knob, the heading selector.
- To or from arrows.
- Compass card.
- Deviation scale (each dot representing 2 degrees of deviation for VOR).
- Lubber line, 45-degree left and right marks, and 90-degree left and right marks.
- Glide-slope deviation scale and dual pointers.

Angular Difference Less Than 45 Degrees

7-108. To determine the intercept heading, locate the bearing from the station presently on. Find the bearing that the aviator wants to intercept, and measure the angular difference.

7-109. If the angular difference is less than 45 degrees, turn toward the desired bearing in the shortest direction with an angle of intercept equal to the computed angular difference. The time to the station will be about equal to the time necessary to complete the intercept (Figure 7-8, page 7-23).

Angular Difference Greater Than 45 Degrees

7-110. The aviator may select any angular interception if timing is not essential, 30 to 45 degrees being generally sufficient (Figure 7-9). If the angular difference is greater than 45 degrees, a series of time-distance check maneuvers (discussed later) may be performed if distance/time to the station is unknown (Figure 7-10, page 7-25).

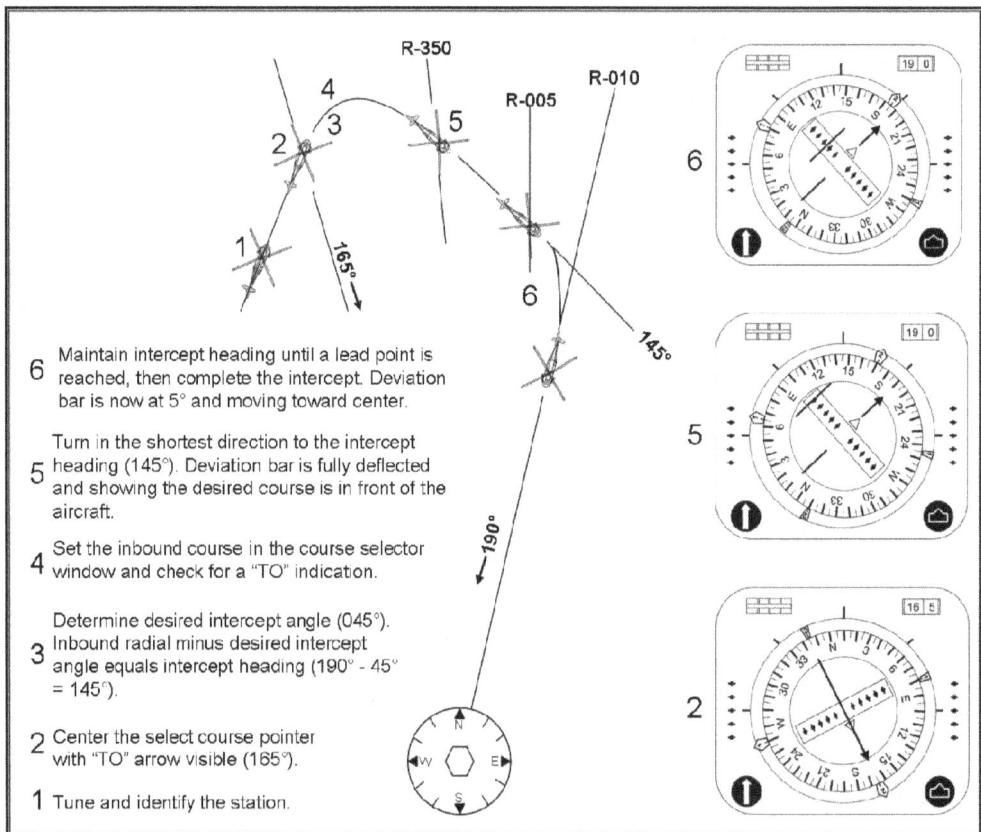

6   Maintain intercept heading until a lead point is reached, then complete the intercept. Deviation bar is now at 5° and moving toward center.

5   Turn in the shortest direction to the intercept heading (145°). Deviation bar is fully deflected and showing the desired course is in front of the aircraft.

4   Set the inbound course in the course selector window and check for a "TO" indication.

3   Determine desired intercept angle (045°). Inbound radial minus desired intercept angle equals intercept heading (190° - 45° = 145°).

2   Center the select course pointer with "TO" arrow visible (165°).

1   Tune and identify the station.

Figure 7-9. Inbound course intercept

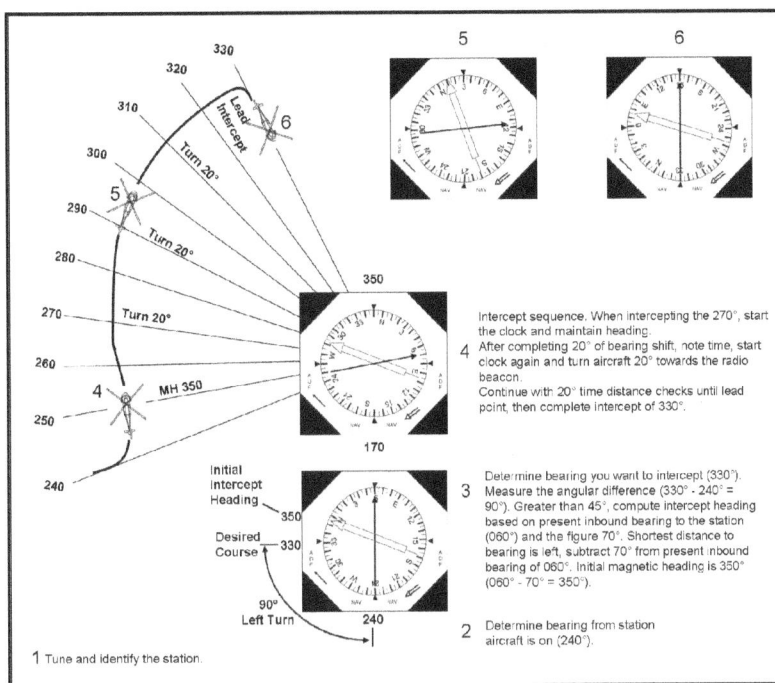

Figure 7-10. Inbound course intercept of greater than 45 degrees

Station Passage

7-111.   When the aircraft is using VOR and VOR/DME, station passage occurs when the TO-FROM indicator makes the first positive change to FROM. For RMI only, station passage is determined when the bearing pointer passes 90 degrees to the inbound course. When the aircraft is using TACAN, station passage is determined when the range indicator stops decreasing. When the aircraft is using NDB, station passage is determined when the bearing pointer passes 90 degrees to the inbound course.

TIME AND DISTANCE CHECK

7-112.   To compute time and distance from a station, first turn the aircraft to place the bearing pointer on the nearest 90-degree index; note time and maintain heading. When the bearing pointer has moved 10 degrees, note the elapsed time in seconds and apply the formulas in the following example to determine time and distance.

Time-Distance Check Example

$$\frac{\text{Time in seconds between bearings}}{\text{Degrees of bearing change}} = \text{Minutes to station}$$

For example, if two minutes (120 seconds) is required to fly a bearing change of 10 degrees, the aircraft is—

$$\frac{120}{10} = 12 \text{ minutes to the station}$$

7-113.   The time from station may also be calculated by using a short method based on the above formula, if a 10-degree bearing change is flown. If the elapsed time for the bearing change is noted in seconds and a 10-degree bearing change is made, the time from the station in minutes is determined by counting off one decimal point. Thus, if 75 seconds are required to fly a 10-degree bearing change, the aircraft is 7.5 minutes from the station. When the bearing pointer is moving rapidly or when several corrections are required to place the pointer on the wingtip position, the aircraft is at station passage.

7-114. The distance from the station is computed by multiplying TAS or ground speed (in miles per minute) by the previously determined time in minutes. For example, if the aircraft is four minutes from station, flying at a TAS of 150 knots or 2.5 nautical miles per minute, the distance from station is 10 nautical miles (2.5 x 4).

7-115. The preceding are methods of computing approximate time and distance. For increased accuracy, use only a small amount of bearing change (about 10 degrees) and correct for existing winds.

7-116. The aviator can determine the ETA over the station by flying a constant heading and checking the time and bearing progression closely. The aviator can also check the position and distance from another station not directly on the flight path.

7-117. The accuracy of time and distance checks is governed by existing wind, degree of bearing change, and accuracy of timing. The number of variables involved causes the result to be an approximation. However, by flying an accurate heading and checking the time and bearing closely, the aviator can get a reasonable estimate of time and distance from the station.

OUTBOUND PROCEDURES

Immediately After Station Passage

7-118. Intercepting courses immediately after station passage does not require large intercept angles. Because of radial convergence, actual aircraft displacement from course is relatively small. For example, a 30-degree off-course indication at 2 nautical miles from the station represents about 1 nautical mile off course.

7-119. Turn to parallel the desired outbound course (compensate for wind). Maintain heading, and allow the bearing pointer to stabilize. Note the number of degrees between the tail of the bearing pointer and the desired course. To correct back on course, use the outbound course interception technique (Figure 7-11).

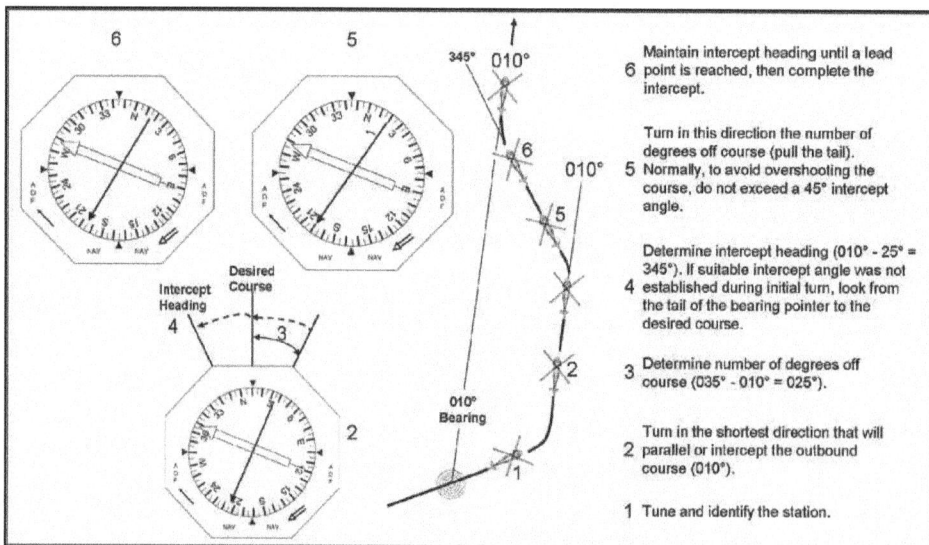

Figure 7-11. Outbound course intercept immediately after station passage

Away From Station

7-120.   Note the position of the bearing pointer tail. Then, on the compass card, look from the tail in the short direction to the desired course. Any heading beyond the desired course is a no-wind intercept heading. Normally, 45 degrees beyond the desired course is a good intercept heading. As in inbound intercepts, consider the known factors of ground speed and distance from the station when selecting an intercept heading. Outbound—away from station procedures are essentially identical to outbound—immediately after station passage, the intercept heading as determined in step 4, Figure 7-12, can be 45 degrees, 30 degrees, or double the angle off the nose intercept.

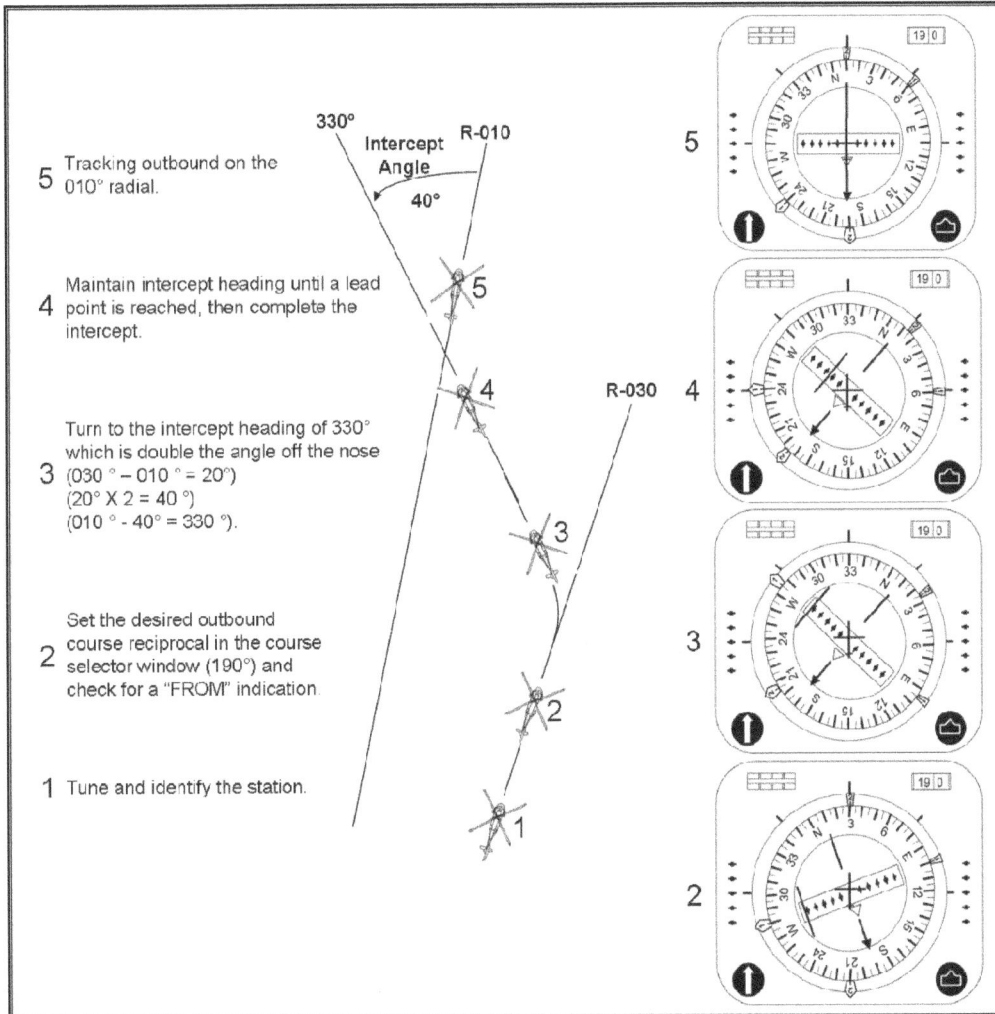

Figure 7-12. Outbound course intercept away from station

ARC INTERCEPTIONS

7-121.   TACAN and VOR/DME arcs are used during all phases of flight. An arc may be intercepted at any angle but is normally intercepted from a radial. An arc may be intercepted when the aircraft is proceeding inbound or outbound on a radial. A radial may be intercepted either inbound or outbound from an arc. The angles of intercept (arc to radial or radial to arc) are about 90 degrees. Because of the large intercept angles, the use of accurate lead points during the interception aids in preventing excessive undershoots or overshoots.

ARC INTERCEPTION FROM A RADIAL

7-122.   Track inbound on the RRS 325-degree radial (Figure 7-13), frequently checking the DME mileage readout. A .5 nautical mile lead is satisfactory for ground speeds of 150 knots or less; start the turn to the arc at 10.5 miles. At higher ground speeds, use a proportionately greater lead. Continue the turn for about 90 degrees. The rollout heading will be 055 degrees in no-wind conditions. During the last part of the intercepting turn, monitor the DME closely. If the arc is being overshot (more than 1 nautical mile), continue through the originally planned rollout heading. If the arc is being undershot, roll out of the turn early. The procedure for intercepting the 10 DME when outbound is basically the same, the lead point being 10 nautical miles minus .5 nautical mile, or 9.5 nautical miles.

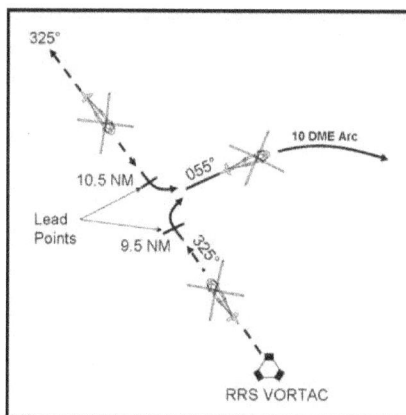

Figure 7-13. Arc interception from a radial

RADIAL INTERCEPTION FROM AN ARC

7-123.   A lead radial is the radial at which the turn from the arc to the inbound course is started. When the aircraft intercepts a radial from a DME arc, the lead radial will vary with arc radius and ground speed. When an aviator flies arcs, such as those depicted on most approach plates, the lead radial will be less than 5 degrees at speeds of 150 knots or less. There is no difference between intercepting a radial from an arc and intercepting from a straight course.

7-124.   Set the course of the radial to be intercepted as soon as possible and determine the approximate lead. Upon reaching this point, start the intercepting turn. Without an RMI, the technique for radial interception is the same except for azimuth information, which is available only from the OBS and CDI.

7-125.   The technique for intercepting a localizer from a DME arc is similar to intercepting a radial. At the depicted lead radial (LR 330 degrees in Figure 7-14, page 7-29), an aviator having a single VOR/LOC receiver should set the localizer frequency. If the aviator has dual VOR/LOC receivers, one unit may be used to provide azimuth information with the other being set to the localizer frequency.

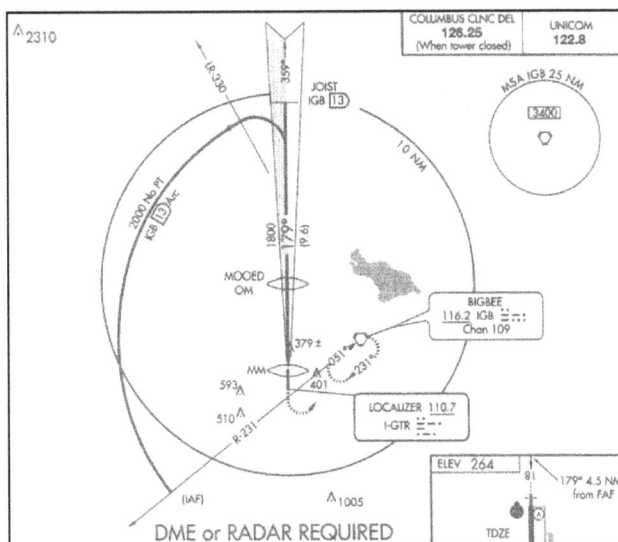

Figure 7-14. Localizer interception from a distance measuring equipment arc

FLYING A DISTANCE MEASURING EQUIPMENT ARC

7-126.   When flying a DME arc with wind, the aviator should keep a continuous mental picture of position relative to the facility. Because the wind-drift correction angle is constantly changing throughout the arc, wind orientation is important. In some cases, wind can be used to return to the desired track. High airspeeds require more aviator attention because of the higher rate of deviation and correction.

7-127.   Maintaining the arc is simplified by keeping slightly inside the curve; thus, the arc is turning toward the aircraft and interception may be accomplished by holding a straight course. If outside the curve, the arc is turning away and a greater correction is required.

7-128.   With an RMI, in a no-wind condition, the aviator should theoretically be able to fly an exact circle around the facility by maintaining an RB of 90 degrees or 270 degrees. In actual practice, a series of short legs are flown. To maintain the arc in Figure 7-15, page 7-30, proceed as the following example describes.

Flying a DME Arc Example

With the RMI bearing pointer on the wingtip reference (90° or 270° position) and the aircraft at the desired DME range, maintain a constant heading and allow the bearing pointer to move 5° to 10° behind the wingtip. DME range should increase slightly.

Turn toward the facility to place the bearing pointer 5° to 10° ahead of the wingtip reference, then maintain heading until the bearing pointer is again behind the wingtip. Continue this procedure to maintain the approximate arc.

If a crosswind is drifting the aviator away from the facility, turn the aircraft until the bearing pointer is ahead of the wingtip reference. If a crosswind is drifting the aviator toward the facility, turn until the bearing is behind the wingtip.

As a guide in making range corrections, correct about 10° to 20° for each ½-mile deviation from the desired arc. For example, in no-wind conditions if the aviator is ½ to 1 mile outside of the arc and the bearing pointer is on the wingtip reference, turn the aircraft 20° toward the facility to return to the arc.

Maintain aircraft position within 2 nautical miles of the desired DME arc.

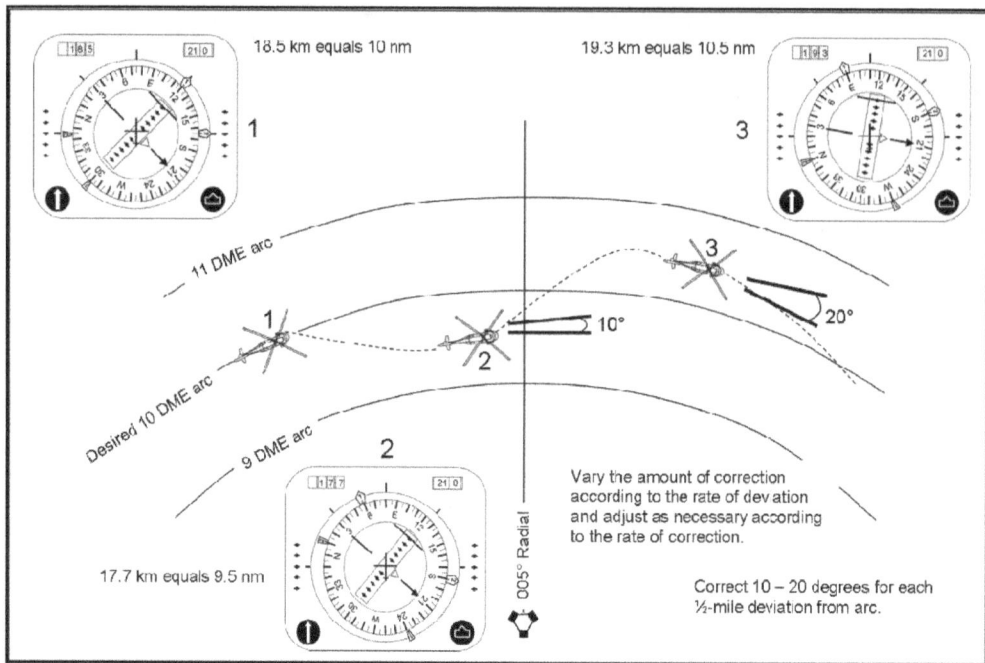

Figure 7-15. Flying a distance measuring equipment arc

AREA NAVIGATION

DESCRIPTION

7-129.   RNAV equipment includes VOR/DME, TACAN, VORTAC, GPS, and INS. RNAV equipment is capable of computing aircraft position, actual track, and ground speed and then presenting meaningful information to the aviator. This information may be in the form of distance, cross-track error, and time estimates relative to the selected track or WP. In addition, RNAV equipment installations must be approved for use under IFR. The appropriate aircraft operator's manual must always be consulted to determine what equipment is installed, approved operations, and details of how to use the equipment. Some aircraft may have equipment allowing input from more than one RNAV source, thereby providing a very accurate and reliable navigation source.

AREA NAVIGATION COMPUTATION

7-130.   VOR RNAV is based on information generated by present VORTAC or VOR/DME systems to create a WP using an airborne computer. As shown in Figure 7-16, page 7-31, the value of side A is the measured DME distance to the VOR/DME. The value of Side B is the distance from the VOR/DME to the WP angle 1 (VOR radial or bearing from the VORTAC to the WP). The bearing from the VOR/DME to the aircraft, angle 2, is measured by the VOR receiver. The airborne computer continuously compares angles 1 and 2 and determines angle 3 and side C, which is the distance in nautical miles and magnetic course from the aircraft to the WP. Guidance information is presented on the cockpit display.

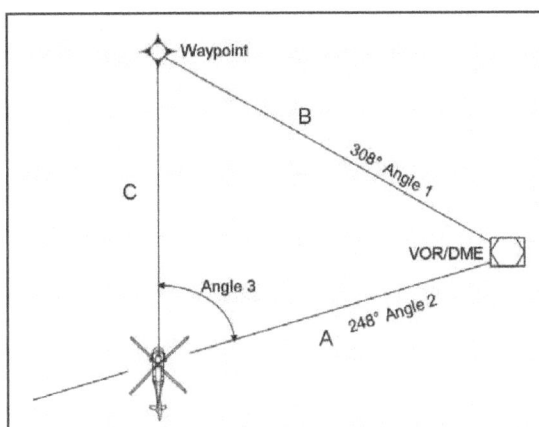

Figure 7-16. Area navigation computation

COMPONENTS

7-131. Although RNAV cockpit instrument displays vary among manufacturers, most are connected to the aircraft CDI with a switch or knob to select VOR or RNAV guidance. The display includes WP, frequency, mode in use, WP radial and distance, DME distance, ground speed, and time to station. Most VOR/DME RNAV systems have the following airborne controls:

- Off/on/volume control to select the frequency of the VOR/DME station to be used.
- MODE select switch used to select VOR/DME mode with one of the following:
  - Angular course width deviation (standard VOR operation).
  - Linear cross-track deviation as standard (± 5 nautical miles full-scale CDI).
- RNAV mode with direct to WP with linear cross-track deviation of ± 5 nautical miles.
- RNAV/APPR (approach mode) with linear deviation of ± 1.25 nautical miles as full-scale CDI deflection.
- WP selection control, which allows selection of any WP in storage; some units allow the storage of more than one WP.
- Data input controls, which allow user input of WP number or identification (IDENT), VOR or LOC frequency, WP radial, and distance.

7-132. DME ground-speed readout in the VOR/DME mode is accurate only when the VOR/DME is tracking directly to or from the station. In RNAV mode, the DME ground-speed readout is accurate on any track.

FUNCTION

7-133. Advantages of the VOR/DME RNAV system stem from the ability of the airborne computer to locate a WP wherever convenient, as long as the aircraft is within reception range of both a nearby VOR and DME facility. A series of these WPs make up an RNAV route. In addition to the published routes, a random RNAV route may be flown under IFR if approved by ATC. To either fly a route or to execute an approach under IFR, the RNAV equipment installed in the aircraft must be approved for the appropriate IFR operations.

7-134. In vertical NAV mode, vertical as well as horizontal guidance is provided in some installations. A WP is selected where the descent begins and another where the descent ends. The RNAV equipment computes rate of descent relative to ground speed and, on some installations, displays vertical guidance information on the glide-slope indicator. When using RNAV during an instrument approach, the aviator must keep in mind that the vertical guidance information provided is not part of the nonprecision approach. Published nonprecision approach altitudes must be observed and complied with, unless otherwise directed by ATC. To fly to a WP using RNAV, observe the procedure described in the following example and illustrated in Figure 7-17.

Aircraft/VORTAC/WP Relationship Example

Select the VOR/DME frequency, the RNAV mode, and the radial of the VOR that passes through the WP (225 degrees). Select the distance from the DME to the WP chosen (12NM). Check and confirm all inputs and that the CDI needle is centered with the TO indicator showing. To keep the CDI needle centered, maneuver the aircraft to fly the indicated heading ± wind correction. The CDI needle indicates distance off course of 1 nautical mile per dot; DME readout indicates distance (NM) from the WP; ground speed reads closing speed (knots) to the WP; and time to station (TTS) reads time to the WP.

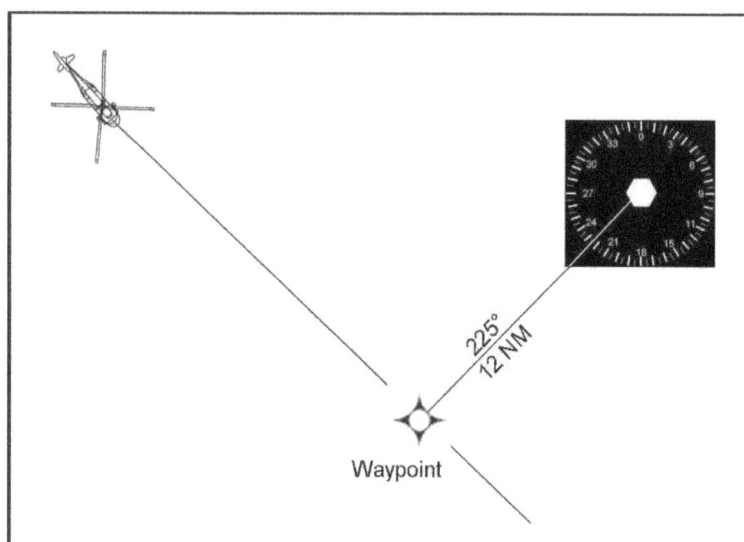

Figure 7-17. Aircraft/very (high frequency) omnidirectional radio range tactical air navigation aid/waypoint relationship

ERRORS

7-135. The limitation of the RNAV system is the reception volume. Published approaches have been tested to ensure that reception volume is not a problem. Descents/approaches to airports distant from the VOR/DME facility may not be possible because during the approach, the aircraft may descend below the reception altitude of the facility at that distance.

GLOBAL POSITIONING SYSTEM NAVIGATION

7-136. GPS equipment used while operating under IFR must meet the standards set forth in Technical Standard Order (TSO) C-129 (or equivalent) and the airworthiness installation requirements and be approved for that type of IFR operation and operated according to the appropriate aircraft operator's manual.

7-137. An updatable GPS database that supports the appropriate operations (en route, terminal, and instrument approaches) is required when the aircraft is operating under IFR. The aircraft GPS navigation database contains WPs from geographic areas where GPS navigation has been approved for IFR operations. The aviator selects the desired WPs from the database and may add user-defined WPs for the flight.

7-138.   Equipment approved according to TSO C-115a, VFR, and hand-held GPS systems do not meet the requirements of TSO C-129 and are not authorized for IFR navigation, instrument approaches, or as a principal instrument flight reference. During IFR operations, these units (TSO C-115a) may only be considered as an aid to situational awareness (SA).

7-139.   Using the calculated range and position information supplied by the satellite, the GPS receiver/processor mathematically determines its position by triangulation from several satellites. The GPS receiver needs at least four satellites to yield a three-dimensional position (latitude, longitude, and altitude) and time solution. The GPS receiver computes navigational values (such as distance and bearing to a WP and ground speed) by using the aircraft's known latitude/longitude and referencing these to a database built into the receiver.

7-140.   The GPS receiver verifies the integrity (usability) of the signals received from the GPS constellation through RAIM to determine if a satellite is providing corrupted information. RAIM needs a minimum of five satellites in view (or four satellites and a barometric altimeter barometrically aiding), to detect an integrity anomaly. For receivers capable of doing so, RAIM needs six satellites in view (or five satellites with barometrically aiding) to isolate and remove a corrupt satellite signal from the navigation solution.

7-141.   Generally there are two types of RAIM messages. One type indicates that there are not enough satellites available to provide RAIM, and another type indicates that the RAIM has detected a potential error exceeding the limit for the current phase of flight. Without RAIM capability, the aviator has no assurance of the accuracy of GPS position.

7-142.   Aircraft using approved GPS navigation equipment during IFR conditions may be required to have an alternate means of navigation. Alternate means of navigation are required when aircraft are operating IFR during the following: domestic en route phase, terminal operations, and certain IAPs. The avionics necessary to receive all ground-based facilities appropriate for the route to the destination airport and any required alternate airport must be installed and operational. Ground-based facilities necessary for these routes must also be operational. Active monitoring of alternative navigation equipment is not required if the GPS receiver uses RAIM for integrity monitoring. Active monitoring of an alternate means of navigation is required when the RAIM capability of the GPS equipment is lost. In situations where the loss of RAIM capability is predicted, the flight must rely on other approved equipment or delay departure or the flight may be cancelled.

INSTRUMENT FLIGHT RULES FLIGHT

7-143.   Preflight preparations ensure that the GPS is properly installed and certified with a current database for the type of operation. The GPS operation must be conducted according to the appropriate aircraft operator's manual. Aviators must be thoroughly familiar with the particular GPS equipment installed in the aircraft.

7-144.   Required preflight preparations include checking NOTAMs relating to the IFR flight when the aviator is using GPS as a supplemental method of navigation. GPS satellite outages are issued as GPS NOTAMs, both domestically and internationally. Aviators may obtain GPS RAIM availability information for an airport by specifically requesting GPS aeronautical information from an AFSS during preflight briefings. GPS RAIM aeronautical information can be obtained for a three-hour period: the ETA and one hour before to one hour after the ETA hour or a 24-hour timeframe for a specific airport. FAA briefers provide RAIM information for a period of one hour before to one hour after the ETA, unless a specific timeframe is requested by the aviator. Aviators should request a RAIM prediction from the departure airport when departing on a published GPS departure procedure. Some GPS receivers can predict RAIM availability. The aviator ensures that the required underlying ground-based navigation facilities, related aircraft equipment appropriate to the route of flight, terminal operations, instrument approaches for the destination, and alternate airports/heliports are operational for the ETA. If the required ground-based facilities and equipment are not available, the flight should be rerouted, rescheduled, or canceled or conducted under VFR.

7-145. Except for programming and retrieving information from the GPS receiver, planning the flight is accomplished in a manner similar to that using conventional NAVAIDs. Departure WP, DP, route, STAR, desired approach, IAF, and destination airport are entered into the GPS receiver according to the manufacturer's instructions. During preflight, additional information may be entered for functions such as ETA, fuel planning, and winds aloft.

7-146. When the GPS receiver is turned on, an internal process of test and initialization is started. When the receiver is initialized, the user develops the route by selecting a WP or series of WPs, verifies the data, and selects the active flight plan. This procedure varies widely among the manufacturer's receivers. GPS is a complex system, offering little standardization between receiver models. The aviator is responsible for being familiar with the operation of the aircraft equipment that he is using.

7-147. The GPS receiver provides navigational values such as track, bearing, ground speed, and distance. These are computed from the aircraft's present latitude and longitude to the location of the next WP. Course guidance is provided between WPs. The aviator has the advantage of knowing the aircraft's actual track over the ground. As long as track and bearing to the WP are matched up (by selecting the correct aircraft heading), the aircraft is going directly to the WP.

SUBSTITUTION

7-148. Aircraft GPS systems, certified for IFR en route phase and terminal operations, may be used as a substitute for ADF, VOR, and DME receivers during the following operations within the United States NAS:

- Determining the aircraft position over a DME fix, which includes en route operations at and above 24,000 feet MSL (FL240) during GPS navigation.
- Flying a DME arc.
- Navigating TO or FROM the NDB/compass locator or VOR.
- Determining the aircraft position over the NDB/compass locator or VOR.
- Determining the aircraft position over a fix defined by the NDB/compass locator bearing crossing a VOR/LOC course.
- Holding over the NDB/compass locator or VOR.

7-149. The following restrictions apply when the aviator uses GPS as a substitute for ADF, VOR, or DME:

- Equipment must be installed according to appropriate airworthiness installation requirements and operated within the provisions of the appropriate aircraft operator's manual.
- The required integrity for these operations must be provided by at least en route RAIM or equivalent.
- WPs, fixes, intersections, and facility locations to be used for these operations must be retrieved from the GPS airborne database, which must be current; if the required positions cannot be retrieved from the airborne database, the substitution of GPS for ADF, VOR, and/or DME is not authorized.
- Procedures must be established for RAIM outages or predicted outages; these outages may require the flight to rely on other approved equipment or the aircraft to be equipped with operational NDB/ADF, VOR, and/or DME receivers. Otherwise, the flight must be rerouted, delayed, or canceled or conducted VFR.
- The course deviation bar or indicator must be set to terminal sensitivity (normally 1 or 1-1/4 nautical miles) during GPS course guidance tracking in the terminal area.

- A non-GPS approach procedure must exist at the alternate airport when one is required; if the non-GPS approaches on which the aviator must rely require DME, VOR, or ADF, the aircraft must be equipped with DME, VOR, or ADF avionics, as appropriate.
- Charted requirements for ADF, VOR, and/or DME can be met using GPS, except for use as the principal instrument approach navigation source.

7-150. To determine the aircraft position over a DME fix, verify that aircraft GPS system integrity monitoring is functioning properly and indicates satisfactory integrity. If the fix is identified by a five-letter name contained in the GPS airborne database, select either the named fix as the active GPS WP or facility establishing the DME fix as the active GPS WP. When the aviator uses a facility as the active WP, the only acceptable facility is the DME facility charted as the one used to establish the DME fix. If this facility is not in the airborne database, the aviator is not authorized to use that facility WP for this operation. If the fix is identified by a five-letter name not contained in the GPS airborne database or if the fix is not named, select the facility establishing the DME fix or another named DME fix as the active GPS WP. If selecting the named fix as the active GPS WP, the aviator is over the fix when the GPS indicates arrival at the active WP. If selecting the DME providing facility as the active GPS WP, the aviator is over the fix when the GPS distance from the active WP equals the charted DME value and the aircraft is on the appropriate bearing or course.

7-151. To fly a DME arc, verify that aircraft GPS system integrity monitoring is functioning properly and indicates satisfactory integrity. Select from the airborne database the facility providing the DME arc as the active GPS WP. The only acceptable facility is the DME facility on which the arc is based. If this facility is not in the airborne database, the aviator is not authorized to perform this operation. Maintain position on the arc by reference to the GPS distance, instead of DME readout.

7-152. To navigate TO or FROM the NDB/compass locator or VOR, verify that aircraft GPS system integrity monitoring is functioning properly and indicates satisfactory integrity. Select the NDB/compass locator or VOR facility from the airborne database as the active WP. If the chart depicts the compass locator collocated with a fix of the same name, use of that fix as the active WP in place of the compass locator facility is authorized. Select and navigate on the appropriate course to or from the active WP.

7-153. To determine the aircraft position over the NDB/compass locator or VOR, verify that aircraft GPS system integrity monitoring is functioning properly and indicates satisfactory integrity. Select the NDB/compass locator or VOR facility from the airborne database. When the aviator uses the NDB/compass locator or VOR, that facility must be charted and in the airborne database. If this facility is not in the airborne database, the aviator is not authorized to use a facility WP for this operation. The aviator is over the NDB/compass locator or VOR when the GPS system indicates he is at the active WP. To determine the aircraft position over a fix made up of the NDB/compass locator bearing crossing a VOR/LOC course, verify that aircraft GPS integrity monitoring is functioning properly and indicates satisfactory integrity.

7-154. A fix made up by crossing an NDB and/or a compass locator bearing is identified by a five-letter fix name. The aviator may select the named fix or NDB/compass locator facility providing the crossing bearing to establish the fix as the active GPS WP. When using the NDB/compass locator, that facility must be charted and in the airborne database. If this facility is not in the airborne database, the aviator is not authorized to use a facility WP for this operation. If selecting the named fix as the active GPS WP, the aviator is over the fix when the GPS system indicates that he is at the WP and the aircraft is on the prescribed track from the non-GPS navigation source. If selecting the NDB/compass locator facility as the active GPS WP, the aviator is over the fix when the GPS bearing to the active WP is the same as the charted NDB/compass locator bearing for the fix when flying the prescribed track from the non-GPS navigation source.

7-155. To hold over the NDB/compass locator or VOR, verify that aircraft GPS system integrity monitoring is functioning properly and indicates satisfactory integrity. Select the NDB/compass locator or VOR facility from the airborne database as the active WP. When using a facility as the active WP, the only acceptable facility is the NDB/compass locator or VOR facility that is charted. If this facility is not in the airborne database, the aviator is not authorized to use a facility WP for this operation. Select nonsequencing (HOLD or OBS) mode and the appropriate course according to the appropriate aircraft operator's manual. Hold using the GPS according to the appropriate aircraft operator's manual.

Chapter 8

Airspace

This chapter provides a general overview of airspace systems. AR 95-1, AIM, Instrument Flying Handbook, Instrument Procedures Handbook, and other FAA/International Civil Aviation Organization (ICAO) publications and Web sites provide specific and detailed information.

SECTION I – NATIONAL AIRSPACE SYSTEM

8-1. The National Airspace System (NAS) is the network of U.S. airspace: air navigation facilities, equipment, services, airports, landing areas, aeronautical charts, rules, regulations, procedures, technical information, manpower, information and/or services, and material. Included are system

Contents

components shared jointly with the military. The system's present configuration is a reflection of the technological advances involving the speed and altitude capability of jet aircraft, as well as the complexity of microchip and satellite-based navigation equipment. To conform to international aviation standards, the U.S. adopted the primary elements of the classification system developed by ICAO.

AIRSPACE CLASSIFICATION

8-2. Airspace classification in the United States is as designated in Figure 8-1, page 8-2. Refer to AR 95-1 for approved cloud clearance and flight visibility for Army aviators.

CLASS A

8-3. Generally, Class A airspace is airspace from 18,000 feet MSL up to and including FL600, including the airspace overlying the waters within 12 nautical miles of the coast of the 48 contiguous states and Alaska. Unless otherwise authorized, all pilots must operate their aircraft under IFR.

CLASS B

8-4. Generally, Class B airspace is airspace from the surface to 10,000 feet MSL surrounding the nation's busiest airports in terms of airport operations or number of passengers. The configuration of each Class B airspace area is individually tailored and consists of a surface area and two or more layers (some Class B airspace areas resemble upside-down wedding cakes) and is designed to contain all published instrument procedures, once an aircraft enters the airspace. An ATC clearance is required for all aircraft to operate in the area, and all aircraft that are cleared receive separation services within the airspace.

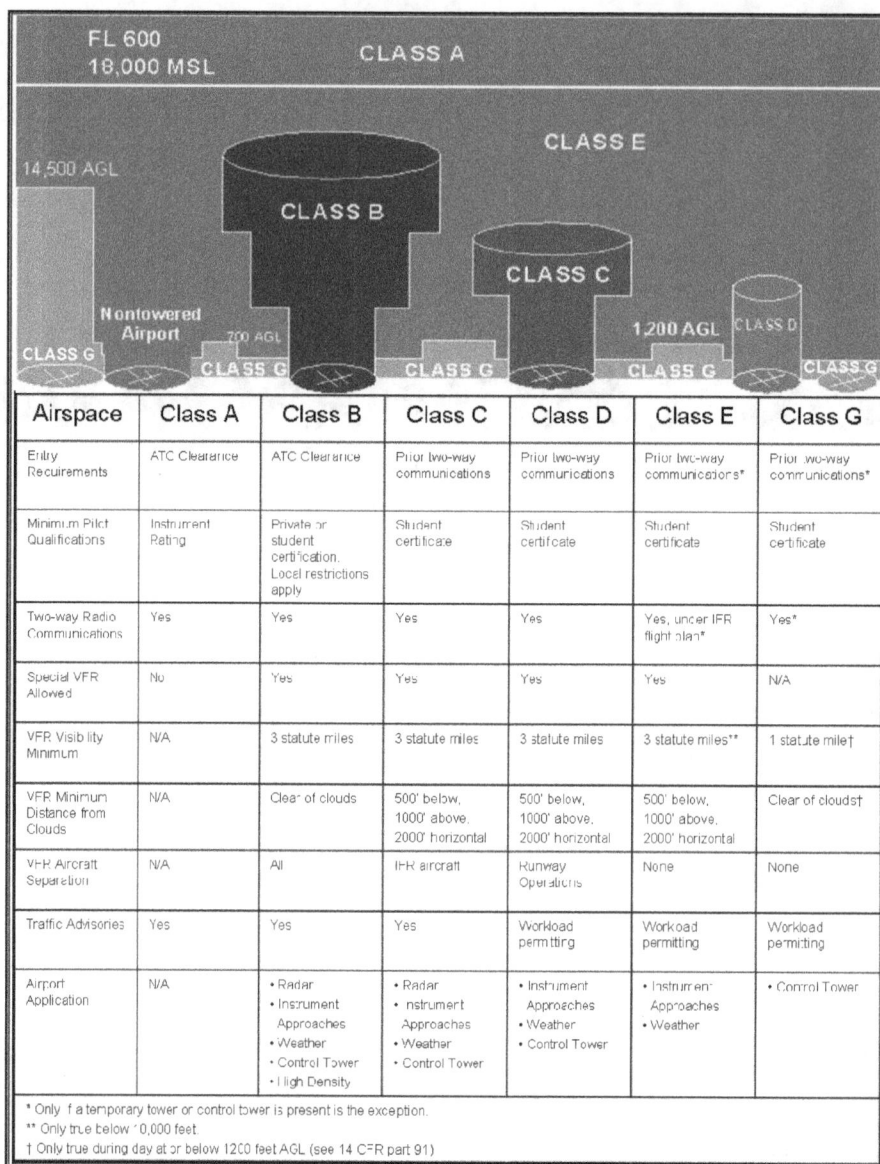

Airspace	Class A	Class B	Class C	Class D	Class E	Class G
Entry Requirements	ATC Clearance	ATC Clearance	Prior two-way communications	Prior two-way communications	Prior two-way communications*	Prior two-way communications*
Minimum Pilot Qualifications	Instrument Rating	Private or student certification. Local restrictions apply	Student certificate	Student certificate	Student certificate	Student certificate
Two-way Radio Communications	Yes	Yes	Yes	Yes	Yes, under IFR flight plan*	Yes*
Special VFR Allowed	No	Yes	Yes	Yes	Yes	N/A
VFR Visibility Minimum	N/A	3 statute miles	3 statute miles	3 statute miles	3 statute miles**	1 statute mile†
VFR Minimum Distance from Clouds	N/A	Clear of clouds	500' below, 1000' above, 2000' horizontal	500' below, 1000' above, 2000' horizontal	500' below, 1000' above, 2000' horizontal	Clear of clouds†
VFR Aircraft Separation	N/A	All	IFR aircraft	Runway Operations	None	None
Traffic Advisories	Yes	Yes	Yes	Workload permitting	Workload permitting	Workload permitting
Airport Application	N/A	• Radar • Instrument Approaches • Weather • Control Tower • High Density	• Radar • Instrument Approaches • Weather • Control Tower	• Instrument Approaches • Weather • Control Tower	• Instrument Approaches • Weather	• Control Tower

* Only if a temporary tower or control tower is present is the exception.
** Only true below 10,000 feet.
† Only true during day at or below 1200 feet AGL (see 14 CFR part 91)

Figure 8-1. Airspace classification

CLASS C

8-5. Generally, Class C airspace is airspace from the surface to 4,000 feet above the airport elevation (charted in MSL) surrounding those airports that have an operational control tower, are serviced by a radar approach control, and have a certain number of IFR operations or passengers. Although the configuration of each Class C area is individually tailored, the airspace usually consists of a surface area with a 5 nautical mile radius, an outer circle with a 10 nautical mile radius that extends from 1,200 feet to 4,000 feet above the airport elevation, and an outer area. Each person must establish two-way radio communications with the ATC facility providing air traffic services before entering the airspace and thereafter maintain those communications while within the airspace.

CLASS D

8-6. Generally, Class D airspace is airspace from the surface to 2,500 feet above the airport elevation (charted in MSL) surrounding those airports that have an operational control tower. The configuration of each Class D airspace area is individually tailored, and when instrument procedures are published, the airspace will normally be designed to contain the procedures. Arrival extensions for IAPs may be Class D or Class E airspace. Unless otherwise authorized, each person must establish two-way radio communications with the ATC facility providing air traffic services before entering the airspace and, thereafter, maintain those communications while in the airspace.

CLASS E

8-7. Generally, if not classified as A, B, C, or D airspace, and it is controlled airspace, then it is Class E. Class E airspace extends upward from either the surface or a designated altitude to the overlying or adjacent controlled airspace. When designated as a surface area, the airspace will be configured to contain all instrument procedures. Also in this class are Federal airways, airspace beginning at either 700 or 1,200 feet AGL used to make the transition to and from the terminal or en route environment and en route domestic and offshore airspace areas designated below 18,000 feet MSL. Unless designated at a lower altitude, Class E airspace begins at 14,500 MSL over the United States, including that airspace overlying the waters within 12 nautical miles of the coast of the 48 contiguous states and Alaska, up to but not including 18,000 feet MSL and the airspace above FL600.

CLASS G

8-8. Class G airspace is airspace not designated as Class A, B, C, D, or E. Class G airspace is essentially uncontrolled by ATC except when associated with a temporary control tower.

SPECIAL-USE AIRSPACE

8-9. Special-use airspace is the designation for airspace in which certain activities must be confined or where limitations may be imposed on aircraft operations that are not part of those activities. Certain special-use airspace areas can create limitations on the mixed use of airspace. The special-use airspace depicted on instrument charts includes the area name or number, effective altitude, time and weather conditions of operation, the controlling agency, and the chart panel location. On NACO en route charts, this information is available on the panel opposite the air/ground (A/G) voice communications.

PROHIBITED AREA

8-10. Prohibited areas contain airspace of defined dimensions within which the flight of aircraft is prohibited. Such areas are established for security or other reasons associated with national welfare. These areas are published in the Federal Register and are depicted on aeronautical charts. The area is charted as a "P" with a number (such as P-123). As the name implies, flight through this airspace is not permitted.

RESTRICTED AREA

8-11. Restricted areas are areas where operations are hazardous to nonparticipating aircraft and contain airspace within which the flight of aircraft, while not wholly prohibited, is subject to restrictions. Activities within these areas must be confined because of either their nature or limitations imposed upon aircraft operations that are not a part of those activities, or both. Restricted areas denote the existence of unusual, often invisible, hazards to aircraft (artillery firing, aerial gunnery, or guided missiles). IFR flights may be authorized to transit the airspace and are routed accordingly. Penetration of restricted areas without authorization from the using or controlling agency may be extremely hazardous to the aircraft and its occupants. ATC facilities apply the following procedures when aircraft are operating on an IFR clearance (including those cleared by ATC to maintain VFR-On-Top) via a route that lies within joint-use restricted airspace:

- If the restricted area is not active and has been released to the FAA, the ATC facility will allow the aircraft to operate in the restricted airspace without issuing specific clearance to do so.
- If the restricted area is active and has not been released to the FAA, the ATC facility will issue a clearance that will ensure that the aircraft avoids the restricted airspace.

8-12. Restricted areas are charted with an "R" followed by a number (such as R-5701) and are depicted on the en route chart appropriate for use at the altitude or FL being flown.

WARNING AREA

8-13. Warning areas are similar in nature to restricted areas; however, the U.S. government does not have sole jurisdiction over the airspace. A warning area is airspace of defined dimensions, extending from 3 nautical miles outward from the coast of the United States, containing activity that may be hazardous to nonparticipating aircraft. The purpose of such areas is to warn nonparticipating pilots of the potential danger. A warning area may be located over domestic or international waters or both. The airspace is designated with a "W" and a number (such as W-123).

MILITARY OPERATIONS AREA

8-14. Military operations areas (MOAs) consist of airspace of defined vertical and lateral limits established for the purpose of separating certain military training activities from IFR traffic. Whenever an MOA is being used, nonparticipating IFR traffic may be cleared through an MOA if IFR separation can be provided by ATC. Otherwise, ATC will reroute or restrict nonparticipating IFR traffic. MOAs are depicted on sectional, VFR terminal area, and en route low-altitude charts and are named rather than numbered (Boardman MOA).

ALERT AREA

8-15. Alert areas are depicted on aeronautical charts with an "A" and a number (A-123) to inform nonparticipating aviators of areas that may contain a high volume of aviator training or an unusual type of aerial activity. Aviators should exercise caution in alert areas. All activity within an alert area shall be conducted according to regulations, without waiver, and aviators of participating aircraft, as well as aviators transiting the area, shall be equally responsible for collision avoidance.

CONTROLLED FIRING AREA

8-16. Controlled firing areas (CFAs) contain activities that, if not conducted in a controlled environment, could be hazardous to nonparticipating aircraft. The distinguishing feature of the CFA, as compared to other special-use airspace, is that its activities are suspended immediately when spotter aircraft, radar, or ground lookout positions indicate that an aircraft might be approaching the area. There is no need to chart CFAs because they do not cause a nonparticipating aircraft to change its flight path.

OTHER AIRSPACE

MILITARY TRAINING ROUTE

8-17. Military training routes (MTRs) are used by military aircraft to maintain proficiency in tactical flying; see Area Planning/1B (AP/1B). These routes are usually established below 10,000 feet MSL for operations at speeds in excess of 250 knots. Some route segments may be defined at higher altitudes for purposes of route continuity. Routes are identified as IR for IFR and VR for VFR, followed by a number. MTRs with no segment above 1,500 feet AGL are identified by four number characters (IR1206, VR1207). MTRs that include one or more segments above 1,500 feet AGL are identified by three-number characters

(IR206, VR207.). IFR low-altitude en route charts depict all IR and VR routes that accommodate operations above 1,500 feet AGL. IR routes are conducted according to IFR, regardless of weather conditions. Refer to DOD FLIP AP/1B.

TEMPORARY FLIGHT RESTRICTION

8-18. Temporary flight restrictions (TFRs) are put into effect when traffic in the airspace would endanger or hamper air or ground activities in the designated area. For example, a forest fire, chemical accident, flood, or disaster-relief effort could warrant a TFR, which would be issued as a NOTAM.

NATIONAL SECURITY AREA

8-19. National security areas (NSAs) consist of airspace of defined vertical and lateral dimensions established at locations where there is a requirement for increased security and safety of ground facilities. Flight in NSAs may be temporarily prohibited by regulation under the provisions of 14 CFR, part 99, and prohibitions will be disseminated via NOTAM.

FEDERAL AIRWAY

8-20. The primary NAVAID for routing aircraft operating under IFR is the Federal Airways System. Each Federal airway is based on a centerline that extends from one NAVAID or intersection to another NAVAID specified for that airway. A Federal airway includes the airspace within parallel boundary lines 4 nautical miles to each side of the centerline. As in all instrument flight, courses are magnetic and distances are in nautical miles. The airspace of a Federal airway has a floor of 1,200 feet AGL, unless otherwise specified. A Federal airway does not include the airspace of a prohibited area.

VICTOR AIRWAY

8-21. Victor airways include the airspace extending from 1,200 feet AGL up to, but not including, 18,000 feet MSL. The airways are designated on sectional and IFR low-altitude en route charts with the letter "V," followed by a number (such as V198). Typically, victor airways are given odd numbers when oriented north/south and even numbers when oriented east/west. If more than one airway coincides on a route segment, the numbers are listed serially (such as V70-194) (Figure 8-2, page 8-6).

JET ROUTE

8-22. Jet routes exist only in Class A airspace, from 18,000 feet MSL to FL450, and are depicted on high-altitude en route charts. The letter "J" precedes a number to label the airway (J12).

OTHER ROUTING

8-23. The latest version of AC 90-91, National Route Program, provides guidance to users of the NAS for participation in the National Route Program (NRP). All flights operating at or above FL290 within the continental United States are eligible to participate in the NRP, the primary purpose of which is to allow operators to plan minimum time/cost routes that may be off the prescribed route structure.

8-24. In addition, international flights to destinations within the United States are eligible to participate in the NRP within specific guidelines and filing requirements. NRP aircraft are not subject to route-limiting restrictions (published preferred IFR routes) beyond a 200 nautical mile radius of their point of departure or destination.

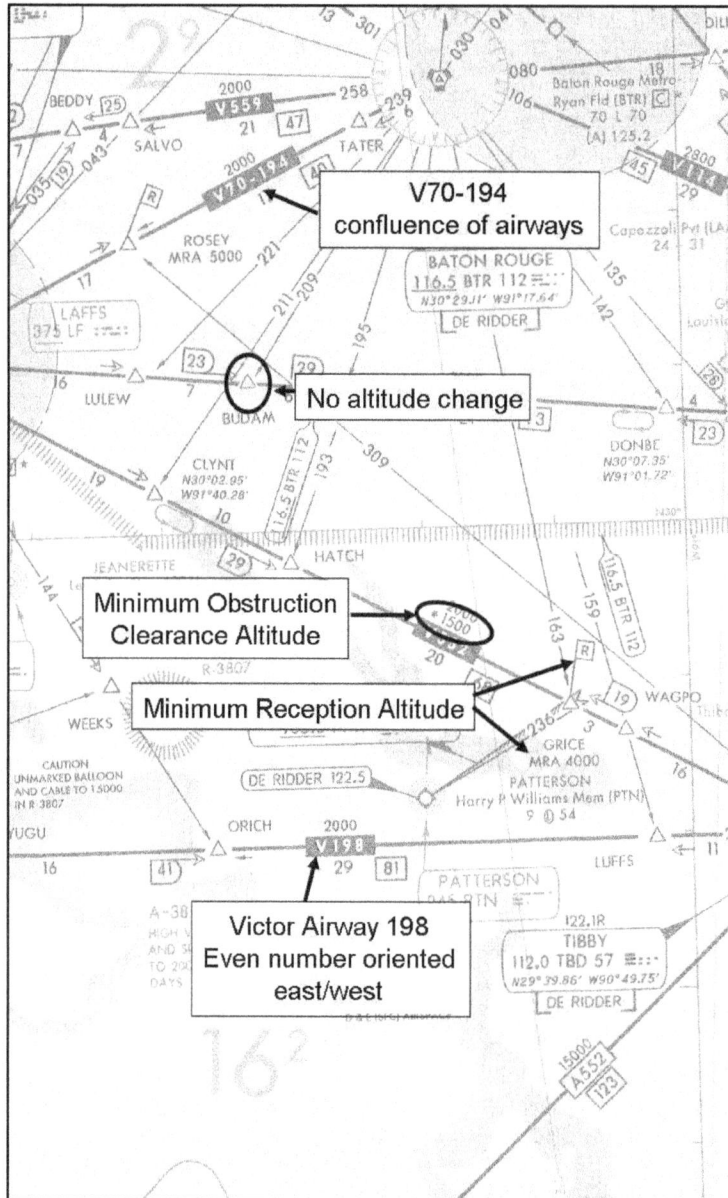

Figure 8-2. Victor airways and charted information

FM 3-04.240

Preferred Instrument Flight Rules Route

8-25. Preferred IFR routes have been established between major terminals to guide pilots in planning their routes of flight, minimizing route changes, and aiding in the orderly management of air traffic on Federal airways. Low- and high-altitude preferred routes are located at the following Web site, http://www.fly.faa.gov/Products/Coded_Departure_Routes/NFDC_Preferred_Routes_Database/nfdc_prefe rred_routes_database.html. To use a preferred route, reference the departure and arrival airports; if a routing exists for the flight, airway instructions will be listed.

Tower En Route Control

8-26. Tower en route control (TEC) is an ATC program that uses overlapping approach control radar services to provide IFR clearances. By using TEC, the aviator is routed by airport control towers. Some advantages include abbreviated filing procedures, fewer delays, and reduced traffic separation requirements. TEC depends on the ATC's workload, and the procedure varies among locales.

SECTION II – INTERNATIONAL CIVIL AVIATION ORGANIZATION

8-27. The ICAO is composed of more than 180 member nations and is a part of the United Nations. Unlike the FAA, whose regulations are directive, ICAO is basically an advisory organization that jointly agrees on procedural criteria. These criteria are published in a document called Procedures for Air Navigation Services-Aircraft Operations (PANS-OPS). Individual ICAO member nations may then comply with all, a part, or none of the criteria published in PANS-OPS. For example, the United States is an ICAO member nation but uses none of the PANS-OPS procedures—instead using the Federal Aviation Regulations (FARs) for procedural guidance. A specific nation's adoption of ICAO criteria makes that criteria directive in that country. When adopted by a participating nation, these procedures are intended to be strictly adhered to by flight crews to achieve and maintain an acceptable level of safety in flight operations. The information provided in this chapter is based on the standards of PANS-OPS.

SAFETY

8-28. Even more so than in the United States, international flying requires good judgment on the part of the aviator. The Army expects and encourages the application of good, sound judgment. The global mission of the Army requires aviators to operate in countries without a well-developed aviation system or into airfields where the ICAO rules have been ignored, replaced, or poorly applied. The pilot-in-command (PC) must necessarily be the final judge of what is safe and prudent for any given mission.

APPLICABILITY

8-29. Procedures described in this chapter apply only in airspace not under FAA control. These procedures are ICAO standard procedures and may be modified by each country.

CURRENT INFORMATION AND PROCEDURES

8-30. Changes to ICAO standard procedures can be numerous and may even vary from airfield to airfield within a country. Area planning FLIP generally contains a comprehensive consolidation of procedural requirements, but a thorough review of all applicable preflight planning sources is essential to ensuring compliance with ICAO, host-nation, and Army requirements.

TERMINAL INSTRUMENT APPROACH PROCEDURES

8-31. There are many different kinds of approaches published in the DOD FLIP books for regions outside of the United States. Some approaches are designed using U.S. TERPS at overseas bases. Other approaches are designed under the civil PANS-OPS criteria while other procedures use host-nation criteria that are different from PANS-OPS. Aircraft executing maneuvers other than those intended by the host-nation approach design could exceed the boundaries of the protected airspace or may cause overflight of unauthorized areas. All ICAO procedures must be flown as depicted.

COMPLIANCE

8-32. When operating in airspace not under FAA control, aviators will apply ICAO procedures. Local procedures may have to be developed for operations in different theaters, airfields, or host nations not under ICAO or FAA jurisdiction.

DEFINITIONS

PROCEDURES FOR AIR NAVIGATION SERVICES-AIRCRAFT OPERATIONS

8-33. PANS-OPS is a two-part document. The first volume is for aviators and is similar to the FAA's AIM. The second volume contains the ICAO TERPS. The document is intended for use by international civilian aviation, not the military. A number of editions of PANS-OPS have been published since the creation of the ICAO, each with significant changes in the details of instrument approach procedure design. Therefore, approaches in different parts of the world have been designed with entirely different rules.

AIRCRAFT CATEGORIES

8-34. Aircraft approach categories play a much larger role in the design of ICAO instrument procedures than they do in the United States. In addition to affecting final approach minimums, PANS-OPS references maximum speeds by category for such operations as holding, departures, and the intermediate segments of instrument approaches. To make matters even more confusing, these additional category restrictions specify speeds that are completely different from the familiar approach speeds on final. The appropriate PANS-OPS category speeds appear in table 8-1, page 8-10, and table 8-2, page 8-15.

TRACK

8-35. Track is the projection on the surface of the earth of the path of an aircraft, the direction of which path at any point is usually expressed in degrees from North. The aviator should apply known wind drift to maintain the ground path.

BANK ANGLE

8-36. Bank angles for ICAO procedures are based on an average achieved bank angle of 25 degrees or the bank angle giving a rate of turn of 3 degrees per second, whichever is less.

ESTABLISHED ON COURSE

8-37. The ICAO defines established on course as being within half full scale deflection for an ILS or VOR/TACAN and within ± 5 degrees of the required bearing for the NDB. Aviators should not consider their aircraft established on course until within these limits. ICAO obstacle clearance surfaces assume that the aviator does not normally deviate from the centerline more than one-half scale deflection after being established on track. Although there is a range of acceptable variation, make every attempt to fly the aircraft on the course centerline and on the glide path. Allowing a more than half-scale deflection (or a more than half-scale fly-up deflection on glide slope), combined with other system tolerances, could place aircraft near the edge or bottom of the protected airspace where loss of protection from obstacles can occur.

DEPARTURE PROCEDURES

SCREEN HEIGHTS

8-38. Accurately determining screen height used for a particular DP may be difficult or impossible. For PANS-OPS, the origin of the obstacle identification surface (OIS) begins at 16 feet (5 meters) above the departure end of the runway (DER). Use this for a default planning reference unless it is determined that a different screen height applies. Use caution, be conservative, and make use of all available resources when attempting to determine the actual screen height.

CLIMB GRADIENT

8-39. ICAO gradients are the same as the FAA, but they are expressed as percent gradients instead of feet/nautical miles. ICAO obstacle clearance during departures is based on a 2.5 percent gradient obstacle clearance (152 feet/nautical miles) and an increasing 0.8 percent obstacle clearance (48 feet/nautical miles). This minimum climb gradient equates to 3.3 percent (200 feet/nautical miles). Minimum climb gradients exceeding 3.3 percent will be specified to an altitude/height, after which the 3.3 percent will be used.

BASIC RULES FOR ALL DEPARTURES

8-40. PANS-OPS uses the same initial departure concept as the U.S. TERPS. Unless the procedure specifies otherwise, the aviator must climb on runway heading at a minimum of 200 feet/nautical miles (3.3 percent) until reaching 400 feet above the DER. Continue to climb at a minimum of 200 feet/nautical miles until reaching a safe en route altitude.

OMNIDIRECTIONAL DEPARTURES

8-41. The PANS-OPS omnidirectional departure is somewhat similar to the FAA's diverse departure; the departure procedure is without any track guidance provided. There are some very important differences, however. An omnidirectional departure may be published although obstacles penetrate the 40:1 OIS. If this is the case, PANS-OPS gives the departure designer a number of ways to publish departure restrictions. These restrictions may be published singly or in any combination.

Standard Case

8-42. Where no obstacles penetrate the 40:1 OIS, then no departure restrictions will be published. Upon reaching 400 feet above DER, the aviator may turn in any direction.

Specified Turn Altitude

8-43. The procedure may specify a 3.3 percent climb to an altitude where a safe omnidirectional turn can be made.

Specified Climb Gradient

8-44. The procedure may specify a minimum climb gradient of more than 3.3 percent to an altitude before turns are permitted.

Sector Departure

8-45. The procedure may identify sectors for which either a minimum turn altitude or a minimum climb gradient is specified. For example, climb straight ahead to 2,000 feet before commencing a turn to the east/sector 180 degrees to 270 degrees.

DEPARTURES WITH TRACK GUIDANCE

8-46. PANS-OPS uses the term standard instrument departure (SID) to refer to departures using track guidance. Minimum climb gradients may apply. Two basic types are straight and turning.

Straight Departures

8-47. Whenever possible, a straight departure will be specified. A departure is considered straight if the track is aligned within 15 degrees of the runway centerline.

Turning Departures

8-48. A turning departure may be constructed where a route requires a turn of more than 15 degrees. Turns may be specified at an altitude, a fix, or a facility. If an obstacle prohibits turning before reaching the DER, an earlier turning point or a minimum turning altitude/height will be specified. When necessary, the aviator will turn to a heading to intercept a specified radial/bearing. The turning departure procedure will specify the turning point, the track to be made, and the radial/bearing to be intercepted.

Maximum Speed Limits

8-49. Maximum speeds may be published by category or by a note. For example, these procedures may be annotated, "Departure limited to CAT B Aircraft" or "Departure turn limited to 165 KIAS maximum." Aviators must comply with the speed limit published on the departure to remain within protected airspace. If a higher speed is required, request an alternate DP.

Aircraft Categories

8-50. If the departure is limited to specific aircraft categories, table 8-1 provides the applicable speeds.

Table 8-1. Aircraft category and maximum airspeed

Category	Maximum Airspeed (KIAS)
A	120
B	165
C	265
D	290
E	300

APPROACH PROCEDURES

PROCEDURAL TRACKS

8-51. Procedural track approaches are the most common ways of making the transition from the en route structure. These approaches are often much more complicated than a comparable United States approach, and may include multiple NAVAIDs, fixes, and course changes.

REVERSAL AND RACETRACK PROCEDURES

8-52. If the instrument approach cannot be designed as a procedural track arrival, then a reversal procedure or a racetrack or a holding pattern is required.

Reversal Procedure

8-53. ICAO reversal procedures are similar in concept to FAA procedure turns. The ICAO recognizes three methods of performing a reversal procedure, each with its own airspace characteristics:
- The 45-degree/180-degree procedure turn.

● The 80-degree/260-degree procedure turn.
● The base turn.

8-54. Entry is restricted to a specific direction or sector. To remain within the airspace provided requires strict adherence to the directions and timing specified. The protected airspace for reversal procedures does not permit a racetrack or holding maneuver to be conducted unless so specified. An aviator may not enter an ICAO procedure turn using the holding technique described in Chapter 10. Instead, refer to the following entry procedures.

The 45-Degree/180-Degree Procedure Turn

8-55. This procedure starts at a facility or fix and consists of the following:

● A straight leg with track guidance (may be timed or limited by a radial or DME distance).
● A 45-degree turn.
● A straight leg without track guidance (timed one minute from the start of the turn for categories A and B aircraft and 1 minute 15 seconds from the start of the turn for categories C, D, and E aircraft).
● Turning 180 degrees in the opposite direction to intercept the inbound track.

8-56. Adjust time or distance on the outbound track to ensure that the reversal is initiated at a point specified on the IAP, if so depicted, or the maneuver is completed within the specified "remain within" distance (Figure 8-3).

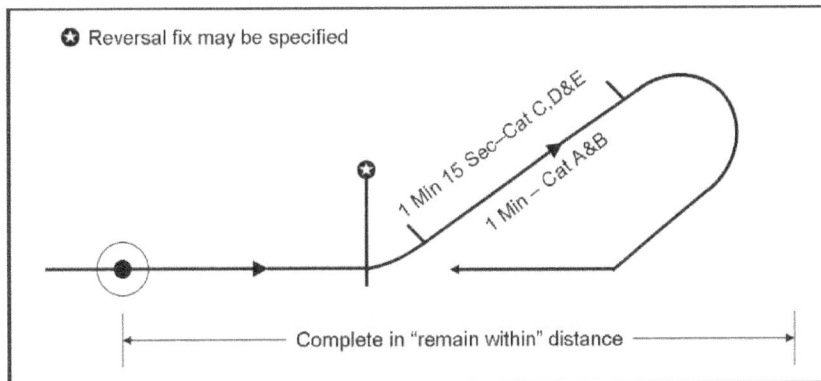

Figure 8-3. The 45-degree/180-degree procedure turn

The 80-Degree/260-Degree Procedure Turn

8-57. This procedure (Figure 8-4, page 8-12) starts at a facility or fix and consists of—

● A straight leg with track guidance (may be timed or limited by a radial or DME distance).
● An 80-degree turn.
● Turning 260 degrees in the opposite direction to intercept the inbound track.

8-58. Adjust time or distance on the outbound track to ensure that the reversal is initiated at a point specified on the IAP, if so depicted, or the maneuver is completed within the specified "remain within" distance.

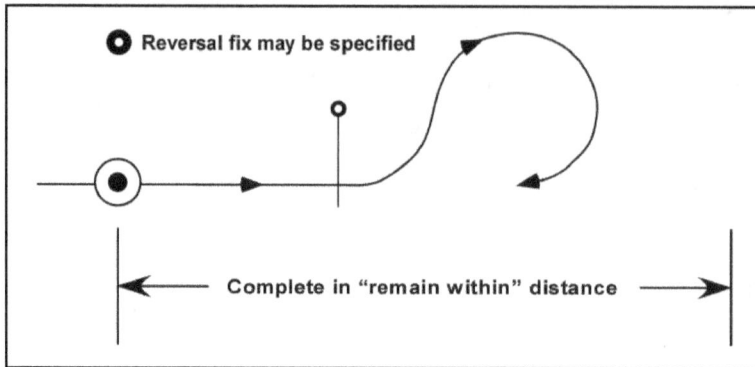

Figure 8-4. The 80-degree/260-degree procedure turn

The Base Turn

8-59. This procedure consists of intercepting and maintaining a specified outbound track, timing from the facility or proceeding to a specified fix, followed by a turn to intercept the inbound track (Figure 8-5). The base turn procedure is not optional. An aviator may not fly one of the procedure turns described above instead of the depicted base turn. More than one track may be depicted, depending on the aircraft category.

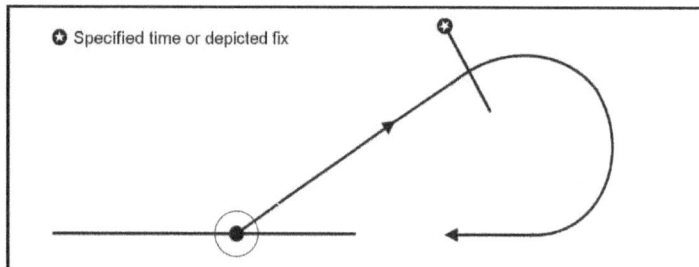

Figure 8-5. Base turn

Reversal Procedure Entry

The 30-Degree Entry Sector

8-60. PANS-OPS specifies this entry sector because, unlike in the United States, the course reversal protected airspace may not include any airspace except on the outbound side of the procedure turn fix. In the United States, protected airspace includes a large entry zone surrounding fix (Figure 8-6, page 8-13).

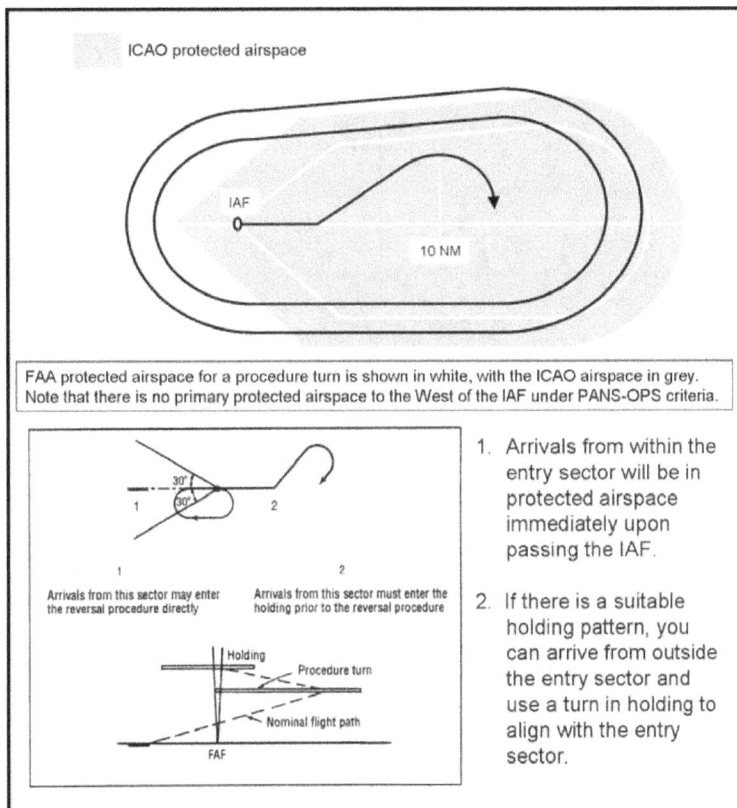

Figure 8-6. Comparison of Federal Aviation Administration and International Civil Aviation Organization protected airspace for a procedure turn

8-61. Unless the procedure specifies particular entry restrictions, the 45-degree/180-degree, 80-degree/260-degree, and base turn reversal procedures must be entered from a track within ± 30 degrees of the outbound reversal track (Figure 8-7, page 8-14). There is a special rule for base turns; for base turns where the ± 30-degree entry sector does not include the reciprocal of the inbound track, the entry sector is expanded to include the reciprocal (Figure 8-8, page 8-14). If the aircraft's arrival track is not within the entry sector—

- Comply with the published entry restrictions or arrival routing.
- Enter holding before the reversal procedure if a suitable arrival holding pattern is published.
- Use good judgment while maneuvering the aircraft into the entry sector if no published routing or suitable holding pattern is available.

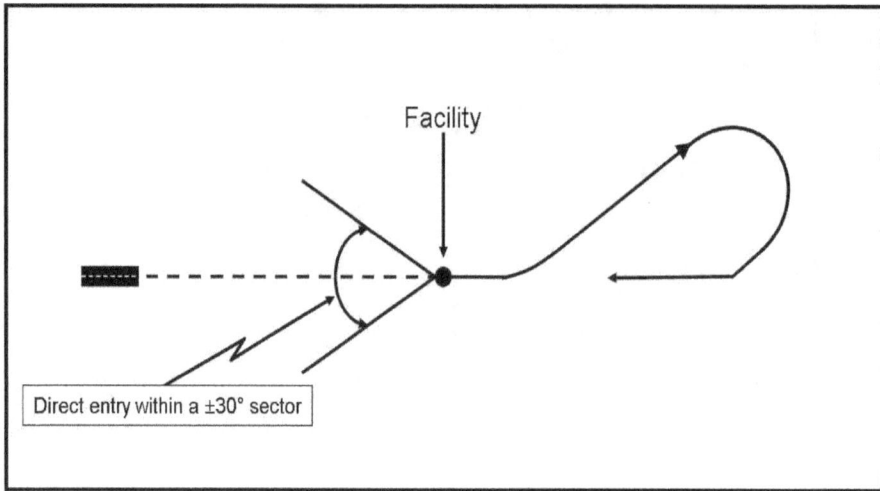

Figure 8-7. Procedure turn entry

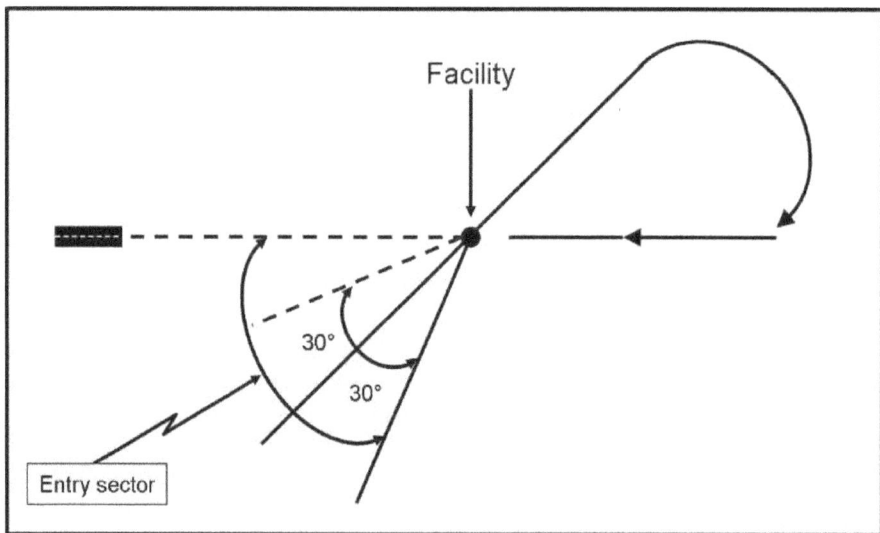

Figure 8-8. Base turn entry

Arriving From Outside the Entry Sector

8-62. There is often some form of published arrival routing into the course reversal IAF such as a STAR, a feeder routing, or an arrival airway. This arrival routing may not fall into the 30-degree entry sector. Such arrival routes will be blended into the reversal approach, and protected airspace is provided to allow the aviator to turn onto the outbound reversal track. Aviators need not request maneuvering airspace to perform an alignment maneuver. Such requests are often met with confusion by ATC. Aviators should remain within protected airspace on the published arrival routing whether maneuvering happens to align the aircraft with the 30-degree entry sector.

8-63. On most ICAO course reversals, a holding pattern is published at or near the IAF to accommodate arrivals from outside the 30-degree sector and not on a published arrival routing. PANS-OPS directs aviators arriving from outside the entry sector to enter holding before the reversal procedure. In most cases, the holding pattern will align the aircraft for the approach.

8-64. If there is no suitable holding pattern, danger arises when the aviator attempts to perform the course reversal upon arriving into the IAF from a direction not anticipated by the approach designer. Sometimes there is no holding pattern published for alignment or there is a holding pattern that does not turn into the entry sector. In this case, the aviator will need to maneuver into the entry sector somehow. The aviator must understand the criticality of how small the protected airspace is, especially when compared to an FAA procedure turn. An aviator may be operating completely outside of protected airspace while proceeding to the IAF, and terrain and obstacle clearance may be totally up to aviator judgment. Use good judgment, consider the published minimum safe/sector altitudes, and do not rely solely on ATC to keep safe. Begin timing to comply with published times, or remain within distances when outbound abeam the facility or fix. If the abeam position cannot be determined while in a turn, start timing after completing the turn.

8-65. A descent can be depicted at any point along a course reversal. When a descent is depicted at the IAF, start descent when abeam or past the IAF and on a parallel or intercept heading to the depicted outbound track. For descents past the IAF, be established on a segment of the IAP before beginning a descent to the altitude associated with that segment.

8-66. According to the ICAO definition, established on a segment is considered being within half full-scale deflection for an ILS or VOR and within ± 5 degrees of the required bearing for the NDB.

8-67. The course-reversal maneuver must be completed within the prescribed "remain-within" distance if one is specified and at or above the altitude specified for its completion. Most ICAO course reversals specify a fix or a time to start the reversal turn instead of a remain-within distance. Comply with all guidance on the IAP. Do not automatically assume an ICAO course-reversal maneuver is treated the same as a procedure turn in the United States.

8-68. Before reaching the IAF, reduce to maneuvering airspeed. Use holding speed if maneuvering speed is not specified for the aircraft. If the procedure is limited to specific aircraft categories, the applicable speeds for these are located in table 8-2.

Table 8-2. Aircraft category and airspeed

Category	Maximum Airspeed (KIAS)
A	110
B	140
C	240
D	250
E	250

8-69. Additional speed restrictions may be charted on individual IAPs. The maximum speeds by category, as shown above, however, will not be exceeded without approval of the appropriate ATC agency.

Racetrack Procedure

8-70. The ICAO racetrack procedure (Figure 8-9, page 8-16) is similar in concept to FAA holding in lieu of procedure turn. This maneuver consists of a holding pattern with outbound leg lengths of one to three minutes, specified in 30-second increments. As an alternative to timing, the outbound leg may be limited by a DME distance or an intersecting radial or bearing.

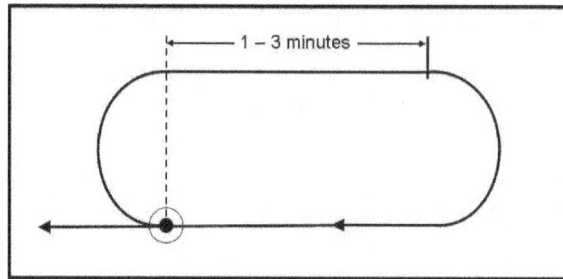

Figure 8-9. Racetrack procedure

Racetrack Entry

8-71. A racetrack procedure is used when aircraft arrive at the fix from various directions. Entry procedures for a racetrack are the same as entry procedures for holding patterns. Exceptions are the following:

- The teardrop offset will not exceed 30 degrees from the inbound course.
- The teardrop entry from sector 2 (Figure 8-10, page 8-18) is limited to one-and-a-half minutes wings level on the 30-degree teardrop track, after which the aviator is expected to turn to a heading to parallel the outbound track for the remainder of the outbound time; if the outbound time is only one minute, the time on the 30-degree teardrop track will also be one minute.
- Parallel entries may not return directly to the facility without first intercepting the inbound track.
- All maneuvering will be done, as much as practical, on the maneuvering side of the inbound track.

8-72. When necessary because of airspace limitations, entry into the racetrack procedure may be restricted to specified routes. When so restricted, the entry routes will be depicted on the IAP. Racetrack procedures are used where sufficient distance is not available in a straight segment to accommodate the required loss of altitude and when entry into a reversal maneuver is not practical. They may also be specified as alternatives to reversal procedures to increase operational flexibility.

Shuttle

8-73. A shuttle is a descent or climb conducted in a holding pattern. A shuttle is normally specified where the descent required between the end of the initial approach and the beginning of the final approach exceeds standard ICAO approach design limits.

Alternate

8-74. Alternate procedures may be specified to any of the procedures described above. IAPs will contain the appropriate depiction and the words "alternative procedure." Aviators should be prepared to execute either procedure. Before accepting clearance for an approach that depicts an alternative procedure, determine which procedure that the controlling agency expects.

Circling

8-75. ICAO circling protected airspace is essentially the same as in the United States. One important distinction to make is between the terms "runway environment" and "airport environment." While circling using an ICAO-designed procedure, the aviator must maintain visual contact with the runway environment (as defined in paragraph 10-184) throughout the entire circling maneuver. In the United States, an aviator is required to maintain visual contact with the airport environment only while circling to land.

LOCALIZER

8-76. PANS-OPS abbreviates the localizer facility as LLZ. The accuracy of the signal generated by the LLZ is the same as an LOC. PANS-OPS normally requires the LLZ final-approach track alignment to remain within 5 degrees of the runway centerline. However, in certain cases, the alignment can exceed 5 degrees. Where required, PANS-OPS allows an increase of the final-approach track to 15 degrees for categories C, D, and E. For aircraft categories A and B, the maximum angle formed by the final-approach track and the runway centerline is 30 degrees.

8-77. Before flying an LLZ, compare the final approach course with runway heading. The airdrome sketch should provide a visual indication of the angle formed between the final-approach track and the runway centerline.

TIMING FOR MISSED APPROACH AND FINAL APPROACH FIX TO MISSED APPROACH POINT

8-78. Some host nations use nonstandard timing for determining the MAP on a procedure. Timing may go from the FAF to the runway threshold or from a step-down fix to the runway threshold. When these host-nation procedures are published in DOD FLIP, these nonstandard timing blocks will be converted to the U.S. standard of FAF to MAP. This conversion can induce some errors because of rounding of numbers. For this reason, when using timing to determine the MAP on a DOD procedure produced by a host nation, crews must correctly determine the timing based on ground speed and then fly that ground speed to avoid exaggerating errors already induced because of the conversion from host-nation to DOD format.

HOLDING

BANK ANGLE

8-79. Make all turns at a bank angle of 25 degrees or at a rate of 3 degrees per second, whichever requires the lesser bank. ICAO procedures do not allow correcting for winds by adjusting bank angle. The triple-drift technique, described in paragraph 10-113, is a good way to correct for winds without varying the bank angle.

TRACKS

8-80. All procedures depict tracks. Attempt to maintain the track by allowing for known winds and applying corrections to heading and timing during entry and while flying in the holding pattern.

LIMITING RADIAL

8-81. When holding away from a NAVAID, where the distance from the holding fix to the NAVAID is short, a limiting radial may be specified. A limiting radial may also be specified where airspace conservation is essential. If encountering the limiting radial first, initiate a turn onto the radial until turning inbound. Do not exceed the limiting DME distance, if published.

HOLDING ENTRY PROCEDURE

8-82. The ICAO holding entry procedure is a mandatory procedure. Aviators must comply with all timing, distances, and limiting radials. Enter the holding pattern based on the heading (±5 degrees) relative to the three entry sectors depicted in Figure 8-10, page 8-18. Upon reaching the holding fix, follow the appropriate procedure for the following entry sectors:

- **Sector 1 (Parallel).** Turn onto an outbound heading for the appropriate time or distance, and then turn towards the holding side to intercept the inbound track or to return to the fix.
- **Sector 2 (Offset).** Turn to a heading making an angle of 30 degrees from the reciprocal of the inbound track on the holding side; fly outbound for the appropriate period of time, until the

correct limiting DME is attained or where a limiting radial is specified, then turn right to intercept the inbound holding track.

- **Sector 3 (Direct).** Turn and follow the holding pattern.

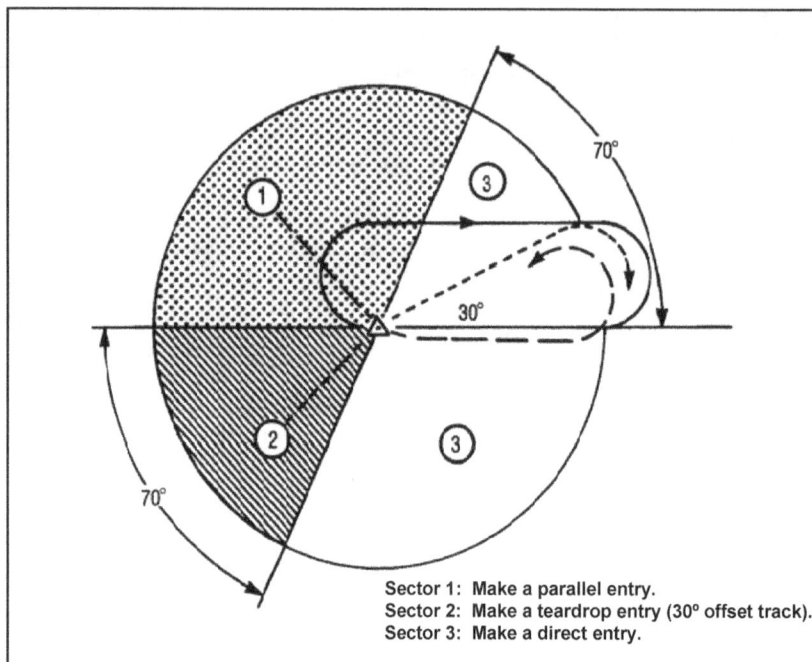

Sector 1: Make a parallel entry.
Sector 2: Make a teardrop entry (30° offset track).
Sector 3: Make a direct entry.

Figure 8-10. International Civil Aviation Organization holding pattern entry sectors

AIRSPEEDS

8-83. There is little standardization of maximum holding airspeeds in PANS-OPS. There are three different tables of holding airspeeds that an approach designer could use, depending on which edition of PANS-OPS was used when the holding pattern was constructed. Furthermore, many countries publish their own holding pattern airspeeds. This information should be published in FLIP but may be quite difficult or impossible to actually find. An aviator must understand, however, that the concept is the same as in the United States. Maximum holding airspeeds are defined by PANS-OPS (or the host country) and have no relation to the holding speed specified in the aircraft operator's manual. Table 8-3 reproduces airspeeds from the second edition of PANS-OPS, which is the one most commonly used.

Table 8-3. Airspeeds

ALTITUDE (feet)	AIRSPEED (Normal Conditions)	AIRSPEED (Turbulence*)
0-14,000 (CAT A and B)	170 KIAS	170 KIAS
0-14,000 (CAT C and D)	230 KIAS	280 KIAS
14,001-20,000	240 KIAS	280 KIAS or 0.8 Mach, whichever is less
20,001-34,000	265 KIAS	280 KIAS or 0.8 Mach, whichever is less
34,001+	0.83 Mach	0.83 Mach
*The speeds published for turbulence conditions shall be used for holding only after prior clearance with ATC, unless the relevant publications indicate the holding area can accommodate aircraft flying at these high holding speeds.		

HOLDING PATTERN LENGTHS

8-84. On the second and subsequent arrivals over the fix, turn and fly an outbound track that will most appropriately position the aircraft for the turn onto the inbound track. Continue outbound until the appropriate limiting distance or time. ICAO outbound legs are the limiting factor for both timed and fixed-distance holding patterns. The times are one minute outbound at or below 14,000 feet MSL or one-and-a-half minutes outbound above 14,000 feet MSL.

WIND CORRECTIONS

8-85. Attempt to correct both heading and timing to compensate for the effects of wind to ensure that the inbound track is regained before passing the holding fix inbound. Indications available from the NAVAID and estimated or known winds should be used in making these corrections. If a limiting radial is published and encountered before the outbound limits, that radial must be followed until a turn inbound is initiated.

ALTIMETER SETTING PROCEDURES

8-86. There are three different methods of reporting the altimeter measurements and four different units of measure used to express altimeter settings. For aircraft having only one type of altimeter scale or for areas where the altimeter setting is not converted for the aviator, the FIH contains conversion tables. Crew members must understand how to apply the conversions before flight into airspace using other than inches of mercury/atmosphere pressure at nautical height (QNH) for altimeter settings. Refer to FLIP AP for specific altimeter setting procedures for each country.

ATMOSPHERIC PRESSURE AT NAUTICAL HEIGHT SETTINGS

8-87. A QNH altimeter setting represents the pressure that would, in theory, exist at sea level at that location by measuring the surface pressure and correcting to sea-level pressure for a standard day. Set the reported QNH when descending through, or operating below, the published MSL transition level. With the proper QNH set, the altimeter will indicate the height above MSL. All DOD approach criteria are based on using QNH altimeter settings.

STANDARD ALTIMETER SETTINGS

8-88. The standard altimeter (QNE) is used to indicate the height above an imaginary plane called the standard datum plane, also known as FL0. The established altimeter setting at FL0 is 29.92 inches of mercury, or 1013.2 millibars. Set QNE (29.92) when climbing through or operating above the transition altitude.

ATMOSPHERIC PRESSURE AT FIELD ELEVATION SETTINGS

8-89. Atmospheric pressure at field elevation (QFE) is the altimeter setting issued to aircraft to indicate the AGL height above the airport. With the proper QFE set, the altimeter should indicate zero on the ground. QFE is commonly used by the Royal Air Force and the Royal Navy in the United Kingdom and in many parts of the Pacific and Eastern Europe.

TRANSITION ALTITUDE

8-90. Transition altitude is the altitude in the vicinity of an airport at or below which the vertical position of an aircraft is determined from an altimeter set to QNH. Transition altitude is normally specified for each airfield by the country in which the airfield exists. Transition altitude will not normally be below 3,000 feet HAA and must be published on the appropriate charts.

TRANSITION LEVEL

8-91. The lowest flight level available for use above transition altitude is called the transition level. Transition level is usually passed to aircraft during approach or landing clearances. The transition layer may be published or supplied by ATC via the ATIS or during arrival. Half flight levels may be used (FL45).

TRANSITION LAYER

8-92. The transition layer is that area between the transition altitude and transition level. Aircraft are not normally assigned altitudes within the transition layer.

TRANSITION BETWEEN FLIGHT LEVELS AND ALTITUDES

8-93. The vertical position of an aircraft at or below transition altitude shall be expressed in altitude (QNH or QFE as appropriate). Vertical position at or above the transition level shall be expressed in terms of flight levels (QNE). When passing through the transition layer, vertical position shall be expressed in terms of flight levels (QNE) when climbing and in terms of altitudes (QNH or QFE as appropriate) when descending. After an approach clearance has been issued and the descent to land is commenced, the vertical positioning of an aircraft above the transition level may be by reference to altitude (QNH or QFE as appropriate), provided that level flight above the transition altitude is not indicated or anticipated. This is intended for turbo jet aircraft where an uninterrupted descent from high altitude is desired and for airfields equipped to reference altitudes throughout the descent.

ALTIMETER ERRORS

8-94. When the altimeter does not indicate the reference elevation or height exactly but is within specified tolerances, no adjustment of this indication should be made either by the pressure adjustment knob or other adjustments on the altimeter during any phase of flight. Furthermore, any error within tolerances noted during preflight check on the ground should be ignored by the aviator in flight.

ALTIMETER USE IN FLIGHT

8-95. Before takeoff, at least one altimeter will be set to the latest QNH/QFE altimeter setting. Set the altimeter to QNE (29.92) climbing through transition altitude. Before commencing the initial approach to an airfield, the number of the transition level should be obtained from the appropriate air traffic services unit. Obtain the latest QNH/QFE before descending below the transition level.

TRANSPONDER OPERATING PROCEDURES

8-96. When an aircraft carries a serviceable transponder, the aviator shall operate the transponder at all times during flight, regardless of whether the aircraft is within or outside airspace where secondary surveillance radar (SSR) is used for air traffic service purposes.

OPERATING CODES

8-97. Operate codes as assigned by ATC on the basis of regional air navigation agreements. In the absence of any ATC directions or regional air navigation agreements, operate the transponder on Mode A, Code 2000.

8-98. The use of Mode A, Code 7700, in certain areas, may result in the elimination of the SSR response of the aircraft from the ATC radar display in cases where the ground equipment is not provided with automatic means for its immediate recognition.

8-99. If an aviator squawks 7600, the controller will try to verify by asking the aviator to IDENT or change the code. If the aviator's receiver is functioning, the controller will communicate with him using the IDENT or code change.

HI-JACK CODES

8-100.   If an aviator experiences an unlawful interference with an aircraft in flight and selects code 7500, ATC will request confirmation of this code. Depending on the circumstances, the aviator can confirm the code or not reply at all. The absence of a reply from the aviator will be taken by ATC as an indication that the use of code 7500 is not due to an inadvertent false code selection.

This page intentionally left blank.

Chapter 9

Air Traffic Control System

This chapter provides a general overview of communication equipment, communication procedures, and ATC facilities and services available for IFR flight in the NAS. Specific and detailed information is provided in FAA Order 7110.10, AIM, Instrument Flying Handbook, Instrument Procedures Handbook, and other FAA/ICAO publications and Web sites.

COMMUNICATIONS

EQUIPMENT

Navigation/Communication Equipment

9-1. Aviators communicate with ATC on VHF and UHF frequencies. If ATC assigns a frequency that cannot be selected on the assigned radio, ask for an alternative frequency. Some AFSSs can be communicated with by transmitting on 122.1 megahertz (selected on the communication radio) and receiving on a VOR frequency (selected on the navigation radio). This is called duplex operation.

Contents

Radar and Transponders

9-2. ATC radars are able to display energy reflected from an aircraft's metallic structure, which is displayed as a primary return. Some ATC radars are also able to display secondary returns. A secondary return, which relies on transponder replies to ground interrogation signals, is able to display aircraft-specific information. This information can be used with automation.

9-3. A transponder is a radar beacon transmitter/receiver installed in the instrument panel. ATC beacon transmitters send out interrogation signals continuously as the radar antenna rotates. When an interrogation is received by the transponder, a coded reply is sent to the ground station for display on the controller's scope. Transponder codes are assigned by ATC.

9-4. When a controller asks the aviator to IDENT and he pushes the IDENT button, the return on the controller's scope is intensified for precise identification of the flight. When requested, briefly push the IDENT button to activate this feature. A good practice is to verbally confirm to ATC that the codes have been changed or the IDENT button has been pushed.

9-5. Secondary radar returns can display Mode C altitude reporting on the control scope if the aircraft is equipped with an encoding altimeter or blind encoder. When the transponder's function switch is in the altitude (ALT) position, the aircraft's pressure altitude is sent to the controller. Adjusting the altimeter's Kollsman window has no effect on the altitude read by the controller. (Primary radar returns provide only range and bearing information from the radar antenna to the target.)

9-6. Transponders must be on whenever the aircraft is operating in controlled airspace. Mode C altitude reporting is required by regulation in Class B and Class C airspace and inside of a 30-mile circle surrounding the primary airport in Class B airspace. Altitude reporting should be on at all times.

PROCEDURES

9-7.   Clarity in communication is essential for safe instrument flight and requires aviators and controllers to use terms understood by both. The pilot/controller glossary in the AIM is the best source of terms and definitions. The AIM is revised twice a year, and new definitions are added. Review the glossary frequently. Because clearances and instructions are composed largely of letters and numbers, a phonetic pronunciation guide has been developed for both.

9-8.   Air traffic controllers must follow the guidance of FAA Order 7110.65 when communicating with aviators. The manual presents the controller with different situations and prescribes precise terminology to be used. This is advantageous for aviators because a recognized pattern or format can be expected. Controllers are faced with a variety of communication styles based on aviator experience, proficiency, and professionalism.

9-9.   Aviators should study the examples in the AIM, listen to other aviators communicate, and apply lessons learned to their own communications with ATC. Aviators should ask for clarification of a clearance or instruction, when needed. Use plain English to ensure understanding, and expect the controller to reply in the same way. A safe instrument flight is the result of cooperation between controller and aviator.

FACILITIES

9-10. The controller's primary responsibility is separation of aircraft operating under IFR. Separation of aircraft is achieved using ATC facilities, which include the AFSS, airport traffic control tower (ATCT), terminal radar approach control (TRACON), and ARTCC.

Automated Flight Service Station

9-11. The first contact with ATC will likely be through AFSS, either by radio or telephone. AFSSs provide pilot briefings, receive and process flight plans, relay ATC clearances, originate NOTAMs, and broadcast aviation weather. Some facilities provide EFAS, take weather observations, and advise United States Customs and Immigration of international flights.

9-12. Telephone contact with flight service is obtained by dialing 1-800-WX-BRIEF anywhere in the United States for connection to the nearest AFSS based on the area code from which the aviator is calling. There are a variety of methods for making radio contact: direct transmission, RCOs, ground communication outlets (GCOs), and using duplex transmissions through NAVAIDs. The best source of information on frequency usage is the A/FD. The legend panel on sectional charts also contains contact information.

9-13. The briefer sends the flight plan to the host computer at the ARTCC. After processing, the computer sends flight strips to the tower, radar facility handling the departure route, and center controller in whose sector the aviator will first enter. These strips are delivered about 30 minutes before the proposed departure time. Strips are delivered to en route facilities 30 minutes before the aviator is expected to enter their airspace. If the aviator fails to open the flight plan, the flight plan will time out 2 hours after the proposed departure time.

9-14. When departing an airport in Class G airspace, the aviator receives IFR clearance from the AFSS by radio or telephone. The clearance contains either a clearance void time (the aviator must be airborne before this time) or a release time (the aviator should not be airborne before this time). Aviators can help the controller by stating how soon they expect to be airborne. If, for example, the void time is 10 minutes past the hour and the aviator is airborne at exactly 10 minutes past the hour, the clearance is void; he must be airborne before the void time. Aviators may ask for a specific void time when filing their flight plan.

Air Traffic Control Towers

9-15. Several controllers in the tower cab are involved in handling instrument flight. Where there is a dedicated clearance delivery position, that frequency is found in the A/FD and on the instrument approach chart for the departure airport. Where there is no clearance delivery position, the ground controller performs this function. At the busiest airports, pretaxi clearance is required; the frequency for pretaxi clearance can be found in the A/FD. Taxi clearance should be requested not more than 10 minutes before proposed taxi time.

9-16. IFR clearances should be read back to the clearance delivery controller. Instrument clearances can be overwhelming when the aviator copies them verbatim. IFR clearances typically begin with the clearance limit (usually the destination airport) and then continue with the route, including any DP; initial altitude; frequency (for departure control); and transponder code. With the exception of the transponder code, most of these items are known before engine start. Clearances will be issued according to FAA Order 7110.65, as appropriate, in the following order:

- Aircraft identification.
- Clearance limit.
- SID.
- Route of flight including preferential departure route/preferential departure arrival route/preferred arrival route, when applied.
- Altitude data in the order flown.
- Holding instructions.
- Any special information.
- Frequency and beacon code information.

9-17. One technique for copying clearances is writing CRAFT (clearance, route, approach, frequency, and transponder code) down the left side of a page. Refer to the following example.

Example of IFR Clearance (using CRAFT)

An aviator has filed an IFR flight plan from Seattle, Washington, to Sacramento, California, via V-23 at 7,000 feet. He notes that traffic is taking off to the north from Seattle-Tacoma (Sea-Tac) airport and, by monitoring the clearance delivery frequency, notes the DP being assigned to southbound flights. The clearance limit will be the destination airport, so he writes "SAC" after the letter C. He writes "SEATTLE TWO–V23" after R for route, because departure control has issued this departure to other flights (the aviator could also call the tower via telephone to ask what departure is in use). He writes "7" after the A and the departure control frequency printed on the approach charts for Sea-Tac after F, and leaves the space after T blank–the transponder code is generated by computer and can seldom be determined in advance. Then he calls clearance delivery and reports ready to copy.

As the controller reads the clearance, the aviator confirms what he has already written down; if there is a change, he draws a line through that item and writes in the changed item. Chances are that changes will be minimal, and he will have copied most of the clearance before keying the microphone. Developing clearance shorthand to cut down on the verbiage that must be copied is worthwhile.

9-18. Either the text or a graphic representation of a DP is required (if one is available) and should be reviewed before accepting a clearance. This is another reason for the aviator to find out beforehand which DP is in use. If the DP includes an altitude or a departure control frequency, those items will not be included in the clearance from the tower cab.

9-19. The last clearance received supersedes all previous clearances. For instance, if the DP is "Climb and maintain 2,000 feet, expect higher in 6 miles" and upon contacting the departure controller, the aviator is told "Climb and maintain 8,000 feet," the 2,000-foot restriction has been canceled. This rule applies in terminal and center airspace. If the aviator is ready to copy the IFR clearance before the strip has been received from the center computer, he will be advised "clearance on request" and the controller will call when the clearance has been received.

9-20. The local controller is responsible for operations in Class D airspace and on active runways. At some towers designated as IFR towers, the local controller has vectoring authority. At VFR towers, the local controller accepts inbound IFR flights from the terminal radar facility and cannot provide vectors. The local controller also coordinates flights in the local area with radar controllers. Although Class D airspace normally extends 2,500 feet above field elevation, towers frequently release the top 500 feet to the radar controllers to facilitate overflights. Accordingly, when a flight is vectored over an airport at an altitude that appears to enter the tower controller's airspace, there is no need to contact the tower controller—all coordination is handled by ATC.

9-21. The departure radar controller may be in the same building as the control tower, but often the departure radar position is remotely located. The tower controller will not issue a takeoff clearance until the departure controller issues a release.

Terminal Radar Approach Control

9-22. TRACONs are considered terminal facilities because they provide the link between the departure airport and en route structure of the NAS. Terminal airspace normally extends 30 nautical miles from the facility with a vertical extent of 10,000 feet; however, dimensions vary widely. Class B and Class C airspace dimensions are provided on aeronautical charts. At terminal radar facilities, the airspace is divided into sectors, each with one or more controllers. Each sector is assigned a discrete radio frequency. All terminal facilities are approach controls and should be addressed as "Approach" except when directed to do otherwise: "Contact departure on 120.4."

9-23. Terminal radar antennas are located on or adjacent to the airport. Terminal controllers can assign altitudes lower than published procedural altitudes, called minimum vectoring altitudes (MVAs). MVAs are not published or accessible to aviators but are displayed at the controller's position. However, if altitude assigned seems too low, confirm before descending.

9-24. When the aviator receives and accepts his clearance and reports ready for takeoff, a controller in the tower contacts the TRACON for a release; the aviator will not be released until the departure controller can fit the flight into the departure flow and may have the aviator hold for release. When the aviator receives takeoff clearance, the departure controller is advised of the flight and awaits a call from the aviator. All of the information that the controller needs is on the departure strip or computer screen; there is no need to repeat any portion of the clearance to that controller. Simply establish contact with the facility when instructed to do so by the tower controller. The terminal facility computer detects and tracks assigned transponder codes; for this reason, the transponder should remain on standby until takeoff clearance has been received.

9-25. The aircraft will appear on the controller's radar as a target with an associated data block that moves as the aircraft moves through the airspace. The data block includes aircraft identification and type, altitude, and airspeed. A TRACON controller uses airport surveillance radar (ASR) to detect primary targets and automated radar terminal systems (ARTSs) to receive transponder signals. These two are combined on the controller's scope.

9-26. At facilities with ASR-3 equipment, radar returns from precipitation are not displayed as varying levels of intensity and controllers must rely on pilot reports and experience to provide weather avoidance information. With ASR-9 equipment, the controller can select up to six levels of intensity. Level 1 precipitation does not require avoidance tactics, but the presence of levels 2 or 3 should cause aviators to investigate further. The returns from higher levels of intensity may obscure aircraft data blocks, and controllers may select the higher levels only on aviator request. When uncertain about the weather ahead, ask the controller if the facility can display intensity levels.

Tower En Route Control

9-27. At many locations, instrument flights can be conducted entirely in terminal airspace. These TEC routes are generally for aircraft operating below 10,000 feet and can be found in the A/FD. Aviators desiring to use TEC should include that designation in the remarks section of the flight plan.

9-28. Aviators are not limited to the major airports at the city pairs listed in the A/FD. For example, a tower en route flight from an airport in New York (NYC) airspace could terminate at any airport within about 30 miles of Bradley International Airport (BDL) airspace such as Hartford (HFD).

9-29. Minimum safe altitude warnings (MSAWs) are a valuable service provided by the automated radar equipment at terminal radar facilities. This equipment predicts aircraft positions with a two-minute lead time based on the present flight-path conditions—the controller issues a safety alert if the aircraft will encounter terrain or obstructions in its projected path. An unusually rapid descent rate on a nonprecision approach can trigger such an alert.

Air Route Traffic Control Center

9-30. Air route traffic control center facilities are responsible for maintaining separation between IFR flights in the en route structure. Center radars (air route surveillance radar) acquire and track transponder returns using the same basic technology as terminal radars.

9-31. Earlier center radars display weather as an area of slashes (light precipitation) and "H"s (moderate rainfall). Because the controller cannot detect higher levels of precipitation, aviators should be wary of areas showing moderate rainfall. Newer radar displays show weather as three levels of blue, and controllers can select the level of weather to be displayed. Weather displays of higher levels of intensity can cause difficulty for controllers in seeing aircraft data blocks; aviators should not expect ATC to display weather continuously.

9-32. Center airspace is divided into sectors in the same manner as terminal airspace; in addition, most center airspace is divided by altitudes into high and low sectors. Each sector has a dedicated team of controllers and selection of radio frequencies because each center has a network of remote transmitter/receiver sites. All center frequencies are found in the back of the A/FD and on en route charts. Each ARTCC's area of responsibility covers several states; when flying from the vicinity of one remote communication site toward another, expect the same controller to talk on different frequencies.

Center Approach/Departure Control

9-33. Most airports with instrument approaches do not lie within terminal radar airspace, and when operating to or from these airports, the aviator communicates directly with the center controller. If the aircraft is departing a tower-controlled airport, the tower controller provides instructions for contacting the appropriate center controller. When an aircraft is departing an airport without an operating control tower, clearance includes instructions such as "Upon entering controlled airspace, contact Houston Center on 126.5." The aviator is responsible for terrain clearance until reaching the controller's MVA and still has this responsibility until he hears his aircraft call sign and "radar contact" from the center controller.

9-34. If obstacles in the departure path require a steeper-than-standard climb gradient (200 FPNM), the aviator should be so advised by the controller. However, the departure airport listing should be checked in the A/FD to determine if there are trees or wires in the departure path; when in doubt, ask the controller for the required climb gradient.

9-35. A common clearance in these situations is "When able, proceed direct to the Astoria VOR." This means that the aviator can proceed when he is able to do so while maintaining terrain and obstruction clearance but not as soon as a signal suitable for navigation is received from the NAVAID. Using the standard climb gradient, the aviator must be 2 miles from the DER before it is safe to turn (400 feet AGL). When a center controller issues either a heading to fly to or a direct route or states "direct when able," the controller becomes responsible for terrain and obstruction clearance.

9-36. Another center clearance is "Leaving (altitude), fly (heading) or proceed direct when able." This clearance keeps the terrain/obstruction clearance responsibility in the cockpit until above the minimum IFR altitude. A controller cannot issue an IFR clearance until the aviator is above the minimum IFR altitude unless the aircraft is able to climb in VFR conditions.

9-37. On a center controller's scope, one nautical mile is about 1/28 of an inch. When a center controller is providing approach/departure control services at an airport many miles from the radar antenna, estimating headings and distances is difficult for center controller. Controllers issuing vectors to final must set the range on their scopes to not more than 125 nautical miles to provide the greatest possible accuracy for intercept headings. At locations farther from a center radar antenna, aviators should expect a minimum of vectoring.

CONTROL SEQUENCE

9-38. The IFR system is flexible and accommodating if an aviator is prepared. As many frequencies as possible are written down before they are needed, and an alternate is determined if the flight cannot be completed as planned. Be familiar with facilities and services available on the flight route (table 9-1). Know where to find the nearest VFR conditions, and be prepared to divert if the situation deteriorates. An IFR flight with departure and arrival at airports with control towers uses ATC facilities and services in the following sequence:

- **AFSS:** Obtain a weather briefing for departure, destination, alternate airports, and en route conditions, and then file a flight plan by calling 1-800-WX-BRIEF.
- **ATIS:** Preflight complete, listen for present conditions and approach in use.
- **Clearance delivery:** Before taxiing, obtain departure clearance.
- **Ground control:** Receive taxi instructions.
- **Tower:** Takeoff checks complete, receive clearance to takeoff.
- **Departure control:** Once the transponder tags up with the ARTS, the tower controller instructs the aviator to contact "Departure" to establish radar contact.
- **ARTCC:** After departing the departure controller's airspace, the aviator is handed off to the center that coordinates the flight while en route. He may be in contact with multiple ARTCC facilities; they coordinate handoffs.
- **EFAS/HIWAS:** Obtain in-flight weather information before leaving the ATC frequency.
- **ATIS:** Obtain ATIS information before leaving the ATC frequency.
- **Approach Control:** Center hands off to approach control where the aviator receives additional information and clearances.
- **Tower:** Once cleared for approach, the aviator is instructed to contact tower control; the flight plan is canceled by the pilot through the tower controller when the aircraft lands.

Table 9-1. Air traffic control facilities, services, and radio call signs

Communications Facility	Description	Frequency
Airport Advisory Area "(AFSS name) RADIO"	AFSS personnel provide traffic advisories to pilots operating within 10 miles of the airport.	122.2, 123.6, and 255.4 MHz.
UNICOM "(airport name) UNICOM"	Airport advisories from an airport without an operating control tower or AFSS.	Listed in A/FD under the city name; also on sectional charts in airport data block.
Air Route Traffic Control Center "CENTER"	En route radar facilities that maintain separation between IFR flights and between IFR flights and known VFR flights. Centers will provide VFR traffic advisories on a workload-permitting basis.	Listed in A/FD and on instrument en route charts.
Approach/Departure Control "(airport name) APPROACH" (unless otherwise advised)	Positions at a terminal radar facility responsible for handling of IFR flights to and from the primary airport (where Class B airspace exists).	Listed in A/FD; also on sectional charts in the communications panel and on terminal area charts.

Table 9-1. Air traffic control facilities, services, and radio call signs

Communications Facility	Description	Frequency
Automatic Terminal Information Service	Continuous broadcast of audiotape prepared by ATC controller containing wind direction, wind velocity, temperature, altimeter setting, runway and approach in use, and other information of interest to pilots.	Listed in A/FD under the city name; also on sectional charts in airport data block, in the communications panel, and on terminal area charts.
Clearance Delivery "(airport name) CLEARANCE"	Control tower position responsible for transmitting departure clearances to IFR flights.	Listed on instrument approach procedure charts.
Common Traffic Advisory Frequency	CTAF provides a single frequency for pilots in the area to use for contacting the facility and/or broadcasting their position and intentions to other pilots.	Listed in A/FD; also on sectional charts in the airport data block (followed by a white C on a blue or magenta background). At airports with no tower, CTAF is 122.9, the "MULTICOM" frequency.
Automated Flight Service Station "(facility name) RADIO"	Provides information and services to pilots, using RCOs and GCOs.	Listed in A/FD and on sectional charts, both under city name and in a separate listing of AFSS frequencies. On sectional charts, listed above the VOR boxes or in separate boxes when remote.
Ground Control "(airport name) GROUND"	At tower-controlled airports, a position in the tower responsible for controlling aircraft taxiing to and from the runways.	Listed in A/FD under city name.
Hazardous Inflight Weather Advisory Service	Continuous broadcast of forecast hazardous weather conditions on selected NAVAIDs. No communication capability.	Black circle with white H in VOR frequency box; notation in A/FD airport listing under "Radio Aids to Navigation."
MULTICOM "(airport name) TRAFFIC"	Intended for use by pilots at airports with no radio facilities. Pilots should use self-announce procedures given in the AIM.	122.9 MHz. A/FD shows 122.9 as CTAF; also on sectional charts, 122.9 is followed by a white C on a dark background, indicating CTAF.
Tower "(airport name) TOWER"	"Local" controller responsible for operations on the runways and in Class B, C, or D airspace surrounding the airport.	Listed in A/FD under city name; also on sectional and terminal control area charts in the airport data block and communications panel.
En Route Flight Advisory Service "FLIGHT WATCH"	In-flight weather information provided by FAA.	122.0 MHz (0600-2200 local time).

9-39. An IFR flight with departure and arrival at airports without operating control towers uses ATC facilities and services in the following sequence:

- **AFSS:** Obtain a weather briefing for departure, destination, alternate airports, and en route conditions, and then file the flight plan by telephone; provide the latitude/longitude description for small airports to ensure that the center is able to locate departure and arrival locations.
- **AFSS or UNICOM:** ATC clearances can be filed and received on the UNICOM frequency if the licensee has made arrangements with the controlling ARTCC; otherwise, file with AFSS via telephone. Be sure preflight preparations are complete before filing. Clearance includes a clearance void time; the aviator must be airborne before the void time.
- **ARTCC:** After takeoff, establish contact with the center. The aviator may be in contact with multiple ARTCC facilities; they coordinate handoffs.
- **EFAS/HIWAS:** Obtain in-flight weather information before leaving the ATC frequency.
- **Approach Control:** Center hands off to approach control, where the aviator receives additional information and clearances. If the aircraft is able to land under VMC, the IFR clearance may be canceled before landing.

LETTERS OF AGREEMENT

9-40. At boundaries between the airspace controlled by different facilities, the location and altitude the aviator is handed off is determined by letters of agreement (LOAs) negotiated between the two facilities. This information is not available in any FAA publication. Note on en route charts the points at which handoffs occur. In each handoff to a different facility, the controller must know aircraft altitude and position.

Chapter 10

Instrument Flight Rules Information and Procedures

No single procedure applies to the planning and preparation involved with all flights conducted IFR. Once an aviator understands the overall operation of IFR flight, the many procedural details can be put into the appropriate sequence. This chapter explains sources for flight planning, conditions associated with instrument flight, and procedures used for each phase of IFR flight: departure, en route, approach, and landing.

SECTION I – SOURCES OF FLIGHT PLANNING INFORMATION

10-1. Aviators consult the appropriate aircraft operator's manual for flight planning information pertinent to the aircraft flown. In case of a conflict between AR 95-1 and FARs, Army aviators are expected to comply with AR 95-1. USAASA has negotiated with the FAA and obtained written authorization to deviate, in certain instances, from requirements stipulated in the FARs.

Contents

DEPARTMENT OF DEFENSE FLIGHT INFORMATION PUBLICATIONS

10-2. DOD FLIP information is provided at: https://164.214.2.62/products/digitalaero/index.cfm#flip. After 1 October 2006, the FLIP and Digital Aeronautical Flight Information File (DAFIF) will no longer be accessible to the public. DOD customers will continue to have web access to all DAFIF and FLIP products through a restricted Web site. Details are available at http://www.nga.mil.

GENERAL PLANNING

10-3. General planning (GP) contains general information on all FLIP terms, explanation of divisions of United States Airspace, flight plans and codes, common worldwide pilot procedures, ICAO procedures, operations and firings over high seas, and aviation weather codes. The GP is published every 32 weeks with planning change notices (PCNs) issued at the 16-week midpoint of the GP book cycle and urgent change notices (UCNs) issued as required.

AREA PLANNING

AP 1, 2, 3, and 4

10-4. These documents contain planning and procedure information for a specific region or geographic area. Area planning (AP)/1, 2, and 3 are published every 24 weeks with PCNs at the 8- and 16-week intervals. AP/4 is published every 48 weeks with PCNs at the 16- and 32-week intervals. UCNs are published as required.

AP 1A, 2A, 3A and 4A (Special-Use Airspace)

10-5. These documents contain all prohibited, restricted, danger, warning, and alert areas listed by country. Military operations and known parachute jumping areas are also listed. These documents are published every 48 weeks with PCNs at the 16- and 32-week intervals. UCNs are published as required.

AP 1B (Military Training Routes, North and South America)

10-6. AP/1B contains information relative to military routes including IRs, VRs, slow-speed, low-altitude training routes (SRs), refueling tracks/anchors/VFR helicopter refueling tracks, and avoidance locations. Charts (seven charts on four sheets) containing graphic depictions of IR, VR, and SR route systems throughout the continental United States and Alaska are also included. These documents are published every eight weeks.

FLIGHT INFORMATION HANDBOOK

10-7. The FIH contains aeronautical information required by DOD aircrews in flight that is not subject to frequent change. Sections include information on emergency procedures, FLIP and NOTAM abbreviation/codes, national and international flight data and procedures, meteorological information, conversion tables, and standard time signals. The handbook is designed for worldwide use with DOD FLIP en route supplements. The publication cycle is every 32 weeks.

INSTRUMENT FLIGHT RULES SUPPLEMENT

10-8. This supplement contains an alphabetical IFR airport/facility directory, special notices, and procedures required to support en route and area charts. The publication cycle is every eight weeks.

INSTRUMENT FLIGHT RULES EN ROUTE LOW-ALTITUDE CHARTS

10-9. These charts portray the airway system and related data required for IFR operations at altitudes below 18,000 feet MSL. Twenty-six variable scale charts are printed on 13 sheets, L-1 through L-26, covering the entire United States. An additional sheet containing Charts L-27 and L-28—duplicating data shown on L-20, L-22, L-24 and L-25—is available for those who frequently plan flights north and south along the east coast within the area of coverage. The publication cycle is every eight weeks.

INSTRUMENT FLIGHT RULES EN ROUTE HIGH-ALTITUDE CHARTS

10-10. These charts portray the airway system and related data required for IFR operations at altitudes at and above 18,000 feet MSL. Six charts are printed on three sheets. The publication cycle is every eight weeks.

TERMINAL HIGH AND LOW ALTITUDE

10-11. Twenty-five bound booklets contain IAPs, airport diagrams, SIDs, and radar instrument approach minimums. The set contains all DOD TERPS and civil TERPS requested by the military. Cross-hatching, displayed along the entire top and bottom borders, denotes high-altitude procedures; cross-hatching, displayed along the upper left half of the top border and lower right half of the bottom border, denotes high- and low-altitude procedures. Publication cycle is every eight weeks. A high-low terminal change notice is published at the four-week midpoint and contains revisions, additions, and deletions to the last complete issue. TERPS are identified to be meaningful to the aviator and permit ready identification of air traffic control phraseology. The types of charts found in these publications follow.

Straight-in Approach

10-12. Procedures meeting criteria for authorization of straight-in landing minima are identified by the type of NAVAIDs that provide final approach guidance and the runway to which the final approach courses are aligned (such as ILS Rwy 18R, LOC BC Rwy 7, TACAN Rwy 4, NDB Rwy 21, VOR Rwy 15, VOR/DME Rwy 6, or ILS or TACAN Rwy 9). A solidus (/) indicates that more than one type of equipment must be used to execute final approach (VOR/DME). When two approaches are on the same chart, the word "or" indicates that either type of equipment may be used to execute the final approach (for example, ILS or TACAN, ILS or NDB, or VOR/DME or TACAN). When the same final approach guidance is used to the same runway, procedures are identified as follows: TACAN 1 Rwy 36, TACAN 2 Rwy 36, VOR 1 Rwy 18, and VOR 2 Rwy 18. Carefully examine all procedures to determine if the aviator is capable of flying the entire procedure. In some instances, Army aircraft may not be equipped to execute missed approach segments that are designated to/from a NAVAID such as TACAN.

Circling Approach

10-13.   When a procedure does not meet criteria for straight-in landing minimums authorization, identification is by the type of NAVAID that provides final approach guidance and an alphabetical suffix. The first procedure formulated bears the suffix A although there may be no intention to formulate additional procedures. If additional procedures are formulated, they are identified alphabetically in sequence (VOR-A, VOR/DME-B, NDB-C, and localizer-type directional aid [LDA]–D). A revised procedure bears its original identification.

Helicopter Procedures

10-14.   Helicopter-only procedures bear an identification that includes the term copter, type of facility providing final approach course guidance, and a final approach course numerical identification (such as COPTER VOR 090, COPTER NDB 270, COPTER PAR 327, and COPTER ASR 327). If the procedure includes an arc final approach, the word ARC is used and followed by a sequential number (COPTER VORTAC ARC 1, COPTER VOR/DME ARC 2, and COPTER TACAN ARC 3).

STANDARD TERMINAL ARRIVALS

10-15.   A single booklet contains all STARs. The publication cycle is every eight weeks.

CIVIL PUBLICATIONS

AERONAUTICAL INFORMATION MANUAL

10-16.   The AIM provides the aviation community with basic flight information and ATC procedures used in the U.S. NAS. An international version, called the Aeronautical Information Publication, contains parallel information, as well as specific information on international airports used by the international community. The AIM is available online at http://www.faa.gov/airports_airtraffic/air_traffic/publications/atpubs/aim/.

AIRPORT/FACILITY DIRECTORY

10-17.   The A/FD contains information on airports, communications, and NAVAIDs pertinent to IFR flight. The A/FD also includes VOR receiver checkpoints, AFSS, weather service telephone numbers, and ARTCC frequencies. Various special notices essential to IFR flight are also included, such as land and hold short operations (LAHSO) data, civil use of military fields, continuous power facilities, and special flight procedures.

10-18.   In major terminal and en route environments, preferred routes have been established to guide aviators in planning their routes of flight, minimizing route changes, and aiding in the orderly management of air traffic using Federal airways. The A/FD lists high- and low-altitude preferred routes.

NOTICES TO AIRMEN PUBLICATION

10-19.   The Notices to Airmen Publication (NTAP) contains current NOTAMs that are essential to flight safety as well as supplemental data affecting other operational publications listed. The NTAP also includes current flight data center (FDC) NOTAMs, which are regulatory in nature, issued to establish restrictions to flight or amend charts or published IAPs.

INSTRUMENT PROCEDURES HANDBOOK

10-20.   The Instrument Procedures Handbook (IPH) is a technical reference for aviators who are conducting IFR operations in the NAS. Instrument flight examiners (IFEs), instructor pilots (IPs), and all Army aviators will find this handbook a valuable training aid that details coverage of instrument charts and procedures including IFR takeoff, departure, en route, arrival, approach, and landing. The IPH is available at http://www.faa.gov/library/manuals/aviation/instrument_procedures_handbook. The IPH introduces advanced information for IFR operations and expands on information contained in FAA H-8083-15 and is available at http://www.faa.gov/library/manuals/aviation/instrument_flying_handbook/.

10-21.   Safety information covering relevant subjects—such as runway incursion, LAHSO, controlled flight into terrain (CFIT), and human factors issues—are also included. Emphasis applies to airplane operations. Guidelines specific to helicopter IFR operations are included in Appendix C. Persons using this handbook must also become familiar with and apply the pertinent parts of the AIM.

AERONAUTICAL CHART USER GUIDE

10-22.   For reference purposes, the Aeronautical Chart User's Guide is now available in Adobe Acrobat format for download at http://www.naco.faa.gov/index.asp?xml=naco/online/aero_guide. The guide is divided into six sections and covers the charts listed in Figure 10-1.

- World aeronautical charts
- IAPs
- Sectional aeronautical charts
- Flyway planning charts
- STARs
- En route low-altitude charts
- En route high-altitude charts
- Area charts
- Oceanic route charts
- Helicopter route charts
- SIDs
- Terminal area charts

Figure 10-1. Types of aeronautical charts

SECTION II – INSTRUMENT FLIGHT RULES FLIGHT PLAN

FILING

PRIOR TO FLIGHT

10-23.   As specified in 14 CFR, part 91, no person may operate an aircraft in controlled airspace IFR unless that person has filed an IFR flight plan. IFR flight plans are filed and IFR flights are conducted according to AR 95-1 and AR 95-2. Flight plans may be submitted to military flight operations in person or to the nearest AFSS or ATCT either in person or by telephone or computer (using the direct user access terminal system [DUATS] at http://www.duats.com/), or by radio if no other means are available. Aviators should file IFR flight plans at least 30 minutes before estimated time of departure to preclude possible delay in receiving a departure clearance from ATC. Chapter 4 provides guidance for completing and filing DD Form 175 (Military Flight Plan) (Figure 10-2) and DD Form 1801 (DOD International Flight Plan) (Figure 10-3, page 10-6). The GP authorizes use of FAA Form 7233-1 (Flight Plan) in lieu of DD Form 175 and of FAA Form 7233-4 (International Flight Plan) in lieu of DD Form 1801 when the aircraft is departing U.S. installations that do not have a military base operations facility. Find DD Form 175 and DD Form 1801 at http://www.dtic.mil/whs/directives/infomgt/forms/formsprogram.htm. The GP provides a blank copy of FAA Form 7233-1 and FAA Form 7233-4 but not specific guidance on completing the form. The AIM provides guidance for completing and filing FAA Form 7233-1 (Figure 10-4, page 10-7); it is available at FSSs and is generally found in flight planning rooms at airport terminal buildings. An electronic version of FAA Form 7233-1 is located at http://forms.faa.gov/forms/faa7233-1.pdf . Specific guidance on completing FAA Form 7233-4 is found at http://www.faa.gov/ats/aat/ifim/ifim0107.htm under flight planning notes, and the blank form is found at http://forms.faa.gov/forms/faa7233-4.pdf.

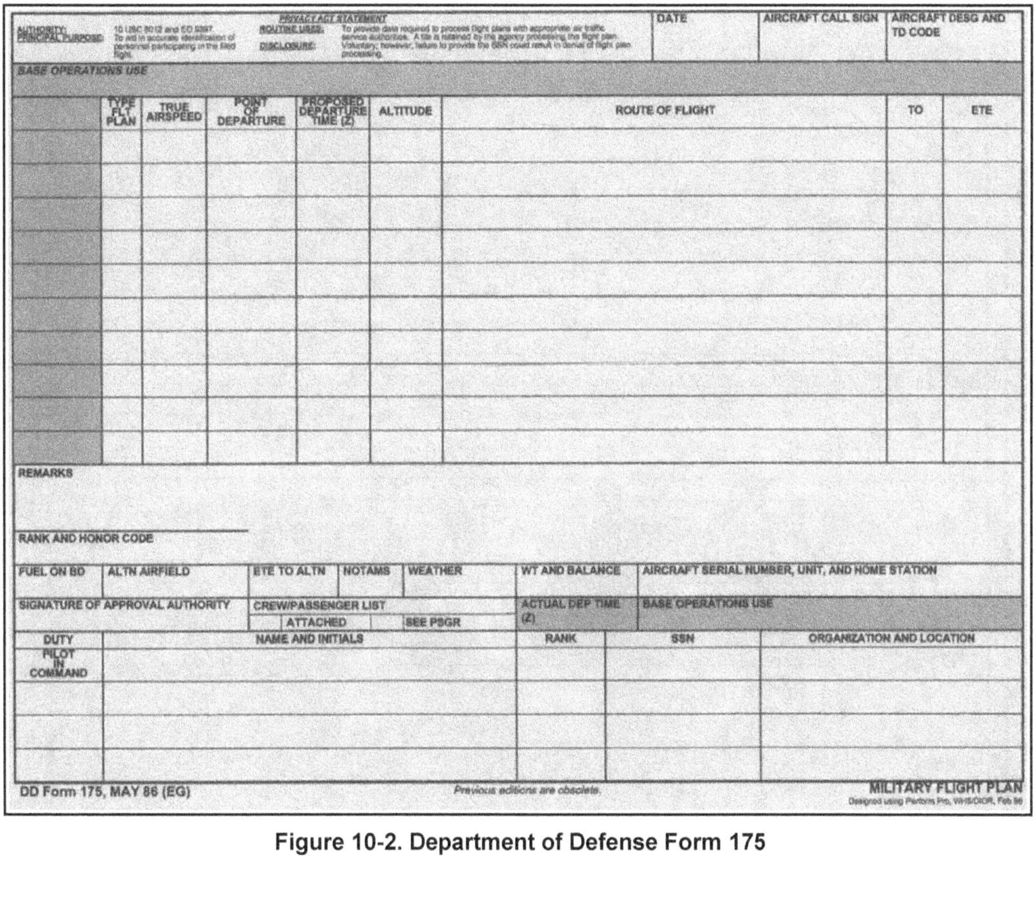
PRIVACY ACT STATEMENT
AUTHORITY: 10 USC 8012 and EO 9397.
PRINCIPAL PURPOSE: To aid in accurate identification of personnel participating in the filed flight.
ROUTINE USES: To provide data required to process flight plans with appropriate air traffic service authorities. A file is retained by the agency processing the flight plan.
DISCLOSURE: Voluntary; however, failure to provide the SSN could result in denial of flight plan processing.
DATE | AIRCRAFT CALL SIGN | AIRCRAFT DESG AND TD CODE
BASE OPERATIONS USE

	TYPE FLT PLAN	TRUE AIRSPEED	POINT OF DEPARTURE	PROPOSED DEPARTURE TIME (Z)	ALTITUDE	ROUTE OF FLIGHT	TO	ETE

REMARKS
RANK AND HONOR CODE
FUEL ON BD | ALTN AIRFIELD | ETE TO ALTN | NOTAMS | WEATHER | WT AND BALANCE | AIRCRAFT SERIAL NUMBER, UNIT, AND HOME STATION
SIGNATURE OF APPROVAL AUTHORITY | CREW/PASSENGER LIST: ATTACHED / SEE PBGR | ACTUAL DEP TIME (Z) | BASE OPERATIONS USE

DUTY	NAME AND INITIALS	RANK	SSN	ORGANIZATION AND LOCATION
PILOT IN COMMAND				

DD Form 175, MAY 86 (EG) — Previous editions are obsolete. — MILITARY FLIGHT PLAN

Figure 10-2. Department of Defense Form 175

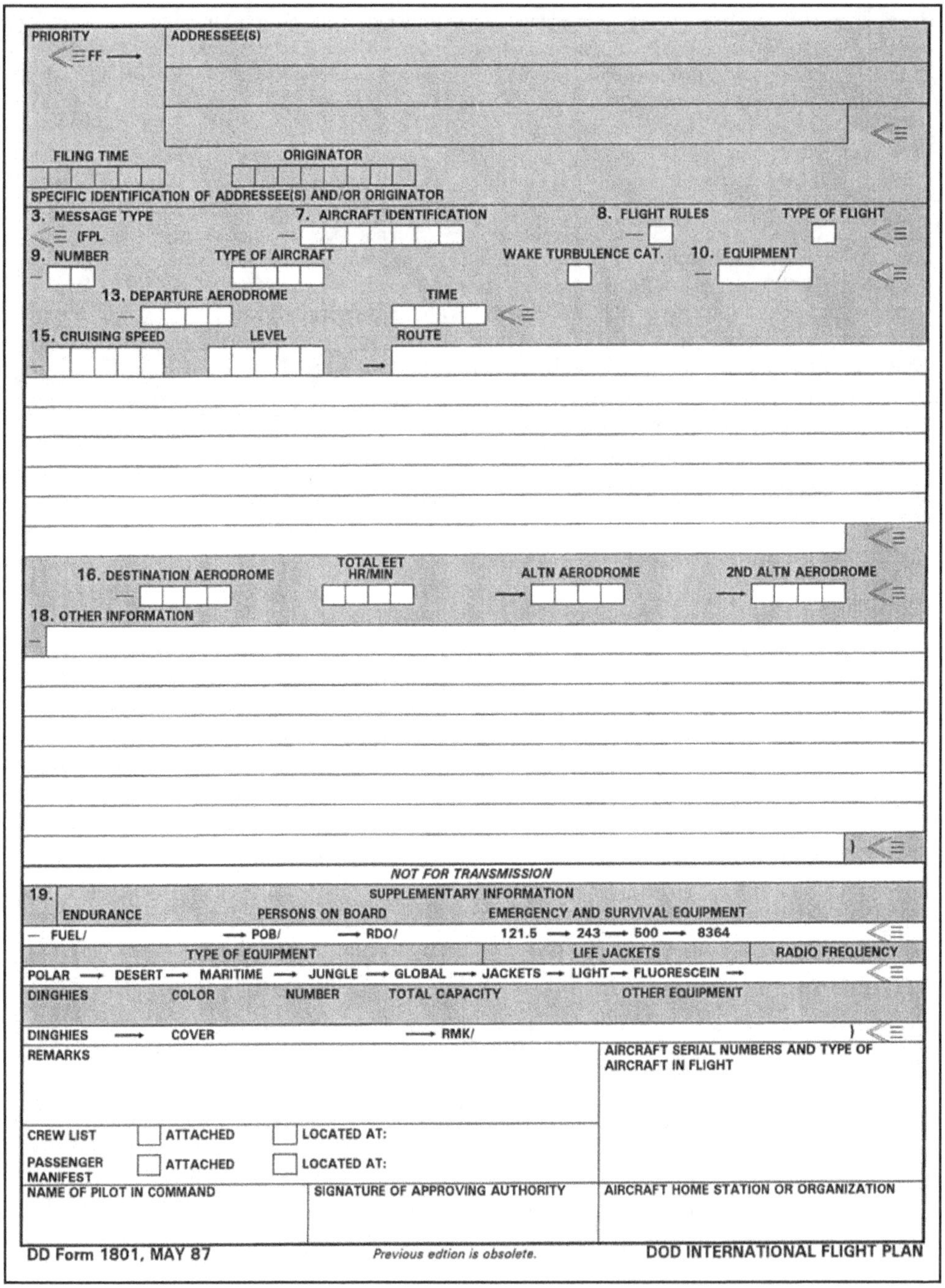

PRIORITY	ADDRESSEE(S)				
≡FF →					

FILING TIME   ORIGINATOR

SPECIFIC IDENTIFICATION OF ADDRESSEE(S) AND/OR ORIGINATOR

3. MESSAGE TYPE	7. AIRCRAFT IDENTIFICATION	8. FLIGHT RULES	TYPE OF FLIGHT
≡ (FPL	—	—	
9. NUMBER	TYPE OF AIRCRAFT	WAKE TURBULENCE CAT.	10. EQUIPMENT
—			— /

13. DEPARTURE AERODROME   TIME

— ≡

15. CRUISING SPEED   LEVEL   ROUTE

—   →

16. DESTINATION AERODROME	TOTAL EET HR/MIN	ALTN AERODROME	2ND ALTN AERODROME
—		→	→

18. OTHER INFORMATION

—

) ≡

NOT FOR TRANSMISSION

19.   SUPPLEMENTARY INFORMATION

ENDURANCE	PERSONS ON BOARD	EMERGENCY AND SURVIVAL EQUIPMENT
— FUEL/	→ POB/ → RDO/	121.5 → 243 → 500 → 8364 ≡

TYPE OF EQUIPMENT	LIFE JACKETS	RADIO FREQUENCY
POLAR → DESERT→ MARITIME → JUNGLE → GLOBAL →	JACKETS → LIGHT→ FLUORESCEIN →	≡
DINGHIES COLOR NUMBER TOTAL CAPACITY	OTHER EQUIPMENT	

DINGHIES   →   COVER   → RMK/   ) ≡

REMARKS	AIRCRAFT SERIAL NUMBERS AND TYPE OF AIRCRAFT IN FLIGHT
CREW LIST ☐ ATTACHED ☐ LOCATED AT:	
PASSENGER MANIFEST ☐ ATTACHED ☐ LOCATED AT:	

NAME OF PILOT IN COMMAND	SIGNATURE OF APPROVING AUTHORITY	AIRCRAFT HOME STATION OR ORGANIZATION

DD Form 1801, MAY 87   *Previous edtion is obsolete.*   DOD INTERNATIONAL FLIGHT PLAN

Figure 10-3. Department of Defense Form 1801

Form Approved   OMB NO. 2120-0026

U.S. DEPARTMENT OF TRANSPORTATION FEDERAL AVIATION ADMINISTRATION	(FAA USE ONLY) ☐ PILOT ☐ VNR	TIME STARTED	SPECIALIST INITIALS
FLIGHT PLAN	☐ STOPOVER		

1. TYPE	2. AIRCRAFT IDENTIFICATION	3. AIRCRAFT TYPE/ SPECIAL EQUIPMENT	4. TRUE AIRSPEED	5. DEPARTURE POINT	6. DEPARTURE TIME		7. CRUISING ALTITUDE
VFR					PROPOSED (Z)	ACTUAL (Z)	
IFR							
DVFR			KTS				

8. ROUTE OF FLIGHT

9. DESTINATION (Name of airport and city)	10. EST. TIME ENROUTE		11. REMARKS
	HOURS	MINUTES	

12. FUEL ON BOARD		13. ALTERNATE AIRPORT(S)	14. PILOT'S NAME, ADDRESS & TELEPHONE NUMBER & AIRCRAFT HOME BASE	15. NUMBER ABOARD
HOURS	MINUTES			
			17. DESTINATION CONTACT/TELEPHONE (OPTIONAL)	

16. COLOR OF AIRCRAFT	CIVIL AIRCRAFT PILOTS. FAR Part 91 requires you file an IFR flight plan to operate under instrument flight rules in controlled airspace. Failure to file could result in a civil penalty not to exceed $1,000 for each violation (Section 901 of the Federal Aviation Act of 1958, as amended). Filing of a VFR flight plan is recommended as a good operating practice. See also Part 99 for requirements concerning DVFR flight plans.

FAA Form 7233-1 (8-82)   CLOSE VFR FLIGHT PLAN WITH _____ FSS ON ARRIVAL

MILITARY STOPOVER (FAA USE ONLY)

TYPE ☐ IFR ☐ VFR	AIRCRAFT IDENTIFICATION	AIRCRAFT TYPE/SPECIAL EQUIPMENT	REMARKS
DEPARTURE POINT	DESTINATION	ETA	

TAS	DEP. PT	ETD	ALTITUDE	ROUTE OF FLIGHT	DESTINATION	ETE	REMARKS
KTS							
KTS							
KTS							
KTS							
REMARKS							INITIALS

FAA Form 7233-1 (8-82)

Figure 10-4. Federal Aviation Administration Form 7233-1

10-24.   Aviators must advise base operations or the tie-in FSS serving the departure, stopover, or en route delay aerodrome when actual departure time will be delayed one hour or more beyond the filed proposed departure time and provide an updated proposed departure time. When departing nonmilitary fields, the aviator must ensure that the actual departure time is passed to the tie-in FSS servicing the departure field. The aviator can request this change through the tower or directly to the tie-in FSS. If takeoff time is not passed to the tie-in FSS, the aircraft will arrive unannounced at the next destination.

IN FLIGHT

10-25.   IFR flight plans may be filed from the air under various conditions including the following:
- A flight outside of controlled airspace before the aircraft proceeds into IFR conditions in controlled airspace.
- A VFR flight with IFR weather conditions expected en route in controlled airspace.

10-26.   In either situation, the flight plan may be filed with the nearest AFSS or directly with the ARTCC. An aviator who files with the AFSS submits the information normally entered during preflight filing, except for point of departure, together with present position and altitude. The items required for an in-flight plan are located on the inside back cover of the DOD FLIP IFR-Supplement. AFSS relays this information to the ARTCC. The ARTCC then clears the aviator from present position or a specified navigation fix.

10-27.   An aviator filing direct with the ARTCC reports present position and altitude and submits only the flight-plan information normally relayed from the AFSS to the ARTCC. Traffic saturation frequently prevents ARTCC personnel from accepting flight plans by radio. In such cases, the aviator is advised to contact the nearest AFSS to file the flight plan.

CANCELING

10-28.   An IFR flight plan may be canceled at any time when the aircraft is operating in VFR conditions outside Class A airspace by stating "cancel my IFR flight plan" to the controller or air-to-ground station with which communicating. After canceling the IFR flight plan, change to the appropriate air-to-ground frequency and transponder code as directed and VFR altitude/flight level.

10-29.   ATC separation and information services (including radar services, where applicable) are discontinued. If an aviator desires VFR radar advisory service, he must specifically request it. Other procedures may apply if the IFR flight plan is canceled within areas such as Class B or Class C airspace.

10-30.   If an aviator is operating on an IFR flight plan to an airport with an operating control tower, the flight plan is canceled automatically upon landing. If operating on an IFR flight plan to an airport without an operating control tower, the aviator must cancel the flight plan. The aviator can cancel the flight plan after landing by telephone or by radio while airborne and able to communicate with ATC. If there is no FSS and air-to-ground communications with ATC are not possible below a certain altitude, the aviator can cancel the IFR flight plan while still airborne and able to communicate with ATC by radio. When following this procedure, be certain that the remainder of the flight can be conducted under VFR. The aviator should expeditiously cancel the IFR flight plan because this allows other IFR traffic to use the airspace.

SECTION III – CLEARANCES

10-31.   An ATC clearance allows an aircraft to proceed under specified traffic conditions within controlled airspace for the purpose of providing separation between known aircraft. A flight filed for a short distance at a relatively low altitude in an area of low traffic density might receive a clearance as in the following example.

Clearance Example 1

"Army 12345, cleared to Andalusia-Opp airport direct, cruise 5,000."

10-32. The term cruise in this clearance means that the aviator is authorized to fly at any altitude from the minimum IFR altitude up to and including 5,000 feet. He may level off at any altitude within this block of airspace. A climb or descent within the block may be made at the aviator's discretion. However, once the aviator has reported leaving an altitude within the block, the aircraft may not return to that altitude without further ATC clearance.

10-33. When ATC issues a cruise clearance with an unpublished route, an appropriate crossing altitude is specified to ensure terrain clearance until the aircraft reaches a fix, point, or route where altitude information is available. The crossing altitude ensures IFR obstruction clearance to the point at which the aircraft enters a segment of a published route or IAP. Once a flight plan is filed, ATC issues clearance with appropriate instructions as in the following clearing examples 2 and 3.

Clearance Example 2

"Army 12345 is cleared to Skyline airport via the Crossville 055 radial, Victor 18, maintain 5,000. Clearance void if not off by 1330."

Clearance Example 3

"Army 12345 is cleared to Wichita Mid-continent airport via Victor 77, left turn after takeoff; proceed direct to the Oklahoma City VORTAC. Hold west on the Oklahoma City 277 radial, climb to 5,000 in holding pattern before proceeding on course. Maintain 5,000 to CASHION intersection. Climb to and maintain 7,000. Departure control frequency will be 121.05. Squawk 0412."

10-34. Suppose that an aviator is awaiting departure clearance at a busy metropolitan terminal (the first IFR departure from this airport). On an average day, the tower at this airport controls departures at a rate of one every two minutes to maintain the required traffic flow. Clearance delivery may issue the abbreviated clearance given in clearing example 4, which includes a DP.

Clearance Example 4

"Army 12345, cleared to La Guardia as filed, RINGOES 8 departure Phillipsburg transition, maintain 8,000. Departure control frequency will be 120.4, Squawk 0700." This clearance may be readily copied in shorthand as follows: "CAF RNGO8 PSB M80 DPC 120.4 SQ 0700."

10-35. The information contained in this DP clearance is abbreviated using clearance shorthand found in the FAA Instrument Flying Handbook. An aviator should be aware of the locations of specified navigation facilities, together with the route and point-to-point time, before accepting the clearance. The DP enables the aviator to study and understand details of the departure before filing an IFR flight plan. The DP provides information necessary to set up communication and navigation equipment and the departure procedures required before requesting IFR clearance.

10-36. Once clearance is accepted, the aviator is required to comply with ATC instructions. He may request a clearance different from that issued if another course of action is more practical or aircraft equipment limitations or other considerations make acceptance of the clearance inadvisable. Aviators should also request clarification or amendment, as appropriate, whenever a clearance is not fully understood or considered unacceptable because of safety of flight. The aviator is responsible for requesting an amended clearance if ATC issues a clearance that would cause an aviator to deviate from a rule or regulation or place the aircraft in jeopardy.

SEPARATIONS

10-37. ATC may or may not be able to provide separation information. Table 10-1, page 10-10, shows ATC parameters regarding separation.

Table 10-1. Air traffic control separation parameters

Air Traffic Control	
Provides an IFR clearance w/separation	*Does not provide clearance for aircraft operating*
• Vertically by assignment of different altitudes. • Longitudinally by controlling time separation between aircraft on the same course. • Laterally by assignment of different flight paths. • By radar including all of the above.	• Outside of controlled airspace. • With VFR-On-Top authorized instead of a specific assigned altitude. • During climb or descent in VFR conditions. • In VFR conditions, because uncontrolled VFR flights may be operating in the same airspace.

10-38.   In addition to heading and altitude assignments, ATC occasionally issues speed adjustments to maintain required separations. Example 1 shows an ATC-issued separation adjustment that involves slowing the aircraft speed.

Separation Example 1
"Army 12345, slow to 100 knots."

10-39.   Aviators who receive speed adjustments are expected to maintain that speed, ±10 knots. If for any reason the aviator is not able to accept a speed restriction, the aviator should advise ATC. ATC may also employ visual separation techniques to keep aircraft safely separated. An aviator obtaining visual contact with another aircraft may be asked to maintain visual separation or to follow the aircraft. A second separation adjustment is given in the following example.

Separation Example 2
"Army 12345, maintain visual separation with that traffic, climb and maintain 7,000."

10-40.   Acceptance of these instructions is an acknowledgment that the aviator will maneuver the aircraft, as necessary, to maintain safe separation. The aviator also acknowledges responsibility for wake turbulence avoidance by accepting these instructions.

10-41.   In the absence of radar contact, ATC relies on position reports to assist in maintaining proper separation. Using data transmitted by the aviator, the controller follows flight progress. ATC must correlate the reports with all others to provide separation; therefore, accuracy of reports can affect the progress and safety of every other aircraft operating in the area on an IFR flight plan.

VISUAL FLIGHT RULES-ON-TOP

10-42.   Aviators on IFR flight plans operating in VFR weather conditions may request VFR-On-Top in lieu of an assigned altitude. VFR-On-Top is an IFR clearance allowing aviators to fly VFR altitudes, which permits them to select an altitude or flight level of their choice (subject to any ATC restrictions).

10-43.   By requesting a climb to VFR-On-Top, aviators can climb through a cloud, haze, smoke, or other meteorological formation and then either cancel their IFR flight plan or operate VFR-On-Top. The ATC authorization will contain either a top report (or a statement that no top report is available), and a request to report upon reaching VFR-On-Top. In addition, the ATC authorization may contain a clearance limit, routing, and an alternative clearance if VFR-On-Top is not reached by a specified altitude.

10-44.   An aviator on an IFR flight plan, operating in VFR conditions, may request to climb/descend in VFR conditions. When operating in VFR conditions with an ATC authorization to maintain VFR-On-Top/maintain VFR conditions, aviators on IFR flight plans must do the following:

- Fly at the appropriate VFR altitude as prescribed in part 91.
- Comply with VFR visibility and distance-from-cloud criteria in part 91.
- Comply with IFRs applicable to this flight (minimum IFR altitudes, position reporting, radio communications, course to be flown, and adherence to ATC clearance).

10-45. Aviators operating on a VFR-On-Top clearance should advise ATC before any altitude change to ensure exchange of accurate traffic information. ATC authorization to maintain VFR-On-Top is not intended to restrict aviators to operating only above an obscuring meteorological formation (layer). The clearance also permits operation above, below, or between layers or in areas where there is no meteorological obscuration. Aviators must understand that clearance to operate VFR-On-Top/VFR conditions does not imply cancellation of the IFR flight plan.

10-46. Aviators operating VFR-On-Top/VFR conditions may receive traffic information from ATC on other pertinent IFR or VFR aircraft. However, when operating in VFR weather conditions, aviators are responsible for remaining vigilant to see and avoid other aircraft. This clearance must be requested by the aviator on an IFR flight plan. VFR-On-Top is not permitted in certain areas (such as Class A airspace); consequently, IFR flights operating VFR-On-Top must avoid such airspace.

VISUAL FLIGHT RULES OVER-THE-TOP

10-47. VFR Over-The-Top is strictly a VFR operation in which the aviator maintains VFR cloud clearance requirements while operating on top of an undercast layer. This situation might occur when the departure airport and destination airport are reporting clear conditions, but a low overcast layer is present in between. The aviator could conduct a VFR departure, fly over the top of the undercast in VFR conditions, then complete a VFR descent and landing at the destination. VFR cloud clearance requirements are maintained at all times, and an IFR clearance is not required for any part of the flight.

SECTION IV – NOTICE TO AIRMEN SYSTEM

10-48. Check applicable NOTAMs for each flight. Flight operations depend on thorough preflight planning. For flight planning purposes, NOTAM information is available from the United States NOTAM System (USNS) via the DOD Internet NOTAM Distribution System (DINS).

10-49. The DINS is composed of a large central data management system deriving information from the U.S. Consolidated NOTAM Office at the FAA Air Traffic Control Command Center located at Herndon, VA. Real-time NOTAM information is maintained and made available through the internet. Coverage includes all military airfields and virtually all domestic, international, and FDC NOTAMs. If not covered by DINS, the airfield does not transmit NOTAM data to the USNS. A plain language notice in red font is displayed advising the user of that fact. In such a case, contact the desired location directly for NOTAM information.

NOTICE TO AIRMEN

10-50. NOTAM is defined in the GP as a notice containing information (not known sufficiently in advance to publicize by other means) concerning the establishment, condition, or change in any component (facility, service, procedures, or hazards in the NAS) of which timely knowledge is essential to personnel concerned with flight operations. NOTAM abbreviations are explained in the FIH and NTAP.

NOTICES TO AIRMEN TYPES

MILITARY FLIGHT SAFETY

10-51. These NOTAMs contain flight safety related information about individual military aerodromes. This information includes runway closures, NAVAID outages, frequency changes, and runway lighting.

FLIGHT DATA CENTER

10-52.   FDC NOTAMs are regulatory documents containing important information such as amendments to published approaches, chart changes, and TFRs. FDC NOTAMs are broken down into the categories of general FDC NOTAMs; ARTCC FDC NOTAMs; airport, facility, and procedural FDC NOTAMs; and special notices.

General Flight Data Center

10-53.   General FDC NOTAMs apply to all aircraft—regardless of departure, destination, or flight route. The general FDC NOTAMs contain information including, but not limited to, changes to U.S. Government FLIPs, hostile airspace advisories, special FAA regulations, changes to SOPs in U.S. airspace, and any other general information that might affect flight operations.

Air Route Traffic Control Center Flight Data Center

10-54.   Applying only to aircraft flying through the associated ARTCC, these FDC NOTAMs are identified by the three-letter center identifier beginning with a Z (ZHU – Houston Center). ARTCC FDC NOTAMs may include, but are not limited to, changes to published minimum altitudes and routings, in-flight hazards and advisories, special-use airspace activity, and airspace changes/restrictions.

Airports, Facilities, and Procedural Flight Data Center

10-55.   These NOTAMs cover civilian and some joint-use fields. They include, but are not limited to, changes to local procedures, changes/revisions/amendments to published instrument approach and departure procedures, and changes/revisions to minimum altitudes.

Special Notices

10-56.   These NOTAMs are FDC NOTAMs. They normally specify special FAA regulations dealing with current events and issues of national security.

ATTENTION NOTICES

10-57.   Attention notices (general notices) are broken into groups (table 10-2). Table 10-2 shows the abbreviations for these groups.

Table 10-2. Attention notice groups

Group	Abbreviation
All	ATTA
North America	ATTN
Caribbean & South America	ATTC

CIVILIAN "D" (DISTANT) SERIES

10-58.   D-Series NOTAMs contain information about individual civilian aerodromes. These include runway closures and lighting, NAVAID outages, and frequency changes.

CIVILIAN "L" (LOCAL) SERIES

10-59.   Equivalent to a military airfield advisory, L-Series NOTAMs contain information that is not widely disseminated and will not prevent use of an airfield's runways. The information may, however, affect the use of other parts of an airfield. Contact the local FSS governing the field to find these NOTAMs.

NOTICES TO AIRMEN PUBLICATION

10-60.   NTAP is available on the Internet at http://www.faa.gov/NTAP/INDEX.HTM. If Internet access is not available, ask base operations personnel for the hard copy. This book consists of four parts:

- Part 1 contains FDC NOTAMs and NOTAMs that meet the criteria of D NOTAMs and are expected to remain in effect for an extended time.
- Part 2 contains revisions to minimum en route IFR altitudes and COPs as well as other information regarding a wide geographic area or not suited for Part 1.
- Part 3 contains significant international NOTAMs including foreign notices, Department of State advisories, and overland/oceanic airspace notices.
- Part 4 contains graphical notices of items that will affect flight operations in the following areas: General Information, Special Military Operations, Major Sporting and Entertainment Events, Northeast United States, Southeast United States, East Central United States, South Central United States, Southwest United States, Northwest United States, Alaska/Hawaii, and Special Airshow Section.

GLOBAL POSITIONING SYSTEM

10-61.   The aviator accesses GPS NOTAMs through the DINS Web page by entering the four-letter identifier KGPS. When entered, this identifier yields individual satellite information useful for updating FMS database information. GPS NOTAM information regarding GPS approach availability is obtained by entering the four-letter ICAO airfield identifier on the NOTAM home page. GPS NOTAMs must be retrieved for all flights using GPS.

INTERNET DISTRIBUTION SYSTEM

10-62.   DINS (https://www.notams.jcs.mil or backup https://www.notams.faa.gov) is the current method for aircrews to obtain real-time NOTAM data validated by the USNS, which includes domestic, international, military, and FDC NOTAMs. DINS is frequently changed to improve content and format of information provided. The information is broken down into multiple pages including the Home Page/United States NOTAM Office, FDC NOTAMs, TFRs, Special Notices, ARTCC NOTAMs, Radius/Flight Path Search, North Atlantic and Pacific Track Systems, reduced vertical separation minimums (RVSM), European Theater, FM Immunity, and ICAO Search/Listing. DINS provides a plain-language notice, highlighted in red, when a requested location is not in the U.S. NOTAM System. If the requested location is not covered, NOTAM information is not transmitted for the USNS. Contact the requested location to receive NOTAM information.

HOME PAGE/UNITED STATES OFFICE PAGE

10-63.   Check for NOTAMs by inputting the four-letter ICAO airfield identifiers in the space provided for Flight Safety & Local NOTAMs. The user can enter up to 10 ICAO identifiers at any one time. Flight information region (FIR) identifiers, MOA names, special-use airspace identifiers, and ARTCC identifiers (to check their NOTAMs as well as KFDC and KGPS to check FDC and GPS NOTAMs respectively) may be entered. GPS NOTAMs must be retrieved before flights using GPS. Click the "View NOTAMs" button to view current NOTAMs for the selections. NOTAMs are displayed in plain-language text with the tracking number unless raw format is selected. When raw format is selected, NOTAMs are presented in the international, machine-readable, ICAO code format with multiple report fields, NOTAM series, and NOTAM tracking numbers displayed.

FLIGHT DATA CENTER PAGE

10-64.   The "FDC TFR, Special Notices and ARTCC" page offers the flexibility to extract TFRs from the FDC NOTAMs and various ARTCC area NOTAMs. Click on the "TFR Only" button, and then select the ARTCCs of interest.

> *Note.* For those interested in all ARTCC TFRs, click on the All ARTCC TFRs button. Use the optional "ARTCC Special Notices" checkbox to add "FDC Special Notices" with the TFR request.

RADIUS/FLIGHT PATH SEARCH

10-65.   The radius search page allows the user to input an ICAO identifier or latitude/longitude and receive NOTAMs within a specified radius of that location. The NOTAMs listed include surrounding airports and NAVAIDs, ARTCCs, universal information regions (UIRs), and FIRs. The flight-path search page allows the user to input ICAO identifiers for departure and arrival fields as well as several en route locations. The user can select to receive any of the NOTAMS specified above within a specified nautical mile buffer in addition to FDC NOTAMs. Special-use airspace NOTAMs are also available with the radius and flight-path search pages.

> *Note.* Local NOTAMs are not displayed on these pages. Check for local NOTAMs from the DINS home page for military airfields or the local FSS for civilian fields.

TRACK SYSTEMS

10-66.   This section provides aircrews with daily message traffic regarding the North Atlantic Track System (NATS) and Pacific tracks. Other parts of the organized track system will be added in the future.

REDUCED VERTICAL SEPARATION MINIMUMS

10-67.   RVSM NOTAMs are broken out by FIR and the controlling ATC center. They are displayed alphabetically by their ICAO identifier. Aircrews are encouraged to frequently check the FAA RVSM Web site at http://www.faa.gov/ats/ato/rvsm1.htm for updates.

> *Note.* There could be as many as 90 active RVSM notices, and it may take about 15 to 20 seconds to retrieve the data.

EUROPEAN THEATER

10-68.   This page provides data from the U.S. Army Flight Operations Detachment Europe (AFOD) and contains NOTAMs on airfields, airspace, navigation/communications, special notices, and updates throughout the European theater. This page also covers FM immunity information for Europe, Africa, and Middle East AOs as well as Bird Activity NOTAMs (BIRDTAMS) issued by the German Military Geophysical Office.

European Central Airspace Reservation Facility Page

10-69.   NOTAMs concerning operations and airspace controlled by the European Central Airspace Reservation Facility (EUCARF) can be obtained through this page. Information includes airspace, refueling tracks, and altitude reservations (ALTRVs) currently reserved through EUCARF.

Frequency Modulation Immunity

10-70.   Covering Europe, Africa, and Middle East AOs, this page provides a consolidated listing of FM immunity NOTAM and country guidance applicable to DOD FLIP. Information is depicted by DOD FLIP documents and followed by individual country limitations, guidance, and NOTAMS. Listed countries require FM-immune receivers unless otherwise noted. Countries not listing any information are assumed to have implemented ICAO Annex 10 requirements for FM immunity.

INTERNATIONAL CIVIL AVIATION ORGANIZATION SEARCH/LISTING PAGES

10-71. Use this site to search the DINS database for an ICAO airport and country by inputting the ICAO identifier. The Listing Page provides a geographic listing of all sites covered by DINS, allowing the user to find the four-letter identifier of the desired airfield by selecting the country (and state in the continental United States [CONUS]) to determine if an airfield is covered by DINS and the USNS. Special-use airspace identifiers are listed at the bottom of each state listing on the Listing Page.

THE FEDERAL ADMINISTRATION AGENCY DISTRIBUTION SYSTEM

10-72. Unlike DINS, which allows aviators to check their own NOTAMs, the FAA NOTAM Distribution System is based on a verbal briefing system. To obtain a verbal briefing, contact a FSS by calling 1-800-WX-BRIEF. The FSS briefer will provide the NOTAM D information for any field requested. NOTAM L information must be requested from the servicing FSS or directly from the airfield. Flight Service Stations maintain a file of FDC NOTAMs affecting conditions within 400 miles of their facility. FDC information concerning conditions more than 400 miles away from the FSS or information that is already published in the NTAP is given only on request. The FSS briefer assumes that the aviator has looked at the appropriate sections of the Notices to Airman Publication. They will not brief the information contained in the NTAP unless specifically requested.

WEB PAGE LIMITATIONS

10-73. The DINS web page, while updating on a real-time basis, does not autorefresh information. This means that while the page is current up-to-the-minute when the aviator originally accesses it, no further updates are received unless the page is refreshed by clicking VIEW—REFRESH or by reentering the selected ICAO identifiers and clicking on "view notices." New NOTAMs will contain a tracking number and should be sorted in increasing numerical order (oldest to newest). Use caution because various numbering formats are used depending on the type of NOTAM displayed. The newest NOTAMs may not necessarily be at the bottom of the complete list of NOTAMs for a particular ICAO location. Recheck the NOTAM Web site before all flights to ensure receipt of the latest NOTAMs.

SECTION V – NAVIGATION OPTIONS IN THE NATIONAL AIRSPACE SYSTEM

10-74. The two methods of navigating in the NAS are on airways and off airways. Specific procedures for filing are found in FLIP General Planning unless noted otherwise.

ON AIRWAYS

10-75. The two fixed route systems established for air navigation purposes are the VOR and low/medium frequency (L/MF) system and the jet route system. To the extent possible, these route systems are aligned in an overlying manner to facilitate transition between each. Unless otherwise authorized by ATC, aviators are required to adhere to the centerline of airways or routes being flown. Special attention must be given to this requirement during course changes. Turns that begin at or after fix passage may exceed airway or route boundaries. Thus, the FAA expects aviators to lead turns and take other actions considered necessary during course changes to adhere as closely as possible to the airways or route being flown. Aviators should attempt to adhere to course centerline whenever possible.

10-76. The VOR and L/MF airway system consists of airways designated from 1,200 feet above the surface (in some instances, higher) up to, but not including, 18,000 feet MSL. These airways are depicted on en route low-altitude charts:

- Except in Alaska and coastal North Carolina, VOR airways are based solely on VOR or VORTAC NAVAIDs and are identified by a "V" (Victor) followed by the airway number

(V12); segments of VOR airways in Alaska and North Carolina (V290) are based on L/MF NAVAIDs and charted in brown, instead of black, on en route charts. To make the transition from one airway to another at an unnamed intersection, enter the designations of the two airways, separated by a space (YKM V4 V187 TCM).

- The L/MF airways (colored airways) are based solely on L/MF NAVAIDs, depicted in brown on aeronautical charts, and identified by color name and number (Amber One). Green and red airways are plotted east and west. Amber and blue airways run north and south. Except for G13 in North Carolina, the colored airway system exists only in Alaska.

10-77.   The Jet Route system consists of jet routes established in Class A airspace. These routes are depicted on en route high-altitude charts. On aeronautical charts, jet routes are depicted in black and are identified by a "J" (Jet), followed by the airway number (J12). Jet routes are based solely on VOR or VORTAC navigation facilities (except in Alaska). Segments of jet routes in Alaska are based on L/MF NAVAIDs and are charted in brown on en route charts.

AREA NAVIGATION ROUTES

10-78.   RNAV is a method of navigation permitting aircraft operations on any desired course within the coverage and capabilities of the aircraft onboard navigation equipment. Designated area navigation routes are permanently published and charted airway routes based on area navigation equipment. They are available to aircraft with RNAV capability.

REQUIRED EQUIPMENT

10-79.   FAA AC 90-45 outlines the RNAV equipment specifications for certification within the NAS. The major types of appropriate equipment are the following:

- VORTAC referenced or course line computer (CLC) systems.
- INS units.
- Microwave landing system (MLS)/RNAV equipment, which provides area navigation with reference to an MLS ground facility; aircraft must stay within range of the navigation station.
- GPS.

OFF AIRWAYS (DIRECT)

10-80.   Aviators can use several methods to fly off the airway system. This system is otherwise known as direct flight.

NAVIGATIONAL AID USE

10-81.   The absence of airway identifiers between fixes/NAVAIDs on a flight plan indicates direct flight. Aircraft may file along a direct course between NAVAIDs as long as the aircraft does not exceed the limitations of the NAVAIDs being used to define the course. For example, an "L" class VORTAC is only usable below 18,000 feet MSL and within 40 nautical miles of the station. NAVAID limitations can be found in the front of the FLIP IFR Supplement.

DEGREE-DISTANCE ROUTE DEFINITION

10-82.   Degree-distance route definition is a military-only privilege that allows certain aircraft to exceed the NAVAID limitations imposed by NAVAID-to-NAVAID filing restrictions. The specific procedures for filing and using degree-distance route definitions are published in FAA Order 7110.65. The use of degree-distance criteria is limited to aircraft performing specialized military missions.

RANDOM AREA NAVIGATION ROUTES

10-83. Random RNAV routes are direct routes flown between any two points, based on aircraft onboard RNAV capability, and defined in terms of latitude/longitude coordinates, degree-distance fixes, or offsets from established routes/airways at a specified distance and direction. Radar monitoring by ATC is required on all random RNAV routes within the National Airspace System. Factors that ATC will consider in approving random RNAV routes include the capability to provide radar monitoring and compatibility with traffic volume and flow. ATC will monitor each flight with radar; however, navigation on the random RNAV route is the responsibility of the aviator. Paragraph 10-79 describes acceptable RNAV equipment.

SECTION VI – DEPARTURES

DEPARTURE PROCEDURES

10-84. DPs are designed to expedite clearance delivery, facilitate transition between takeoff and en route operations, and ensure adequate obstacle clearance. DPs provide aviators with departure routing clearance information in both graphic and textual form. To simplify clearances, DPs are established for the most frequently used departure routes in areas of high traffic activity. A DP will normally be used where such departures are available because this is advantageous to both users and ATC (Figure 10-5, page 10-18).

10-85. DPs can be found after the charted approaches for a particular airport/airfield in DOD FLIP (Terminal) Low Altitude United States volumes. The aviator should remember the following points when filing IFR out of terminal areas where DPs are in use:

- Aviators operating IFR aircraft from locations where DP procedures are in effect may expect an ATC clearance containing a DP; the use of a DP requires aviator possession of at least the textual description of the approved DP.
- If an aviator does not possess a preprinted DP or, for any other reason, does not wish to use a DP, the aviator is expected to advise ATC; notification is accomplished by filing "NO DP" in the remarks section of the filed flight plan or by advising ATC.
- When accepting a DP in the clearance, the aviator must comply with the DP.

DIVERSE DEPARTURE

10-86. An aviator may have to file a flight plan from an airfield where diverse departures are not authorized. If so, he is required to fly the approved DP assigned by ATC.

10-87. When an instrument approach is initially developed for an airport, the procedure designer also does an assessment for departures. If an aircraft turns in any direction from a runway and is clear of obstacles, that runway meets diverse departure criteria and no DP is developed. At busier airports, there may be a need to develop DPs to increase efficiency and reduce communications and departure delays as opposed to obstacle avoidance.

10-88. If no IFR DP is published, climb runway heading to 400 feet above the departure end of runway elevation; turn in the shortest direction to the first filed point. This procedure keeps the aircraft clear of terrain and obstructions as long as the climb is at 200 FPNM, unless the aircraft is required to level off by a crossing restriction, until it reaches the minimum IFR altitude. The 40:1 OIS begins at the DER and slopes upward at 152 FPNM until the aircraft reaches the minimum IFR altitude or entering the en route structure.

03303

OPPTO-ONE DEPARTURE (VECTOR) (OPPTO1·OPPTO)

CAIRNS AAF (KOZR)
FORT RUCKER, ALABAMA

ATIS 111.2 316.15
CLNC DEL
118.075 380.1
GND CON
121.9 288.25
CAIRNS TOWER *
135.2 (CTAF) 248.55
DEP CON
133.45 239.4
JACKSONVILLE CENTER
120.2 346.4

SL-577 [USA]

MONTGOMERY
112.1 MGM
Chan 58

MONROEVILLE
116.8 MVC
Chan 115
Cross as assigned
L-18

280°
(46)

R-268

ANDAL
Cross as assigned

R-185

R-100

(15)

R-041

OPPTO
(23)
Cross as assigned

268°

HANCHEY AHP

CAIRNS
AAF

Aprx dist fr
tkof area

CAIRNS
111.2 OZR
Chan 49

221°
(37)

CRESTVIEW
115.9 CEW
Chan 106

L-18

DEPARTURE ROUTE DESCRIPTION

TAKE-OFF RWY 6: Turn left heading 270°....
TAKE-OFF RWY 18: Turn right heading 205°....
TAKE-OFF RWY 24: Turn right heading 300°....
TAKE-OFF RWY 36: Turn left to heading 270°....
TAKE-OFF PAD A: Fly heading 310°....
TAKE-OFF PAD D2: Fly heading 360°....
Maintain 2000, expect clearance to requested altitude/flight level ten (10) minutes after departure.
Expect Radar vector to intercept OZR R-268. Thence via _____ (transition).
ANDAL TRANSITION: (OPPTO1 • ANDAL) Proceed via OZR R-268 to ANDAL INT, cross ANDAL at _____ (as assigned).
CEW TRANSITION: (OPPTO1 • CEW) Proceed via OZR R-268 to OPPTO INT, thence via CEW R-041 to CEW. Cross CEW VOR at _____ (as assigned).
MVC TRANSITION: (OPPTO1 • MVC) Proceed via OZR R-268 to ANDAL INT, thence via MVC R-100 to MVC. Cross MVC VOR at _____ (as assigned).

OPPTO-ONE DEPARTURE (VECTOR) (OPPTO1 • OPPTO)

FORT RUCKER, ALABAMA
CAIRNS AAF (KOZR)

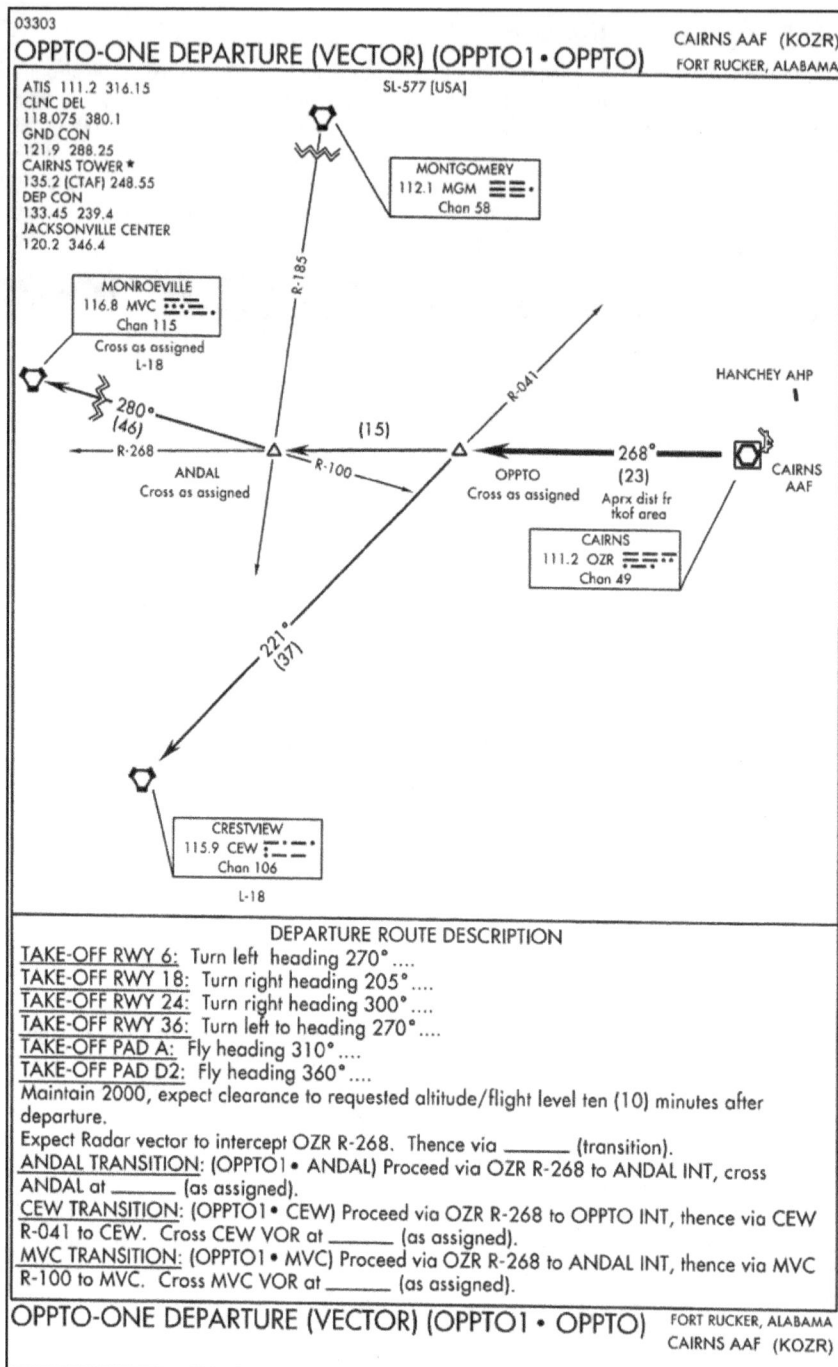

Figure 10-5. Departure procedure

10-89.   If diverse departures are not authorized, consider AIM information and make the following checks:

- Before departing an airport on an IFR flight, consider the type of terrain and other obstacles on or near the departure airport.
- Comply with nonstandard IFR minimums and DPs.
- Always follow the specific ATC departure instructions.

10-90.   Aviators must be aware that diverse departure criteria are based solely on an aircraft's ability to operate within the standard departure envelope for that specific category of aircraft and do not consider degraded climb capability because of equipment malfunction, terminal aid to navigation degradation, or special aircrew qualification requirements. The AIM indicates that obstacle clearance responsibility rests with the aviator when choosing to climb in visual conditions in lieu of flying a DP and/or depart under increased takeoff minima rather than fly the DP.

RADAR CONTROLLED DEPARTURE

10-91.   An aviator departing IFR from airports in congested areas normally receives navigational guidance from departure control by radar vector. When the departure is to be vectored immediately following takeoff, the aviator is advised before takeoff of the initial heading to be flown. This information is vital in the case two-way radio communications are lost during departure.

10-92.   Following takeoff, contact departure control on the assigned frequency when advised to do so by the control tower. At this time, departure control verifies radar contact and gives headings, altitude, and climb instructions to move the aircraft quickly and safely out of the terminal area. Fly the assigned headings and altitudes until the controller provides aircraft position with respect to the route given in the clearance, whom to contact next, and to "resume your own navigation." Departure control vectors the aircraft to either a navigation facility or an en route position appropriate to the departure clearance, or the flight is transferred to a controller with further radar surveillance capabilities.

10-93.   A radar-controlled departure does not relieve aviator responsibilities as PC. Be prepared before takeoff to conduct navigation according to ATC clearance with navigation receivers checked and properly tuned. While under radar control, monitor instruments to ensure continuous orientation to the route specified in the clearance and record the time over designated checkpoints.

DEPARTURE FROM AIRPORTS WITHOUT AN OPERATING CONTROL TOWER

10-94.   When departing from airports that have neither an operating tower nor an FSS, telephone the flight plan to the nearest ATC facility at least 30 minutes before the estimated departure time. If weather conditions permit, the aviator could depart VFR and request IFR clearance as soon as radio contact is established with ATC. If weather conditions make flying VFR undesirable, again telephone and request clearance. In this case, the controller issues a short-range clearance, pending establishment of radio contact, and might restrict the departure time to a certain period (for example, "Clearance void if not off by 0900"). This authorizes departure within the allotted period and authorization to proceed according to the clearance. In the absence of any specific departure instructions, the aviator is expected to proceed on course via the most direct route.

SECTION VII – EN ROUTE

PROCEDURES

10-95.   Procedures en route vary according to the proposed route, traffic environment, and ATC facilities controlling the flight. Some IFR flights are under radar surveillance and controlled from departure to arrival, while others rely entirely on aviator navigation. Where ATC has no jurisdiction, an IFR clearance will not be issued. ATC has no control over the flight nor does the aviator have any assurance of separation from other traffic.

POSITION REPORTS

10-96.   The aviator is required to furnish a position report over certain reporting points unless in radar contact with ATC. Position reports are required over each compulsory reporting point (shown on the chart as solid triangle figures ▲) along the route being flown, regardless of altitude, including those with a VFR-On-Top clearance. Along direct routes, IFR flight reports are required over each point used to define the route. Reports at reporting points (shown as open triangle figures △) are made only when requested by ATC. Position reports should include the following items (inside back cover of IFR supplement):

- Identification.
- Position.
- Time.
- Altitude/FL.
- Type of flight plan.
- Next reporting point and ETA.
- The name only of the next succeeding (required) reporting point along the flight route.
- Pertinent remarks.

10-97.   Submit en route position reports to ARTCC controllers via direct controller-to-pilot communications channels. Use appropriate ARTCC frequencies listed on the en route chart.

10-98.   Whenever an initial center contact is to be followed by a position report, the name of the reporting point is included in the communication. Including the reporting point alerts the controller that information is forthcoming (for example, "Cleveland Center, Army 12345 at HARWL intersection").

ADDITIONAL REPORTS

10-99.   The aviator will make the following reports to ATC or FSS facilities without a specific ATC request (found in the FIH):

- When departing a previously assigned altitude/flight level for a newly assigned altitude/flight level.
- When an altitude change will be made if operating on a clearance specifying "VFR-On-Top."
- When unable to climb/descend at a rate of at least 500 feet per minute.
- When the approach has been missed (request clearance for specific action—to alternate airport, another approach).
- When the change in the average TAS (at cruising altitude) varies by 5 percent or 10 knots (whichever is greater) from the filed flight plan.

Note. Aviators of aircraft involved in instrument training at military terminal area facilities may omit the reports in the next two bulleted sentences when radar services are provided.

- Upon reaching a holding fix or point to which cleared, report time and altitude or flight level.
- When leaving any assigned holding fix or point.
- After any loss of VOR, TACAN, ADF, LF navigation receiver capability in controlled airspace, complete or partial loss of ILS receiver capability, or impairment of air-to-ground communications capability; reports include aircraft identification, equipment affected, degree to which the capability to operate under IFR in the ATC system is impaired, and the nature and extent of assistance desired from ATC.

Note. Other equipment installed in an aircraft may effectively impair safety and/or the ability to operate IFR. If such equipment (airborne weather radar) malfunctions and if the aviator judges safety or IFR capabilities to be affected, reports are made as above.

- Any safety-of-flight information.

10-100. The following reports are required when the aviator is not in radar contact:

- When leaving FAF inbound on final approach (nonprecision approach) or when leaving the outer marker or fix used in lieu of the outer marker inbound on final approach (precision approach).
- Whenever it becomes apparent that a previously submitted estimate is in error by more than three minutes, the aviator submits a corrected estimate.

10-101. Aviators encountering unforecast weather conditions or forecast hazardous conditions are expected to forward a report of such weather to ATC. ICAO position reporting is found in the FIH, after the FAA position reporting requirements.

PLANNING DESCENT AND APPROACH

10-102. ATC arrival procedures and cockpit workload are affected by weather conditions, traffic density, aircraft equipment, and radar availability. When landing at airports with approach control services and where two or more IAPs are published, aviators are provided, in advance of arrival, with information on the type of approach to expect or if the aircraft will be vectored for a visual approach. This information is broadcast either on ATIS or by a controller. It is not furnished when visibility is 3 miles or better and the ceiling is at or above the highest initial approach altitude established for any low-altitude IAP for the airport. Although this information helps plan arrival actions, it is not an ATC clearance or commitment and is subject to change. Fluctuating weather, shifting winds, or blocked runways are conditions that may result in changes to the approach information previously received. Advise ATC immediately if unable to execute the approach or if another type of approach is preferred. If the destination is an airport without an operating control tower but has automated weather data with broadcast capability, monitor the ASOS/AWOS frequency to determine current weather. Advise ATC, once receipt of the broadcast weather is obtained, and state future intent.

10-103. Upon deciding which approach to execute, plan for descent before reaching the IAF or transition route depicted on the IAP. When flying the transition route, maintain the last assigned altitude until hearing "cleared for the approach" and intercepting a segment of the approach. The aviator may "request lower" to bring the transition route closer to the required altitude for the initial approach altitude. When ATC uses the phrase, "at pilot's discretion" in the altitude information of a clearance, the aviator has the option to start a descent at any rate and may level off temporarily at any intermediate altitude. However, once vacating an altitude, the aviator may not return to that altitude. When ATC has not used the term "at pilot's discretion" nor imposed any descent restrictions, initiate descent promptly upon acknowledgment of the clearance.

10-104. Descend at an optimum rate (consistent with the operating characteristics of the aircraft) to 1,000 feet above the assigned altitude. Then attempt to descend at a rate of between 500 and 1,500 FPM until the assigned altitude is reached. If unable to descend at a rate of at least 500 FPM or if necessary to level off at an intermediate altitude during descent, advise ATC. When required for speed reduction, descend at an optimum rate except when leveling off at 10,000 MSL during descent or 2,500 feet above airport elevation (before entering a Class B, Class C, or Class D surface area).

STANDARD TERMINAL ARRIVAL ROUTES

10-105. STARs are established to simplify clearance delivery procedures for arriving aircraft at certain areas having high-density traffic. A STAR serves a purpose parallel to that of a DP for departing traffic (Figure 10-6, page 10-23). The following points regarding STARs are important to remember:

- All STARs are found in the TPP or http://www.naco.faa.gov/index.asp?xml=naco/online/d_tpp , along with IAP charts for the destination airport. The AIM also describes STAR procedures.
- If the destination is a location for which STARs are published, the aviator may be issued a clearance containing a STAR whenever ATC deems appropriate; the aviator must possess the approved textual description.
- It is the aviator's responsibility to accept or refuse an issued STAR; if the aviator does not wish to use a STAR, he should advise ATC by placing "NO STAR" in the remarks section of the filed flight plan or when first contacting ATC by radio.
- When accepting a STAR in the clearance, the aviator must comply.

INOPERATIVE/UNUSABLE COMPONENTS SUBSTITUTION

10-106. The basic ground components of an ILS are the localizer, glide slope, outer marker, middle marker, and inner marker (when installed). A compass locator or precision radar may be substituted for the outer or middle marker. DME, VOR, or NDB fixes authorized in the standard IAP or surveillance radar may be substituted for the outer marker.

10-107. In addition, IFR-certified GPS equipment, operated according to AC 90-94, may be substituted for ADF and DME equipment, except during NDB IAP. Specifically, GPS can be substituted for ADF and DME equipment when—

- Flying a DME arc.
- Navigating to/from an NDB.
- Determining the aircraft position over an NDB.
- Determining the aircraft position over a fix made up of a crossing NDB bearing.
- Holding over an NDB.
- Determining aircraft position over a DME fix.

HOLDING PROCEDURES

10-108. Holding is maneuvering an aircraft in relation to a navigation fix while the aviator awaits further clearance. The standard no-wind holding pattern is flown by following a specified holding course inbound to the holding fix. This procedure is done by making a 180-degree turn to the right, flying a heading outbound to parallel the holding course, and making another 180-degree turn to the right to intercept and following the holding course to the fix (Figure 10-7, page 10-24). The holding pattern is nonstandard when turns are made to the left. Unless otherwise instructed by ATC, aviators are expected to hold in a standard pattern. The standard no-wind length of the inbound leg of the holding pattern is one minute at or below 14,000 feet MSL and one-and-a-half minutes above 14,000 feet MSL. DME holding patterns specify the outbound leg length. If holding at a DME fix without specified outbound leg length, use the timing procedures listed above. Depending on traffic and weather conditions, holding may be required. The ATC clearance always specifies left turns if a nonstandard pattern is to be flown.

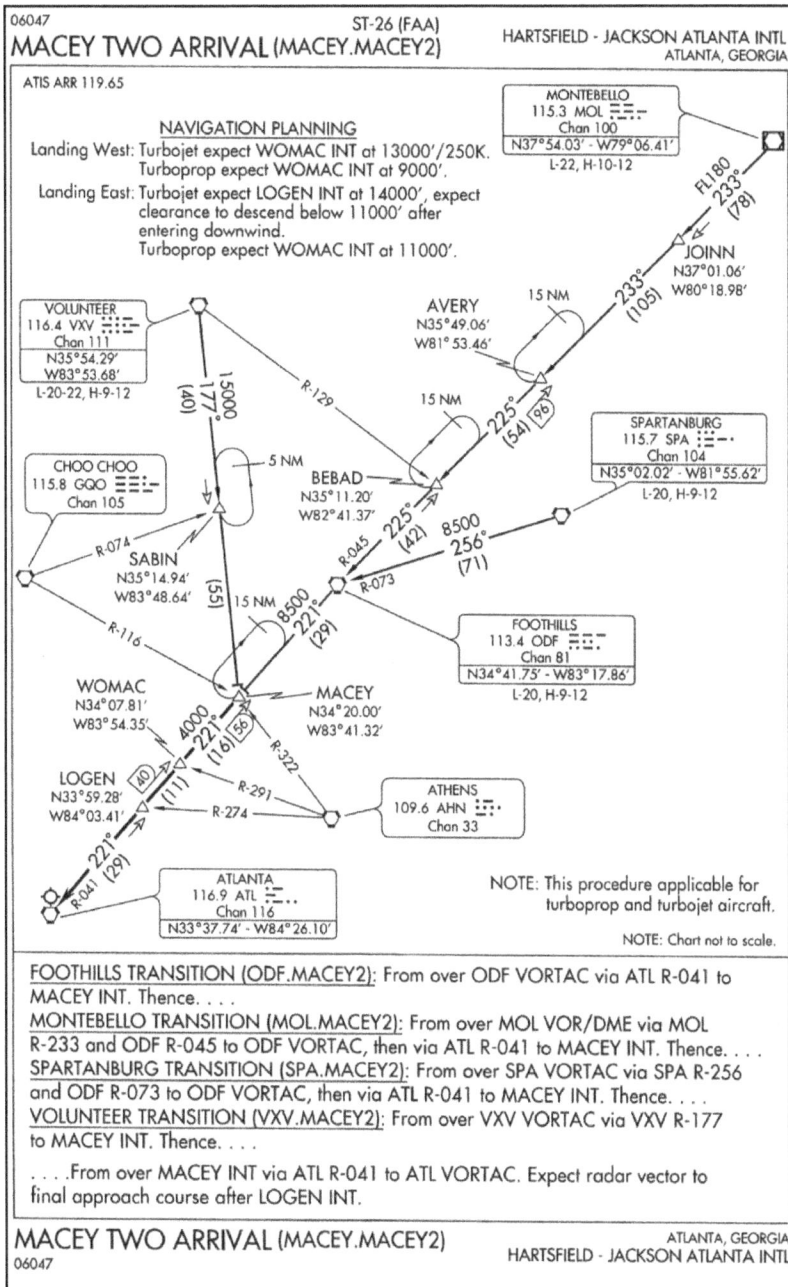

Figure 10-6. Standard terminal arrival route

STANDARD HOLDING PATTERN (NO WIND)

10-109. The standard holding pattern is a racetrack pattern (Figure 10-7). The aircraft follows the specified course inbound to the holding fix, turns 180 degrees to the right, flies a parallel straight course outbound for one minute, turns 180 degrees to the right, and flies the inbound course to the fix.

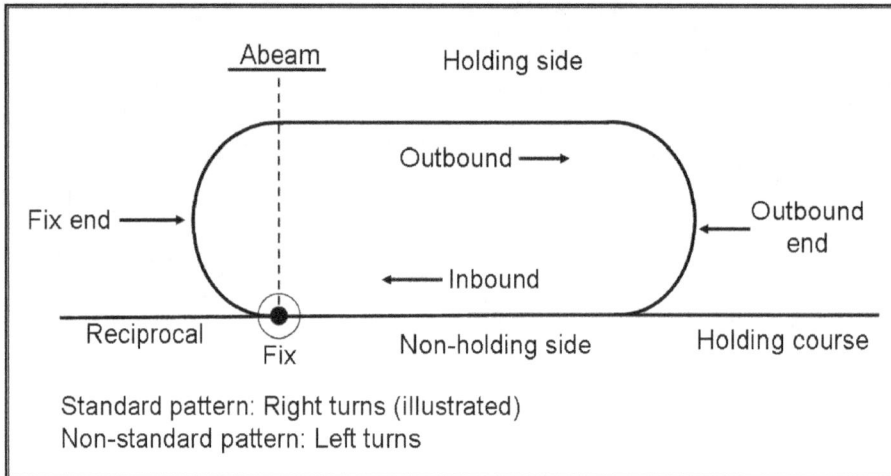

Figure 10-7. Standard holding pattern—no wind

STANDARD HOLDING PATTERN (WITH WIND)

10-110. When complying with the holding pattern procedures given in the AIM, aviators may not be able to fly a symmetrical racetrack pattern when wind exists. Aviators are expected to—

- Compensate for the effect of a known wind except when turning.
- Adjust outbound timing to achieve a one minute (one-and-a-half minutes above 14,000 feet MSL) inbound leg; see Figures 5-6 and 5-7, page 5-5, for examples of calculating outbound time. See Figure 10-10, page 10-28, regarding when to start outbound time.

10-111. Figure 10-8, page 10-25, illustrates the asymmetrical track that an aviator must fly to compensate for a left crosswind. The aviator can compensate for wind by applying drift corrections to the inbound and outbound legs and time allowances to the outbound leg.

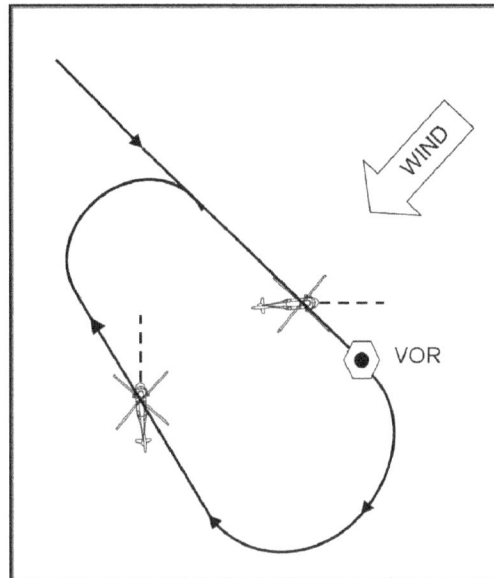

Figure 10-8. Standard holding pattern with drift correction

DRIFT CORRECTIONS

10-112. Knowledge of drift correction and TAS relationship can be useful, especially when course guidance is not available (for example, during the outbound legs of a holding pattern or procedure turn). The following technique may be used to determine approximate drift correction when the crosswind component is known: Divide crosswind component by aircraft speed in nautical miles per minute as shown in the following example.

Example of Drift Correction
30 knots crosswind and 180 KTAS [3NM per minute]
30 ÷ 3 = 10 degrees drift correction.

10-113. The aviator should compensate for wind effect primarily by drift correction on the inbound and outbound legs. When the aircraft is outbound, triple the inbound drift correction; if correcting left by 8 degrees when inbound, correct right by 24 degrees when outbound as shown in the following example.

HOLDING INSTRUCTIONS

10-114. When the aircraft arrives at the clearance limit before receiving clearance beyond the fix, ATC expects the aircraft to maintain the last assigned altitude and begin holding according to the depicted holding pattern. If no pattern is depicted, the aviator begins holding in a standard holding pattern on the course upon which the fix is approached. Immediately request further clearance. When no delay is anticipated, ATC will issue holding instructions at least five minutes before estimated arrival at the fix. When an aircraft is three minutes or less from a clearance limit and a clearance beyond the fix has not been received, the aviator is expected to start a speed reduction so that the aircraft crosses the fix at or below the maximum holding airspeed. If holding instructions are not received upon arrival at the fix, hold according to procedures in FLIP. For two-way radio failure holding procedures, refer to the FIH.

10-115. Where a holding pattern is depicted, ATC clearances specify the direction of holding from the fix. The clearance is given in terms of the eight cardinal compass points (N, NE, E, SE) along with the name of the holding fix (for example, "Cleared to DARED, hold south as published.").

10-116. When a holding pattern is not depicted, ATC clearances specify the direction of holding from the fix in terms of the eight cardinal compass points, the holding fix (the fix may be omitted if included at the beginning of the transmission as the clearance limit), and the radial, course, bearing, airway, or route on which the aircraft is to hold. ATC also provides the leg length in miles if DME or RNAV is to be used (leg length is specified in minutes on aviator request or if deemed necessary by the controller), and the direction of turn (for left turns, the aviator requests or the controller states direction if necessary).

10-117. Time to expect further clearance (EFC) and any pertinent additional delay information is issued for either a charted or uncharted holding pattern. ATC instructions are also issued when a delay will exceed one hour or a revised EFC is necessary. In a terminal area having a number of NAVAIDs and approach procedures, a clearance limit may not indicate clearly which approach procedures to use. On initial contact, or as soon as possible thereafter, approach control advises the aviator of the approach type anticipated. Ceiling/visibility is reported as being at or below the highest circling minimums established for the airport concerned. ATC transmits a current weather conditions report and subsequent changes, as necessary. Aircraft holding while awaiting approach clearance are advised if reported weather conditions are below minimums applicable to their operation. In this case, ATC issues suitable instructions to aircraft desiring to continue holding or proceed to another airport. According to AR 95-1, aviators may initiate an approach regardless of ceiling and visibility.

STANDARD ENTRY PROCEDURES

10-118. Entry procedures in the AIM evolved from extensive experimentation under a wide range of operational conditions. By following these standardized procedures, the aircraft remains within the boundaries of the prescribed holding airspace.

10-119. Reduce airspeed to holding speed within three minutes of ETA at the holding fix. Speed reduction prevents overshooting the holding airspace limits, especially at locations where adjacent holding patterns are close together. The exact time to reduce speed is not important as long as arrival at the fix occurs at the preselected holding speed within three minutes of the submitted ETA. If speed reduction and preparation for fix identification take longer, adjust entry to the pattern and report the amended ETA. The aviator should advise ATC if the aircraft exceeds maximum holding speed. All aircraft may hold at the altitudes and maximum holding airspeeds shown in table 10-3.

Table 10-3. Holding altitudes and airspeeds

Altitude (MSL) (feet)	Airspeed (KIAS)
MHA–6,000	200
6,001–14,000	230
14,001 and above	265

10-120. Maximum holding airspeeds can be limited by the following:

- Maximum airspeed of 210 KIAS in holding patterns from 6,001 to 14,000 feet (as depicted by an icon).
- Maximum airspeed of 175 KIAS in holding patterns (as depicted by an icon) that are generally found on IAPs applicable to Category A and B aircraft only.
- Maximum airspeed of 310 KIAS in holding patterns at Air Force airfields and 230 KIAS in holding patterns at Navy airfields unless otherwise depicted.
- Maximum airspeed of 100 KIAS in holding patterns during copter/short takeoff and landing (STOL) only approaches.

FEDERAL AVIATION ADMINISTRATION ENTRY PROCEDURES

10-121. Entry procedures enable the aircraft to enter the holding pattern and remain within protected airspace. The FAA recommends parallel, teardrop, and direct entries into holding (see Figure 10-9).

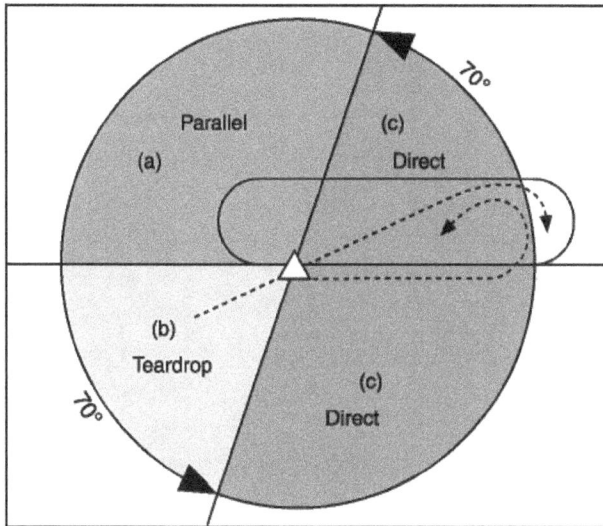

Figure 10-9. Holding pattern entry procedures

Parallel Entry

10-122. When approaching the holding fix from sector (a) in Figure 10-9, turn to a heading to parallel the holding course outbound on the nonholding side for about one minute. Turn in the direction of the holding pattern through more than 180 degrees, and return to the holding fix or intercept the holding course inbound.

Teardrop Entry

10-123. When approaching the holding fix from sector (b) in Figure 10-9, fly to the fix, turn outbound using course guidance, when available, or to a heading for a 30-degree teardrop entry within the pattern (on the holding side) for about one minute, then turn in the direction of the holding pattern to intercept the inbound holding course.

Direct Entry

10-124. When approaching the holding fix from sector (c) in Figure 10-9, fly directly to the fix and turn to follow the holding pattern. All turns during entry and while holding are made at 3 degrees per second, a 30-degree bank angle, or a bank angle provided by a flight director system.

TIME FACTORS

10-125. The holding pattern entry time reported to ATC is the initial time of arrival over the fix. Upon entering a holding pattern, the initial outbound leg is flown for one minute at or below 14,000 feet MSL and for one-and-a-half minutes above 14,000 feet MSL. Timing for subsequent outbound legs is adjusted, as necessary, to achieve proper inbound leg time. Aviators begin outbound timing over or abeam the fix, whichever occurs later. If the abeam position cannot be determined, start timing when the turn to outbound is completed (Figure 10-10). Timing inbound begins at the completion of the outbound-end turn, wings level (see Figure 10-6, page 10-23, for identification of the outbound end).

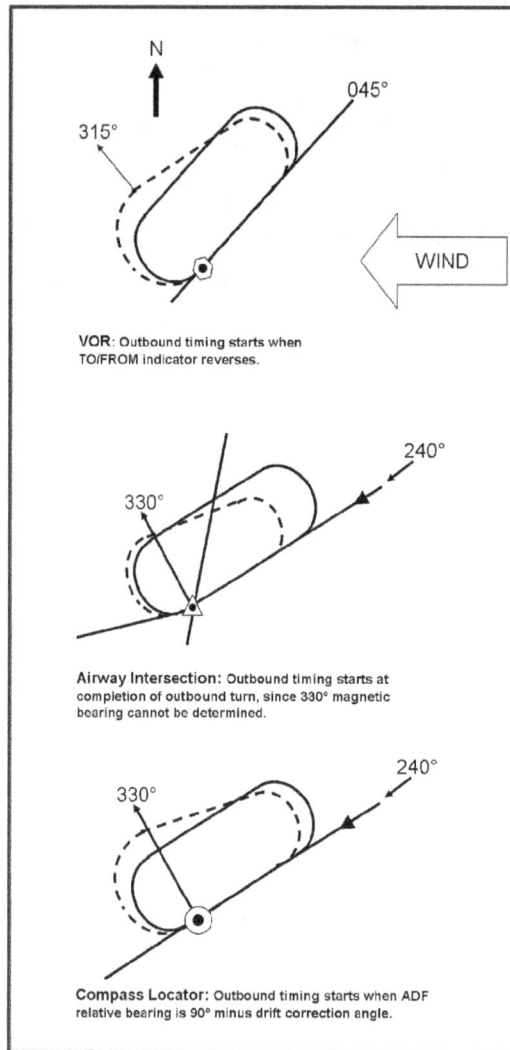

Figure 10-10. Holding and outbound timing

10-126. ATC issues an EFC time in holding clearances. The purpose of the EFC time is twofold. First, the EFC lets the aviator know how long that he is expected to remain in a holding pattern. Second, it provides him with a clearance time to leave the holding pattern if two-way radio communications failure occurs. ATC may provide an earlier clearance to depart the holding pattern and should provide a clearance to depart as EFC time approaches. If an aviator does not receive further clearance before reaching the EFC, he should request clearance to leave holding or a revised EFC time from ATC. ATC must know the time leaving the holding fix before succeeding aircraft can be cleared to the airspace that the aircraft has vacated. Leave the holding fix—

- When ATC issues either further clearance en route or approach clearance.
- As prescribed in part 91 (for IFR operations; two-way radio communications failure, and responsibility and authority of the PC).

●   After canceling the IFR flight plan, if holding in VFR conditions.

DISTANCE MEASURING EQUIPMENT HOLDING

10-127. The same entry and holding procedures apply to DME holding except distances (nautical miles) are used instead of time values. The length of the outbound leg is specified by the controller, and the end of this leg is determined by the DME readout.

SECTION VIII – APPROACHES

PUBLISHED PROCEDURE COMPLIANCE

10-128. Compliance with procedures on approach charts provides necessary navigation guidance for alignment with final approach courses as well as obstruction clearance. Under certain conditions, a course reversal maneuver or procedure turn may be necessary. This procedure is not authorized when—

●   "No PT" appears on the approach course on the plan view of the approach chart.
●   Radar vectoring is provided to the final approach course.
●   A holding pattern is published in lieu of a procedure turn.
●   A timed approach is executed from a holding fix.
●   Otherwise directed by ATC.

APPROACHES TO AIRPORTS

INSTRUMENT LETDOWN

10-129. Unless otherwise authorized, when an instrument letdown to an airport is necessary, aviators should use a standard IAP prescribed for that airport. IAPs are depicted on IAP charts and found in the TPP or DOD FLIP (Terminal).

10-130. ATC approach procedures depend on facilities available at the terminal area, the type of instrument approach executed, and existing weather conditions. ATC facilities, NAVAIDs, and associated frequencies appropriate to each standard instrument approach are given on the approach chart. Individual charts are published for standard approach procedures associated with the facilities in Figure 10-11.

10-131.

```
• NDB
• LDA*
• VORTAC
• RNAV
• ILS
• VOR
• LOC
• VOR/DME
• SDF**
• GPS

* Localizer-type directional aid
** Simplified directional facility
```

Figure 10-11. Facilities with standard approach procedures

Full Approach

10-132. An IAP can be flown as a full approach or with the assistance of radar vectors. When flown as a full approach, aviators conduct their own navigation using routes and altitudes depicted on the instrument approach chart. This procedure allows the aviator to make the transition from the en route phase to the instrument approach and then to a landing with minimal assistance from ATC. A full approach is requested by the aviator and is most often used in areas without radar coverage, providing the aviator with a means of completing an instrument approach during a communications failure.

Radar Vectors

10-133. When an approach is flown with radar vectors, ATC provides guidance in the form of headings and altitudes to position the aircraft to intercept final approach. The aviator resumes navigation, intercepts the final approach course, and completes the approach using the IAP chart. This method is often more expedient than the full approach and allows ATC to sequence arriving traffic. An aviator operating in radar contact can generally expect assistance of radar vectors to the final approach course.

WITHOUT AN OPERATING CONTROL TOWER

10-134. When approaching a facility without a control tower (Figure 10-12, page 10-31), monitor the AWOS/ASOS (if available) for the latest weather conditions. When direct communication between the aviator and controller is no longer required, the ARTCC or approach controller clears the aircraft for an instrument approach and advises "change to advisory frequency approved." Aviators should expeditiously change to the CTAF frequency because the ATC facility will not have runway in use or airport traffic information. If arriving on a cruise clearance, ATC will not issue further clearance for approach and landing.

10-135. If an approach clearance is required, ATC authorizes the aviator to execute his choice of standard instrument approach (if more than one is published) with the phrase "cleared for the approach" and the communications frequency change required, if any. From this point, the aviator has no contact with ATC and should close the IFR flight plan before landing, if in VFR conditions, or by telephone after landing. Unless otherwise directed by ATC, the aviator is expected to execute the complete IAP shown on the chart.

10-136. Inbound aircraft should initiate contact about 10 miles from the airport and continue to monitor the appropriate frequency until after landing and clear of the movement area. If the aircraft has only one radio capable of transmitting on the ATC and CTAF frequency, do not leave the assigned ATC frequency until instructed to do so. Inbounds should—

- Report altitude, aircraft type, and location relative to the airport.
- Indicate whether landing or over flight.
- Request airport advisory (if UNICOM or FSS).

10-137. Make position reports at the following locations on the approach:

- When departing the final approach fix inbound.
- When established on the final approach segment or immediately upon being released by ATC.
- Upon completion or termination of the approach.
- Upon executing the missed approach procedure.
- When exiting the active runway.

10-138. Most VFR pilots operating in the vicinity of the airport will not be familiar with fix names. Locations should be referred to in the simplest terms that the average VFR pilot will understand. For example, use the terminology "5 miles east" instead of "Kirby Intersection."

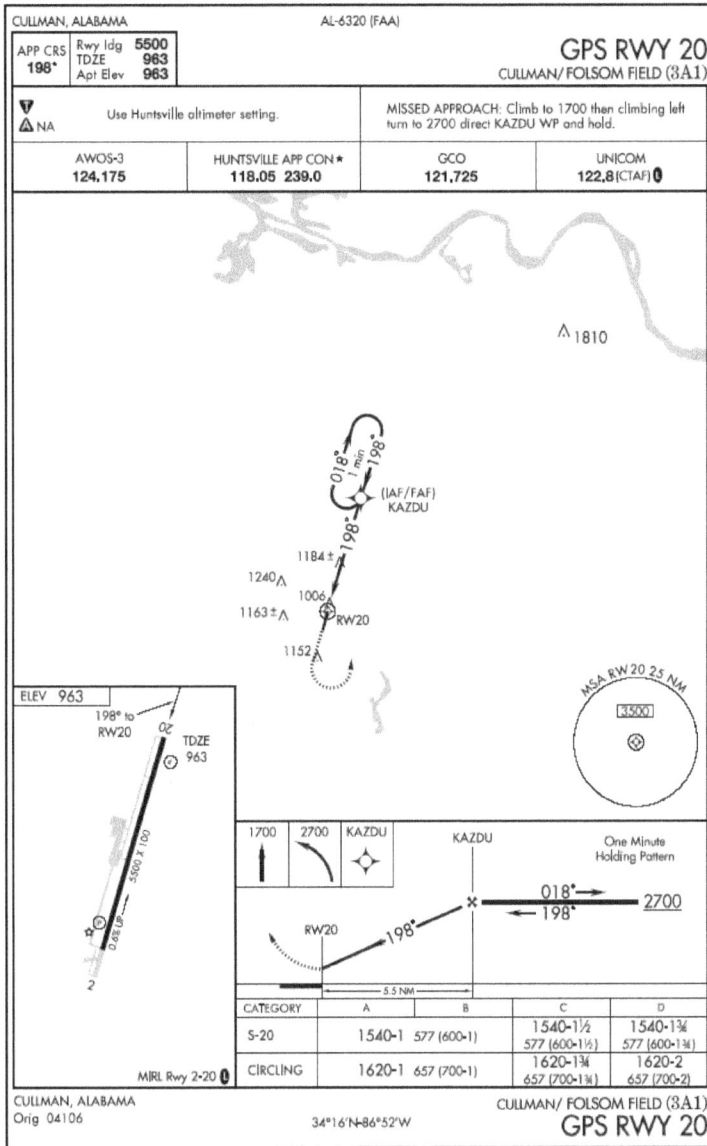

Figure 10-12. Approach procedure without an operating control tower

10-139. When self-announcing the aviator's position, as in the example, the aviator uses the following format:

- Name of the airport, followed by the word "traffic."
- The aviator's call sign.
- The aircraft type in terms that the average VFR pilot will understand.
- The aviator's location in terms that the average VFR pilot will understand.
- The aviator's intentions.
- Name of the airport repeated.

Example of CTAF Call
"Folsom Field traffic, Army 12345, white Cessna King—Air, 5 miles north on the straight-in GPS Runway 20, touch and go, Folsom Field."

Approach Control Present

10-140. Radar approved for approach control service is used to provide vectors with published IAPs. Radar vectors provide course guidance and expedite traffic to the final approach course of any established IAP. Figure 10-13, page 10-33, shows an IAP chart with maximum ATC facilities available. Approach control facilities provide radar services and clear arriving aircraft to an outer fix most appropriate to the route being flown with vertical separation. If required, approach control facilities also issue holding information. If radar handoffs are effected between ARTCC and approach control or between two approach control facilities, aircraft are cleared to the airport or to a fix located so that the handoff is completed before the time that the aircraft reaches the fix. When radar handoffs are used, successive arriving flights may be handed off to approach control with radar separation in lieu of vertical separation. After handoff to approach control, aircraft are vectored to the appropriate final-approach course. Radar vectors and altitude/flight levels are issued, as required, for spacing and separating aircraft; therefore, aircraft must not deviate from headings issued by approach control.

10-141. Normally, an aviator is informed when necessary to vector the aircraft across the final-approach course. When the determined approach course crossing is imminent and the aviator has not been informed, the controller should be questioned. Do not turn inbound on the course unless approach control issues a clearance. The clearance includes the final vector for interception of the final approach course allowing the aircraft to establish this course before reaching the FAF. If the aircraft is already inbound, the aviator is issued clearance before reaching the FAF. After the flight is established inbound on the final approach course, radar separation is maintained with other aircraft. The aircraft is expected to complete the approach using the NAVAID designated in the clearance (ILS, VOR, NDB, or GPS) as the primary means of navigation. After passing the FAF inbound, proceed direct to the airport and complete the approach or execute the published missed approach procedure. Radar service is automatically terminated when the landing is complete or the tower controller has the aircraft in sight, whichever occurs first.

LOW-ALTITUDE APPROACHES

10-142. Low-altitude approaches are used for aircraft to make the transition from a low-altitude environment to final approach for landing. Low-altitude IAPs assist in guiding aircraft to the FAF on course, on altitude, and in final-approach configuration. ATC usually provides radar vectors to final; however, be prepared to execute the full procedure when appropriate. The two broad categories of low-altitude approaches are course reversals and procedure tracks. Before reviewing each type in detail, listed below are guidelines applying to low-altitude approaches.

INITIAL-APPROACH FIX

10-143. Most approaches begin at an IAF. ATC normally clears the aircraft to the appropriate IAF and then for the approach. Unless ATC specifically clears the aircraft otherwise, the aircraft is expected to fly to the IAF and execute the full IAP as published.

FINAL-APPROACH SEGMENT

10-144. Some approaches depict only a final-approach segment starting at the FAF. In these cases, radar is required to ensure proper alignment with the final-approach course at the appropriate altitude. When ATC clears for the approach, maintain the last assigned altitude until established on a segment of the published IAP.

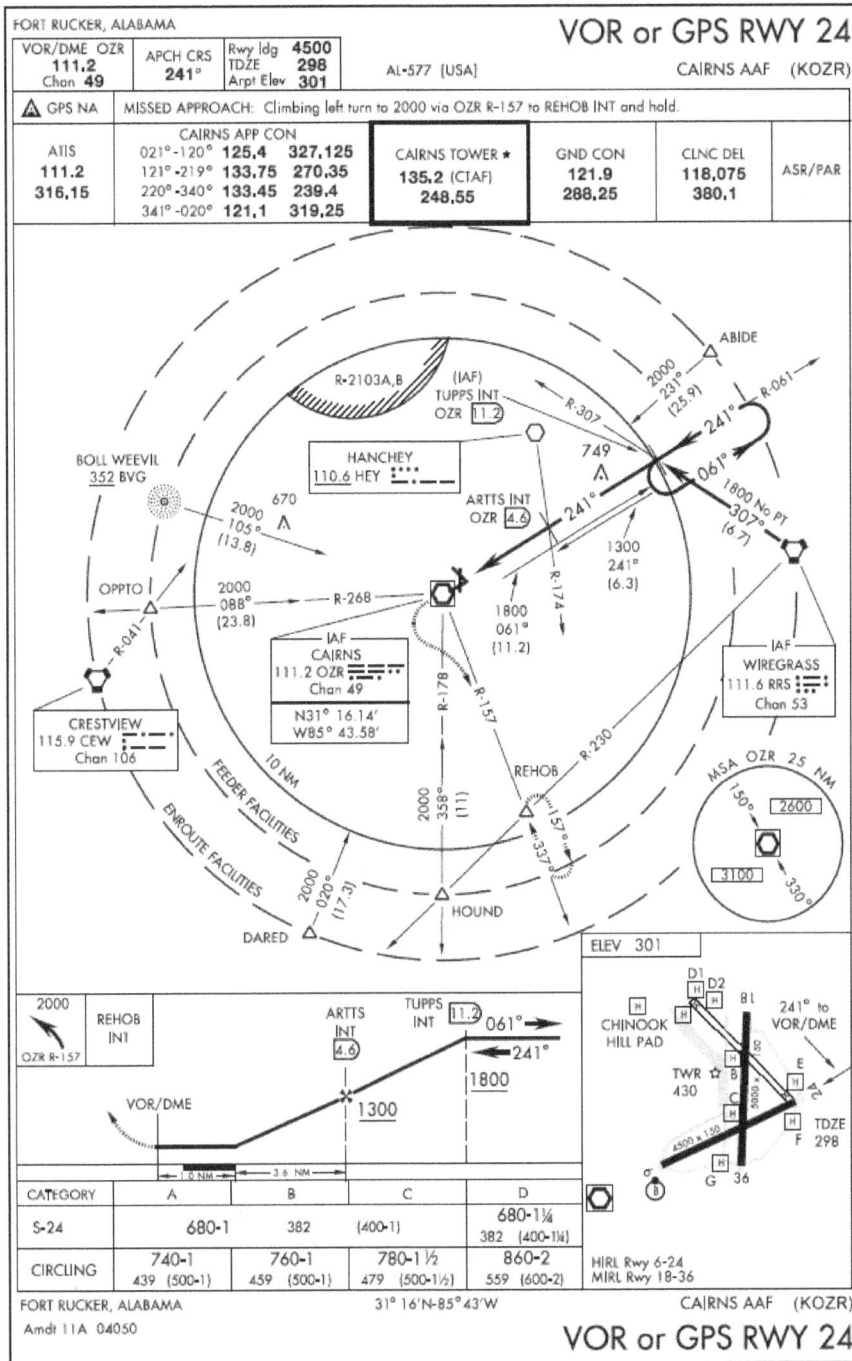

Figure 10-13. Instrument approach procedure chart with maximum air traffic control facilities available

ESTABLISHED ON COURSE

10-145. Established on course is defined as being within that instrument maneuver course standard as specified within the aircraft specific ATM. For example, a UH-60 aviator would be considered established on course when within 2.5 degrees of course centerline IAW TC 1-237, Task 1178, Standard number 2. For an instrument landing system (ILS) approach, intercept and maintain the localizer course within 2.5 degrees of course centerline (two dots on the horizontal situation indicator [HSI]).

COURSE REVERSALS

10-146. The two common types of course reversals are the PT and the holding in lieu of procedure turn. Do not execute either procedure in the following situations:

- When ATC gives clearance for a straight-in approach.
- When flying the approach via No PT routing.
- When the aircraft is established in holding and subsequently cleared for the approach and the holding course and procedure turn course are the same.
- When ATC provides radar vectors to the final-approach course.
- When ATC clears the aircraft for a timed approach (when the aircraft is established in a holding pattern and the aviator is given a time to depart the FAF inbound).

10-147. In any of the previous bulleted situations, proceed over the FAF at the published FAF altitude. Continue inbound on the final approach course without making a procedure turn, holding pattern, or any other aligning maneuver until the aircraft reaches the FAF unless otherwise cleared by ATC. If necessary to make additional circuits in a published holding pattern or to become better established on course before departing the FAF, it is the aviator's responsibility to request such maneuvering from ATC. Historically, these restrictions have created confusion between aviators and controllers. If ever in doubt about what ATC expects, query the controller.

PROCEDURE TURN

10-148. One of the most common types of low-altitude course reversals is the procedure turn. Procedure turns are depicted in the plan view of U.S. Government charts with a barb symbol (⟍⟋), indicating the direction or side of the outbound course on which the procedure turn or maneuvering is to be accomplished. The absence of the procedure-turn barbed arrow in the plan view indicates that a procedure turn is not authorized for that procedure. The procedure-turn fix is identified on the profile view of the approach at the point where the IAP begins. The FAA recommends a maximum airspeed of 200 KIAS during procedure-turn course reversals. Four common techniques for executing a procedure turn (course reversal) are the following:

- Teardrop pattern.
- Standard 45-degree turn (45/180).
- The 80/260 course reversal.
- Holding/racetrack pattern (see standard holding pattern above).

10-149. The outbound course direction of turn, distance within which the turn must be completed, and minimum altitude are specified in the procedure. However, the point at which the turn may be commenced and the type and rate of turn are left to the discretion of the aviator.

10-150. Regardless of the method chosen, plan the outbound leg to allow enough time for configuration and any descent required before the aircraft arrives at the FAF. Ensure that the outbound leg length is adjusted so that the flight stays inside the "remain within distance" noted on the profile view of the approach plate. Remain-within distance is measured from the procedure turn fix unless the IAP specifies otherwise. Turn to intercept the procedure-turn course inbound at the completion of the outbound leg.

10-151. When the NAVAID is on the field and no FAF is depicted, plan the outbound leg so that the descent to MDA can be completed with sufficient time to acquire the runway and position the aircraft for a normal landing. Consideration should be given to configuring on the outbound leg to minimize aviator tasking on final approach. When flying this type of approach, the aviator can consider the FAF to be the descent point from the procedure-turn completion altitude. Establish approach configuration and airspeed before departing procedure-turn completion altitude unless the aircraft operator's manual procedures require otherwise.

10-152. Begin timing once the aircraft is outbound abeam the procedure turn fix. If the abeam position cannot be determine while in the turn, start timing after completing the outbound turn. Fly one to three minutes for the outbound leg. Do not descend from the procedure-turn fix altitude (published or assigned) until the aircraft is abeam the procedure-turn fix heading outbound. If determining when the aircraft is abeam is not possible, start descent after completing the outbound turn. Do not descend from the procedure turn completion altitude until the flight is established on the inbound segment of the approach.

Teardrop Pattern

10-153. For the teardrop entry, start timing at A for two minutes from A to B (Figure 10-14). Reduce airspeed to holding speed in this interval. At B, enter standard-rate turn for a 30-degree change of heading. Time is one minute from B to C. At C, enter standard-rate turn for a 210-degree change of heading, rolling out on the reciprocal of the original entry heading.

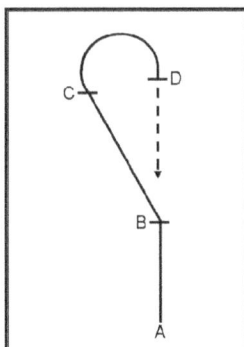

Figure 10-14. Teardrop pattern

Standard 45-Degree Turn (45/180) and 80/260 Course Reversal

10-154. Two other methods used to accomplish a procedure turn approach are the 45/180 (Figure 10-15, page 10-36) and 80/260 (Figure 10-16, page 10-36) course reversal maneuvers (table 10-4). Procedures for flying each maneuver are identical with the exception of the actual course reversal.

Table 10-4. Course reversal steps

45/180 course reversal	80/260 course reversal
Start timing at A for 2 minutes from A to B (Figure 10-15).	Start timing at A for 2 minutes from A to B (Figure 10-16).
At B, turn 45° (standard rate). After roll-out, fly 1 minute to C.	At B, enter a left standard-rate turn for a heading change of 80°.
At C, turn 180°.	
At completion of turn, time 45 seconds from D to E.	At the completion of the 80° turn at C, immediately turn right for a heading change of 260°, rolling out on the reciprocal of the entry heading.
Start turn at E for a 45° change of heading to reciprocal of heading at beginning of maneuver.	

10-155.

10-156.

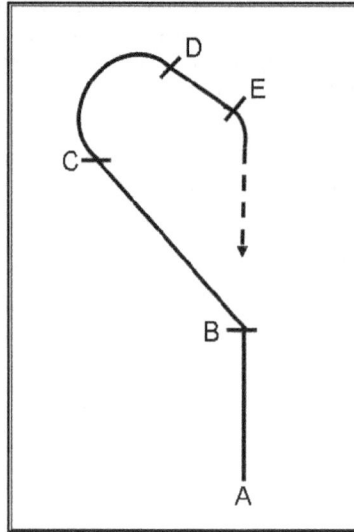

Figure 10-15. 45/180 procedure turn

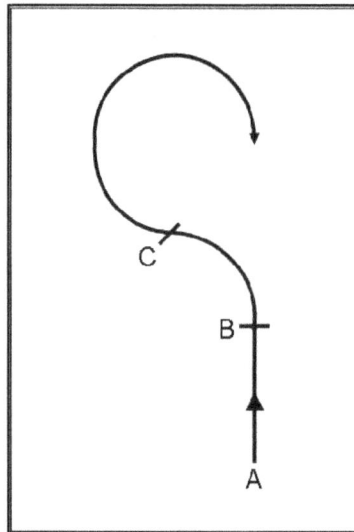

Figure 10-16. 80/260 procedure turn

10-157. Upon reaching the procedure-turn fix, turn in the shortest direction to intercept the procedure-turn course outbound. Intercept and maintain the course outbound as soon as possible after passing the procedure-turn fix. Do not descend from the fix altitude (published or assigned) until abeam the fix and on a parallel or intercept heading to the outbound track. Do not descend from the procedure-turn completion altitude until the aircraft is established on the inbound segment of the approach. At the appropriate time on the outbound leg, begin the course-reversal maneuver. In both cases, comply with the published remain-within distance.

Note. When flying procedure turns designed in FAA airspace, the aviator is not required to wait until the aircraft is on a parallel or intercept heading to begin descent from the procedure turn fix altitude; however, when the aviator flies these types of course reversals in ICAO airspace, this procedure is mandatory because of different TERPS criteria.

Holding in Lieu of Procedure Turn

10-158. Holding in lieu of procedure turn is another common way to execute a low-altitude course reversal. Holding in lieu of procedure turn is depicted like any other holding pattern except the holding pattern track is printed with a heavy black line (←270° / 090°→) in the plan view. The depiction of the approach in the profile view varies, depending on where descent should begin. Enter and fly the holding in lieu of procedure turn according to procedures previously described.

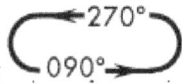

10-159. Descent from the minimum holding altitude is depicted two ways: descent at the holding fix (Figure 10-17) or descent on the inbound leg (Figure 10-18). When a descent is depicted on the inbound leg, the aircraft must be established on the inbound segment of the approach before the aviator begins the descent.

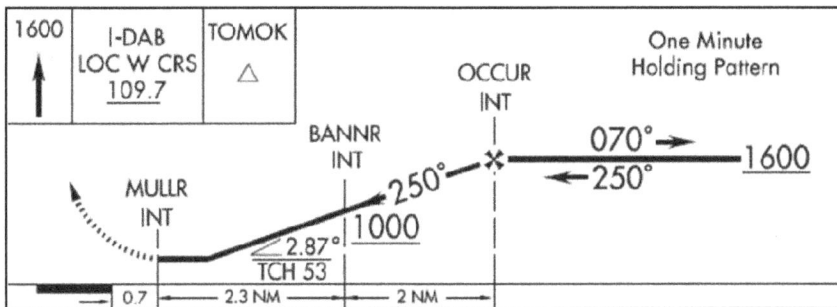

Figure 10-17. Descent at the holding fix

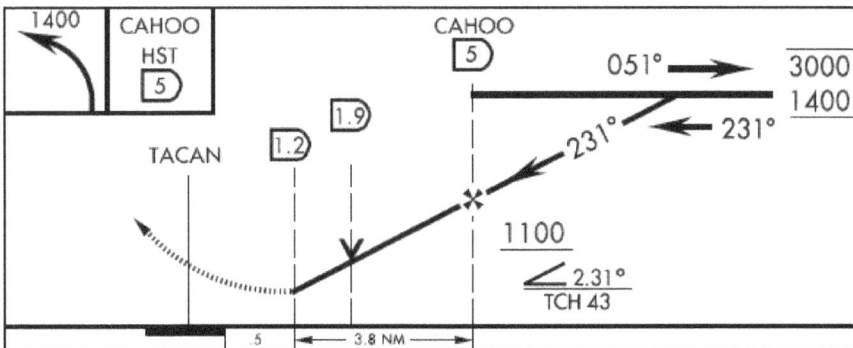

Figure 10-18. Descent on the inbound leg

10-160. If cleared for the approach while holding in a published holding in lieu of procedure turn, complete the holding pattern and commence the approach without making additional turns in the holding pattern (altitude permitting). If an additional turn is needed to lose excessive altitude, request clearance from ATC because additional circuits of the holding pattern are not expected by ATC. If the aircraft is at an altitude from which the approach can be safely executed and the aviator is ready to turn inbound immediately, he may request approval for an early turn from ATC.

PROCEDURAL TRACKS

10-161. There is no specific depiction for a procedural track, and it may employ arcs, radials, courses, or turns. When a specific flight path is required, procedural track symbology is used to depict the flight path between the IAF and FAF. The depiction, a heavy black line, shows the intended aircraft ground track (Figure 10-19, page 10-39).

10-162. When over the IAF, turn immediately in the shorter direction to intercept the published track. If the heading is within 90 degrees of the procedure track course, use normal lead points to intercept the course. If the heading is not within 90 degrees of the course, overfly the fix and turn in the shorter direction to intercept the procedure track course.

10-163. Conform to the specific ground track shown on the IAP. Where a teardrop turn is depicted, turn to the inbound course at any time unless otherwise restricted by the approach plate (Figure 10-20, page 10-40). Determine when to turn by using aircraft turn performance, winds, and the amount of descent required on the inbound course; however, do not exceed the published remain-within distance.

10-164. A descent can be depicted at any point along the procedural track. When the descent is depicted at the IAF, start descent when abeam or past the IAF and on a parallel or intercept heading to the procedural track course. Except for initial descents at an IAF, be established on the appropriate segment of the procedural track before descending to the next altitude shown on the IAP.

10-165. Low-altitude approaches may include arc-to-radial and radial-to-arc combinations. An arc-to-radial altitude restriction applies only while the aircraft is established on that segment of the IAP. Once a lead point is reached and a turn to the next segment is begun, consider the aircraft established on the next segment and descend to the next applicable altitude. When an altitude restriction is depicted at a fix defined as an intersection of a radial and an arc, the restriction must be complied with no later than the completion of the lead turn associated with that fix. If the restriction is met during the lead turn, consider the aircraft established on the next segment and continue to descend to the next applicable altitude restriction.

10-166. Maximum designed obstacle clearance is based on the ability to maintain the course centerline; use position orientation and judgment to determine when to descend while attempting to intercept the procedural track. Where a teardrop is depicted, do not descend from the turn altitude until established on the inbound segment of the procedural track.

HIGH-ALTITUDE APPROACH

10-167. An en route descent or high-altitude instrument approach (Figure 10-21, page 10-41) enables an aircraft to make the transition from a high-altitude structure to a position on and aligned with an inbound course to the FAF, at FAF altitude in the final approach configuration. ATC will issue clearance for a specific type of approach; omission of the clearance indicates that any published instrument approach may be used. Unless ATC provides an appropriate clearance to deviate, fly the entire instrument approach procedure starting at the IAF.

10-168.

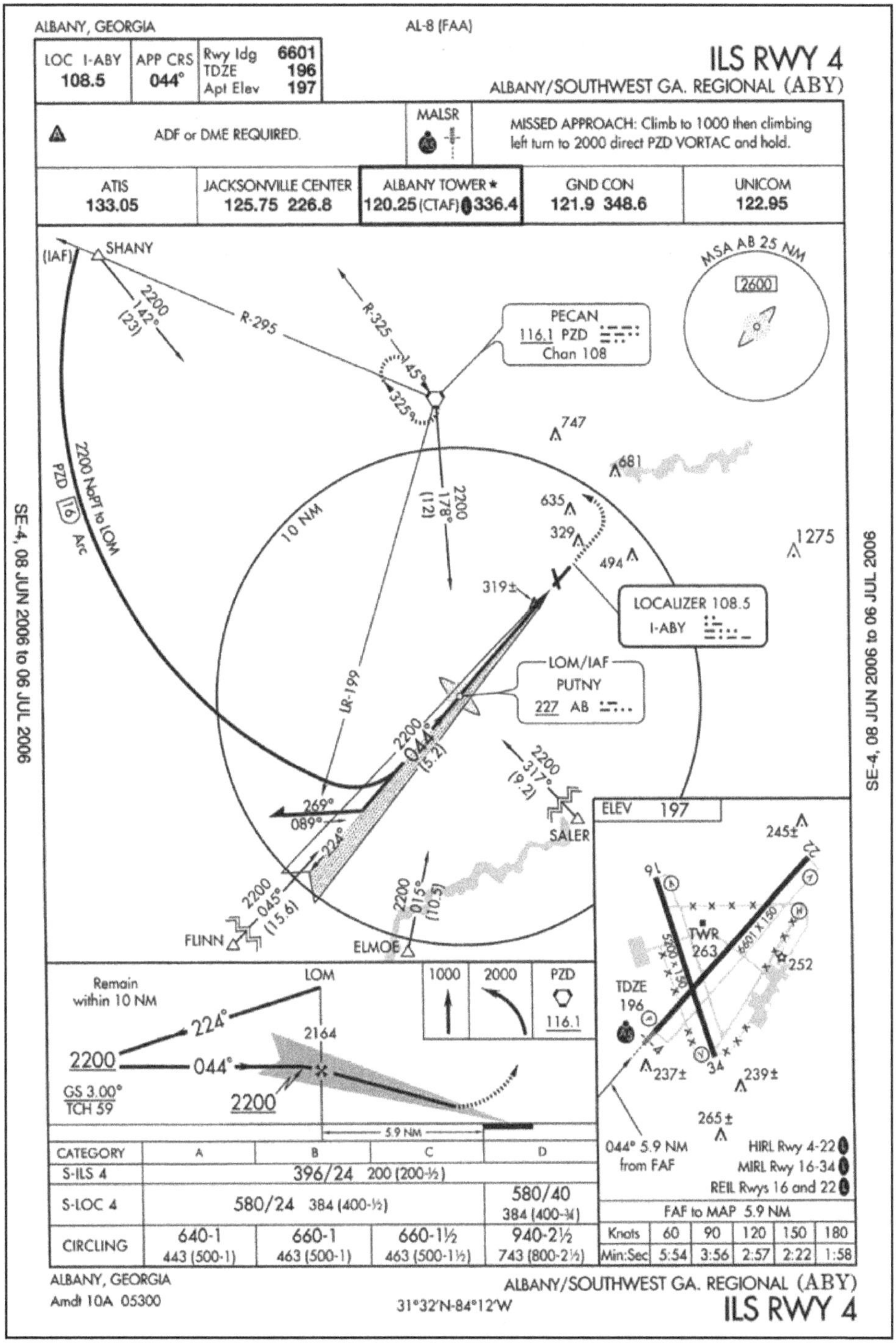

Figure 10-19. Procedural track approach—arcing final

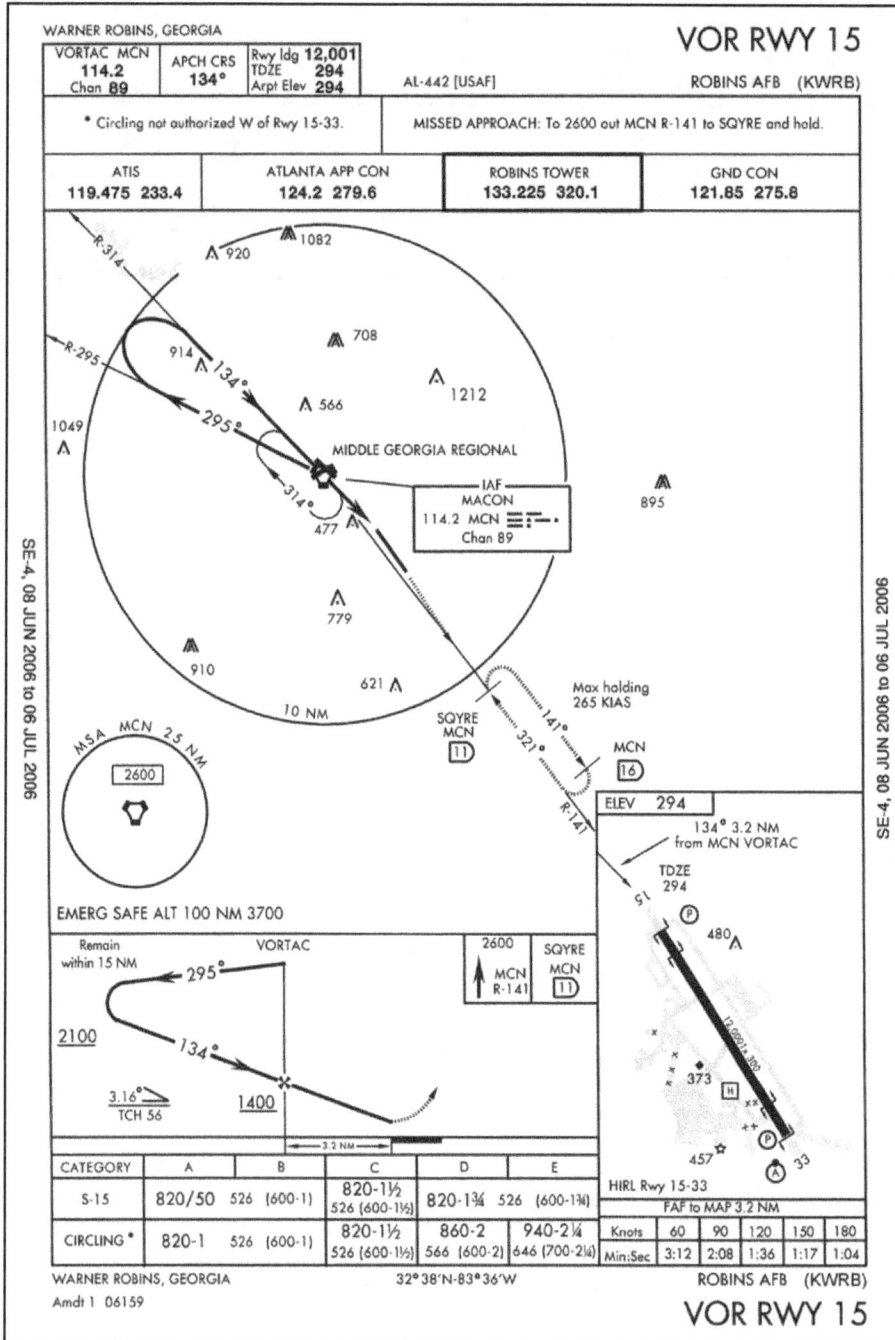

Figure 10-20. Procedural track approach—teardrop turn

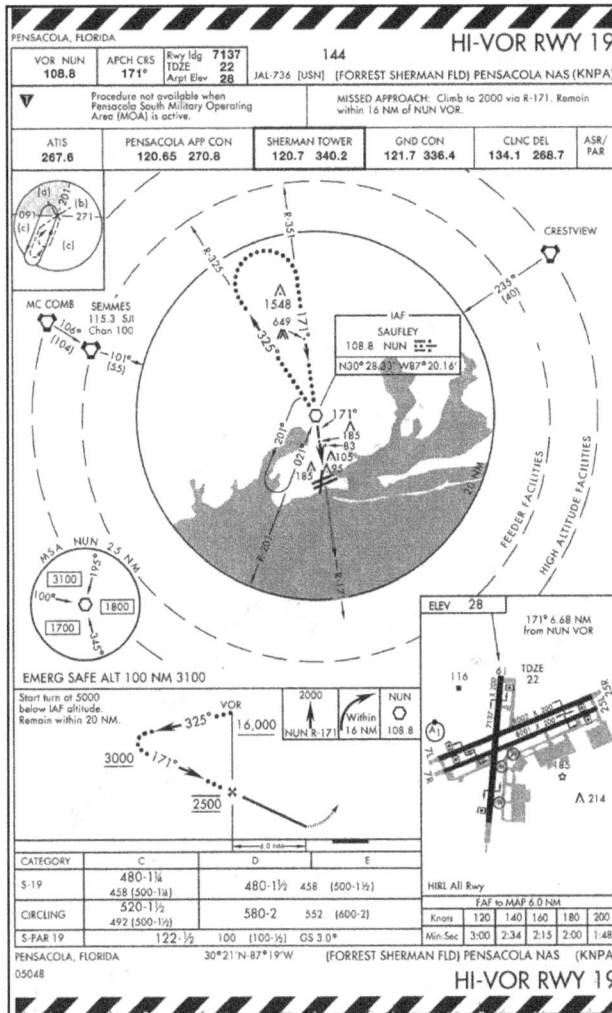

Figure 10-21. High-altitude instrument approach plate

NON-DISTANCE MEASURING EQUIPMENT TEARDROP APPROACHES

10-169. Teardrop approaches are usually associated with VOR or NDB facilities.

Station Passage

10-170. When station passage occurs at the IAF, turn immediately in the shorter direction toward the outbound course and attempt to intercept. Begin descent when the aircraft is established on a parallel or intercept heading to the approach course and outbound from the IAF. When arriving at the IAF at an altitude below that published, maintain altitude and proceed outbound 15 seconds for each 1,000 feet that the aircraft is below the published altitude before starting the descent. When arriving at an altitude above that published, the aviator should descend to the published IAF altitude before starting the approach. If descent is required at the IAF, obtain clearance to descend in a holding pattern. Set the altimeter according to FLIP.

Note. Use a descent gradient of 800 to 1,000 feet/nautical miles (8 to 10 degrees) to ensure that the aircraft remains within protected airspace.

Fly Off

10-171. Some approaches use a fly-off (altitude or range) restriction before the aircraft starts descent. Attempt to intercept the outbound course and comply with altitudes depicted on the approach chart unless otherwise instructed by ATC. Because the aviator cannot be expected to determine accurate ground speed during a constantly changing true airspeed descent, depicted range restrictions should not be shown on non-DME teardrop high-altitude approaches. Penetration turns are annotated "left or right turn at (altitude)." When a penetration-turn altitude is not published, start the turn after descending one-half the total altitude between the IAF and FAF altitudes. One technique to determine the start-turn altitude is to add the IAF and FAF altitudes and divide by two. Before reaching the penetration-turn altitude, set up the navigation equipment to intercept the published inbound approach course. Recheck the altimeter and the direction of the penetration turn.

Penetration Turn

10-172. Fly the penetration turn in the direction published. A 30-degree bank angle is used during the penetration turn; however, bank may be shallower if undershooting course. If it is apparent that the aircraft will undershoot the inbound penetration course, roll out on an intercept heading. Use normal inbound course interception procedures to intercept the course.

Note. If a penetration-turn completion altitude is depicted, do not descend below depicted the altitude until the aircraft is established on the inbound segment of the published approach procedure. Obstacle clearance is based on attempting to maintain course centerline; an aviator must use position orientation and judgment to determine when to descend while attempting to intercept the course.

Descent

10-173. Continue descent to FAF altitude. Establish approach configuration and airspeed before reaching the final approach fix unless the aircraft operator's manual procedures require otherwise.

RADIAL APPROACHES

10-174. Radial approaches are associated with TACAN or VORTAC facilities. The entire approach track is formed by one or more radials.

Crossing the Initial Approach Fix

10-175. When over the IAF, turn immediately in the shorter direction toward the approach course. Intercept the published approach course using appropriate course-intercept procedures. When the heading is within 90 degrees of the approach course, the aviator is not required to overfly the IAF and may use normal lead points to intercept the course.

Descent

10-176. Start descent when the aircraft is abeam or past the IAF on a parallel or intercept heading to the approach course. For DME approaches, crossing the arc is considered abeam the IAF. Intercept the course and comply with altitudes depicted on the approach chart. Aircraft configuration and airspeed requirements before the aircraft reaches the FAF are the same as non-DME teardrop.

RADIAL AND ARC COMBINATION APPROACHES

10-177. Flight procedures are the same for both radial and arc combination approaches when using an arc intercept. However, if established in a holding pattern and the IAF is located on an arc or a radial at a distance less than required for a normal lead point, the aviator may turn early to intercept the arc. Start descent when the aircraft is established on an intercept to the arc and abeam or past the IAF in relation to the initial approach track. Aircraft configuration and airspeed requirements before the aircraft reaches the FAF are the same as the non-DME teardrop. An arc or radial altitude restriction only applies while the aircraft is established on that segment of the approach to which the altitude restriction applies. Once a lead point is reached and a turn to the next segment is initiated, the aviator may descend to the next applicable altitude restriction. These restrictions may be especially important to facilitate a reasonable rate of descent to FAF altitude.

Note. When an altitude restriction is depicted at a fix defined as an intersection of a radial and an arc, the restriction must be complied with no later than the completion of the lead turn associated with that fix. If the restriction is met during the lead turn, consider the aircraft established on the next segment and continue to descend to the next applicable altitude restriction.

MULTIPLE FACILITY APPROACHES

10-178. The multiple facility type approach uses a combination of two or more VORs, NDB, and TACANs to provide the track. Approach entry procedures are the same as prescribed for non-DME teardrop approaches. The entire approach must be flown as depicted to comply with all course and altitude restrictions. Aircraft configuration and airspeed requirements before the aircraft reaches the FAF are the same as for non-DME teardrop approaches.

FINAL APPROACH

10-179. There are numerous types of differing final-approach guidance. In this chapter, final-approach guidance is categorized as nonradar approaches, radar approaches, and procedures with a visual component.

NONRADAR APPROACHES

Nonprecision

10-180. Nonprecision, nonradar approaches include VOR, TACAN, and NDB. Other approaches include VOR/DME, localizer, back course localizer, and GPS.

10-181. The final approach starts at the FAF and ends at the MAP. The optimum length of the final approach is 5 miles; the maximum length is 10 miles. According to AR 95-1, dual VOR equipment requirements specified on approach charts do not apply to Army aircraft. Off tuning from the approach aid to identify an approach fix is authorized. Dual VOR approach minimums apply.

10-182. Nonprecision approach procedures published with an ILS cannot always clearly depict the FAF crossing altitude. Carefully review the IAP using the following guidance. The minimum altitude to be maintained until crossing the fix following the glide-slope intercept point (normally the FAF will be the next fix) is the published glide-slope intercept altitude, altitude published at that fix, or ATC assigned altitude. For most nonprecision approaches, the glide-slope intercept altitude is the minimum FAF crossing altitude.

Time

10-183. Avoid rapid descent requirements on final by crossing the FAF at the published altitude. Timing is required when final approach does not terminate at a published fix as is the case with VOR, NDB, and localizer. If timing is required for MAP identification, begin timing when passing the FAF or the starting point designated in the timing block of the approach plate. This point is usually the FAF but may be a fix not colocated with the FAF such as a LOM, NDB, crossing radial, DME fix, or outer marker. Time and distance tables on the approach chart are based on ground speed; therefore, existing wind and TAS are considered to accurately time final approach. If timing is published on the approach plate, such published timing is a valuable backup in case of DME loss or other events precluding determination of the MAP; if not, do not use timing to identify the MAP. If timing is not specifically depicted on the IAP, this is not an authorized means of MAP identification. Timing is the least precise method for identification; therefore, when it is not authorized for a particular approach because of TERPS considerations, timing information is not published. If other means of identifying the MAP are published (DME), they become the primary means to determine the MAP. When reaching the published DME depicting the MAP, do not delay in executing the missed approach just because timing is not reached.

Minimum Descent Altitude

10-184. When a turn is required over the FAF, turn immediately and intercept the final-approach course to ensure that obstruction clearance airspace is not exceeded. Do not descend to the MDA or step down fix altitude until passing the FAF, if published.

Visual Descent Point

10-185. Arrive at MDA with enough time and distance remaining to identify the runway environment. Depart MDA from a normal VDP to touch down at a rate normally used for a visual approach in the aircraft.

Runway Environment

10-186. Descent below MDA is not authorized until sufficient visual reference with the runway environment has been established and the aircraft is in a position to execute a safe landing. Thorough preflight planning aids the aviator in locating the runway environment (lighting, final approach displacement from runway). The definition of runway environment for nonprecision and precision approaches is the same and consists of one or more of the following elements:

- Approach light system—the aviator may not descend below 100 feet above the TDZE using approach lights as a reference unless red termination bars or red side-row bars are visible and identifiable.
- Threshold, threshold markings, or threshold lights.
- Runway end identifier lights.
- Touchdown zone, touchdown zone markings, or touchdown zone lights.
- Runway or runway markings, and runway lights.
- Visual approach slope indicator.

Note. Most approach lighting systems serving runways where there is no electronic glide-path guidance do not have red termination bars or red side row bars; therefore, one other element of the runway environment must be sighted to descend below 100 feet above the TDZE.

Depending on the location of the MAP, descent from the MDA (once the runway environment is sighted) has to be initiated before reaching the MAP to execute a normal (roughly 3 degrees) descent to landing.

10-187. In many cases, the minimum visibility required for the approach will not permit viewing of the runway environment until the aircraft is beyond the VDP, accentuating the need to compute a VDP and determine a point along the approach when the aviator no longer attempts to land. A common error is to establish a high descent rate once the runway environment is in sight. This descent rate can go unnoticed during an approach without visual glide-path guidance and may lead to a short and/or hard landing. Caution is used to avoid accepting a long touchdown and landing roll.

Alignment

10-188. The final approach course on a nonradar final may vary from the runway heading as much as 30 degrees and still be published as a straight-in approach. The exception is a localizer approach.

Step-Down Fix

10-189. A step-down fix between the FAF and missed approach point is sometimes used. According to AR 95-1, dual VOR equipment requirements specified on approach charts do not apply to Army aircraft. Off-tuning from the approach aid to identify an approach fix is authorized. Dual VOR approach minimums apply. Fixes requiring radar for identification are depicted with the word RADAR appearing next to the fix. Only ground-based radar, such as airport surveillance, precision, or air route surveillance radar, is used to position the aircraft.

GLOBAL POSITIONING SYSTEM APPROACH PROCEDURES

Receiver Autonomous Integrity Monitoring

10-190. If predictive RAIM is not available, another navigation and approach system must be used, another destination selected, or the trip delayed until RAIM is predicted to be available on arrival. A predictive RAIM check is accomplished before arrival to allow for crews to plan for an alternate means of navigation. If a RAIM failure/status annunciation occurs before the final approach waypoint (FAWP), do not commence the approach; coordinate for an alternate clearance.

10-191. If the receiver does not make the transition from armed to approach mode before the aircraft reaches the FAWP (usually the transition occurs 2 nautical miles before), do not commence the approach. If a RAIM failure/status annunciation occurs before the aircraft reaches the FAWP, do not descend to MDA; instead, proceed to the missed approach waypoint (MAWP), via the FAWP, and perform a missed approach. Contact ATC as soon as practical to coordinate for an alternate clearance.

10-192. If a RAIM failure occurs after the FAWP, the receiver, based on equipage, can continue operating without an annunciation for up to five minutes to allow completion of the approach. Check the receiver operator's manual to ensure that the aircraft has this capability; if not and a RAIM flag/status annunciation appears after the FAWP, climb to the missed approach altitude, proceed to the MAWP, and execute a missed approach.

Flying the Approach

10-193. Do not fly the approach unless retrieved in its entirety from a current approved database. Cross-check database waypoints against the published approach plate. If discrepancies exist, do not fly the approach except when the FAWP altitude is raised above that shown on the published chart to ensure adequate clearance at a step-down fix.

10-194. Before commencing the approach, determine which area of the TAA that the aircraft will enter, using bearing and distance to the IF/IAF. Fly the full approach from an initial approach waypoint (IAWP) or feeder fix unless specifically cleared otherwise. Entry from other than an IAWP does not assure terrain clearance.

10-195. Some receivers automatically arm the approach mode, while others require manual arming. Arming the approach mode switches the aircraft to terminal course deviation indicator scaling (+1 nautical mile). If the IAWP is beyond 30 nautical miles from the airfield, course deviation indicator sensitivity will not change until the aircraft is within 30 nautical miles of the airport reference point. Feeder route obstacle clearance is predicated on terminal sensitivity and RAIM at the IAWP. For manual systems, aircrews must ensure that the approach is loaded before being established on any portion of the approach.

10-196. When within 2 nautical miles of the FAWP with the approach mode armed, the receiver automatically initiates a RAIM check and switches to approach sensitivity and RAIM (0.3 nautical miles). Distance is provided based on active WP. Aviators must cross-check the active WP identifier to ensure SA. Some operations (such as holding course-reversal maneuvers) may require manual intervention to stop or resume automatic waypoint sequencing. Ensure that the receiver is sequenced to the appropriate waypoint, especially if not flying the full procedure. If the aircraft is on vectors to final approach, ensure that the receiver is set according to flight manual procedures. Being established on the final-approach course before initiation of the sensitivity change at 2 nautical miles from the FAWP aids aviators in course deviation indicator interpretation before descent to MDA/DA. Requesting or accepting vectors that causes the aircraft to intercept the final approach course within 2 nautical miles of the FAWP is not recommended. When the aviator receives vectors to final approach, most receiver operating manuals suggest placing the receiver in nonsequencing mode before the aircraft reaches the FAWP and setting the course manually. This setting provides an extended final approach course when vectors place the aircraft outside of any existing segment aligned with the runway. Maintain altitudes until established on a published segment of the approach. Required altitudes at waypoints outside of the FAWP or step-down fixes are also considered.

10-197. Flying point to point on the approach does not assure compliance with published procedure; proper RAIM sensitivity will not be available. The course deviation indicator sensitivity will not automatically change to +0.3 nautical miles. Manually setting indicator sensitivity does not automatically change RAIM sensitivity on some receivers.

10-198. Loss of final-approach guidance on an RNAV or a GPS approach procedure is annunciated differently, depending on the particular avionics installation. In some aircraft, the CDI centers when the "GPS Integrity" light illuminates and gives the illusion that the aircraft is on course. Ensure thorough familiarity with aircraft failure annunciations, and discontinue approach immediately if course guidance is questionable.

Final Approach

10-199. Do not descend to MDA, DA, or step-down fix altitude until passing the FAF. VNAV guidance may be used to LNAV minimums; however, the aircraft must level off at the MDA if the runway environment is not in sight. Because of temperature and pressure-altitude effects, aviators shall not use VNAV guidance below published MDA or DA. Comply with step-down fixes depicted on the IAP. VNAV guidance should provide clearance from all step-down fix altitudes; however, crews must monitor altitude at step-down fixes to ensure compliance.

Missed Approach

10-200. To execute a missed approach, activate the missed approach after crossing the MAWP. GPS missed approach procedures require aviator action to sequence from the MAWP to the missed approach procedure. If the missed approach is not activated, the GPS receiver displays an extension of the inbound final-approach course and displayed distance will increase from the MAWP. Do not activate the missed approach before reaching the MAWP. Once the missed approach is activated, course deviation indicator sensitivity is set to 1 nautical mile. Missed approach routings where the first track is via a course, rather than direct to the next waypoint, require additional action from the aviator to set the course. Consult the aircraft operator's manual. Do not turn off the final-approach course before the aircraft crosses the MAWP.

INSTRUMENT LANDING SYSTEM

10-201. The ILS is a precision, nonradar approach. In the United States, the glide slope, localizer, and outer marker are required components for an ILS (Figure 10-22, page 10-47). If the outer marker is inoperative or not installed, it may be replaced by DME, another NAVAID, a crossing radial, or radar if these substitutes are depicted on the approach plate or identified by NOTAM. If the glide slope fails or is unavailable, the approach reverts to a nonprecision approach system. If the localizer fails, the procedure is not authorized. If the OM or one of its substitutes is not available, the procedure is not authorized.

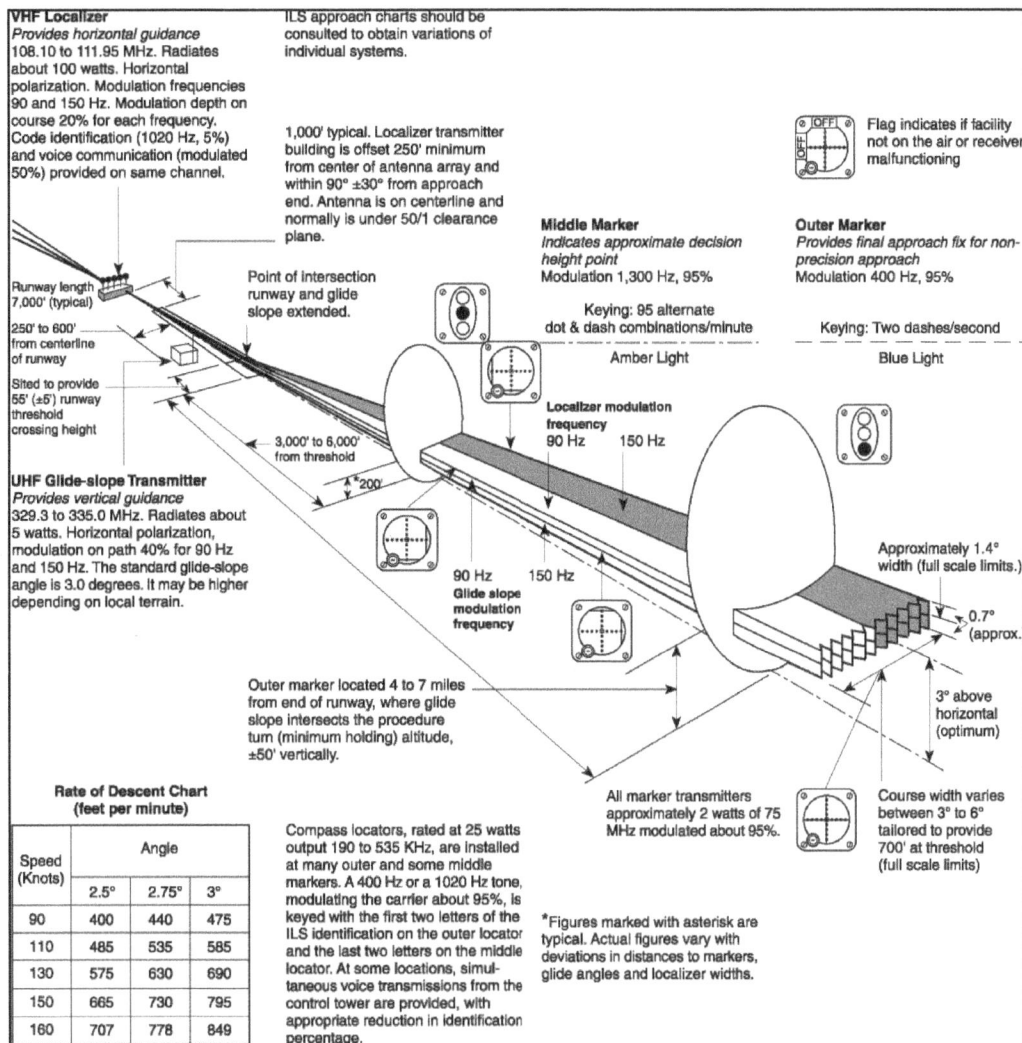

VHF Localizer
Provides horizontal guidance
108.10 to 111.95 MHz. Radiates about 100 watts. Horizontal polarization. Modulation frequencies 90 and 150 Hz. Modulation depth on course 20% for each frequency. Code identification (1020 Hz, 5%) and voice communication (modulated 50%) provided on same channel.

ILS approach charts should be consulted to obtain variations of individual systems.

1,000' typical. Localizer transmitter building is offset 250' minimum from center of antenna array and within 90° ±30° from approach end. Antenna is on centerline and normally is under 50/1 clearance plane.

Flag indicates if facility not on the air or receiver malfunctioning

Middle Marker
Indicates approximate decision height point
Modulation 1,300 Hz, 95%
Keying: 95 alternate dot & dash combinations/minute
Amber Light

Outer Marker
Provides final approach fix for non-precision approach
Modulation 400 Hz, 95%
Keying: Two dashes/second
Blue Light

Runway length 7,000' (typical)
250' to 600' from centerline of runway
Sited to provide 55' (±5') runway threshold crossing height

Point of intersection runway and glide slope extended.

3,000' to 6,000' from threshold

Localizer modulation frequency 90 Hz 150 Hz

UHF Glide-slope Transmitter
Provides vertical guidance
329.3 to 335.0 MHz. Radiates about 5 watts. Horizontal polarization, modulation on path 40% for 90 Hz and 150 Hz. The standard glide-slope angle is 3.0 degrees. It may be higher depending on local terrain.

*200'

90 Hz 150 Hz
Glide slope modulation frequency

Approximately 1.4° width (full scale limits.)
0.7° (approx.)
3° above horizontal (optimum)

Outer marker located 4 to 7 miles from end of runway, where glide slope intersects the procedure turn (minimum holding) altitude, ±50' vertically.

All marker transmitters approximately 2 watts of 75 MHz modulated about 95%.

Course width varies between 3° to 6° tailored to provide 700' at threshold (full scale limits)

Rate of Descent Chart
(feet per minute)

Speed (Knots)	Angle		
	2.5°	2.75°	3°
90	400	440	475
110	485	535	585
130	575	630	690
150	665	730	795
160	707	778	849

Compass locators, rated at 25 watts output 190 to 535 KHz, are installed at many outer and some middle markers. A 400 Hz or a 1020 Hz tone, modulating the carrier about 95%, is keyed with the first two letters of the ILS identification on the outer locator and the last two letters on the middle locator. At some locations, simultaneous voice transmissions from the control tower are provided, with appropriate reduction in identification percentage.

*Figures marked with asterisk are typical. Actual figures vary with deviations in distances to markers, glide angles and localizer widths.

Figure 10-22. Instrument landing system

Transition to the Instrument Landing System Localizer Course

10-202. The transition to the instrument landing system localizer course is performed by using radar vectors or a published approach procedure. First, tune the ILS, as soon as practical during the transition, and monitor the identifier during the entire approach. Set the published localizer front course in the course selector window before attempting localizer interception. If the aviators is using a flight director system or flight management system, the switches are positioned according to instructions in the aircraft operator's manual for intercept and final-approach modes of operation. Normally, manual selection of the final-approach mode is delayed until the aircraft heading is within 15 degrees of the localizer course and the course deviation indicator is within one dot of center. Use any available navigation facility (TACAN) to aid in remaining position oriented in relation to the localizer course and glide-slope intercept point. The glide slope has a usable range of 10 miles.

Accomplishing the Approach

10-203. Once the localizer course is intercepted, reduce heading corrections as the aircraft continues inbound. Heading changes made in increments of 5 degrees or less usually result in more precise course control. When on the localizer course, maintain glide-slope intercept altitude (published or assigned) until intercepting the glide slope. Published glide-slope intercept altitudes may be minimum, maximum, mandatory, or recommended altitudes and are identified by a lightning bolt ($\nearrow$). When the glide-slope intercept altitude is a recommended altitude, only comply with other IAP altitudes (FAF altitude for example) until established on the glide slope. When on glide slope, cross-check the aircraft altitude with the published glide-slope altitude at the outer marker/FAF to ensure that the aircraft is established on the correct glide slope. Do not descend below a descent restrictive altitude (minimum or mandatory) if the course deviation indicator indicates full-scale deflection. On approaches where the glide-slope altitude at the outer marker/FAF is not published, use all means available to ensure that the aircraft is on the proper glide slope and a normal descent rate is established. Airborne marker beacon receivers having a selective sensitivity feature should operate in low-sensitivity position to ensure proper reception of ILS marker beacons.

Using the Glide-Slope Indicator

10-204. Prepare to intercept the glide slope as the glide-slope indicator moves downward from its upper limits. Determine the approximate rate of descent to maintain the glide slope. The vertical velocity required depends on aircraft ground speed and ILS glide-slope angle. Slightly before the glide-slope indicator reaches center position, coordinate pitch and power control adjustments to the desired rate of descent.

10-205. Pitch adjustments made in increments of 2 degrees or less usually result in more precise glide-path control. As the approach progresses, smaller pitch and bank corrections are required for a given course or glide-slope indicator deviation. During the latter part of the approach, pitch changes of 1 degree and heading corrections of 5 degrees or less prevent overcontrolling.

Steering Commands

10-206. If using pitch and bank steering commands supplied by a flight director system, monitor flight-path and aircraft performance instruments to ensure that the desired flight path is being flown and aircraft performance is within acceptable limits. A dangerous error often occurs when the aviator is flying an ILS approach on the flight director system: the aviator concentrates on the steering bars and ignores flight path and aircraft performance instruments.

WARNING

Failure of the flight director computer (steering bars) may not always be accompanied by the appearance of warning flags.

Cross-Check

10-207. Maintain a complete instrument cross-check throughout the approach, with increased emphasis on the altimeter during the latter part. DA/DH is determined by the barometric altimeter. Establish a systematic scan for the runway environment before reaching DA/DH.

Decision Altitude/Decision Height

10-208. DA/DH is the height at which a decision must be made during a precision approach to continue the approach or execute a missed approach. Continued descent below DA/DH is not authorized until sufficient visual reference with the runway environment has been established. A momentary deviation below DA/DH without the runway environment in sight is only authorized with a proper missed approach initiated at DA/DH.

RADAR APPROACHES

Precision and Surveillance Approaches

10-209. The two basic radar approaches are the PAR and ASR. The precision approach provides the aviator with precise course, glide slope, and range information; the surveillance approach provides course and range information and is classified as a nonprecision approach. Upon request, the controller provides recommended altitudes on final approach to the last whole mile that is at or above the published MDA. Recommended altitudes are computed from the start descent point to the runway threshold. At the MAP, the straight-in surveillance system approach error may be as much as 500 feet from the runway edges.

Lost Communications

10-210. In preparation for radar approach, select a backup approach compatible with existing weather and the aircraft, where available. Be prepared to fly this approach in case of radar failure or lost communications. When experiencing lost communications, the aviator is automatically cleared to fly any published approach unless the controller previously issued a specific lost-communications approach. Attempt contact with the controlling agency if no transmissions are received for about one minute while being vectored to final, 15 seconds while on final for ASR approach, and 5 seconds on final for PAR approach.

Backup Approach

10-211. If unable to reestablish communications and maintain VFR, make the transition to backup approach. Intercept the approach at the nearest point that allows a normal rate of descent without compromising safety. Maintain the last assigned altitude or the minimum safe/sector altitude (emergency safe altitude if more than 25 nautical miles from the facility), whichever is higher, until established on the published approach.

No Backup Approach

10-212. If no backup approaches are compatible with the weather or the aircraft, the aviator advises the controller, upon initial contact, of his intent in case of lost communications. If local conditions dictate, the controller may specify the approach to fly when the aviator loses communications. The aviator is responsible for determining the adequacy of any issued lost-communications instructions.

Voice Procedures

10-213. The radar approach is predicated on voice instructions from approach control or radar controller. Repeat headings, altitudes (departing and assigned), and altimeter settings until the final controller advises "do not acknowledge further transmissions." During high-density radar operations, communication time is limited. Keep transmissions brief and specific, commensurate with safety of flight. Do not sacrifice aircraft control to acknowledge receipt of instructions.

Making the Transition to Final

10-214. The transition to final segment of the approach includes all maneuvering up to a point where the aircraft is inbound and about 8 nautical miles from touchdown. A dogleg to final is considered to be part of the transition to final segment.

10-215. During the transition to final approach, the radar controller directs heading and altitude changes, as required, to position the aircraft on final approach. Turns and descents should be initiated immediately after instructed. Perform turns by establishing a bank angle on the attitude indicator, which approximates a standard rate turn for the TAS flown but does not exceed 30 degrees of bank. When aircraft or mission characteristics dictate low turn rates, inform the controller; he can assist in clarifying lead points for turns or corrections.

10-216. Weather information issued by the radar controller includes altimeter setting, ceiling, and visibility. The controller is required to issue ceiling and visibility only when the ceiling is below 1,500 feet (1,000 feet at civil airports) or below the highest circling minimum, whichever is greater, or if the visibility is less than 3 miles. The controller furnishes pertinent information on known field conditions considered necessary for safe aircraft operation. Request additional information, as necessary, to make a safe approach. Use available NAVAIDs to remain position-oriented in relation to the landing runway and the glide-slope intercept point. The controller advises of aircraft position at least once before starting final approach.

10-217. Start the before-landing checklist (landing check), review approach minimums, and tune navigation equipment to comply with lost communication instructions when practical. Determine the approximate initial descent rate required on final approach by referring to the rate-of-descent chart located inside the back cover of the DOD FLIP (Terminal) IAP volumes or by using one of the formulas for two common glide slopes:

- A 3-degree glide slope equals ground speed multiplied by 10, then divided by 2, as shown in the following example.
- A 2½-degree glide slope equals ground speed multiplied by 10, minus 100, then divided by 2.

Example of Glide-Slope Formula

For a final approach ground speed of 180 knots and a 3-degree glide slope, 180 times 10, divided by 2, equals a 900 FPM rate of descent.

Accomplishing the Approach

Nonprecision (Airport Surveillance Radar)

10-218. The controller informs the aviator of the approach runway, the straight-in MDA (if a straight-in approach is being made), and the MAP location and issues advance notice where the descent to MDA begins. When the approach will terminate in a circling approach, furnish the controller with the aircraft category. The controller will issue the circling MDA. Circling MDA for ASR approaches is found in the DOD FLIP (Terminal) volumes. The circling MDA found on the individual IAP refers only to nonradar approaches.

10-219. When the aircraft reaches the descent point, the controller advises descent to MDA. If a descent restriction exists, the controller specifies the prescribed restriction altitude. When the aircraft is past the altitude limiting point, the controller advises to continue descent to MDA. The descent rate should be sufficient to allow the aircraft to arrive in time to see the runway environment and make a normal descent to landing.

10-220. Because of possible different locations of the MAP, recommended altitudes may position the aircraft at MDA at or slightly before reaching the MAP. Consider this in relation to the normal VDP required for the aircraft. The controller issues course guidance, when required, and gives range information each mile while the aircraft is on final approach. Approach guidance is provided until the aircraft is over the MAP unless a discontinuation of guidance is requested. The controller informs the aviator when the aircraft is at the MAP. Fly the aircraft at or above MDA until arrival at the MAP or until establishing visual contact with the runway environment. The aviator may be instructed to report the runway in sight; if the runway environment is not in sight, report it and missed approach instructions will be given. Depending on MAP location, descent from the MDA (once the runway environment is in sight) is often initiated before reaching the MAP to execute a normal (about 3 degrees) descent to landing.

Precision Approach Radar

10-221. The precision final approach, which normally occurs at 8 miles from touchdown, starts when the aircraft is within range of the precision radar and contact is established with the final controller. About 10 to 30 seconds before final descent, the controller advises the aircraft that it is approaching the glide path. When the aircraft reaches the point to start final descent, the controller states "begin descent." At this point, establish the predetermined rate of descent. Adjust power or use drag devices, as required, to maintain desired airspeed or angle of attack. When the airspeed or angle of attack and glide path are stabilized, note the power, attitude, and vertical velocity. Use these values as guides during the approach.

10-222. The controller issues course and glide-path guidance, and often informs the aviator of any deviation from course or glide path. Controller terminology includes "on course," "on glide path," "slightly/well above/below glide path," or "slightly/well left/right of course." Controllers may also issue trend information to assist in conducting precision approach radar (PAR) approach. Examples of trend information phraseologies used are the following: "going above/below glide path," "holding above/below glide path," "holding left/right or course." Trend information may be modified by using the terms "rapidly" or "slowly" as appropriate. The terms "slightly" or "well" are used with trend information.

10-223. Corrections are made immediately after instructions are given or when deviation from established attitude or desired performance is noted. Avoid excessive throttle, pitch, or bank changes. Normally, pitch changes of 1 degree are sufficient to correct back to glide path.

10-224. Accurate heading control is important for runway alignment during the final approach phase. When instructed to make heading changes, make them immediately. Heading instructions are preceded by the phrase "turn right" or "turn left." To prevent overshooting the desired course, the bank angle should approximate the number of degrees to be turned, not to exceed a one-half standard-rate turn. At high final-approach speeds, a large bank angle may be required to prevent a prolonged correction. In any case, do not exceed the one-half standard-rate turn. After a new heading is directed, the controller assumes that it is being maintained. Additional heading corrections are based on the last assigned heading.

10-225. The controller advises the aviator when the aircraft reaches the published DA/DH. DA/DH is determined in the cockpit either as read on the altimeter or when advised by the controller, whichever occurs first. The controller continues to provide advisory course and glide-path information until the aircraft passes over the landing threshold, at which time the controller advises "over landing threshold." To provide a smooth transition from instrument to visual conditions, a systematic scan for runway environment should be integrated into the cross-check before reaching DA/DH.

10-226. The controller ceases providing course and glide path guidance when—

- The aviator reports the runway/approach lights in sight.
- The aviator requests to or advises that he will proceed visually ("Cairns radar, runway in sight, taking over visual.").

10-227. An aviator's report of "runway in sight" or "visual" alone does not constitute a request/advisement to proceed visually, and the controller continues to provide course and glide-path guidance. If the decision is made to discontinue the approach, based on aviator judgment or radar controller guidance, advise the controller as soon as practical during execution of the missed approach.

No-Gyro Approach (heading indicator inoperative)

10-228. If the heading indicator fails during flight, advise the radar controller and request a no-gyro approach. The final approach may be either precision or surveillance. Perform turns during the transition to final by establishing an angle of bank on the attitude indicator that approximates a standard rate turn, not to exceed 30 degrees of bank. Perform turns on final by establishing an angle of bank on the attitude indicator that approximates a half standard-rate turn. If unable to comply with these turn rates, inform the controller so that ATC may determine lead points for turn and heading corrections. Initiate turns immediately upon hearing "turn right" or "turn left." Stop the turn on receipt of "stop turn." Acknowledge controller commands to start or stop turns until advised not to acknowledge further transmissions. Do not use half standard-rate turns on final approach until instructed; the controller may want standard-rate turns even on final approach if abnormal conditions exist (such as strong crosswinds and turbulence).

OTHER APPROACHES

TIMED APPROACHES FROM A HOLDING FIX

10-229. Timed approaches from a holding fix are conducted when many aircraft are waiting for an approach clearance. Although the controller will not specifically state "timed approaches are in progress," the assigning of a time to depart the FAF inbound (nonprecision approach), or outer marker or fix used in lieu of the outer marker inbound (precision approach) indicates that timed approach procedures are being used.

10-230. In lieu of holding, the controller may use radar vectors to the final-approach course to establish a distance between aircraft, ensuring an appropriate time sequence between the FAF and outer marker or fix used in lieu of the outer marker and airport. Each aviator in the approach sequence is given advance notice about the time that he should leave the holding point on approach to the airport. When a time to leave the holding point is received, the aviator should adjust the flight path to leave the fix as closely as possible to the designated time. Timed approaches may be conducted when—

- A control tower is in operation at the airport where the approaches are conducted.
- Direct communications are maintained between the aviator and center or approach controller until the aviator is instructed to contact the tower.
- If more than one missed approach procedure is available, none require a course reversal.
- If only one missed approach procedure is available, the following conditions are met:

Course reversal is not required.

Reported ceiling and visibility are equal to or greater than the highest prescribed circling minimums for the IAP.

- When cleared for the approach, aviators should not execute a procedure turn.

APPROACHES TO PARALLEL RUNWAYS

10-231. Procedures permit ILS instrument approach operations to dual or triple parallel runway configurations. Parallel approaches are an ATC procedure that permits parallel ILS approaches to airports with parallel runways separated by at least 2,500 feet between centerlines. When parallel approaches are in progress, aviators are informed that approaches to both runways are in use. During parallel approaches, ATC diagonally separates or staggers aircraft; in simultaneous approaches, ATC directs aircraft side-by-side on the approach (Figure 10-23, page 10-53).

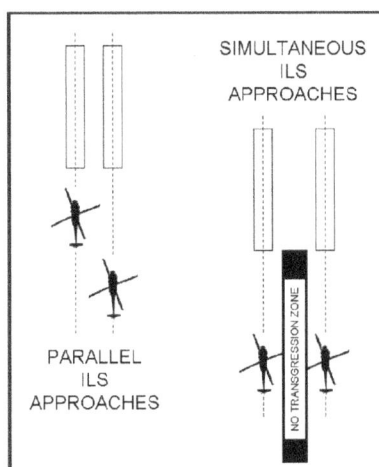

Figure 10-23. Parallel and simultaneous instrument landing system approaches

10-232. Simultaneous approaches are permitted to runways—
- With centerlines separated by 4,300 to 9,000 feet.
- Equipped with final monitor controllers.
- That require radar monitoring to ensure separation of aircraft on the adjacent parallel approach course.

10-233. The approach procedure chart includes the note "simultaneous approaches authorized runways 14L and 14R," identifying appropriate runways. When advised that simultaneous parallel approaches are in progress, aviators must advise approach control immediately of malfunctioning or inoperative components.

10-234. Parallel approach operations demand heightened aviator SA. The proximity of adjacent aircraft conducting simultaneous parallel approaches mandates strict compliance with all ATC clearances and approach procedures. Aviators must pay particular attention to the following approach chart information: name and number of approach, localizer frequency, inbound course, glide-slope intercept altitude, DA/DH, missed approach instructions, special notes/procedures, and the assigned runway location and proximity to adjacent runways. Aviators exercise strict radio discipline, which includes continuous monitoring of communications and avoidance of lengthy, unnecessary radio transmissions.

SIDE-STEP MANEUVER

10-235. ATC may authorize a side-step maneuver to either one of two parallel runways that are separated by 1,200 feet or less, followed by a straight-in landing on the adjacent runway. Aircraft that execute a side-step maneuver will be cleared for a specific approach procedure and landing on the adjacent parallel runway. For example, "Cleared ILS runway seven left approach, side-step to runway seven right." Aviators are expected to commence the side-step maneuver as soon as possible after the runway or runway environment is in sight. Landing minimums to the adjacent runway are based on nonprecision criteria and are higher than precision minimums to the primary runway but are normally lower than published circling minimums.

CIRCLING APPROACH

10-236. Landing minimums are listed on the approach chart under "CIRCLING." Circling minimums apply when it is necessary to circle the airport or maneuver for landing or when no straight-in minimums are specified on the approach chart. The circling minimums published on the instrument approach chart provide a minimum of 300 feet of obstacle clearance in the circling area (Figure 10-24, page 10-54).

During a circling approach, maintain visual contact with the runway of intended landing and fly no lower than the circling minimums until in position to make a final descent for a landing. If the ceiling allows, fly at an altitude that more nearly approximates the aircraft's VFR traffic pattern altitude. This altitude makes maneuvering safer and brings the view of the landing runway into a more normal perspective.

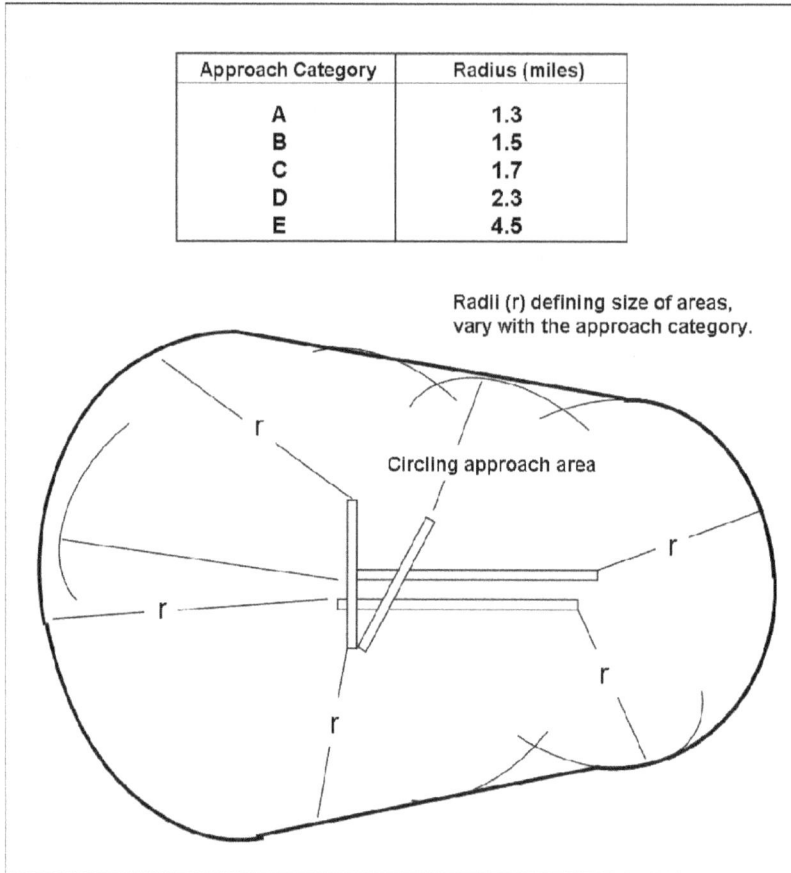

Approach Category	Radius (miles)
A	1.3
B	1.5
C	1.7
D	2.3
E	4.5

Radii (r) defining size of areas, vary with the approach category.

Circling approach area

Figure 10-24. Circling approach area radii

10-237. Figure 10-25, page 10-55, shows patterns that can be used for circling approaches. Pattern "A" can be flown when the final approach course intersects the runway centerline at less than a 90-degree angle and the aviator sights the runway early enough to establish a base leg. When sighting the runway too late to fly pattern "A," circle as shown in "B." Fly pattern "C" if desirable to land opposite the direction of the final approach and the runway is sighted in time for a turn to downwind leg. If the runway is sighted too late for a turn to downwind, fly pattern "D." Regardless of the pattern flown, the aviator must maneuver the aircraft to remain within the designated circling area.

10-238. Sound judgment and knowledge of the capabilities and performance of the aircraft are the criteria for determining the pattern flown in each instance. It is necessary to consider all factors when an aviator flies a circular approach to include airport design, ceiling and visibility, wind direction and velocity, final approach course alignment, distance from the FAF to the runway, and ATC instructions.

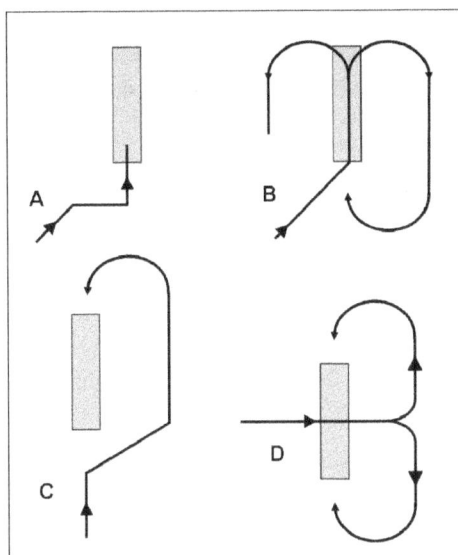

Figure 10-25. Circling approaches

MISSED APPROACHES

10-239. A missed approach procedure is formulated for each published instrument approach allowing the aviator to return to the airway structure while remaining clear of obstacles. The procedure is shown on the approach chart in text and graphic form and should be studied and mastered before beginning the approach.

10-240. When the aviator initiates a missed approach procedure at the MAP, the aviator establishes a climb pitch attitude while setting climb power. Configure the aircraft for climb, turn to the appropriate heading, advise ATC that the aircraft is executing a missed approach, and request further clearances. If initiating the missed approach before reaching the MAP (unless otherwise cleared by ATC), continue to fly the IAP as specified on the approach plate at or above the MDA or DA/DH before beginning a turn. If visual reference is lost while circling to land IFR, execute the appropriate missed approach procedure. Make the initial climbing turn toward the landing runway and maneuver to intercept and fly the missed approach course. Aviators should immediately execute the missed approach procedure when—

- The runway environment is not in sight.
- Unable to make a safe landing.
- Directed by the controlling agency.

10-241. Missed approach procedures are related to FAF location. When the FAF is not located on the field, the missed approach procedure specifies distance from the facility to the MAP. The airport diagram on the IAP shows the time from the facility to the missed approach at various ground speeds, which are determined from airspeed, wind, and distance values. This time determines when to report and execute a missed approach if applicable minimums are not available. Missed approach instructions are provided before starting final approach of an ASR or a PAR approach.

10-242. If an aviator decides to execute a missed approach before reaching the missed approach point, the aviator should continue along the IAP routing at or above the MDA/DA/DH until reaching the missed approach point. Climb to the missed approach altitude while following the IAP routing. Do not initiate any turns on the missed approach until reaching the missed approach point. If ATC issues a vector on the missed approach, consider this the new clearance.

SECTION IX – LANDING

10-243. ATC provides current visibility reports appropriate to the runway in use. These reports may be in the form of prevailing visibility, runway visual value (RVV), or RVR. However, only the aviator can determine if flight visibility meets landing requirements indicated on the approach chart. If flight visibility meets the minimum prescribed for the approach, then the approach may be continued to a landing. If flight visibility is less than that prescribed for the approach, the aviator must execute a missed approach, regardless of reported visibility.

10-244. The landing minimums published on IAP charts are based on full operation of all components and visual aids associated with the instrument approach chart being used. Higher minimums are required with inoperative components or visual aids. For example, if the approach lighting with sequenced flashing lights (ALSF)-1 approach lighting system is inoperative, visibility minimums for an ILS are increased by one-quarter mile. If more than one component is inoperative, each minimum is raised to the highest minimum required by any single inoperative component. ILS glide-slope inoperative minimums are published on instrument approach charts as localizer minimums. Consult the "Inoperative Components or Visual Aids Table" (printed on the inside front cover of each TPP) or "Inop Components Table" in the supplementary enclosures of the DOD FLIP (Terminal) IAP charts for a complete description of the effect of inoperative components on approach minimums.

LAND AND HOLD SHORT OPERATIONS

10-245. LAHSO includes landing and holding short of an intersecting runway or taxiway, or some other predetermined point on the runway other than specifically on a runway or taxiway. Previously, simultaneous operations on intersecting runways (SOIR) were used exclusively to describe simultaneous operations on two intersecting runways–either two aircraft landing simultaneously or one aircraft landing and another departing. The term LAHSO incorporates SOIR and is expanded to include holding short of a taxiway and predetermined points on the runway. Additional operations are outlined in FAA Order 7210.3, chapter 10.

10-246. U.S. Army aircraft are not authorized to accept LAHSO clearances because of safety concerns. Army aircraft types were omitted from FAA Order 7210.3, chapter 10, for these reasons.

LANDING FEES

10-247. Check the FLIP for airfields of intended use to determine if a landing fee is charged. If so, have sufficient funds but consider that CFR Title 14, Part 152, appendix D, paragraph 26 states, in part, that "All facilities of the Airport developed with Federal aid and all those usable for the landing and taking off of aircraft, will be available to the United States at all times, without charge, for use by government aircraft in common with other aircraft, except that if use by government aircraft is substantial, a reasonable share, proportional to such use, of the cost of operating and maintaining facilities so used, may be charged." If paying a landing fee, obtain a receipt. If possible, relay the person's name, organization, airport name, and telephone numbers to the USAASA, Airspace Support Division.

Note. If using fixed base operator (FBO) services or facilities, payment may be required. Marshaling and use of restrooms and lounge are not considered landing fees.

Chapter 11

Emergency Operations

Changing weather conditions, ATC, aircraft, and aviators are variables that make instrument flying an unpredictable and challenging operation. Safety of the flight depends on the aviator's ability to manage these variables while maintaining positive aircraft control and adequate situational awareness. This chapter discusses recognition and suggested remedies for emergency events related to unforecasted, adverse weather, aircraft system malfunctions, communication/navigation system malfunctions, loss of SA, and inadvertent instrument meteorological conditions (IIMCs).

SECTION I – EMERGENCIES

11-1. An emergency can be either a distress or urgency condition as defined in the pilot/controller glossary:

Contents

- **Distress**—a condition of being threatened by serious and/or imminent danger and requiring immediate assistance.
- **Urgency**—a condition of being concerned about safety and requiring timely but not immediate assistance; a potential distress condition.

11-2. Aviators do not hesitate to declare an emergency when faced with distress conditions such as fire, mechanical failure, or structural damage. However, some are reluctant to report an urgency condition when encountering situations that may not be immediately perilous but are potentially catastrophic. An aircraft is in an urgency condition the moment that the aviator becomes doubtful about position, fuel endurance, weather, or any other condition that could adversely affect flight safety. This is the time to request assistance—not after the situation has developed into a distress condition.

11-3. The PC is responsible for crew, passengers, and operation of the aircraft at all times. Both AR 95-1 and FAR 91.3 allow deviations from regulations during emergencies. This leeway allows the PC to make the best decision to ensure safety of all personnel during these contingencies. Also, by declaring an emergency during flight, that aircraft becomes a priority to land safely. Aviators who become apprehensive for their safety for any reason should request assistance immediately. Assistance is available in the form of radio, radar, direction finding stations, and other aircraft.

UNFORECASTED ADVERSE WEATHER

INADVERTENT THUNDERSTORM ENCOUNTER

11-4. An aviator should avoid flying through a thunderstorm of any intensity. However, certain conditions may be present that could lead to an inadvertent thunderstorm encounter. For example, flying in areas where thunderstorms are embedded in large cloud masses may make thunderstorm avoidance difficult, even when the aircraft is equipped with thunderstorm detection equipment. Aviators must be prepared to deal with inadvertent thunderstorm penetration. At the very least, a thunderstorm encounter subjects the aircraft to turbulence that could be severe. The aviator, as well as the crew and any passengers, should tighten seat belts and shoulder harnesses and secure any loose items in the cabin.

11-5. As with any emergency, the first order of business is to fly the aircraft. The aviator workload will be high; therefore, increased concentration is necessary to maintain an instrument scan. Once in a thunderstorm, it is better to maintain a course straight through the thunderstorm rather than turning around. A straight course will most likely get the aviator out of the hazard in the least amount of time, and turning maneuvers only increase structural stress on the aircraft.

11-6. Reduce power to a setting that will maintain a recommended turbulence penetration speed as described in the appropriate aircraft operator's manual, and try to minimize additional power adjustments. Concentrate on keeping the aircraft in a level attitude while allowing airspeed and altitude to fluctuate. Similarly, if using autopilot, disengage altitude and speed hold modes because they only increase the aircraft's maneuvering–which increases structural stress.

11-7. During a thunderstorm encounter, the potential for icing also exists. As soon as possible, turn on anti-icing/deicing equipment, if the aircraft is equipped with it. Icing can be rapid at any altitude and may lead to power failure and/or loss of airspeed indication.

11-8. Lightning is also present in a thunderstorm and can temporarily blind an aviator. To reduce risk, turn up cockpit lights to the highest intensity, concentrate on flight instruments, and resist urge to look outside.

INADVERTENT ICING ENCOUNTER

11-9. Because icing is unpredictable, aviators may find themselves in icing conditions although they have done everything to avoid the condition. To stay alert to this possibility while operating in visible moisture, aviators should monitor the outside air temperature (OAT).

11-10. Anti-icing/deicing equipment is critical to safety of the flight. If anti-icing/deicing equipment is used before sufficient ice has accumulated, it may not be able to remove all ice accumulation. Use of anti-icing/deicing will reduce power availability. Refer to the appropriate aircraft operator's manual for use of anti-icing/deicing equipment.

11-11. Before entering visible moisture with temperatures at 5 degrees above freezing or cooler, activate appropriate anti-icing/deicing equipment in anticipation of ice accumulation; early ice detection is critical. Detecting ice may be particularly difficult during night flight. The aviator may need to use a flashlight to check for ice accumulation on the wings, fuselage, landing gear, and horizontal stabilizer. At the first indication of ice accumulation, the aviator must act to circumvent icing conditions. Options for action once ice has begun to accumulate on the aircraft are the following:
- Move to an altitude with significantly colder temperatures.
- Move to an altitude with temperatures above freezing.
- Fly to an area clear of visible moisture.
- Change the heading, and fly to an area of known nonicing conditions.

11-12. If these options are not available, consider an immediate landing at the nearest suitable airport. Anti-icing/deicing equipment does not allow aircraft to operate in icing conditions indefinitely; it only provides more time to evade icing conditions.

PRECIPITATION STATIC

11-13. P-static occurs when accumulated static electricity discharges from extremities of the aircraft. This discharge has the potential to create problems for the instrument aviator. These problems range from serious, such as complete loss of VHF communications and erroneous magnetic compass readings, to the annoyance of high-pitched audio squealing and St. Elmo's fire.

11-14. P-static is caused when an aircraft encounters airborne particles during flight (rain or snow) and develops a negative charge. It can also result from atmospheric electric fields in thunderstorm clouds. When a significant negative voltage level is reached, the aircraft discharges it, creating electrical disturbances. To reduce problems associated with P-static, the aviator ensures that the aircraft's static wicks are maintained and accounted for. Broken or missing static wicks are replaced before an instrument flight.

AIRCRAFT SYSTEM MALFUNCTIONS

11-15. Preventing aircraft system malfunctions that might lead to an in-flight emergency begins with a thorough preflight inspection. In addition to items normally checked before VFR flight, aviators intending to fly IFR should pay particular attention to antennas, static wicks, anti-icing/deicing equipment, pitot tube, and static ports. During taxi, verify operation and accuracy of all flight instruments. The aviator must ensure that all systems are operational before departing into IFR conditions.

GENERATOR

11-16. Depending on aircraft being flown, a generator failure is indicated in different ways. Some aircraft use an ammeter that indicates the state of charge or discharge of the battery. A positive indication on the ammeter indicates a charge condition; a negative indication reveals a discharge condition. Other aircraft use a loadmeter to indicate the load being carried by the generator. If the generator fails, a zero load indication is shown on the loadmeter. As a minimum, a caution light is installed to indicate a generator failure. Review the appropriate aircraft operator's manual for information on the type of systems installed in the aircraft.

11-17. Once a generator failure is detected, the aviator must reduce electrical load on the battery and land as soon as practical. Depending on electrical load and condition of the battery, sufficient power may be available for an hour or more of flight or for only a matter of minutes. The aviator must be familiar with systems requiring electricity to run and which continue to operate without power. The aviator can attempt to troubleshoot generator failure by following established procedures published in the appropriate aircraft operator's manual. If the generator cannot be reset, inform ATC of an impending electrical failure.

INSTRUMENT

11-18. System or instrument failure is usually identified by a warning indicator or an inconsistency between indications on the attitude indicator, supporting performance instruments, and instruments at the other pilot station, if so equipped. Aircraft control must be maintained while the aviator identifies the failed components. Expedite cross-check including all flight instruments. The problem may be individual instrument failure or a system failure affecting several instruments.

11-19. One method of identification involves an immediate comparison of the attitude indicator with rate-of-turn indicator and VSI. Along with providing pitch-and-bank information, this technique compares the static system with the pressure system and electrical system. Identify failed components, and use remaining functional instruments to maintain aircraft control.

11-20. Attempt to restore inoperative components by checking the appropriate power source, changing to a backup or alternate system, and resetting the instrument if possible. Covering failed instruments may enhance the ability to maintain aircraft control and navigate the aircraft. ATC is advised of the problem and, if necessary, declares an emergency before the situation deteriorates beyond the ability to recover.

PITOT/STATIC SYSTEM

11-21. A pitot or static system failure can also cause erratic and unreliable instrument indications. When a static system problem occurs, it affects the airspeed indicator, altimeter, and VSI. In the absence of an alternate static source in an unpressurized aircraft, the aviator could break the glass on the VSI. The VSI is not required for instrument flight, and breaking the glass provides the altimeter and airspeed indicator a source of static pressure. Breaking the glass could cause additional instrument errors.

COMMUNICATION/NAVIGATION

TWO-WAY RADIO FAILURE

11-22. Avionics equipment has become very reliable, and the likelihood of a complete communications failure is remote. However, each IFR flight should be planned and executed in anticipation of a two-way radio failure. At any point during a flight, the aviator must know exactly what route and altitude to fly and when to continue beyond a clearance limit. The FIH describes procedures to be followed in case of two-way radio communications failure.

COMMUNICATION/NAVIGATION MALFUNCTION

11-23. Reports are made to ATC or FSS facilities of any loss in controlled airspace of VOR, TACAN, ADF, LF navigation receiver capability, complete or partial loss of ILS receiver capability, or impairment of air-to-ground communications capability. Reports include aircraft identification, equipment affected, degree to which the capability to operate under IFR in the ATC system is impaired, and nature and extent of assistance desired from ATC.

LOSS OF SITUATIONAL AWARENESS

11-24. SA is an overall assessment of environmental elements and how they affect flight. A knowledgeable aviator makes proactive decisions. SA permits the aviator to make decisions ahead of time and allows evaluation of several different options. Conversely, an aviator missing important pieces of the puzzle makes reactive decisions. Poor SA means that this aviator lacks vision regarding future events; the aviator is forced to make decisions quickly, often with limited options. During a typical IFR flight, an aviator operates at varying levels of SA. An aviator may be en route to a destination with a high level of SA when ATC issues an unexpected STAR. Because the STAR is unexpected and the aviator is unfamiliar with the procedure, SA is reduced. However, after becoming familiar with the STAR and resuming normal navigation, the aviator returns to a higher level of SA.

11-25. Factors reducing SA include distractions, unusual or unexpected events, complacency, high workload, unfamiliar situations, and inoperative equipment. In some situations, a loss of SA may be beyond an aviator's control. With an electrical system failure and associated loss of an attitude indication, an aviator may find the aircraft in an unusual attitude. In this situation, established procedures are used to regain SA. Aviators must be alert to loss of SA especially when hampered by a reactive mindset. To regain SA, reassess the situation and work toward understanding. The aviator may need to seek additional information from other sources, such as navigation instruments, other crew members, or ATC.

INADVERTENT INSTRUMENT METEOROLOGICAL CONDITION

11-26. Some aviators have the misconception that IIMC does not apply to an IFR flight. Two potential scenarios are below:
- Aircraft has entered VMC during an IAP and while circling to land encounters IMC.
- During a nonprecision IAP, the aircraft is VMC while continuing at MDA and the aviator on the controls has made the transition to visual too soon; as the aircraft is slowed for landing, it climbs back up into IMC.

11-27. To survive an encounter with IIMC, an aviator must recognize and accept the seriousness of the situation. The aviator needs to immediately commit to the instruments and perform recovery procedures according to the appropriate ATM.

RECOGNITION

11-28. When an aviator is in IMC, he is unable to maintain aircraft attitude control by reference to the natural horizon. During IMC encounters, whether inadvertent or intentional, the aviator is unable to navigate or establish geographical positions by visual reference to landmarks on the surface. IIMC must be accepted as a genuine emergency, requiring appropriate action. When IIMC is encountered, the crew must commit to instruments and applicable recovery procedures.

MAINTAINING AIRCRAFT CONTROL

11-29.   Once the crew members recognize the situation, they commit to controlling the aircraft by using and trusting flight instruments. Attempting to search outside the cockpit for visual confirmation can result in spatial disorientation and complete control loss. The crew must rely on instruments and depend on crew coordination to facilitate that transition. Although the task at hand may appear overwhelming and the situation may be compounded by extreme apprehension, the crew must consciously commit to maintaining aircraft control.

11-30.   The most important concern, along with maintaining aircraft control, is to initiate a climb immediately. An immediate climb will provide a greater separation from natural and man-made obstacles, as well as improve radar reception of the aircraft by ATC. An immediate climb should be appropriate for the current conditions, environment, and known or perceived obstacles.

11-31.   The five basic procedures listed below assist in maintaining aircraft control after encountering IIMC with the most critical action being to immediately announce IIMC and begin a substantial climb while procedures are being performed. These procedures are performed nearly simultaneously:
- **Attitude** – Level wings on the attitude indicator.
- **Heading** – Maintain heading; turn only to avoid known obstacles or as briefed for multiship operations.
- **Torque** – Adjust torque as necessary for desired climb rate.
- **Airspeed** – Adjust airspeed as necessary.

Complete the IIMC recovery according to local regulations and policies.

11-32.   The aviator must trust flight instruments concerning the aircraft's attitude regardless of intuition or visual interpretation. The vestibular sense (motion sensing by the inner ear) can confuse the aviator. Because of inertia, sensory areas of the inner ear cannot detect slight changes in aircraft attitude nor can they accurately sense attitude changes that occur at a uniform rate over time. Conversely, false sensations often push the aviator to believe that the attitude of the aircraft has changed when, in fact it has not, resulting in spatial disorientation.

ASSISTANCE

11-33.   After aircraft control is stabilized, other duties can be performed such as the following:
- Changing the transponder to the appropriate code.
- Contacting ATC on guard (if the frequency is not known).
- Complying with local directives and guidance.
- Tuning required navigational radios.
- Preparing the crew for IAP to be performed.

RECOVERY

11-34.   In case of IIMC, aviators must be prepared to execute preplanned recovery procedures according to AR 95-1, the applicable ATM, and local rules and regulations. Aviators may have limited or multiple options for recovery based on availability of approved IAP, NAVAIDs, and installed/operational aircraft equipment. The first option is to use approved DOD/U.S. Government IAP. The second option is to use FAA, ICAO, or host-nation IAP. Third, if operating in areas where no approved IAP exists, commanders should contact USAASA, which can develop and approve IAP for those areas. While operating in areas that do not facilitate the use of an approved IAP or flying aircraft that are not equipped to fly approved IAP, the aviator can use an emergency GPS recovery procedures as a last resort. Commanders determine the need for an emergency GPS recovery procedure, task an instrument examiner to develop the procedure, and have the procedure approved by the first 06 in the chain of command according to AR 95-1. Emergency GPS recovery procedures should be used only for training during VMC or actual emergencies when no other approved approach is available. The emergency GPS recovery procedure is developed using a simple calculation that meets or exceeds TERPS requirements. ATMs provide more detailed instructions for developing emergency GPS recovery procedures.

SECTION II – AIR TRAFFIC CONTROL REQUIREMENTS AND RESPONSIBILITIES

11-35. ATC personnel can help aviators during in-flight emergency situations. Aviators should understand the services provided by ATC and the resources and options available. These services enable aircrews to focus on aircraft control and help them make better decisions in a time of stress.

PROVIDE INFORMATION

11-36. During emergency situations aviators should provide as much information as possible to ATC. ATC uses the information to determine what kind of assistance it can provide with available assets and capabilities. Information requirements vary depending on the existing situation. ATC requires at a minimum, the following information for in-flight emergencies:

- Aircraft identification and type.
- Nature of the emergency.
- Aviator's desires.

11-37. The aviator, if time and the situation permit, should provide ATC with more information. Figure 11-1 lists additional information that would help ATC in further assisting the aviator.

```
• Aircraft altitude
• Point of departure and destination
• Airspeed
• Fuel remaining in time
• Heading since last known position
• Visible landmarks
• NAVAID signals received
• Time and place of last known position
• Aircraft color
• Aviator reported weather
• Emergency equipment on board
• Number of people on board
• Aviator capability for IFR flight
• Navigation equipment capability
```

Figure 11-1. Additional ATC information

REQUEST ASSISTANCE

11-38. When the aviator requests, or when deemed necessary, ATC can enlist services of available radar facilities and DF facilities operated by the FAA and military services. ATC can also coordinate with other agencies, such as the Federal Communications Commission and local authorities, and request their emergency services and facilities.

RADAR ASSISTANCE

11-39. Radar is a invaluable asset that can be used by aviators during emergencies. With radar, ATC can provide navigation assistance to aircraft and provide last-known location during catastrophic emergencies. If a VFR aircraft encounters, or is about to encounter, IMC weather conditions, the aviator can request radar vectors to VFR airports or VFR conditions. If the aviator determines that he is qualified for and the aircraft is capable of conducting IFR flight, the aviator should file an IFR flight plan and request a clearance from ATC to the destination airport as appropriate. If the aircraft has already encountered IFR conditions, ATC can inform the aviator of appropriate terrain/obstacle clearance minimum altitude. If the aircraft is below appropriate terrain/obstacle clearance minimum altitude and sufficiently accurate position information has been received or radar identification is established, ATC can furnish a heading or radial on which to climb to reach appropriate terrain/obstacle clearance minimum altitude.

EMERGENCY AIRPORT

11-40. ATC personnel consider the following factors when recommending an emergency airport to aircraft requiring assistants.
- Remaining fuel in relation to airport distances.
- Weather conditions.

Note. Depending on the nature of the emergency, certain weather phenomena may deserve weighted consideration. An aviator may elect to fly further to land at an airport with VFR conditions instead of closer airfield with IFR conditions.

- Airport conditions.
- NAVAID status.
- Aircraft type.
- Aviator's qualifications.
- Vectoring or homing capability to the emergency airport.

11-41. In addition, ATC and aviators should determine which guidance can be used to fly to the emergency airport. The following options may be available:
- Radar.
- DF.
- Following another aircraft.
- NAVAIDs.
- Pilotage by landmarks.
- Compass headings.

EMERGENCY OBSTRUCTION VIDEO MAP

11-42. The emergency obstruction video map (EOVM) is intended to facilitate advisory service in an emergency situation when appropriate terrain/obstacle clearance minimum altitude cannot be maintained. The EOVM, and the service provided, are used only under the following conditions:
- The aviator has declared an emergency.

- The controller has determined an emergency condition exists or is imminent because of the aviator's inability to maintain an appropriate terrain/obstacle clearance minimum altitude.

Note. Appropriate terrain/obstacle clearance minimum altitudes may be defined as minimum IFR altitude (MIA), MEA, MOCA, or MVA.

11-43. When providing emergency vectoring service, the controller advises the aviator that any headings issued are emergency advisories intended only to direct the aircraft toward and over an area of lower terrain/obstacle elevation.

Note. Altitudes and obstructions depicted on the EOVM are actual altitudes and locations of the obstacle/terrain and contain no lateral or vertical buffers for obstruction clearance.

RESPONSIBILITY

11-44. ATC, in communication with an aircraft in distress, should handle the emergency and coordinate and direct the activities of assisting facilities. ATC will not transfer this responsibility to another facility unless that facility can better handle the situation.

11-45. When an ATC facility receives information about an aircraft in distress, they will forward detailed data to the center in the area of the emergency. Centers serve as central points for collecting information, coordinating with SAR, and distributing information to appropriate agencies.

11-46. Although 121.5 megahertz and 243.0 megahertz are emergency frequencies, the aviator should keep the aircraft on the initial contact frequency. The aviator should change frequencies only when a valid reason exists. When necessary and if weather and circumstances permit, ATC should recommend that aircraft maintain or increase altitude to improve communications, radar, or DF reception.

ESCORT

11-47. An escort aircraft, if available, should consider and evaluate an appropriate formation. Special consideration must be given if maneuvers take the aircraft through clouds. Aircraft should not execute an in-flight join up during emergency conditions unless both crews involved are familiar with and capable of formation flight and can communicate and have visual contact with each other.

COMMUNICATIONS FAILURE

11-48. When an IFR aircraft experiences two-way radio communications failure, air traffic control is based on anticipated aviator actions. Aviator procedures and recommended practices are set forth in the AIM, CFRs, and pertinent military regulations such as the FIH. When the aviator of an aircraft equipped with a coded radar beacon transponder experiences a loss of two-way radio capability, the aviator is expected to adjust the transponder to reply on Mode 3/A Code 7600. ATC takes the following actions, as appropriate, if two-way radio communications are lost with an aircraft:

- For aircraft under immediate control jurisdiction, use all means available to reestablish communications with the aircraft; these may include, but are not limited to, emergency frequencies, NAVAIDs equipped with voice capability, FSS, and Aeronautical Radio Incorporated (ARINC).
- Broadcast clearances through available means of communications including the voice feature of NAVAIDs.
- Attempt to reestablish communications by having aircraft use its transponder or make turns to acknowledge clearances and answer questions; request any of the following in using the transponder:
    Request aircraft to reply Mode 3/A IDENT.

Request aircraft to reply on Code 7600 or, if already on Code 7600, appropriate stratum code. Request aircraft to change to stand-by for sufficient time to ensure the lack of a target is the result of requested action.

- Broadcast a clearance for aircraft to proceed to its filed alternate airport at the MEA if the aircraft operator concurs.

This page intentionally left blank.

Appendix A

Instrument Flight Rules Operations

Planning for an IFR flight depends on the nature of the mission, type and number of aircraft, distance to be flown, selected route, weather conditions, and navigational facilities. The checklist presented in this appendix applies to instrument flight planning within the United States. Aviator proficiency and judgment dictate necessary modifications to these procedures and techniques. When assigned a mission, the flight is planned to arrive at a fixed destination at a definite time. The type of aircraft, load, and personnel onboard are often predetermined; however, when aviators plan proficiency flights, they usually choose aircraft, destination, route, time, and other factors that affect the flight. When possible, variable factors affecting the mission are controlled to produce optimum flight conditions.

FLIGHT PLANNING

WEATHER BRIEFING SOURCES

A-1. All aviators are responsible and accountable for procurement and analysis of aeronautical weather reports and forecasts, including recognizing critical weather situations and estimating visibility while in flight. Local commanders establish policies specifying when DD Form 175-1 (Flight Weather Briefing) is required to be filed with the DD Form 175 flight plan (AR 95-1). Weather information for DD 175-1 is obtained from a military weather facility. If a military forecaster is not available, the PC will obtain a weather forecast according to DOD/U.S. Government FLIP. Army priority for obtaining a formal DD 175-1 weather briefing is the following:

- U.S. military weather forecaster.
- Combat weather team or supporting operational weather squadron (OWS).
- Other military or Government weather service.

A-2. If departing a location with no military or Government weather briefing and NOTAM services, obtain information by—

- Contacting the OWS for that area (see FIH, section C).
- Obtaining real-time NOTAM updates at https://www.notams.jcs.mil .

Note. Current operational publications should be checked for procedures and listings.

WEATHER DATA BRIEFING

A-3. The weather briefing includes the forecast for destination and alternate airfields at ETA to include the following elements of the forecast:

- Ceiling and visibility—applicable regulations should be checked for compliance; the destination forecast determines the requirement for selecting an alternate. If minimum conditions specified in AR 95-1 exist at the destination, an alternate airport is not required.
- Weather phenomena producing low ceilings and visibility.
- Hazards to flight such as thunderstorms, icing, gusty winds, and high-density altitude.
- Height of cloud tops.

A-4. The weather briefing forecast covers en route conditions to destination and alternate airfields to include the following elements:

- Hazards to flight.
- Freezing level.
- Height of cloud tops and bases.
- Flight-level winds and temperatures.

A-5. With the aid of a forecaster, a clear mental picture of the overall weather situation should be obtained, including locations of frontal systems and high- or low-pressure areas. The rate and direction of their movement and the associated weather conditions should be clearly understood.

AIRCRAFT EQUIPMENT

A-6. Check the aircraft logbook or other available source for onboard navigational equipment. Check for restrictions that might affect the mission (such as oil samples due and inoperative equipment).

FLIGHT INFORMATION PUBLICATION RESEARCH

A-7. The list provided is not all-inclusive and should be modified according to pertinent publications:

- Check the appropriate en route supplement (IFR or VFR) for departure, destination, and alternate if required.
- Check availability of fuel at destination and alternate.
- Check low-altitude en route chart for effective control zone hours.
- Check NOTAMs—flight information bulletins are no longer a source of NOTAM data.
- Review SIDs, published nonstandard DPs and weather minimums, and approach plate for departure airfield; this information assists in maintaining obstruction clearance during the takeoff and departure phases and aids in planning an orderly transition to the en route phase.
- Review approach plate for destination and alternate. Become familiar not only with the approach planned but also other available approaches; check for outlying IAFs or published feeder routes that may provide an orderly transition from en route to approach phases.

ROUTE SELECTION

A-8. Select the best route based on weather conditions and preferred routes. Check current operational publications for listings. Deviate from preferred routes only when safety or the mission requires. Departure and IAF and feeder route information are also considered. The closest available IAF or transition fix should be planned because it is normally assigned by ATC.

A-9. File for direct flight only if the mission requires or if considerable savings of fuel or time can be realized. If the flight penetrates uncontrolled airspace, ATC will not provide traffic separation.

ROUTE SURVEY

A-10. Conduct a route survey to destination and alternate airfields using navigational charts to determine the following:

- Primary radio aids for en route navigation. List frequencies, station identifiers, courses, and radials on the flight log.
- Supplementary radio aids to be used for position fixing and secondary navigation.
- Availability of ATC and weather radar en route.
- Distance between reporting points and total flight distance—total distance is computed from takeoff to the destination airport via the flight planned route.
- MEA, MOCA, MAA, MRA, and MCA.

ALTITUDE SELECTION

A-11. Select the best altitude for the flight based on the following:

- **Weather conditions.** Avoid altitudes where icing and turbulence will be hazardous.
- **Direction.** Unless otherwise required to avoid flight hazards or if requested by ATC, direction of flight in controlled airspace is based on the hemispherical rule. Hemispherical rule application in controlled airspace considers overall flight direction rather than individual legs that may vary from easterly to westerly directions; in uncontrolled airspace, hemispherical rule is mandatory for each individual leg.
  - Odd altitudes apply to magnetic courses, from 0 to 179 degrees.
  - Even altitudes apply to magnetic courses, from 180 to 359 degrees.
- **MEA, MOCA, MAA, MRA, and MCA**:
  - Select altitudes that comply with published minimum altitudes applicable to the flight.
  - On direct flights, determine minimum altitude based on charted obstacles and regulation requirements; when direct routes are planned, there are two basic considerations: FAR 91.177 must be complied with to ensure obstruction clearance, and NAVAID ranges and restrictions must be researched to ensure reception for the entire leg.
  - Do not plan a flight at the MEA if the flight-level temperature will be significantly below standard. Lowering of pressure levels in air significantly colder than standard results in true altitude being significantly lower than indicated altitude; request an altitude assignment above the MEA under these cold air temperature conditions.
- **Aircraft performance and equipment.** In selecting a flight altitude, consider the following:
  - Optimum operating conditions for the aircraft.
  - Oxygen availability.
  - Radio equipment limitations (such as range and altitude).
- **Air traffic control.**
  - Avoid relatively low altitudes that may conflict with approach control service in complex terminal areas.
  - Do not request unnecessary altitude changes.

DEPARTURE

A-12. Plan departures to comply with SIDs at airports where established. ATC normally employs SIDs, because it may assign a departure other than the one requested. Check availability of departure control (conventional or radar). Note appropriate frequencies. Study the local area chart, if published, or the departure area on the en route chart. Be familiar with radio facilities and intersections within the departure area.

PERFORMANCE PLANNING CARD

A-13. Consult the aircraft operator's manual to determine the performance planning card (PPC) information required to include TAS, Vne, cruise power setting, and cruise fuel consumption. Compute and file the TAS accurately. Later in flight, compute TAS to verify preflight calculations. If the actual TAS varies more than 10 knots from the filed TAS, notify ATC of the difference.

GROUND SPEED

A-14. Compute ground speed for each leg of the flight by combining forecast winds with the planned course and TAS (see Chapter 5).

ESTIMATED TIME EN ROUTE

A-15. Based on ground speed and distance, compute estimated time en route (ETE) for each leg of the flight between reporting points (see Chapter 5). On the initial leg, allow sufficient additional time for the planned departure and climb to flight altitude. If en route climbs are made at reduced airspeed, allow additional time for significant changes on the leg. Compute total ETE for the flight. This is the estimated time required en route from the airport of departure to the destination airport based on the flight plan route. Remember that the ETE is exclusive of the time required for planned en route delays. The ETE to the alternate airfield should include time from the—

- MAP to the missed approach holding point to include one circuit in the holding pattern.
- Missed approach holding point to the alternate including approach and landing time.

FUEL

A-16. Compute the fuel-on-board flight plan entry by subtracting the warm up, takeoff, and taxi fuel allowance (see the aircraft operator's manual) from the total fuel onboard (see Chapter 5). Divide this quantity by the cruise consumption rate. The cruise consumption rate is determined by cruise conditions and aircraft gross weight as explained in the aircraft operator's manual. Compute total fuel required for the flight based on the appropriate consumption rate specified in the operator's manual and include allowance for the following:

- Warm up and taxi.
- Initial climb (consult aircraft operator's manual for extended climbs).
- En route cruise to destination and alternate. Allow time, in addition to ETE, for known en route delays required by the mission; en route ATC delays usually cannot be anticipated. Also allow time for the approach.
- Fuel reserves required for IFR flight.

A-17. Compute surplus fuel by subtracting total fuel required from total fuel capacity. Surplus fuel is important because en route traffic delays and holding at the destination are not provided for in the fuel requirements. The purpose of reserve fuel is for unforeseen circumstances; do not plan to use reserves for routine delays.

TERMINAL AREA

A-18. If an area chart is published for the destination, study it carefully to become familiar with radio facilities, intersections, published transitions, and STARs. Study all published destination approaches that the aircraft is equipped to make. Become familiar with the following:

- Transitions.
- Final approach courses.
- Procedure turns.
- Approach minimums (DA/DH or MDA, ceiling, and visibility).
- Restrictions, warning, caution, and notes.

AIRCRAFT FLIGHT PLAN

A-19. Army aviators use a military flight plan according to DOD FLIP. FAA flight plans may be used in lieu of military forms when aviators depart from U.S. installations not having a military base operations facility.

SAMPLE INSTRUMENT FLIGHT RULES PLANNING REQUIREMENTS

A-20. Table A-1 provides techniques used in planning and preparation of flight under IFR conditions. It is not all-inclusive or aircraft specific but provides a starting point of common aircraft items.

Table A-1. Sample instrument flight rules planning requirements

Aircraft Capabilities	
Installed navigation equipment (ADF, VOR, DME, GPS)	PPC data (hover, cruise airspeed/fuel flow, arrival)
Weight/balance (AR 95-1, Chapter 5)	Anti-ice/deice equipment
Maintenance requirements (inspections, torque checks)	
Aircrew Capabilities	
Pilot takeoff minimums (AR 95-1, chapter 5)	
Required publications (DA Pam 738-751; AR 95-1, Chapter 5)	
Physical limitations (illness, crew endurance)	
Weather Planning	
Departure (AR 95-1, Chapter 5)	En route
Arrival (AR 95-1, Chapter 5)	Hazards to flight (TRW, icing, turbulence)
FLIP/NOTAM Research	
En route supplement (airfield data, fuel, PPR, NAVAIDs)	
En route chart (airways, direct routing, altitudes, course changes, MEA/MOCA changes)	
IAP (approach selection, weather/visibility, alternate requirements)	
FIH (lost communications, position reporting)	
AP3 (theater-specific procedures)	
GP (flight-plan preparation, aviator responsibilities, weather interpretation)	
NOTAMs	
Departure	
Standard/nonstandard departures (IAP; AR 95-1, Chapter 5)	
Weather requirements	
Departure IAP for emergencies	
En Route	
Route selection (airways, direct routing, IAPs, transitions)	
Altitudes (airway, hemispherical, ORTCA)	
En route weather hazards (DD Form 175-1)	
Course changes	
MEA, MOCA, MRA changes	
Arrival	
IAP availability (based on weather [WX], NOTAMS, aircraft equipment)	
Weather requirements	
Transitions from en route phase	
Alternate requirements (AR 95-1, Chapter 5)	
Inoperative components	
Estimated Time En Route Planning	
Times based on ground speed according to winds for each leg of flight	
Adjust for climbs/radar vectors	
Missed approach/alternate planning	
Calculate total time	
Fuel Requirements	
ETE-based	
Alternate/missed approach planning	
Reserve requirement (AR 95-1, Chapter 5)	
Flight Plan Preparation	
According to GP, Chapter 4; and AR 95-1, Chapter 5	

This page intentionally left blank.

Appendix B

Instrument Flight in a Theater of Operations

An Army aviator conducts a flight under instrument flight rules in an FAA or ICAO environment. Conversely, an Army aviator may experience IIMC during the initial entry phase of a combat operation and need to execute an emergency GPS recovery. Instrument flight may be required in a theater of operation in which a country's aviation infrastructure ranges from fully intact and operational to completely destroyed or nonexistent. This appendix provides information on what the aviator can expect from ATC upon entry.

ATC OPERATIONS

B-1. Air traffic command and control is crucial to the effectiveness of aviation operations and must be outlined, synchronized, and integrated effectively to meet the service or joint force commander's requirements. A typical theater of operation is composed of and operates as a joint force. These operations are set forth in FM 3-52.3, which provides multiservice ATC procedures. An airspace integration entity and Regional Air Movement Control Center (RAMCC), especially for nations with a nonfunctioning civil ATC system, is created to ensure that ATC issues are handled competently. A command-and-control relationship is identified between each of the four services and ATC. ATC operations occur during initial entry, transition, and sustainment operations.

INITIAL ENTRY

B-2. The Army, Marine Corps, and Air Force—either jointly or on their own—can provide an initial airfield ATC capability. Initial ATC forces are normally of short duration and require follow-on sustainment (less than 14 days). An ATC team can usually complete an initial stand-up with limited IFR capability within 12 to 72 hours, depending on the following factors:

- Joint force commander (JFC) risk acceptance.
- Flyability check.
- Required flight check.

B-3. All services can initially deploy systems that allow ATC radio communications and limited airfield IFR airfield abilities. These systems are matched to very specific aircraft systems such as TACAN, the Marine Corps ARA-63 airborne radar, Marine remote area automatic landing system (MRAALS), Army NDB, or Air Force mobile microwave landing system (MMLS). The Marine Corps and Air Force special tactics teams (STTs) have packable/portable airfield lighting systems organic to their units, allowing them to provide a complete initial airfield operating package. The Navy has onboard ATC communications, IFR capability, and lighting systems available on the amphibious assault ship, landing platform helicopter (LPH), multipurpose amphibious assault ships (LHDs), and general-purpose amphibious assault ships (LHAs). Initial service ATC capabilities are outlined in table B-1, page B-2.

Table B-1. Initial air traffic control capabilities

Service	Voice Communication (Secure)			Deployable NAVAIDs	Runway Lighting	VFR	Limited IFR
	VHF	UHF	FM				
Army	Yes	Yes	Yes	NDB, PAR	No	Yes	Yes
Air Force	Yes	Yes	Yes	MMLS, TACAN	Yes	Yes	Yes
Marine Corps	Yes	Yes	Yes	MRAALS, TACAN	Yes	Yes	Yes
Navy*	Yes	Yes	Yes	PAR, ILS	Yes	Yes	Yes
*Navy ship availability is based on the ship's proximity, patrol area, and time on station/in assigned area.							

B-4. The Marine Corps MRAALS is an all-weather instrument landing system. It transmits azimuth, distance, and elevation data in the J-band (15.412 to 15.680 gigahertz) and DME/station identification data in the D-band (962 to 1213 megahertz). It provides 40-degree azimuth and 20-degree elevation guidance out to 10 nautical miles on final approach to aircraft equipped with the ARA-63 airborne radar system. It also provides 360-degree DME and station identification information out to 40 nautical miles.

B-5. The Air Force MMLS is similar to an ILS. It has a glide-slope antenna, known as an elevation station, and a localizer antenna, known as an azimuth station. Coverage extends to a distance of at least 15 nautical miles. MMLS has 200 discrete channels in the range of 5000 to 5150 megahertz.

B-6. Navy ATC facilities (sea-based) are resident in numerous ships capable of launching and recovering aircraft. The two largest platforms are the aircraft carrier and large deck amphibious assault carrier. If an Army aircraft experiences IIMC and is routed to a Navy ship, the aircraft is most likely to be sequenced to a member of the large deck amphibious assault carrier ship class, specifically, an LHA, LHD, or LPH. Smaller ships do launch and recover aircraft; however, capabilities are generally restricted to terminal approach and landing on their specific platform.

ARMY NAVIGATIONAL AIDS

RADIO BEACON SET

B-7. The AN/TRN-30 radio beacon set transmits a homing signal, which is used in airborne direction-finding equipment installed in Army aircraft. The radio beacon provides an amplitude-modulated radio frequency signal on any one of 964 channels in the frequency range of 200 to 535.5 and 1605 to 1750.5, tunable in 500-Hertz increments. The RF output is automatically keyed into four-letter Morse code characters selected by the operator or manually keyed.

Radio Beacon Set Version 1

B-8. The pathfinder configuration consists of both the 15-foot and 30-foot antenna configurations that the AN/TRN 30 (V1) is capable of operating in. The power requirements are 24 volts direct current (DC). The V1 beacon requires a cleared area of 128 feet in diameter. Operating in the 15-foot antenna configuration, the beacon operates in the frequency range of 1605 to 1750.5 only and has a transmission range of 28 kilometers, or 15 nautical miles. Operating in the 30-foot antenna configuration, the beacon uses frequency ranges of 200 to 535.5 and 1605 to 1750.5 and has a transmission range of 46 kilometers, or 25 nautical miles.

Radio Beacon Set Version 2

Tactical Mode

B-9. The tactical configuration uses a 60-foot antenna configuration in the AN/TRN 30 (V2) radio beacon set and is a semipermanent NAVAID. The power requirements are 28 volts DC. The V2 beacon tactical configuration operates on the frequency range of 200 to 535.5 only and has a transmission range of 93 kilometers, or 50 nautical miles.

Semifixed Mode

B-10. The semifixed mode uses the 60-foot antenna configuration and continues to require 28 volts DC as its power requirement. The frequency range in this mode of the V2 beacon remains 200 to 535.5, but the transmission distance is 185 kilometers, or 100 nautical miles.

AIR TRAFFIC NAVIGATION, INTEGRATION, AND COORDINATION SYSTEM

B-11. The Air Traffic Navigation, Integration, and Coordination System (ATNAVICS) provides continuous, near all weather, precision landing assistance and departure recovery capability at Army tactical airfields and landing areas. In addition, the AN/TPN-31 provides area surveillance and aircraft identification capability for a 25 nautical mile radius of all sites and a 10 nautical mile precision approach radar capability. The system consists of three integrated radars: ASR, PAR, and SSR.

TRANSITION OPERATIONS

B-12. Transition operations are operations during the period that initial entry ATC resources require replacement, replenishment, augmentation, or upgrade of ATC services until sustainment ATC forces are established. Transitional ATC operations may be extended based on the intended time frame of the operation or availability of airlift or sealift resources to deploy sustainment ATC forces. Initial ATC forces require relief within 72 hours to reconstitute the initial entry capability and provide a sustained or more capable conventional airfield environment. Timelines for replacement of initial ATC forces are situation dependent.

B-13. Under ideal conditions, ATC operations flow from initial to sustained operations, without the need for a distinct transition phase. After the initial entry phase, which lasts about 72 hours, there is a typical timeline progression from initial through transition and into the sustained phase. This transition is shown in table B-2.

Table B-2. Transition to sustained air traffic control operations

Action	Timeline in Days			
	3-7	8-14	15-25	45+
Sustainment ATC forces and equipment arrive	X			
Air Force combat communications established	X			
Marine ATC established	X			
Army ATC established	X			
Transitional ATC begins		X		
Transition to sustainment forces begins			X	
Initial ATC forces relieved/forward deployment/reassigned			X	
Sustainment NAVAIDS operational			X	
GCA/radar approach control (RAPCON) operational			X	
PAR operational			X	
TACAN/NDB/MMLS operational			X	
PAR/GCA/TERPS approaches approved			X	
Host nation resumes ATC services				X
Sustainment ATC redeploys				X

SUSTAINMENT OPERATIONS

B-14. Sustained ATC operations occur when the desired operational capability is achieved. They terminate when services are no longer required. Services can provide VFR and IFR service to all aircraft through mobile control towers, radar systems, and communications connectivity. All forces are limited by the extent that they can be resupplied/maintained. Navy shipboard systems (FM 1-564) are limited only by the ship's ability to remain on station and maintain the operational health of its systems. Air Force and Marine ATC sustainment equipment provides complete ATC service to support a theater airbase mission; however, it requires extensive airlift to deploy. Currently, the Army does not have the capability to provide an approach control and airfield lighting. However, the Army can provide a fully instrumented airfield, which includes a tower and radar services. Table B-3 shows service capabilities and references.

Table B-3. Service capabilities and references

Service	Approach	GCA	Tower	Reference
Army		X	X	FM 1-120 and FM 3-52.3, Appendix B
Air Force	X	X	X	AFMAN 13-220
Marine Corps	X	X	X	MCWP 3-25.8
Navy	X	X	X	FM 1-564
Army manuals: AKO. Air Force manuals: http://www.e-publishing.af.mil/afpubs.asp. Marine Corps manuals: https://www.doctrine.quantico.usmc.mil/. Navy manuals: https://www.natec.navy.mil/.				

B-15. ATC units begin transition and restoration back to civil ATC services as soon as possible after conclusion of military operations. ICAO surveys airfields and ATC facility infrastructures to determine needed improvements and ensure that these facilities meet ICAO standards and recommended practices (SARPs). During the transition from military ATC personnel and equipment to host-nation or contracted services, military ATC personnel continue to be present, providing oversight, quality-assurance evaluation, procedures review, and host-nation agreements.

THEATER AIRSPACE COMMAND AND CONTROL

AIRSPACE CONTROL SYSTEM

B-16. There is a distinct difference between tactical flight procedures in a combat zone and IFR flight in a sovereign nation's airspace. During initial combat operations, Army ATS units establish IFR procedures within a combat zone under supervision and control of the combined forces air component commander (CFACC). Many of these procedures are published in loose-leaf format or an Aviator Procedures Guide (APG) rather than in the DOD FLIP. As the theater matures and civil authorities begin to reestablish airspace control, tactical flight procedures or FAA-developed approaches may be replaced by host-nation procedures. At the same time, the APG or loose-leaf procedures may be replaced by published FLIP procedures. This maturing of the airspace control system is either ongoing in a number of theaters of operation or complete. FLIP account managers and unit operations officers must be aware of the status of airspace control in their area of responsibility (AOR) and obtain sufficient FLIP products to operate in and around the theater. AR 95-1 requirements to use DOD/United States Government FLIP for all Army missions are not waived during contingency operations. Unprepared units may find it difficult or impossible to conduct IFR flight operations.

DEPARTMENT OF DEFENSE FOREIGN CLEARANCE GUIDE

B-17. Another source of information for operating outside of continental United States (OCONUS) or during contingency operations is the Department of Defense Foreign Clearance Guide (DOD 4500.54-G) accessible with a user name and password at https://www.fcg.pentagon.mil/. The DOD FCG, which may contain sensitive information, is based on bilateral arrangements between the United States and foreign government officials and is not releasable outside the United States government unless approved by a competent authority. This document provides necessary information for aircraft international mission planning and execution, personnel travel to foreign countries, as well as general information on foreign locations. Because the DOD FCG is directive for all DOD and DOD-sponsored travel abroad, travelers must ensure that they comply with this guide.

THEATER OF OPERATION PROCEDURES

B-18. The pace of operating tempo (OPTEMPO) and deployments to contingency operations continues to challenge the capabilities of Army aviation and ATS units across the force. Before deploying to an operational area, operations officers and FLIP account managers must complete several steps to ensure continued support. The unit's FLIP account changes to support operations in areas away from home station. United States Army units should contact the USAASA FLIP manager to suspend or curtail United States FLIP distribution amounts before deploying from home base and upon arriving or receiving a valid APO mailing address for the new location. Point of contact information is in the front of DOD FLIP publications or at usaasade@hq.hqusareur.army.mil. Traditional distribution methods for DOD FLIP products often are not feasible in fast-moving contingency operations caused by mail system delays. To overcome this delay, USAASA may set up FLIP distribution points in the theater of operations to ensure unit access to required FLIP information and/or FLIP information, which can be downloaded from https://164.214.2.62/products/digitalaero/index.cfm#plan. Specific procedures for a given theater of operations or country are found in the appropriate DOD FLIP Area Planning publication (Iraq information is located in AP/3), and new information is updated/posted according to the print cycle.

This page intentionally left blank.

Weather Reports and Risk Management

SECTION I – WEATHER REPORTS USED FOR PLANNING

DEPARTMENT OF DEFENSE FORM 175-1

C-1. Unless directed by higher headquarters or local operating procedures, all entries in individual blocks are at the discretion of the briefer, based on aircrew requirements and the weather situation. Entries on the DD Form 175-1, or equivalent briefing form, must be horizontally and vertically consistent, showing sound meteorological reasoning. For example, if a weather warning or advisory for surface wind is indicated in block 11, the surface wind forecast in block 9 should reflect the warning or advisory wind criteria, along with the warning or advisory number entered in block 13. Enter all times in UTC, all winds in five digits (six for wind speeds over 99 knots), and record all heights in hundreds of feet with the surface level as SFC.

PART I - TAKEOFF DATA

C-2. Enter the general forecast for takeoff one hour either side of the estimated time of departure (ETD). Figure C-1 reflects part I of the flight weather briefing. Table C-1, page C-2, explains these blocks. Meteorological codes can be found in AFMAN 15-124.

FLIGHT WEATHER BRIEFING								
PART I - TAKEOFF DATA								
1. DATE	2. ACFT TYPE/NO.	3. DEP PT/ETD	4. RWY TEMP	5. DEWPOINT	6. TEMP DEV	7. PRES ALT	8. DENSITY ALT	
060215	UH60/12345	KOZR/1400 Z	+7 °F/C	+5 °F/C		+20 FT	FT	
9. SFC WIND M	10. CLIMB WINDS		11. LOCAL WEATHER WATCH/WARNING/ADVISORY				12. RSC/RCR	
29012G18	24025 (SFC-060) 21035 (060-100)		NONE				N/A	
13. REMARKS/TAKEOFF ALTN FCST								

Figure C-1. Takeoff data

Table C-1. Takeoff data block explanation

Block No. and Explanation
1. Date
Enter UTC departure date in the format needed for operational use & communication with command and control (C2) systems (YYMMDD, DD/MMM/YYYY, & YYYY/MM/DD).
2. ACFT type/no.
Enter aircraft type (UH-60, CH-47) & radio call sign, mission #, or last three digits of tail #.
3. Dep PT/ETD
Enter ICAO ID# & ETD. Enter departure grid point or latitude/longitude for locations not having location identifiers.
4. RWY temp
Enter runway temperature (prefixed with + or -, as applicable) & designate °F/C used.
5. Dew point
Enter dew-point temperature (prefixed with + or -, as applicable) & designate °F/C used.
6. Temp deviation
Enter temperature deviation in °C unless requested in Fahrenheit.
7. Pres alt
Enter pressure altitude in feet, prefixed with + or -, as applicable.
8. Density alt
Enter density altitude in feet, prefixed with + or -, as applicable.
9. SFC wind
Enter surface wind direction in magnetic heading for missions departing the airfield & in true direction for missions departing another airfield. Designate "M" for magnetic or "T" for true. Enter surface wind direction to nearest 10° in 3 digits & surface wind speed (including gust) in 2 or 3 digits. Ensure that wind entries use a minimum of 5 digits (3 digits for direction & 2 digits for speed). Surface winds have 2 digits to represent gusts, while winds aloft use 3 digits for speed when winds exceed 99 kt. Enter VRB for forecast variable wind direction & CALM when winds are forecast to be calm.
10. Climb winds
Enter true direction & representative wind or winds from takeoff to cruise altitude. Input wind direction to nearest 10° in 3 digits & wind speed in 2 or 3 digits to nearest 5 kt. Input climb winds in layers if significant differences exist (wind speed changes of ≤ 20 kt &/or wind direction changes ≤ 30°& wind speed expected to be more than 25 kt) from 1 stratum to another.
11. Local weather watch/ warning/ advisory
Enter any known forecast/observed weather watch, warning, or advisory valid for ETD +/- 1 hour. When watch, warning, & advisory data for a location are not available (remote briefing), enter check with local flight agencies. Inform aircrew that status of local weather watches, warnings, &/or advisories is undeterminable, & recommend checking with local ATC or airfield operations.
12. RSC/RCR*
Enter latest reported RSC/RCR for departure airfield, if available. Runway condition codes can be found AFMAN 15-124. When the RSC/RCR is not available, enter N/A.
13. Remarks/takeoff ALTN FCST
Enter remarks on weather affecting takeoff & climb (such as inversions, icing, turbulence, and low-level wind shear). Ensure that briefing contents & local TAF are consistent. If requested, enter forecast for specific takeoff alternate & time.
*RSC-Runway Surface Condition; RCR- Runway Condition Reading

PART II – EN ROUTE AND MISSION DATA

C-3. Enter data for the duration of the mission and entire route of flight. Brief hazards for the specific mission, if applicable, and en route that are within 25 miles either side of the route and within 5,000 feet above and below the planned flight level. Insert or attach forecasts for drop zones, ranges, or low-level routes that apply to the specific mission. Figure C-2 reflects part II of the flight weather briefing. Table C-2 explains the blocks.

PART II - ENROUTE & MISSION DATA									
14. FLT LEVEL/WINDS/TEMP 060 23015/-02		SEE ATTACHED	**15. SPACE WEATHER**				**16. SOLAR/ LUNAR**	LOCATION	
				NO IMPACT	MARGINAL	SEVERE	BMNT 15/0531 z	SR 15/0624 z	MR 15/1952 z
			FREQ					SS 15/1730 z	MS 15/0724 z
			GPS					EENT 15/1823 z	ILLUM 92 %
			RAD						

17. CLOUDS AT FLT LEVEL			**18. OBSCURATIONS AT FLT LEVEL RESTRICTING VISIBILITY**			
YES	☒ NO	IN AND OUT	YES	☒ NO	TYPE	

19. MINIMUM CEILING - LOCATION 100 DHN FT AGL	**20. MAXIMUM CLOUD TOPS - LOCATION** 180 CSG FT MSL	**21. MINIMUM FREEZING LVL - LOCATION** 100 DHN FT MSL

22. THUNDERSTORMS			**23. TURBULENCE**			**24. ICING**				**25. PRECIPITATION**				
CHART 28 OWS 15/1000Z			CHART 28 OWS 15/1000Z			CHART 28 OWS 15/1000Z				CHART				
☒ NONE	AREA	LINE	☒ NONE	IN CLEAR	IN CLOUD	☒ NONE	RIME	MIXED	CLEAR	☒ NONE	DRIZZLE	RAIN	SNOW	PELLET
ISOLATED 1 - 2%			LIGHT			TRACE				LIGHT				
FEW 3 - 15%			MODERATE			LIGHT				MODERATE				
SCATTERED 16 - 45%			SEVERE			MODERATE				HEAVY				
NUMEROUS - MORE THAN 45%			EXTREME			SEVERE				SHOWERS				
HAIL, SEVERE TURBULENCE & ICING, HEAVY PRECIPITATION, LIGHTNING & WIND SHEAR EXPECTED IN AND NEAR THUNDERSTORMS.			LEVELS			LEVELS				FREEZING				
LOCATION			LOCATION			LOCATION				LOCATION				

Figure C-2. En route and mission data

Table C-2. En route and mission data block explanation

Block No. and Explanation
14. Flight level/winds/temp
Enter planned flight level in hundreds of ft in 3 digits (280 for 28,000 ft, 080 for 8,000 ft). Enter true wind direction at flight level in tens of degrees and speed to nearest 5 kt. Enter forecast flight-level temperature in °C (prefixed with + or -, as applicable). For significant wind-speed direction changes, break forecast into legs (BLV-MXF 27025/-15). Otherwise, brief a representative wind & temperature for entire route (32020/-18).
15. Space weather
Check appropriate block indicating frequency (FREQ), GPS, & radiation (RAD) that apply to mission. Indicate boundaries of degradation (UHF 20N180W to Paya Lebar). When weather forecasters use a High Altitude Radiation Dosage Chart, 10.0 to less than 100.0 millirems per hour constitute marginal, & 100.0 millirems per hour & greater constitute severe. A second option is to check appropriate blocks & attach applicable space weather charts to DD Form 175-1. Indicate attachments by writing SEE ATTACHED in block 15 (Figure C-2), & check "Yes" in block 34 (Figure C-4).
16. Solar/lunar
Enter location specified by aircrew, beginning morning nautical twilight (BMNT), sunrise (SR), sunset (SS), ending evening nautical twilight (EENT), moonrise (MR), moonset (MS), & percentage of moon illumination (ILLUM).
17. Clouds at flight level
Check appropriate block for flight level. "Yes" implies flight in clouds at least 45% of the time; "No," in clouds<1%, or "In & Out," in clouds between 1% & 45%.

Table C-2. En route and mission data block explanation

Block No. and Explanation
18. Obscurations at flight level restricting visibility
Check appropriate block. If "Yes," enter forecast obscurations type (such as fog, haze, and smoke) that could potentially restrict in-flight visibility along planned route or mission flight level. Specify intensity and location if applicable.
19. Minimum ceiling
Enter lowest ceiling en route for mission (if applicable) in hundreds of ft AGL & geographical location (060 ft BLV-MXF). For minimum ceiling over mountainous or hilly terrain, or in thunderstorms, indicate 010 ft BOSTON MTS or 020 ft SW KY TSTMS.
20. Maximum cloud tops
Enter maximum tops of cloud layers (exclusive of thunderstorm tops) with more than 4/8 coverage in hundreds of ft MSL and geographical location.
21. Minimum freezing level
Enter height and geographical location of lowest freezing level en route for mission (if applicable) in hundreds of ft MSL. If lowest freezing level is at surface, enter SFC & geographical location.
22. Thunderstorms
Enter name & date-time group (DTG) of thunderstorm product used (Air Force Weather Agency (AFWA)/OWS products, radar summary, satellite imagery, or National Weather Service (NWS) or foreign weather service in-flight weather advisories). Enter type, extent, maximum tops, & geographical location of thunderstorms affecting route or mission.
23. Turbulence
Enter name and DTG of turbulence forecast product used (such as AFWA/OWS products or NWS or foreign in-flight weather advisories). Enter type, intensity, levels, & locations of turbulence affecting route or mission.*
24. Icing
Enter name and DTG of icing forecast product used (such as AFWA/OWS products or NWS or foreign in-flight weather advisories). Enter type, intensity, levels, & locations of icing affecting route or specific mission.**
25. Precipitation
Enter type, intensity, character, & geographical location of precipitation areas affecting route/mission, & precipitation encountered at flight level not at surface.

* Not associated with thunderstorms.
**Like AFWA & OWS forecast products, in-flight weather advisories should be used as guidance when preparing the en route forecast. Carefully evaluate & temper all available data (such as radar, PIREPs/air reports [AIREPs], upper air soundings, and online resources) to determine potential effects on the mission & aircraft. Weather personnel must alert aircrews to all existing in-flight weather advisories, even if not used as a basis for the forecast, affecting the mission. If the weather briefer disagrees with the advisory, annotate in block 35 (Figure C-4). Whether the condition described is potentially hazardous to a particular flight is for the aviator to evaluate based on experience, mission, & operational limits of the aircraft. See the FAA AIM for detailed information on NWS in-flight weather advisories.

PART III - AERODROME FORECASTS

C-4. Brief the worst conditions expected during the valid period for the destination and alternate aerodrome. The forecaster ensures that the aircrew is briefed and fully understands the entire weather situation at the destination and alternate airport/location. The need for and selection of an alternate is an aviator decision. The forecaster enters forecasts for subsequent stops and alternates on request, advising the aviator of updates as necessary. Figure C-3, page C-5, shows part III of the flight weather briefing. Table C-3, page C-5, explains the blocks.

PART III - AERODROME FORECASTS							
26.	27. VALID TIME	28. SFC WIND	29. VSBY/WEA	30. CLOUD LAYERS	31. ALTIMETER	RWY TEMP	PRES ALT
DEST/ALTN ~~KOZR~~	Z TO Z 1200 – 1830	24025 M *	7	BKN100 OVC250	INS 30.18	ºF/C	FT
DEST/ALTN	Z TO Z	M T			INS	ºF/C	FT
DEST/ALTN ~~KLSF~~	Z TO Z 1200 – 1830	14015 M *	7	BKN100 OVC250	INS 30.02	ºF/C	FT
~~DEST/ALTN~~ TEMPO	Z TO Z 1200 – 1500	M T	5BR	SCT080 BKN100 OVC2500	INS	ºF/C	FT
DEST/ALTN	Z TO Z	M T			INS	ºF/C	FT
DEST/ALTN	Z TO Z	M T			INS	ºF/C	FT
DEST/ALTN	Z TO Z	M T			INS	ºF/C	FT
DEST/ALTN	Z TO Z	M T			INS	ºF/C	INS

Figure C-3. Aerodrome forecasts

Table C-3. Aerodrome forecasts block explanation

Block No. and Explanation
26. DEST/ALTN
Enter appropriate station identifier for destination (DEST) or alternate (ALTN) aerodrome forecast. Designate DEST or ALTN used. Place conditions described by a TEMPO group under appropriate station identifier, line through DEST/ALTN, & enter TEMPO in the block. In Army multistop missions, if the forecast for all stops is similar, enter A/S (for all stops) & the worst condition and location expected along the route. These entries imply that conditions at all other stops are the same or better.
27. Valid time
Briefings for Army missions require a valid time from ETA through 1 hour after ETA. For A/S entries, valid times are determined from original ETD to last stop, ETA plus 1 hour.
28. SFC wind
Enter true wind direction if destination is an airfield other than own. If flight departs from & terminates at own airfield with no intermediate stops, enter wind direction. Designate M for magnetic or T for true. Enter wind direction to nearest 10° & speed (including gusts) to nearest whole knot. For A/S missions, enter highest wind speed expected (including gusts) & location.
29. VSBY/WEA
Enter lowest prevailing visibility & weather expected during the valid period. Represent in SM for CONUS & overseas U.S. locations, & in meters for other overseas locations, unless otherwise specified by aircrew.
30. Cloud layers
Enter lowest prevailing sky condition expected during the valid period. Weather briefer must fully evaluate all NWS probability groups (PROB30/40%) & indigenous variations of the TAF code. If necessary, use Remarks section to record the briefer assessment & translation of these conditions.
31. Altimeter/RWY TEMP/PRES ALT
Enter lowest altimeter setting expected during the valid period in all cases except where impossible to obtain or determine. Enter forecast runway temperature (RWY TEMP), & designate ºF/C used (prefixed with + or -, as applicable). Enter forecast pressure altitude (PRES ALT) for arrival time at the destination.

PART IV - COMMENTS/REMARKS

C-5. Figure C-4, page C-6, reflects part IV of the flight weather briefing. Table C-4, page C-6, explains the blocks.

PART IV - COMMENTS/REMARKS								
32. BRIEFED RSC/RCR	YES	✗	NOT AVAILABLE	33. PMSV UHF 348.8	34. ATTACHMENTS	YES	✗	NO
35. REMARKS Max Temp: +16C Max PA (KOZR): +60FT Max DA (KOZR): +300FT For weather updates/briefs at Lawson AAF, call 28th OWS at DSN 965-0588 or commercial at 1-803-895-0588.								

Figure C-4. Comments/remarks

Table C-4. Comments/remarks block explanation

Block No. and Explanation
32. Briefed RSC/RCR
Check appropriate block, & enter latest available RSC/RCR value briefed to aircrew for destination & alternate in Remarks section.
33. PMSV
Enter Pilot-To-Metro Service (PMSV) frequency &/or phone patch number of weather unit providing brief. If requesting pilot (weather) reports (PIREPs) for specific areas, enter areas in Remarks (Request PIREP DURGC [during climb]).
34. Attachments
Check appropriate block, indicating if attachments are provided with briefing.
35. Remarks
Enter other significant data (data for which there was insufficient space in other blocks & specialized mission forecasts). Weather briefings provided electronically (faxed, posted on Web page, or e-mailed) must include following statement: Call (airfield weather forecaster) at DSN ###-#### or commercial (###) ###-#### for weather update. Include data on how to get weather support at the next location (for weather updates/briefs at Lawson AAF, call 28th OWS at DSN 965-0588 or commercial at 1-803-895-0588).

PART V - BRIEFING RECORD

C-6.   Figure C-5 reflects part V of the flight weather briefing. Table C-5, page C-7, explains the blocks.

PART V - BRIEFING RECORD			
36. WX BRIEFED TIME E1045/1100 z	37. FLIMSY BRIEFING NO.	38. FORECASTER'S INITIALS RS	39. NAME OF PERSON RECEIVING BRIEFING
40. VOID TIME 1145/1230 z	41. EXTENDED TO/INITIALS z	42. WX REBRIEF TIME/INITIALS z	43. WX DEBRIEF TIME/INITIALS z

Figure C-5. Briefing record

Table C-5. Briefing record block explanation

Block No. and Explanation
36. WX briefed time
Enter time that brief was provided. For briefings sent electronically, enter time that brief was faxed, posted on a Web page or local LAN or passed to a central dispatch facility (such as AMOCC). Append an E in front of time (E1045Z) if crew was not verbally briefed. If calling later for verbal briefing, put a (/) after E time & enter verbal brief time (E1045Z/1100Z).
37. Flimsy briefing no.
If a flight weather briefing folder, flimsy, or computer flight plan (CFP) was prepared, enter folder, flimsy, or CFP identification number.
38. Forecaster's initials
Enter initials of weather briefer/forecaster preparing & disseminating briefing.
39. Name of person receiving briefing
(Remote briefings only). If available, enter receiver's name &, if applicable, military grade.
40. Void time
Add 1:30 to weather briefed time. For Army briefings sent electronically, calculate void time from E time (block 36). If crew calls later for verbal briefing, recalculate void time from verbal briefing time & enter new void time after the first time (1145Z/1230Z).
41. Extended to/initials
When asking for an extension, recheck weather entries, rebrief, & indicate required changes (highlight/bold if electronic, green ink if paper). Enter initials of forecaster providing extension. Extensions follow same rule as void time.
42. WX rebriefed time/initials
(Not required for Army; Army equivalent is "extended to.") If weather rebriefed is different from that originally briefed, indicate changes to original weather entries as specified in block 41 & enter rebrief time & initials of forecaster providing rebrief.
43. WX debrief time/initials
Enter time & initials of debriefing forecaster.

METEOROLOGICAL AVIATION REPORT

C-7. The meteorological aviation report (METAR) is the weather observer's interpretation of weather conditions at a given site and time. The METAR is used by aviators and the NWS to determine the airport's flying category and to produce the terminal area forecast (TAF). Flying categories consist of VFR, marginal visual flight rules (MVFR), and IFR.

C-8. Although the METAR code is being adopted worldwide, each country is allowed to make modifications or exceptions to the code for use in that particular country. The United States reports temperature and dew point in degrees Celsius and continues to use current units of measurement for the remainder of the report.

C-9. The elements in the body of a METAR report are separated by a space. The only exception is temperature and dew point, which are separated by a solidus (/). An element not occurring or not observed is omitted. Figure C-6, page C-8, denotes elements of a METAR.

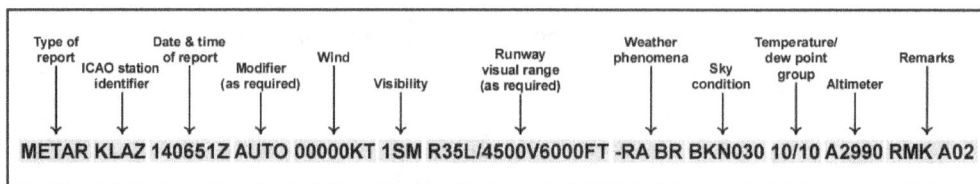

Figure C-6. Meteorological aviation report

TYPE OF REPORT

C-10. The two types of reports are the METAR and aviation selected special weather report (SPECI). The METAR is observed hourly between 45 minutes after the hour until the hour. It is transmitted between 50 minutes after the hour until the hour and encoded as a METAR even if it meets SPECI criteria (table C-6). It is a nonroutine aviation weather report taken when any SPECI criteria have been observed.

Table C-6. Special weather report criteria

Report Element and Criteria	
Wind	
Wind direction changes by 45° or more in less than 15 minutes, & wind speed is 10 kt or more throughout wind shift.	
Visibility	
Surface visibility decreases to less than or, if below, increases to equal or exceed 3, 2, or 1 mile or lowest standard IAP minimum as published in the National Ocean Service U.S. Instrument Procedures. If not published, use ½ mile.	
Ceilings	
The ceiling forms or dissipates below or, if below, increases to equal or exceed 3,000, 1,500, 1,000, or 500 feet or lowest standard IAP minimum as published in the National Ocean Service U.S Instrument Procedures. If not published, use 200 ft.	
RVR	**Tornado, Funnel Cloud, Waterspout**
Changes to above or below 2,400 ft.	When observed or when disappears from sight (ends).
Thunderstorm	**Squalls**
Begins or ends.	When they occur.
Precipitation	**Sky Condition**
When freezing precipitation or ice pellets begin, end, or change intensity or hail begins or ends.	A layer of clouds or obscuring phenomenon aloft that forms below 1,000 ft.
Volcanic Eruption	**Aircraft Mishap**
When an eruption is first noted.	Upon notification of an aircraft mishap, unless of an intervening observation.
Miscellaneous	
Any other meteorological situation designated by the agency or, in observer's opinion, is critical.	

INTERNATIONAL CIVIL AVIATION ORGANIZATION STATION IDENTIFIER

C-11. The METAR code uses ICAO four-letter station identifiers that follow the type of report. In the contiguous United States, the three-letter identifier is prefixed with K (for example, Los Angeles [LAX] becomes KLAX). Elsewhere, the first one or two letters of the ICAO identifier indicate in which region of the world and country (or state) that the station is located. Pacific locations—such as Alaska, Hawaii, and the Mariana Islands—start with P, followed by an A, an H, or a G respectively. The last two letters reflect the specific reporting station identification. For example, Anchorage (ANC) becomes PANC; Canadian station identifiers start with C, and Mexican and western Caribbean station identifiers start with M. For a complete worldwide listing, see ICAO Document 7910.

DATE AND TIME OF REPORT

C-12. The date and time that the observation is taken are transmitted as a six-digit date-time group appended with Z to denote Universal Time Coordinated (UTC), also known as Zulu (Z) time or Greenwich Mean Time (GMT). The first two digits are the date followed with two digits for the hour and two digits for the minutes. A corrected report bears the time of the previously distributed erroneous report.

MODIFIER (AS REQUIRED)

C-13. The modifier element, if used, follows the date-time element. The modifier AUTO identifies an automated weather report with no human intervention. If AUTO is shown in the body of the report, AO1 or AO2 will be encoded in the remarks section of the report to indicate the type of precipitation sensor used at the station. The remark AO1 indicates a report from a station without a precipitation discriminator, and an AO2 remark indicates a report from a station with a precipitation discriminator. The absence of AUTO indicates that the report was made manually or the automated report had human augmentation/backup. The modifier COR identifies a corrected report that is sent out to replace an earlier report with an error (METAR KLAX 140651Z COR...).

WIND

C-14. Wind element is reported as a five-digit group (six digits if speed is over 99 knots). The first three digits are the direction from which the wind is blowing in tens of degrees referenced to true north. Directions less than 100 degrees are preceded with a zero. The next two digits are the average speed in knots or, if over 99 knots, the next three digits (340105KT). Abbreviation KT is appended to denote the use of knots for wind speed. Other countries may use kilometers per hour or meters per second.

C-15. If the wind speed is less than 3 knots, the wind is reported as calm (00000KT). If the wind is gusty, 10 knots or more between peaks and lulls, G denoting gust is reported after the speed followed by the highest gust reported (08012G25KT). If the wind direction is variable by 60 degrees or more and the speed is greater than 6 knots, a variable group consisting of the extremes of the wind directions separated by V follows the wind group (08012G25KT 040V120).

C-16. The wind direction may also be considered variable if wind speed is 6 knots or less and varying in direction (the 60-degree rule does not apply). Variable wind speeds is indicated with the abbreviation VRB (VRB04KT).

Wind Remarks

C-17. Facilities with a wind recorder or automated weather reporting system report peak winds exceeding 25 knots in the Remarks element of the report following the event. The peak wind remark includes three digits for direction and two or three digits for speed, followed by the time in hours and minutes of occurrence. If the hour can be inferred from the report time, only the minutes are reported (PK WND 28045/15).

C-18. A wind shift is indicated by a change in wind direction of 45 degrees or more in less than 15 minutes with sustained winds of 10 knots or more. When a wind shift occurs, WSHFT is included in the Remarks element followed by the time that the wind shift began. If the hour can be inferred from the report time, only the minutes are reported. The contraction FROPA is entered following the time if the wind-shift is the result of a frontal passage (WSHFT 30 FROPA).

VISIBILITY

C-19. Prevailing visibility is reported in statute miles or fractions of statute miles, as needed, followed by SM. Other countries may use meters or kilometers. Prevailing visibility is considered representative of the visibility conditions at the observing site. Prevailing visibility is the greatest visibility equaled or exceeded throughout at least half the horizon circle, which need not be continuous. When visibilities are less than 7 miles, the restriction to visibility is shown in the weather element. Observations of volcanic ash, low-drifting dust, sand, or snow (regardless of visibility) are shown in the weather element.

Visibility Remarks

C-20. If tower or surface visibility is less than 4 statute miles, the lesser of the two is reported in the body of the report; the greater is reported in the Remarks element (TWR VIS 1 1/2 or SFC VIS 1 1/2). Automated reporting stations show visibility less than 1/4 statute mile (M1/4SM) and visibility 10 statute miles or greater. For automated reporting stations having more than one visibility sensor, site-specific visibility (which is lower than the visibility shown in the body) is shown in the Remarks element (VIS 2 1/2 RWY 11).

C-21. When the prevailing visibility rapidly increases or decreases by 1/2 statute mile or more during the observation and average prevailing visibility is less than 3 statute miles, the visibility is variable. Variable visibility is shown in the Remarks element with minimum and maximum visibility values separated by a V (VIS 1/2V2).

C-22. Sector visibility is shown in the Remarks element when it differs from the prevailing visibility and either the prevailing or sector visibility is less than 3 miles (VIS NE 2 1/2).

RUNWAY VISUAL RANGE (AS REQUIRED)

C-23. RVR, when required, is reported in the following format:
- R – Identifies the group.
- "35" – Runway heading.
- L – Identifies the parallel runway designator, if needed.
- 4500V6000FT – Identifies the visual range in feet (meters in other countries) and any variation required.

C-24. RVR is shown in a METAR/SPECI if the airport has RVR equipment and whenever the prevailing visibility is 1 statute mile or less and/or the RVR value is 6,000 feet or less.

Note. When RVR varies by more than one reportable value, the lowest and highest values are shown with V between them.

C-25. When RVR observed is above the maximum value that can be determined by the system, it should be reported as P6000 where 6,000 is the maximum value for this system. When RVR observed is below the minimum value that can be determined by the system, it should be reported as M0600 where 600 is the minimum value for this system.

WEATHER PHENOMENA

C-26. Weather phenomena in the METAR can be broken down into two parts. The qualifiers, the first part, are intensity, proximity, and/or descriptors. Actual weather descriptions, the second part, are precipitation, obscurations, and other weather conditions. Additional weather information—weather begins/ends and hailstone size—may be included in the Remarks.

Qualifiers

Intensity

C-27. Intensity may be shown with most precipitation types light (-), moderate, and heavy (+). When more than one type of precipitation is present, intensity refers to the predominant precipitation (+TSRA is a thunderstorm with heavy rain and not a heavy thunderstorm with rain).

Proximity

C-28. Proximity is reported only for weather phenomena occurring in the vicinity of the airport. Airport vicinity is defined for obscuration to be between 5 and 10 miles of the usual observation point and precipitation just beyond the observation point up to 10 miles and is denoted by VC. Intensity and VC are never shown in the same group, for example—

- VCSH indicates showers in the vicinity of the airport.
- VCFG indicates fog in the vicinity of the airport.

Descriptor

C-29. Eight descriptors (table C-7) further identify weather phenomena and are used with certain types of precipitation and obscurations. TS and SH are used with precipitation and may be preceded with an intensity symbol.

Table C-7. Descriptor qualifiers

Descriptor			Descriptor		
MI	Shallow	Describes fog that has little vertical extent (less than 6 ft)	DR	Low drifting	When dust, sand, or snow is raised by wind to less than 6 ft
BC	Patches	Describes fog that has little vertical extent & reduces horizontal visibility	BL	Blowing	When dust, sand, snow, and/or spray is raised by wind to a height of 6 ft or more
SH	Showers		TH	Thunderstorm	
FZ	Freezing		PR	Partial	

Weather Descriptions

C-30. If more than one significant weather phenomenom is observed, entries are listed in order of decreasing predominance, and, except precipitation, separate weather groups are shown in the report. No more than three weather groups are used to report weather phenomena at or in the vicinity of the station. If more than one type of precipitation is observed, the appropriate contractions are combined into a single group with the predominant type being reported first. In such a group, any intensity refers to the first type of precipitation in the group (refer to Tables C-9 through C-11 while reading the remainder of this section). Examples include the following:

- TSRA indicates thunderstorm with moderate rain.
- +SHRA indicates heavy rain showers.
- -FZRA indicates light freezing rain.

Precipitation

C-31. Precipitation is any form of water particle, whether liquid or solid, that falls from the atmosphere and reaches the ground. Table C-8, page C-12, shows precipitation types.

Table C-8. Precipitation types

Precipitation					
DZ	Drizzle	**SG**	Snow grains	**GR**	Hailstones*
RA	Rain	**IC**	Ice crystals	**GS**	Small hail or snow pellets*
SN	Snow	**PL**	Ice pellets	**UP**	Unknown precipitation**

*Refers to hailstone size.
**Used only at automated sites when light precipitation is falling but precipitation discriminator cannot determine type. This situation usually occurs when rain and snow are falling at the same time.

Obscurations

C-32. Obscurations are any atmospheric phenomena, other than precipitation, that reduce horizontal visibility. Table C-9 shows the types of obscuration.

Table C-9. Obscuration types

Obscuration							
BR	Mist*	**DU**	Dust	**HZ**	Haze	**VA**	Volcanic ash
FG	Fog**	**SA**	Sand	**PY**	Spray	**FU**	Smoke

*Indicates mist restricting visibility & used only when visibility is from 5/8 mile to 6 miles.
**Indicates fog restricting visibility & used only when visibility is less than 5/8 mile.

Other Weather Conditions

C-33. The other weather phenomena are reported when they occur. Table C-10 shows these other types of weather phenomena.

Table C-10. Other types of weather phenomena

PO	Dust/Sand whirls	**FC**	Funnel cloud	**SS**	Sandstorm
SQ	Squall*	**+FC**	Tornado or Waterspout	**DS**	Dust storm

*Denotes sudden increase in wind speed of at least 16 kt, speed rising to 22 kt or more, & lasting at least 1 minute.

Weather Begins/Ends

C-34. The Remarks element shows the beginning and ending times of any type of precipitation or thunderstorms. Types of precipitation may be combined if beginning or ending times are the same (RAB05E30SNB30E45). Because the METAR is generated every hour, only minutes are used to denote beginning (B) and ending (E) times. Refer to table C-8 for precipitation types.

Hailstone Size

C-35. When hailstones are shown in the body of a report, the largest hailstone size is shown in the Remarks element in 1/4-inch increments and identified with the contraction GR (GR 1 ¾). Hailstones less than 1/4 inch are shown in the body of a report as GS, and no remarks are entered indicating hailstone size.

SKY CONDITION

C-36. Sky condition is reported in amount/height/type format. It can also be reported in indefinite ceiling/height (vertical visibility) format.

Amount

C-37. A clear sky, a layer of clouds, or an obscuring phenomenon is reported by one of six sky-cover descriptions. The summation of the cloud layers from below and at higher levels determines what sky covers are reported. The amount of sky cover is reported in eighths of the sky (table C-11).

Table C-11. Reportable descriptions for sky cover

Reportable descriptions	Meaning	Summation amount
*SKC or CLR	Clear	0 or 0 below 12,000 feet
FEW	Few	>0 but < 2/8
SCT	Scattered	3/8 – 4/8
BKN	Broken	5/8 – 7/8
OVC	Overcast	8/8
VV	Vertical Visibility (indefinite ceiling)	8/8

*SKC will be reported at manual stations. The abbreviation CLR shall be used at automated stations when no clouds below 12,000 ft are detected.

Note. For aviation purposes, ceiling is defined as the height AGL of the lowest broken or overcast layer aloft or vertical visibility into an obscuration.

Height

C-38. Cloud bases are reported with three digits in hundreds of feet AGL (SCT020). Clouds above 12,000 feet cannot be detected by automated reporting systems. At reporting stations located in the mountains, if the cloud layer is below the station level, the height of the layer is shown as three solidi (SCT///).

Type (as Required)

C-39. If towering cumulus (TCU) or cumulonimbus (CB) clouds are present, they are reported after the height representing their base. Examples of these reports are SCT040TCU or BKN025CB.

Indefinite Ceiling/Heights (Vertical Visibility)

C-40. The height into an indefinite ceiling is preceded with VV followed by three digits indicating the vertical visibility in hundreds of feet AGL (VV002). Indefinite ceiling indicates total obscuration.

Partial Obscurations

C-41. The amount of obscuration is reported in the body of the METAR when the sky is partially obscured by a surface-based phenomenon by indicating the amount of obscuration as FEW, SCT, or BKN followed by three zeros. The type of obscuring phenomenon is stated in the Remarks element and precedes the amount of obscuration and three zeros. For example, if fog is hiding >1/8 to 2/8 of the sky, it is coded in the body of the METAR as FEW000. Because fog is partially obscuring the sky, a remark is required (FG FEW000).

C-42. Sky covers and ceiling, as determined from the ground, represent—as nearly as possible—what the aviator should experience in flight. An aviator flying at or above a reported ceiling layer (BKN or OVC) should see less than half of the surface below. An aviator descending through a surface-based total obscuration should first see the ground directly below from the height reported as vertical visibility into the obscuration. However, because of the differing viewpoints of the aviator and the observer, observed values and what the aviator sees do not always exactly agree.

Additional Sky-Condition Remarks

C-43. These remarks are included when—

- The ceiling is below 3,000 feet and is variable; the remark ceiling (CIG) is shown in the Remarks element, followed by the lowest and highest ceiling heights, separated with a V (CIG 005V010).

- An automated station uses meteorological discontinuity sensors; site-specific sky conditions that differ from the ceiling height in the body of the report are shown in the Remarks element (CIG 002 RWY 11).

- A layer is varying in sky cover; the variability range is shown in the Remarks element. If there is more than one cloud layer of the same coverage, the variable layer is identified by including the layer height (BKN014 V OVC).

- Significant clouds are observed; the following cloud types are described in the Remarks element:

  - Towering cumulus, TCU, and direction from the station (TCU W).

  - Cumulonimbus, CB; or cumulonimbus mammatus (CBMAM); direction from the station; and direction of movement (if known). If the clouds are beyond 10 miles from the airport, DSNT indicates that they are distant (CB DSNT E or CBMAM E MOV NE).

  - Altocumulus castellanus, ACC; standing lenticular (stratocumulus, SCSL; altocumulus, ACSL; or cirrocumulus, CCSL); or rotor clouds, ROTOR CLD; describe the clouds (if needed) and the direction from the station (ACC NW or ACSL SW).

TEMPERATURE/DEW POINT GROUP

C-44. Temperature/dew point is reported in a two-digit form in whole degrees Celsius separated by a solidus (/). Temperatures below zero are prefixed with an M, which indicates a negative reading. If temperature is available but dew point is missing, temperature is shown followed by a solidus. If temperature is missing, the group is omitted from the report.

ALTIMETER

C-45. The altimeter element is reported in a four-digit format representing tens, units, tenths, and hundredths of inches of mercury prefixed with A. The decimal point is not reported or stated.

Altimeter Remarks

C-46. When pressure is rising or falling rapidly at the time of observation, Remarks element shows PRESRR or PRESFR respectively. Some stations also include the sea-level pressure (which is different from altimeter). It is identified in the Remarks element as SLP followed by the sea-level pressure in hectopascals (SLP982).

REMARKS (AS REQUIRED)

C-47. Remarks (RMK) are included, when appropriate, in the order presented in table C-13, page C-21. Time entries are shown as minutes past the hour if the time reported occurs during the same hour the observation is taken. If the hour is different, hours and minutes are shown. Locations of phenomena within 5 statute miles of the point of observation are reported as at the station. Phenomena between 5 and 10 statute miles are reported as in the vicinity, VC. Phenomena beyond 10 statute miles are shown as distant (DSNT). Direction of phenomena is indicated with the eight points of the compass. Distance remarks are in statute miles except for automated lightning remarks that are in nautical miles. Movements of clouds or weather are indicated by the direction toward which the phenomenon is moving.

Categories of Remarks

C-48. There are two categories of remarks. One category is automated, manual, and plain language. The other category is additive and automated maintenance data.

Automated, Manual, and Plain Language Remarks

C-49. This group of remarks is generated from either manual or automated weather reporting stations and generally elaborates on parameters reported in the body of the report. Table C-12 shows examples of these type of remarks and their meaning.

Table C-12. Automated, manual, and plain language remarks

Example Remark	Remark meaning
Mt. Augustine volcano 70 miles SW erupted 231505 large ash cloud extending to approximately 30,000 ft moving NE	Volcanic Eruptions
TORNADO B13 6 NE	Tornado, Funnel Cloud, or Waterspout
AO1 or AO2	Automated Station Type
PK WND 28045/15	Peak Wind
WSHFT 30 FROPA	Wind shift
TWR VIS 1 ½ or SFC VIS 1 ½	Tower Visibility or Surface Visibility
VIS 1/2V2	Variable Prevailing Visibility
VIS NE 2 ½	Sector Visibility
VIS 2 ½ RWY 11	Visibility at Second Site
OCNL LTGICCG OHD or FRQ LTGICCCCG W	Lightning
RAB05E30SNB20E55	Beginning and Ending of Precipitation
TSB05E30	Beginning and Ending of Thunderstorm
TS SE MOV NE	Thunderstorm Locations
GR 1 ¾	Hailstone Size
VIRGA NE	Virga (see note)
CIG 005V010	Variable Ceiling Height
FU BKN000	Obscurations
BKN014 V OVC	Variable Sky Condition
CB W MOV E or CBMAM S MOV E or TCU W or ACC NW or ACSL SW-W	Significant Cloud Types
CIG 002 RWY 11	Ceiling Height at Second Location
PRESRR or PRESFR	Pressure Rising or Falling Rapidly
SLP982	Sea-Level Pressure
(ACFT MSHP)	Aircraft Mishap
NOSPECI	No SPECI Report Taken
SNINCR 2/10	Snow Increasing Rapidly
Any other information that will affect aviation operations	Other Significant Information

Note. Virga is precipitation falling from a cloud but evaporating before reaching the ground. It results when air below the cloud is very dry. Virga associated with showers suggests strong downdrafts with possible moderate or greater turbulence.

Additive and Automated Maintenance Data Remarks

C-50. Additive data groups are reported only at designated stations. Maintenance data groups are reported only from automated weather reporting stations. Additive data and maintenance groups are not used by the aviation community. The example shows the METAR along with what the aviator hears. The aviator will not hear any remark information. Optional phrases are in parentheses.

> **Example**
> METAR KMKL 021250Z 33018KT 290V360 1/2SM R31/2600FT SN BLSN FG VV008 00/M03 A2991 RMK RAESNB42 SLPNO T00111032
>
> "Jackson (Tennessee), (one two five zero observation), wind three three zero at one eight, wind variable between two niner zero and three six zero, visibility one half, runway three one RVR, two thousand six hundred, moderate snow, blowing snow, fog, indefinite ceiling eight hundred, temperature zero, dew point minus three, altimeter two niner niner one."

TERMINAL AREA FORECAST

C-51. A TAF (Figure C-7) is a concise statement of expected meteorological conditions within a 5 statute mile radius from the center of an airport's runway complex during a 24-hour time period. Some airfields/airports cover a larger area, such as Cairns (KOZR) TAF, which is valid to a radius of 15 statute miles. TAFs use weather codes found in METAR weather reports. U.S. Air Force generated TAFs include forecast elements for icing, turbulence, maximum/minimum temperature, and minimum altimeter.

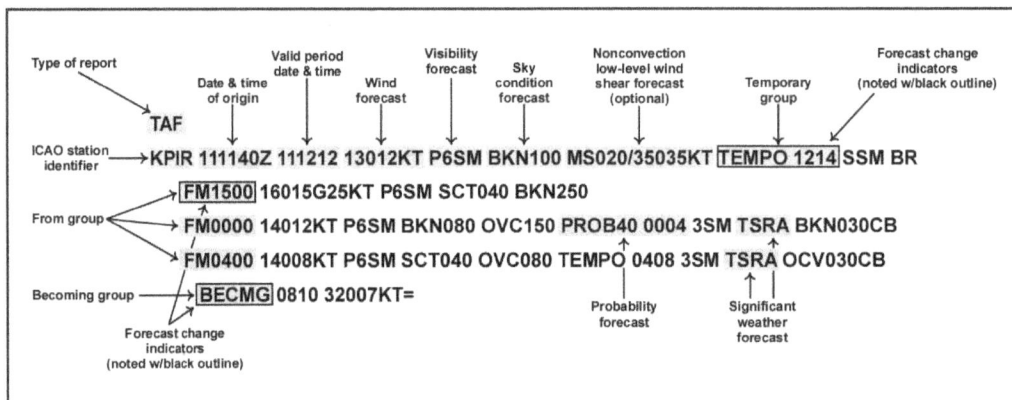

Figure C-7. Terminal area forecast

C-52. The NWS requires that an airport have two consecutive METAR observations, not less than 30 minutes apart nor more than one hour apart, before a TAF is issued. After it is issued, the forecaster uses available weather data sources to maintain the TAF. If, during this time, part or all of the METAR is missing, the forecaster can use other weather sources to maintain the TAF. However, if the forecaster feels that these sources do not provide necessary information, the forecaster will discontinue the TAF.

C-53. International and U.S. military TAFs also contain forecasts of maximum and minimum temperature, icing, and turbulence. These three elements are not included in N3WS-prepared TAFs. For forecast icing and turbulence, see the in-flight aviation weather advisories located at the National Weather Service Web site http://aviationweather.gov/.

TYPE OF REPORT

C-54. This element denotes the TAF type. Two types of TAF reports are a routine forecast, TAF, and an amended forecast, TAF AMD. An amended TAF is issued when the forecaster feels that the TAF is not representative of current or expected weather conditions. An equal sign appears at the end of the TAF report.

INTERNATIONAL CIVIL AVIATION ORGANIZATION STATION IDENTIFIER

C-55. The TAF code uses ICAO four-letter location identifiers. Paragraph C-11 contains more information on ICAO identifiers.

DATE AND TIME OF ORIGIN

C-56. This element is the date and UTC that the forecast is prepared. The format is a two-digit date and four-digit time followed by the letter Z. Routine TAFs are prepared and filed about one-half hour before scheduled issuance times (111140Z for a forecast prepared on the eleventh day of the month at 1140Z or 050530Z for a forecast prepared on the fifth day of the month at 0530Z).

VALID PERIOD DATE AND TIME

C-57. The valid period of the forecast is a two-digit date followed by the two-digit beginning and two-digit ending hours in UTC. Routine TAFs are valid for 24 hours and are issued daily at 0000Z, 0600Z, 1200Z, and 1800Z. Currently, most TAFs are changing over to three times a day at 0000Z, 0600Z, and 1800Z. All ending times throughout the TAF of 00Z are indicated by the number 24; for example—

- Forecast valid from the eleventh at 12Z to the twelfth at 12Z is indicated by 111212.
- Forecast valid from the thirtieth at 00Z to the first at 00Z is indicated by 300024.

Amended, canceled, or delayed forecasts may have valid periods less than 24 hours; for example—

- Forecast valid from the twenty-third at 15Z to the twenty-fourth at 12Z is indicated by 231512.
- Forecast valid from the ninth at 10Z to the tenth at 06Z is indicated by 091006.

C-58. For airports with less than 24-hour observational coverage for which part-time terminal forecasts are provided, the TAF is valid until the end of the scheduled forecast even if observations have ceased before that time. Amendment not scheduled (AMD NOT SKED) or no amendment (NIL AMD) is issued after the forecast information. Amendment not scheduled after closing time (AMD NOT SKED AFT Z) is used if the observation times are known and judged reliable. During the time that the station is closed and a TAF is issued, there is no forecast as indicated by NIL (no TAF) after the valid date and time group. Only after two METARs observations are disseminated is a TAF issued. Amendment limited to clouds, visibility, and wind (AMD LTD TO CLD VIS AND WIND) is used at observation sites having part-time manual augmentation, meaning that there will be amendments only for clouds, visibility, and wind and not for thunderstorms or freezing/frozen precipitation.

WIND FORECAST

C-59. The surface wind forecast is the wind direction in degrees from true north (first three digits) and mean speed in knots (last two or three digits if 100 knots or greater). KT denotes the units of wind speed in knots. Wind gusts are noted by the letter G appended to the mean wind speed followed by the highest expected gust (two or three digits if 100 knots or greater). Calm winds are encoded as 00000KT. A variable wind is encoded as VRB when wind direction fluctuates because of convective activity or low wind speeds (3 knots or less). Examples include 13012KT, 18010KT, 35012G26KT, or VRB16G28KT.

VISIBILITY FORECAST

C-60. The prevailing visibility is forecasted in whole and fractions of statute miles followed by SM to note the units of measurement (5SM). Statute miles followed by fractions of statute miles are separated with a space (1 1/2SM, 2 1/4SM). Forecasted visibility greater than 6 statute miles is indicated by coding P6SM. If prevailing visibility is 6 statute miles or less, one or more weather phenomena must be included in the significant weather forecast. If volcanic ash is forecasted, the visibility must also be forecasted even if the visibility is greater than 6 statute miles. Sector or variable visibility is not forecasted.

SIGNIFICANT WEATHER FORECAST

C-61. Expected weather phenomena are coded in TAF reports using the same format, qualifiers, and phenomena contractions as METARs (except unknown precipitation [UP]). Obscurations to vision are forecasted whenever the prevailing visibility is forecasted to be 6 statute miles or less. Precipitation and volcanic ash will always be included in the TAF regardless of the visibility forecasted; for example—

- FM2200 18005KT 1SM BR SKC.
- FM0100 12010KT P6SM -RA BKN020.
- FM1500 22015KT P6SM VA SCT100.

C-62. If no significant weather is expected to occur during a specific time in the forecast, the weather group is omitted. However, if after a period in which significant weather has been forecasted, a change to a forecast of no significant weather (NSW) appears as the weather included in becoming (BECMG) or TEMPO groups. NSW is not used in the initial time period of a TAF or in FM groups (FM0600 16010KT 3SM RA BKN030 BECMG 0810 P6SM NSW).

C-63. If the forecaster determines weather that affects aviation is within the vicinity of the airport, the forecaster will include those conditions after the weather group. The letters VC describe conditions that will occur within the vicinity of an airport (5 to 10 statute miles) and are used only with fog, showers, or thunderstorms (such as P6SM VCFG, 5SM BR VCSH, and P6SM VCTS).

SKY CONDITION FORECAST

C-64. TAF sky condition forecasts use the METAR format. Cumulonimbus (CB) clouds are the only cloud type forecasted in TAFs. Examples include BKN100, SCT040 BKN030CB, or FEW008 BKN015.

C-65. When the sky is obscured because of a surface-based phenomenon, vertical visibility (VV) into the obscuration is forecasted. The format for vertical visibility is VV followed by a three-digit height in hundreds of feet. Partial obscurations are not forecasted. Remember that a ceiling is the lowest broken or overcast layer or vertical visibility (VV008).

NONCONVECTIVE LOW-LEVEL WIND-SHEAR FORECAST (OPTIONAL DATA)

C-66. A forecast of nonconvective low-level wind shear is included immediately after the cloud and obscuration group when wind-shear criteria have been or will be met. The forecast includes the height of the wind shear followed by the wind direction and wind speed at the indicated height. Height is given in hundreds of feet AGL up to and including 2,000 feet. Wind shear is encoded with the contraction WS, followed by a three-digit height, solidus (/), and winds at the height indicated in the same format as surface winds (WS020/36035KT). The wind-shear element is omitted if not expected to occur.

FORECAST CHANGE INDICATORS

C-67. If a significant change in any of the elements is expected during the valid period, a new time period with the changes is included. The following change indicators are used when either a rapid, gradual, or temporary change is expected in some or all of the forecasted meteorological conditions.

From Group

C-68. The "From" (FM) group is used when a rapid and significant change, usually occurring in less than one hour, in prevailing conditions is expected. Appended to the FM indicator is the four-digit hour and minute that the change is expected to begin. The forecast is valid until the next change group or until the end of the current forecast.

C-69. The FM group will mark the beginning of a new line in a TAF report. Each FM group shall contain a forecast of wind, visibility, weather (if significant), sky condition, and wind shear (if warranted). FM groups will not include the contraction NSW. The following are examples of FM groups:

- FM1500 16015G25KT P6SM SCT040 BKN250.
- FM0200 32010KT 3SM TSRA FEW010 BKN030CB.

Becoming Group

C-70. The BECMG group is used when a gradual change in conditions is expected over a period not to exceed two hours. The time when the change is expected to occur is a four-digit group containing the beginning and ending hours of the change that follows the BECMG indicator. The gradual change will occur at an unspecified time within the period. Only the changing forecasted meteorological conditions are included in BECMG groups. Omitted conditions are carried over from the previous time group (FM2000 18020KT P6SM BKN030 BECMG 0103 OVC015).

C-71. This BECMG group describes a gradual change in sky condition from BKN030 to OVC015. The change in sky conditions occurs between 01Z and 03Z. Refer to the FM2000 group for the wind and visibility conditions. The forecast after 03Z will be as follows: 18020KT P6SM OVC015. The report will read as in the following example.

```
FM0400 14008KT P6SM SCT040 OVC080 TEMPO 0408 3SM TSRA OVC030CB
    BECMG 0810 32007KT=
```

This BECMG group describes a gradual change in wind direction only beginning between 08Z and 10Z. Refer to the previous forecast group (in this case, the FM0400 group) for the prevailing visibility, weather, and sky conditions. The forecast after 10Z will be 32007KT P6SM SCT040 OVC080.

Temporary Group

C-72. The temporary (TEMPO) group is used for temporary fluctuations of wind, visibility, weather, or sky condition expected to last for generally less than an hour at a time (occasional), and expected to occur during less than half the time period. The TEMPO indicator is followed by a four-digit group giving the beginning and ending hours of the time period during which the temporary conditions are expected. Only the changing forecasted meteorological conditions are included in TEMPO groups. The omitted conditions are carried over from the previous time group such as in the following example.

```
FM1000 27005KT P6SM SKC TEMPO 1216 3SM BR.
```

This temporary group describes visibility and weather between 12Z and 16Z. The winds and sky condition have been omitted. Go back to the previous forecast group (FM1000) to obtain the wind and sky condition forecast. The forecast between 12Z and 16Z is 27005KT 3SM BR SKC. The report will read as in the following example.

```
FM0400 14008KT P6SM SCT040 OVC080 TEMPO 0408 3SM TSRA OVC030CB
    BECMG 0810 32007KT=
```

C-73. This temporary group describes visibility, weather, and sky condition between 04Z and 08Z. The winds have been omitted. Go back to the previous forecast group (FM0400) to obtain the wind forecast. The forecast between 04Z and 08Z is 14008KT 3SM TSRA OVC030CB.

PROBABILITY FORECAST

C-74. The probability (PROB30 or PROB40) forecast describes the probability or chance of thunderstorms or other precipitation events occurring, along with associated weather conditions (wind, visibility, and sky conditions). The probability forecast will not be used in the first six hours of the TAF. Probability forecasts are not used in U.S. Air Force generated TAFs. Probability forecasts will be seen in TAFs generated by the NWS.

C-75. The PROB30 or PROB40 group is used when the occurrence of thunderstorms or precipitation is in the 30 percent to less than 40 percent or 40 percent to less than 50 percent ranges, respectively. If the thunderstorm or precipitation chance is greater than 50 percent, it is considered a prevailing weather condition and is included in the significant weather section or the TEMPO change indicator group. PROB30 or PROB40 is followed by a four-digit time group giving the beginning and ending hours of the period during which the thunderstorms or precipitation is expected.

C-76. An example is FM0600 0915KT P6SM BKN020 PROB30 1014 1SM RA BKN015; this example depicts a 30 percent to less than 40 percent chance of 1 statute mile, moderate rain, and a broken cloud layer (ceiling) at 1,500 feet between the hours of 10 to 14Z. Another example is FM0000 14012KT P6SM BKN080 OVC150 PROB40 0004 3SM TSRA BKN030CB; in this example, there is a 40 percent to less than 50 percent chance of visibility 3 statute miles, thunderstorms with moderate rain showers, and a broken cloud layer (ceiling) at 3,000 feet with cumulonimbus between the hours of 00 to 04Z.

SECTION II – EN ROUTE WEATHER REPORTS

AUTOMATED SURFACE OBSERVING SYSTEM

C-77. ASOS is sponsored by the FAA, NWS, and DOD. A total of 569 FAA-sponsored and 313 NWS-sponsored ASOSs are installed at airports throughout the country.

C-78. Automated observing systems provide aviators and other users with airport weather observations (temperature, dew point, wind, altimeter setting, visibility, sky condition, and precipitation) and critical aviation weather parameters (the runway touchdown zone on the airport) when and where needed. The systems work nonstop, updating observations every minute, 24 hours a day, every day of the year. By providing atmospheric information at increasing locations, these systems improve aviation mission safety and efficiency and weather forecasts and warnings.

C-79. The automated observing system routinely and automatically provides computer-generated voice directly to aircraft in the vicinity of airports using FAA VHF ground-to-air radio or attached to the ATIS broadcast. The same information is available via landline, and most data is found on the national weather data network.

AUTOMATED WEATHER OBSERVING SYSTEM

C-80. AWOS is a suite of sensors that measures, collects, and disseminates weather data. The information assists meteorologists, aviators, and flight dispatchers in preparing and monitoring weather forecasts, planning flight routes, and providing takeoff and landing information. AWOSs supply a minute-to-minute update usually provided to aviators by a VHF radio on frequencies between 118 and 136 megahertz. AWOSs are categorized as Federal or non-Federal. Federal AWOSs are purchased and maintained by the FAA. Nonfederal AWOSs are purchased and maintained by state, local, and private organizations. The sensors measure weather parameters such as wind speed and direction, temperature and dew point, visibility, cloud heights and types, precipitation, and barometric pressure. The AWOS does not predict weather, but many send current information to weather offices where forecasts are produced using compiled information. Every hour on the hour, AWOS data is made available to off-site users by those AWOSs on Service A (long line telephone communication) or satellite uplink.

C-81. Six AWOS types are available; each includes a different sensor array. Table C-13, page C-21, lists the differences in models, which correspond to systems described in FAA Advisory Circular 150/5220-16C. Federal AWOSs are all AWOS III. The AWOS data acquisition system (ADAS) for the Federal AWOS is a powerful microprocessor-based computer system that collects and processes data from AWOS. It then formats the data for output and dissemination into the NAS.

Table C-13. Automated weather observing system models

Broadcast Information	AWOS Types					
	I	II	III	III-P	III-T	III-P-T
Wind speed	X	X	X	X	X	X
Wind gust	X	X	X	X	X	X
Wind direction	X	X	X	X	X	X
Variable wind direction	X	X	X	X	X	X
Temperature	X	X	X	X	X	X
Dew point	X	X	X	X	X	X
Altimeter setting	X	X	X	X	X	X
Density altitude	X	X	X	X	X	X
Visibility		X	X	X	X	X
Variable visibility		X	X	X	X	X
Sky condition			X	X	X	X
Cloud height and type			X	X	X	X
Present weather				X		X
Precipitation identification				X		
Thunderstorm & lightning detection					X	
Present weather & lightning detection						X

SECTION III – WEATHER RISK MANAGEMENT AND DECISION MAKING

C-82. Many weather providers and weather products make it difficult for aviators to screen out nonessential data, focus on key facts, and correctly evaluate the risk. The *perceive-process-perform* risk management framework is a guide for preflight weather planning and in-flight weather decision making:

- **Perceive** weather hazards that could adversely affect the flight.
- **Process** information to determine whether hazards create risk, which is the potential effect of a hazard not controlled or eliminated.
- **Perform** by acting to eliminate the hazard or mitigate the risk.

PREFLIGHT WEATHER PLANNING

PERCEIVE – UNDERSTANDING WEATHER INFORMATION

C-83. When planning a mission, first check if weather conditions are suitable by collecting information about current and forecast conditions along the intended route and then develop an understanding of weather conditions expected along the flight route. If no military weather information is available at the point of departure, other resources are accessible to aviators. This information becomes even more crucial when weather becomes questionable.

Television and Internet

C-84. For long-range weather planning, many aviators start with televised weather such as The Weather Channel (TWC). TWC is not an FAA-approved source of weather information, but its television and Internet offerings provide tactical and strategic summaries and forecasts (up to 10 per day). The data is compact and easy to use and can supplement approved sources; for example, one TWC Internet page includes a weather map with color-coding for IFR and MVFR conditions at airports around the country. This and other TWC features provide a useful first snapshot of weather conditions needing to be evaluated more closely. The National Weather Service's Aviation Weather Center is another useful source of initial weather information. The AIRMET and SIGMET watch boxes quickly provide a list of marginal or instrument weather areas.

C-85. A printed version of the FSS briefing package is available by obtaining a standard briefing for the route on the DUATS. Free and accessible to all aviators via the Internet at www.duat.com or www.duats.com, this resource provides weather information in an FAA-approved format and records the transaction as an official weather briefing. Printing out selected portions of the DUATS computer briefing provides for closer study and easy reference when an aviator speaks with an FSS briefer.

C-86. Aviation Digital Data Service (ADDS) is a joint effort of the National Oceanic and Atmospheric Administration (NOAA) Forecast Systems Laboratory, National Center for Atmospheric Research (NCAR) Research Applications Program (RAP), and the National Centers for Environmental Prediction (NCEP) Aviation Weather Center (AWC). Available at http://adds.aviationweather.noaa.gov, ADDS combines information from NWS aviation observations and forecasts, making the data available on the Internet, along with visualization tools, for practical flight planning.

Operational Weather Squadron

C-87. OWSs are located worldwide to be the primary 24-hour weather-briefing source. Contact the OWS responsible for the area. Local base/post weather flights may also assist the aviator if higher priority tasking and local mission support allow. Contact information is listed in the FIH, section C. When talking to a military forecaster, provide the following information at least two hours before the desired brief time:

- Name of person calling.
- Aircraft type and call sign.
- VFR or IFR and proposed altitude.
- ETD for departure point and ETA for destination and alternates.
- Route.
- En route stops, if applicable (in order, with ETAs).

Federal Aviation Administration

C-88. The FAA FSS is a source of comprehensive weather information. FSS creates briefing packages derived from NWS data and other flight planning sources. FSS offers four basic briefing packages:

- Outlook (for flights more than six hours away).
- Standard (for most flights).
- Abbreviated (to update specific items after a standard briefing).
- Telephone information briefing service (TIBS), which provides recorded weather information.

C-89. The specific weather information packaged in a standard briefing includes a weather synopsis, sky conditions (clouds), and visibility and weather conditions at the departure, en route, and destination points. Also included are adverse conditions, altimeter settings, cloud tops, dew point, icing conditions, surface winds, winds aloft, temperature, thunderstorm activity, precipitation, precipitation intensity, visibility obscuration, PIREPs, AIRMETs, SIGMETs, convective SIGMETS, and NOTAMs, including any TFRs.

C-90. A FSS weather briefing can be difficult to absorb via telephone. Pictures display complex, dynamic information such as cloud cover and precipitation; therefore, it is helpful to begin the preflight planning process by viewing weather products from a range of providers. The preflight planning process develops an overall mental picture of current and forecast weather conditions and identifies areas that require help from the FSS briefer.

Flight Service Station Briefing

C-91. If a local military weather forecaster and OWS are not available, contact an FSS. Once the weather conditions for the trip are assessed, call FSS. If a DUATS briefing is obtained or the weather situation and mission are simple, an abbreviated briefing is appropriate. If not, ask for a standard briefing. Armed with information obtained from the self-briefing process, the aviators finds it easier to absorb new information from the briefer and can ask questions that are more relevant and specific. Guidelines for obtaining weather data from FSS include the following:

- Contact the right FSS. When dialing the standard number from a cellular phone, the caller is connected to the FSS associated with the cellular telephone's area code, not necessarily to the FSS nearest to present position; when using a cellular telephone outside its normal calling area, check the airport/facility directory for the specific telephone number of the nearest FSS.

- Identify what is needed so that the right briefing package (outlook, standard, or abbreviated) is requested.

- Use the standard flight plan form (FAA Form 7233-1) to provide background to the briefer; review the form before calling, and develop estimates for items such as altitude, route, and estimated time en route to ensure receipt of accurate information.

- Be honest about any limitations in skill or aircraft capability.

- Inform the FSS specialist if new to the area or unfamiliar with the typical weather patterns, including seasonal characteristics; if unfamiliar with the area, have VFR or IFR navigation charts available while talking to the specialist to help sharpen the mental picture of the location of weather hazards in relation to the departure airport, proposed route of flight, and destination.

- Ask questions, and clarify any unclear item. Less experienced aviators are sometimes less assertive; smart aviators ask questions to resolve ambiguities in the weather briefing. The worse the weather, the more data needed to develop options.

- Obtain all weather information needed; if flying in IMC or MVFR that could deteriorate, do not end the briefing without identifying which direction (north, south, east, west) to turn to fly toward for better weather and how far it is to reach.

PROCESS—ANALYZING WEATHER INFORMATION

C-92. After obtaining weather information, study and evaluate the information and how it relates to the circumstances. Aviator training includes weather theory and use of weather products in aviation; however, it takes continuous study and experience to develop skills in evaluating and applying weather data to a specific flight. Approach the task of practical, real-world weather analysis with certain concepts in mind.

Weather Elements

C-93. Six basic elements of weather are the following:
- Temperature (warm or cold).
- Wind (a vector with speed and direction).
- Moisture (or humidity).
- Clouds.
- Precipitation.
- Pressure.

C-94. Temperature differences (uneven heating) support development of low-pressure systems, which can affect wide areas. Surface low-pressure systems usually have fronts associated with them. A front is the zone between two air masses that contain different combinations of the basic elements. Because weather is associated with fronts, which are, in turn, associated with low-pressure systems, possible conditions are revealed by identifying where the low-pressure systems are in relation to the route.

Effects of Weather

C-95. Temperature, wind, and moisture combine to varying degrees to create conditions that affect aviators. The range of possible combinations is nearly infinite, but weather affects aviators in only three ways. Specifically, basic weather elements can—
- Reduce visibility.
- Create turbulence.
- Reduce aircraft performance.

Evaluate Weather

C-96. Review weather data in terms of how current and forecast conditions will affect visibility, turbulence, and aircraft performance for the specific flight. For example, suppose the mission is to fly from Cincinnati Municipal Airport (KLUK) to Ohio State University Airport in Columbus, Ohio (KCMH). The departure from KLUK is around 1830Z and flies VFR at 5,500 MSL. ETE is about one hour. See table C-14 for the weather briefing.

C-97. Aviators have the option of receiving this information in plain English format, if preferred, rather than in code. Whichever format is selected, the first step is to view the weather data in terms of the three specific ways that weather can affect flight: ceiling visibility, aircraft performance, and turbulence.

Table C-14. Weather briefing

Weather Briefing
METARs:
KLUK 261410Z 07003KT 3SM -RA BR OVC015 21/20 A3001
KDAY 261423Z 14005KT 3SM HZ BKN050 22/19 A3003
KCMH 261351Z 19005KT 3SM HZ FEW080 BKN100 OVC130 22/17 A3002

TAFs:
KLUK 261405Z 261412 00000KT 3SM BR BKN015
TEMPO 1416 2SM -SHRA BR
FM1600 14004KT 5SM BR OVC035
TEMPO 1618 2SM -SHRA BR BKN015
FM1800 16004KT P6SM BKN040
FM0200 00000KT 5SM BR BKN025
TEMPO 0912 2SM BR BKN018
KDAY 261303Z 261312 06003KT 5SM BR SCT050 OVC100
TEMPO 1315 2SM -RA BR BKN050
FM1500 15006KT P6SM BKN050
TEMPO 1519 4SM -SHRA BR BKN025
FM1900 16007KT P6SM BKN035
FM0200 14005KT 5SM BR BKN035
FM0600 14004KT 2SM BR BKN012
KCMH 261406Z 261412 19004KT 4SM HZ SCT050 BKN120
FM1800 17006KT P6SM BKN040
TEMPO 1922 4SM -SHRA BR
FM0200 15005KT 5SM BR BKN035
FM0700 14004KT 2SM BR BKN012

WINDS ALOFT (Direction/Speed [in knots] at Various Altitudes [in feet]):

	3000	6000	9000	12000	15000	18000	21000	24000	27000
CMH	1910	2108+15	2807+10	2712+05	2922-07	2936-17	2945-32	2945-40	3138-51
CVG	2310	2607+16	2811+11	2716+06	3019-05	2929-16	2934-30	2932-40	2936-52

C-98. The aviator can organize the information from the weather brief (table C-14) into a locally produced table, as depicted in table C-15, page C-25, that allows for easier comparisons. The column headings in the top row, arranged to match the order in which the briefing information is presented, assist in quickly identifying specific weather hazards possible on the trip. The aviator may convert Zulu (UTC) times to local times.

Table C-15. Derived mission information

Current Conditions							
Place	Time	Turbulence	Ceiling & Visibility			Visibility & Performance	Trends
		Wind	Visibility	Weather	Ceiling (feet in hundreds)	Temp/Dewpt (°C)	Altimeter
KLUK	1410Z	07003KT	3SM	RA, BR	OVC015	21/20	A3001
KDAY	1432Z	14005KT	3SM	HZ	BKN050	22/19	A3003
KCMH	1351Z	19005KT	3SM	HZ	FEW080, OVC130	22/17	A3002

Forecast Conditions					
Place	Time	Turbulence	Ceiling & Visibility		
		Wind	Visibility	Weather	Ceiling (feet in hundreds)
KLUK	FM1800Z	16004KT	P6 SM		BKN040
KDAY	TEMPO 1519Z	--	4SM	-SHRA	BKN025
	FM1900Z	16007KT	P6 SM	--	BKN035
KCMH	FM1800Z	17006KT	P6 SM	--	BKN040
	TEMPO 1922Z	--	4SM	-SHRA, BR	--

Winds Aloft			
Place	Altitude (in feet)	Turbulence	Visibility & Performance
		Wind (direction/ knots)	Temp °C
CVG	6,000	260/07	16
CMH	6,000	210/08	15

Ceiling and Visibility

C-99. The first columns to view are the weather data elements reporting ceiling and visibility. In the case of the proposed VFR flight from KLUK to KCMH, current visibility at the departure and destination airports is marginal and the small temperature/dew point spread should trigger a mental red flag for potentially reduced visibility. The forecasts call for conditions to improve at the departure airport, KLUK, by the time of planned takeoff (1830Z).

C-100. It is possible to encounter marginal conditions, including light rain showers, en route and also at the destination (KCMH). Because the forecast ceilings will probably not allow VFR flight at the planned altitude (5,500 feet MSL), this part of the analysis indicates terrain and obstacle avoidance planning (discussed in the next section) will be necessary if this flight departs at the originally scheduled time.

Aircraft Performance

C-101. Current and forecast temperatures for departure, en route, and destination points are reviewed for possible adverse effect on aircraft performance. In high temperatures, knowledge and planning for the effects of high-density altitude—especially on takeoff, climb, and landing—are imperative. If temperatures are low and flight is planned in the clouds, pay special attention to known or forecast icing and freezing levels.

C-102. In the sample VFR flight from KLUK to KCMN, temperatures on the surface and at the planned altitude are moderate. In those conditions, performance problems associated with density altitude or icing are not likely.

Turbulence

C-103. Review wind conditions for departure airport, en route, and destination airport. A mental picture of vertical wind profiles is also required to select the best altitudes for cruise flight and to determine whether wind shear is present.

C-104. For the sample flight from KLUK to KCMH, the chart format shows that there are light southerly surface winds at the departure and destination airports. Winds aloft will also be light but from a westerly direction. There are no indications for wind shear or convective activity (thunderstorms); therefore, it is safe to conclude that turbulence is not likely to be a hazard.

PERFORM – MAKING A WEATHER PLAN

C-105. The third step is to perform an honest evaluation of crew/aircraft capability and the challenge posed by the particular set of weather conditions. Aviators should consider the adequacy of the combined crew-aircraft team. For example, the crew may be very experienced, proficient, and current, but its weather flying ability is limited by the aircraft model. On the other hand, the aircraft may be technically advanced—with moving map GPS, weather data link, and autopilot—but the crew does not have much weather flying experience. An airplane's capability can never fully compensate for lack of experience. The crew must be fully proficient in the use of onboard equipment and verify proper function.

C-106. Self-check the decision (regardless of experience). If the result of the evaluation process leaves any doubt, then develop safe alternatives. Think of the preflight weather plan as a strategic, overarching exercise. The goal is to ensure that all of the weather-related hazards for this particular flight are identified and that ways to eliminate or mitigate each one are planned. There are several items to include in the weather flying plan.

Escape Options

C-107. A good aircrew knows where to find good weather within the aircraft's range and endurance capability. The aircrew must know where it is, which direction to turn to get there, and how long it will take to get there. When the weather is IMC (ceiling less than 1,000 feet or visibility less than 3 statute miles), identify an acceptable alternative airport for each 25 to 30 nautical-mile segment of the route.

Reserve Fuel

C-108. Identifying the location of VFR weather does no good unless there is adequate fuel to reach it. Flight planning for only a legal fuel reserve could significantly limit options if weather deteriorates. More fuel means access to more alternatives and frees the aircrew from the worry (and distraction) of fuel exhaustion when weather has already increased the cockpit workload.

Terrain Avoidance

C-109. Recognize altitude limitations to avoid encountering terrain and/or obstacles. Consider a terrain avoidance plan for any flight involving the following conditions:
- Weather at or below MVFR (ceiling 1,000 to 3,000 feet; visibility 3 to 5 miles).
- A temperature/dew-point spread of 4°C or less.
- Any expected precipitation.
- Operating at night.

C-110. Identify the MSA for each segment of the flight. All VFR sectional charts include a maximum elevation figure (MEF) in each quadrangle. The MEF is determined by locating the highest obstacle (natural or manmade) in each quadrangle and rounding up 100 to 300 feet. Charts for IFR navigation include an MEA and an MOCA. Jeppesen (civilian) charts depict a minimum off route altitude (MORA), while FAA/NACO charts show an OROCA that guarantees a 1,000-foot obstacle clearance in nonmountainous terrain and a 2,000-foot obstacle clearance in mountainous terrain. In addition, many GPS navigators (panel mounted and handheld) include a feature showing the MSA, en route safe altitude (ESA), or MEA relative to the aircraft's position. If there is access to such equipment, an understanding of how to access and interpret the information regarding safe altitudes is necessary.

Passenger Plan

C-111. A number of weather accidents have been associated with external or peer pressures such as reluctance to disappoint passengers eager to make or continue a mission. There is almost always pressure to launch and pressure to continue. Even the small trip to the hangar can create pressure to avoid wasted time. For this reason, weather planning should include briefing the passengers (and anyone waiting at the destination) in addition to preflighting the aircraft. By jointly planning for weather contingencies and briefing passengers before boarding the aircraft, the aviator will be under less pressure to continue in deteriorating weather conditions. Suggestions include the following:

- Understand the minimums that help build the toughest go/no-go and continue/divert decisions well in advance of any flight.
- Understand that the presence of others can influence decision making and willingness to take risks; emphasize to passengers that safety is the priority.
- Establish weather checkpoints every 25 to 30 nautical miles along the route, at which to reevaluate conditions; if possible, have passengers assist by tracking progress and conditions at each weather checkpoint.
- Use preestablished minimums to determine exactly what conditions will trigger a diversion at any given weather checkpoint; let passengers know what these conditions are.
- Decide specific actions to take if diversion is required at any particular point, and inform passengers during the briefing; preflight is the time to make alternative arrangements if weather conditions worsen.
- Inform personnel at the destination that plans are flexible and they will be kept informed; be sure they understand that safety is the priority and that a delay or cancellation is possible if weather becomes a problem.
- Wait out bad weather, especially involving weather fronts; bad weather normally does not last long, and waiting just a day can often make the difference between attempting a high weather risk flight and a flight that falls within safety guidelines.

IN-FLIGHT DECISION MAKING

PERCEIVE—OBTAINING IN-FLIGHT WEATHER INFORMATION

C-112. Often, weather is not forecast to be severe enough to cancel the mission so aviators often choose to take off and evaluate the weather in flight. It is not necessarily incorrect to take off and evaluate the situation, but it is important to stay alert to weather changes. Aviators and their aircraft operate in (rather than above) most weather. At typical aircraft speeds, a 200-mile trip can leave a two- to three-hour weather information gap between the preflight briefing and the actual flight. Therefore, this gap makes in-flight updates vital.

Visual Updates

C-113. Survey the weather, and determine whether conditions around the aircraft match conditions reported or forecasted. Sometimes there are local deviations in weather conditions (such as isolated cells and fog) that may not be immediately known to the weather briefer or may not appear on weather-product depictions, especially if there is no weather-reporting capability at the departure point. Next Generation Weather Radar (NEXRAD) information is at least 6 to 10 minutes old when it reaches the display—and is older still by departure time.

En Route Weather Conditions

C-114. To monitor conditions en route, aviators can listen to ATIS and ASOS/AWOS broadcasts along the route. These broadcasts help update and corroborate preflight weather information about conditions along the route of flight.

En Route Flight Advisory Service or Flight Watch and Pilot-To-Metro

C-115. Available on 122.0 CONUS from 5,000 AGL to 17,500 MSL (124.67 at higher altitudes), EFAS (addressed as Flight Watch) is a service that provides en route aircraft with timely and meaningful weather advisories pertinent to the type of flight intended, route of flight, and altitude. Request permission from ATC to leave the frequency to contact EFAS, and then provide EFAS with the aircraft identification and name of the VOR nearest to the position of the aircraft. Consult the FIH for current Pilot-to-Metro Service frequencies and instructions.

Air Traffic Control

C-116. Monitoring ATC frequencies along the way keeps the aircrew abreast of changing weather conditions. Monitor if other aircraft along the route are requesting diversions. Aviators can also request information on the present location of weather, which the controller will try to provide if workload permits. When requesting weather information from ATC, be aware that radar, the controller's primary tool, has limitation, and that operational considerations (use of settings that reduce the magnitude of precipitation returns) will affect what the controller sees on radar.

Datalink and Weather Avoidance Equipment

C-117. Radar and lightning detectors, available in some aircraft for many years, contribute significantly to weather awareness in the cockpit. An increasing number of aircraft are now equipped with weather data link equipment, which uses satellites to transmit weather data—such as METARs, TAFs, and NEXRAD radar—to the cockpit. It is often shown as an overlay on the multifunction display (MFD). Handheld devices with weather data link capability are also a popular source of en route weather information.

PROCESS—EVALUATING AND UPDATING IN-FLIGHT CONDITIONS

Visual Updates

C-118. Humans are conditioned to believe what they see. The eyes perceive weather during flight, but prior visual experience largely determines our ability to see things. Like other sensory organs, the eye responds best to changes. It adapts to circumstances that do not change or those that change in a gradual or subtle way by reducing its response. Just as the skin becomes acclimated to the feel of clothing, the eye becomes accustomed to progressive small changes in light, color, and motion so that it no longer visualizes an accurate picture. In deteriorating weather conditions, reduction in visibility and contrast occurs quite gradually and it may be some time before the aviator senses that weather conditions have deteriorated significantly. Therefore, aviators must learn how to look past the visual illusion and see what is really there.

In-Flight Weather Information

C-119. In-flight weather information obtained from ATIS and ASOS/AWOS broadcasts can contribute useful pieces to the en route weather picture; however, this information is only a weather snapshot of a limited area. ATIS and ASOS/AWOS broadcasts are primarily intended to provide information on conditions in the airport vicinity.

C-120. The information reported is derived from an array of sensors. While designed to be as accurate as possible and becoming increasingly sophisticated, these automated systems actually monitor a very small area on the airfield and report only what the sensors can see. For example, sensors measuring visibility actually measure a section of air less than 24 inches wide. Even a dense fog on a portion of the airfield will go undetected by the system unless the fog obscures the sensors. The system will not identify an approaching thunderstorm until it is almost directly over the automated site's ceiling instruments.

En Route Flight Advisory Service

C-121. If deteriorating conditions are suspected or encountered while en route, contact EFAS–Flight Watch or PMSV for additional information. EFAS can be a helpful resource, but interpreting and applying the information received while flying the aircraft—especially in adverse or deteriorating conditions with no autopilot—can be difficult. The aviator needs to understand where the weather is in relation to present position and flight path, where it is going, and how fast it is moving. It is good practice to have an aeronautical chart, with the route clearly marked, readily available before calling Flight Watch/PMSV. The chart helps the aviator visualize where weather conditions are located in relation to current position and intended route of flight and determine whether (and where) a deviation from the original plan is required.

Air Traffic Control

C-122. Radar identifies only entities that reflect energy, including precipitation, the density of which is indicated by the strength of the return. Radar does not detect turbulence, but its existence may sometimes be implied by the intensity of a precipitation return: the stronger the return, the more likely the presence of turbulence. In addition, icing is not directly evident but may be inferred by the presence of moisture, clouds, and precipitation at temperatures at or below freezing.

C-123. ATC radar capacity is limited by the kind of equipment in use. Older radars only depict primary radar returns, and controllers using these units often use a device known as circular polarization (CP) to reduce the magnitude of precipitation returns so that aircraft targets are more clearly visible. In these cases, the weather information displayed is reduced and understated. In general, TRACON radar systems have greater weather capability than ATTC radar with respect to depicting weather. Terminal ATC facilities equipped with the latest radar systems can measure precipitation intensity and display it to the controller in six levels of intensity (table C-16).

Table C-16. Radar system precipitation intensity levels

Level	Intensity	Level	Intensity
1.	Light precipitation	4.	Heavy rain
2.	Light to moderate rain	5.	Very heavy rain; hail possible
3.	Moderate to heavy rain	6.	Very heavy rain and hail; large hail possible

C-124. Interpreting weather information from ATC is facilitated through a thorough understanding of pilot-controller communications. In recent years, several general aviation accidents have occurred in which the effectiveness of information provided by ATC was diminished because aviators and controllers interpreted the same terms in different ways. Never make assumptions regarding ATC-provided en route information. Be specific, and do not hesitate to ask questions to clarify points not understood.

Datalink and Weather Avoidance Equipment

C-125. The quality of datalink and weather avoidance equipment information depends heavily upon update rate, resolution, and coverage area. When an aviator is flying an aircraft that has datalink equipment, safe and accurate interpretation of information received depends on understanding of each of these parameters.

C-126. Data link does not provide real-time information. Although weather and other navigation displays can give aviators an unprecedented quantity of high-quality weather data, their use is safe and appropriate only for strategic decision making (attempting to avoid the hazard altogether). Data link is not accurate or current enough to be safely used for tactical decision making (negotiating a path through a weather hazard area such as a broken line of thunderstorms). Be aware that onboard weather equipment can inappropriately influence the decision to continue a flight. No matter how thin a line of storms appears to be or how many holes appear on the display, there is no safe path through them.

PERFORM—PUTTING IT ALL TOGETHER

C-127. During the preflight planning process, the aircrew develops a strategic, overarching flight plan based on weather data and analysis. During the en route phase, use the data and analysis to make tactical weather decisions. Tactical weather flight requires perception of the conditions, processing (interpreting) their effect on the flight, and performing by taking appropriate action at each stage. Steps include the following:

- Reassess weather on a continuous basis; designate specific fixes (airports) on or near the flight path as weather checkpoints, and use in-flight resources to get updated information.
- Take action if deteriorating weather is suspected:
    - Trust the eyes if weather conditions appear to be deteriorating.
    - Contact EFAS/PMSV for detailed information.
    - Proceed to the nearest airport if clouds form at a lower altitude, or if there are gray or black areas ahead, hard rain or moderate turbulence, or clouds forming above that require descent; reevaluating and implementing a new plan are easier from the safety of an airport.
- Contribute to the system by making PIREPs. Format is not important; offer the information, and the specialist will put it into the appropriate format for distribution.

Air Traffic Control

C-128. If ATC help is necessary to avoid or escape bad weather, ask sooner rather than later. Guidelines include the following:

- Be sensitive to ATC communications workload, but keep controllers advised of weather conditions; tell the controller if deviation is required to avoid a weather hazard.
- Navigational guidance information issued to a VFR flight is advisory; suggested headings do not authorize violation of regulations and do not guarantee clearance of all weather.
- Ask questions, and ask for clarification if a point is not understood.
- Do not assume that the controller is knowledgeable about the flight:
    - If ATC is needed to avoid convective weather, inform the controller that the aircraft has no onboard weather avoidance equipment.
    - If given to another controller while on a suggested heading for weather avoidance, confirm that the next controller knows the original request was for weather avoidance assistance; for example, the initial call might be: "Center, Army 12345, level 5,000, 020 heading for weather avoidance."
    - Never assume that "cleared direct when able" means flying a direct course at that time will keep the aircraft clear of weather; to ATC, "direct when able" means to fly direct when able to navigate directly to the fix. When in doubt, ask if a direct course will keep the aircraft clear of moderate and heavy radar return areas indicative of thunderstorm activity.
    - Words such as showers and precipitation are misleading. Some aviators mistakenly assume that these words indicate areas of rain with no thunderheads present. Do not proceed into areas of showers or precipitation without clarifying the level of precipitation or a descriptor such as light, moderate, or heavy; the difference between Level 1 precipitation and Level 4 precipitation can be fatal.

POSTFLIGHT WEATHER REVIEW

C-129. After a challenging flight in weather, an aviator's initial impulse may be to go home and unwind; however, the immediate postflight period is one of the best opportunities to increase weather knowledge and understanding. Studies show that aviators sometimes fly into bad weather because they lack relevant experience and did not recognize certain weather cues that might create a safety hazard to the flight. Make it a point to learn something from every weather encounter. At the end of a flight involving weather, mentally review the flight and reflect on what was learned from the experience. A possible postflight weather after action report (AAR) can consist of the following questions:

- What weather conditions/hazards existed, and how did they affect this flight? (Examples include turbulence and winds, ceilings and visibility, and aircraft performance.)
- How did the conditions encountered during this flight compare to information obtained in the preflight briefing?
- Which sources of preflight weather information provided the best (or most useful, most accurate, most relevant) data for this flight?
- Which sources of en route weather information provided the best (or most useful, most accurate, most relevant) data for this flight?

C-130. Aviators can also develop weather experience and judgment by observing and analyzing the weather every day. Look out the window or go outside to observe the clouds. What are they doing? Why are they shaped as they are? Why is their altitude changing? This simple habit helps develop the ability to read clouds and understand how shape, color, thickness, and altitude can be valuable weather indicators. As cloud-reading skill develops, try to correlate temperature, dew point, humidity, and time of day to the types of clouds forming. Take note of the wind, and try to visualize how it wraps around the tree or whips around the corner of a building. This exercise increases awareness of wind at critical points in the flight. Developing weather knowledge and expertise helps keep the crew and passengers safe.

This page intentionally left blank.

Appendix D

Internet Resources

D-1. The list provided in table D-1 is not meant to be all inclusive. This appendix provides a starting point for aviators to obtain the latest, accurate information needed to conduct flight operations. Bookmarked web sites addresses do change periodically. Some of these sites are nongovernmental; Web sites without .mil or .gov extensions should be used with discretion by the aviator.

Table D-1. Internet resources for flight operation planning

Proponent	Internet Address
Air Force	
Publications	http://www.e-publishing.af.mil/afpubs.asp
Weather Agency	https://login.afwa.af.mil/front_door/knock.cgi
AOPA	
Web site	http://www.aopa.org/
Online Courses	http://www.aopa.org/asf/online_courses/
Army	
USAASA	http://www.usaasa.belvoir.army.mil/
ASOS/AWOS	
Trainer's Tool Box	http://www.nws.noaa.gov/asos/toolkt.htm
FAA	http://www.NWS.noaa.gov/asos/index.html
DUATS	
CSC DUATS	http://www.duats.com/
(CPU-26A/P)	
Emulator	http://www.csgnetwork.com/e6bcalc.html
FAA	
Air Traffic Publications	http://www.faa.gov/atpubs/
FLIP	
FAA	http://www.naco.faa.gov/index.asp?xml=naco/online/d_tpp
NGA	http://164.214.2.62/products/usfif/index.html
General	
AVweb	http://www.avweb.com/
FAA	http://www.faa.gov/
Whittsflying (Gene Whitt's Web site)	http://www.whittsflying.com/
GPS	
U.S. Army program manager site (GPS)	https://gps.army.mil/gps/menu.cfm
FAA	http://gps.faa.gov/
ICAO	
ICAO	http://www.icao.int/
NOTAMs	
DOD	https://www.notams.jcs.mil/
FAA	https://www.notams.faa.gov/
Planning	

Table D-1. Internet resources for flight operation planning

Proponent	Internet Address
enflight	http://www.enflight.com/index.php
FAA	https://pilotweb.nas.faa.gov/distribution/atcscc.html
Baseops Network	http://www.baseops.net/
Distance calculations	http://www.fai.org/distance_calculation/
Fuel	http://usapc.army.mil/
RVSM	
FAA	http://www.faa.gov/ats/ato/rvsm_documentation.htm
Training	
Aeromedical	http://usasam.amedd.army.mil/RT/req_training.htm
Tutorials	http://stoenworks.com/Tutorials/
Flight Simulator Navigation	http://www.navfltsm.addr.com/index.htm
Approach charts	http://www.volpe.dot.gov/opsad/iapchart.html
Weather	
Intellicast	http://www.intellicast.com/Aviation/
METAR/TAF information	http://metar.noaa.gov/index.jsp
NOAA National Weather Center Aviation site	http://aviationweather.gov
Pilot's Guide FAA/NWS	http://www.nws.noaa.gov/om/brochures/pilot.htm

Appendix E

Aircrew Coordination and Instrument Flight

This appendix describes the background of crew coordination development, crew coordination elements, basic qualities, and objectives as found in the Army Aircrew Coordination Training Enhancement (ACTE) Program. The focus is crew coordination as it applies to instrument flight.

Note. Digitization of crew compartments has expanded and redefined the lines of responsibility for each crew member. The ability of either crew member to perform most aircraft/system functions from his crew station breaks down the standard delineation of duties, allowing the crew added capabilities in training and combat. A crew member can attempt to resolve an unforeseen circumstance without the assistance of another crew member; therefore, good communication among crew members is necessary. The PC must brief specific duties before stepping into the aircraft.

CREW COORDINATION BACKGROUND

E-1. Many aircraft accidents result from one or more crew coordination errors committed before or during the mission. Often, an accident is the result of a sequence of undetected crew errors that combines to produce a catastrophic result. Continued research shows that even when accidents are avoided, crew coordination errors result in degraded mission performance. A systematic analysis of error patterns indicates specific areas that crew-level training could improve. Improved training can reduce the occurrence of such errors and can break the chain of errors that cause accidents and poor mission performance.

CREW COORDINATION ELEMENTS

E-2. Broadly defined, aircrew coordination is the interaction between crew members necessary for safe, efficient, and effective performance of tasks. The essential elements of crew coordination include the following:

- **Communicate positively**. Good cockpit teamwork requires clear communication among crew members; when the sender directs, announces, requests, or offers information, the receiver acknowledges the message while the sender confirms it based on the receiver's acknowledgment.
- **Direct assistance**. A crew member directs assistance when he cannot maintain aircraft control. (During ITO, pilot on the controls [P*] calls for the copilot to call out airspeed, torque, and climb rate); he also directs assistance when aircraft systems are not operating properly and assistance is required of the other crew member.
- **Announce actions**. Effective and well-coordinated actions in the aircraft require all crew members to be aware of expected crew movements and unexpected individual actions; each crew member announces actions affecting the duties of other crew members.
- **Offer assistance**. A crew member provides assistance or information, when requested.
- **Acknowledge actions**. Communications in the aircraft must include supportive feedback to ensure that crew members correctly understand announcements or directives.

- **Be explicit**. Crew members use clear terms and phrases and positively acknowledge critical information. Avoid using terms having multiple meanings, such as "Right," "Back up," or "I have it." Also avoid statements such as "Do you see that?" or "You are coming in a little fast/slow."
- **Provide aircraft control and obstacle advisories.** Although the P* is responsible for aircraft control, other crew members should provide aircraft control information regarding airspeed, altitude, or heading.
- **Coordinate action sequence and timing.** Proper sequencing and timing ensures that the actions of one crew member will mesh with the actions of another crew member.

CREW COORDINATION BASIC QUALITIES

E-3. Crew coordination elements are further broken into a set of 13 basic qualities. Each basic quality is defined in terms of observable behaviors that support the elements.

FLIGHT TEAM LEADERSHIP AND CREW CLIMATE

E-4. Aircrews have a designated leader with clear lines of authority and responsibility. The PC sets the tone for the crew and maintains the working environment. Effective leaders use their authority but do not operate without the participation of other crew members. When crew members disagree on a course of action, they must effectively resolve the disagreement. Specific goals include the following:

- The PC actively establishes an open climate in which crew members talk freely and ask questions.
- Crew members value each other for their expertise and judgment; they do not allow differences in rank and experience to influence their willingness to speak up.
- Alternative viewpoints are normal and part of crew interaction; crew members must handle disagreements in a professional manner, and avoid personal attacks or defensive posturing.
- The PC actively monitors attitudes of crew members and offers feedback, when necessary; each crew member should display appropriate concern for balancing safety with mission accomplishment.

PREMISSION PLANNING AND REHEARSAL

E-5. Premission planning includes all preparatory tasks associated with planning the mission. These tasks include planning for VFR or IFR flight. They also include assigning crew member responsibilities and conducting all required briefings and back briefs. Premission rehearsal involves the crew collectively visualizing and discussing expected and possible events for each phase of the mission. Specific goals include the following:

- The PC ensures that all actions, duties, and mission responsibilities are clearly assigned to specific crew members. Each crew member actively participates in the mission planning process to ensure a common understanding of mission intent and operational sequence; the PC prioritizes planning activities so that critical items are addressed within the available planning time.
- Crew members identify alternate courses of action in anticipation of potential weather changes. Crew members must be prepared to implement contingency plans when required. Crew members mentally rehearse the entire mission by visualizing and discussing potential problems, contingencies, and responsibilities.
- The PC ensures that crew members take advantage of periods of low workloads to rehearse upcoming flight segments; crew members continuously review remaining flight segments to identify and implement required adjustments.

DECISION MAKING

E-6. Decision making is the act of rendering a solution to a problem and defining a plan of action; it must involve risk assessment. The quality of decision making and problem solving, throughout the planning and execution phases of the mission, depends on information available, time constraints, and level of involvement and information exchange among crew members. Although the entire crew should be involved in the decision making and problem-solving process, the PC is the decision maker. Specific goals include the following:

- Under high stress, crew members rely on a pattern-recognition decision process to produce timely responses. They minimize deliberation, consistent with available decision time. Crew members focus on the most critical factors influencing their choice of responses. They efficiently prioritize their specific information needs within the available decision time.
- Under moderate to low stress, crew members rely on an analytical decision process to produce high-quality decisions. They encourage deliberation when time permits. Arriving at the most unbiased decision possible, crew members consider all important factors influencing their choice of action. They consistently seek all available information relative to factors being considered.

WORKLOAD PRIORITY

E-7. This quality addresses the effectiveness of time and workload management. It assesses the extent to which the crew, as a team, avoids distractions from essential activities, distributes and manages workload, and avoids individual task overload. Specific goals include the following:

- Crew members are able to identify and prioritize competing mission tasks. They appropriately delay low-priority tasks until those tasks do not compete with more critical tasks. Crew members consistently avoid nonessential distractions so that they do not affect task performance.
- The PC actively manages distribution of mission tasks to prevent overloading any crew member, especially during critical phases of flight. Crew members watch for workload buildup on others and react quickly to adjust distribution of task responsibilities.
- The PC ensures that all crew members do not focus on the same urgent task, such as an emergency procedure, leaving no one to fly the aircraft.

UNEXPECTED EVENTS

E-8. This quality addresses crew performance under unusual circumstances that may involve high levels of stress. Technical and managerial aspects of coping with the situation are important. Specific goals include the following:

- Crew actions reflect extensive rehearsal of emergency procedures in prior training and premission planning and rehearsal. Crew members coordinate their actions and exchange information with minimal verbal direction from the PC.
- Each crew member appropriately adjusts individual workload and task priorities with minimal verbal direction from the PC. The PC ensures that each crew member is used effectively when responding to the emergency and that the workload is efficiently distributed.

STATEMENTS AND DIRECTIVES

E-9. This quality refers to the completeness, timeliness, and quality of information transfer. It includes crew use of standard terminology and feedback techniques to verify information transfer. Emphasis is on the quality of instructions and statements associated with navigation, obstacle clearance, and instrument readouts. Specific goals include the following:

- Crew members consistently make recommended callouts; statements and directives are always timely.
- Crew members use standard terminology in all communications; statements and directives are clear and concise.

- Crew members actively seek feedback from unresponsive crew members to obtain acknowledgement and understanding of intent; crew members can request additional clarification when necessary.

MISSION SITUATIONAL AWARENESS

E-10. Mission situational awareness considers the extent to which crew members keep each other informed regarding aircraft status and mission. Information reporting helps the aircrew maintain a high level of SA. The information reported includes aircraft position and orientation, equipment and personnel status, environmental and battlefield conditions, and changes to mission objectives. SA by the entire crew is essential to safe flight and effective crew performance. Situational awareness is enhanced by the following:

- Crew members routinely update each other and highlight and acknowledge changes; they take personal responsibility for scanning the entire flight environment, considering their assigned workload and areas to scan.
- Crew members actively discuss conditions and situations that can compromise SA; these include—but are not limited to—stress, boredom, fatigue, and anger.

DECISIONS AND ACTIONS

E-11. This quality addresses the extent to which crew members are kept informed of decisions and actions by other crew members. Crew members should respond verbally or by appropriately adjusting their behaviors, actions, or control inputs to clearly indicate that they understand when a decision has been made and what it is. Failure to do so may confuse fellow crew members and lead to uncoordinated operations. Specific goals include the following:

- Crew members announce decisions and actions, stating rationale and intentions as time permits; the P verbally coordinates the transfer of, or inputs to, controls before action.
- Crew members acknowledge announced decisions or actions and provide feedback on how these decisions or actions will affect other crew tasks if necessary, they promptly request clarification of decisions or actions.

SUPPORTING INFORMATION

E-12. This quality addresses the extent to which supporting information and actions are sought from the crew by another crew member, usually the PC. Crew members should feel free to raise questions during the flight regarding plans, revisions to plans, actions to be taken, and status of key mission information. Specific goals include the following:

- The PC encourages crew members to raise issues or offer information about safety or the mission; crew members anticipate impending decisions and actions and offer information as appropriate.
- Crew members always request assistance from others before they become overloaded with tasks or before they must divert attention from a critical task.

CREW MEMBER ACTIONS

E-13. This quality addresses the extent to which crew members cross-check each other to break the sequence of events (error chains) that leads to accidents or degraded mission performance. Crew members must be capable of detecting each other's mistakes. Cross monitoring is particularly important when crews are tired or overly focused on critical task elements and, thus, prone to mistakes. Specific goals include the following:

- Acknowledging crew error is a common occurrence, and active involvement of the entire crew is required to detect and break error chains leading to accidents; crews constantly watch for errors affecting flight safety or mission performance by monitoring their own performance as well as the performance of others. When noting an error, quickly and professionally inform and assist the crew member committing the error.

- The crew thoroughly discusses the two-challenge rule before mission execution. When required, effectively implement the two-challenge rule with minimal compromise to flight safety.

CREW SUPPORTING INFORMATION

E-14. This quality addresses the extent to which crew members anticipate and offer supporting information and actions to the decision maker, usually the PC, when a decision must be made or an action taken. A specific goal for crew members is to anticipate the need to provide information, warnings, or assistance to the PC or P* during critical phases of flight. They provide required information in a timely manner.

ADVOCACY AND ASSERTION

E-15. This quality concerns the extent to which crew members are proactive in advocating a course of action they consider best, even when others may disagree. Specific goals include the following:

- Maintaining a professional atmosphere, crew members state the rationale for recommended plans and courses of action, as time permits; they request feedback to ensure that others correctly understand their statements or rationale. Time permitting, other crew members practice good listening habits and wait for explanations before commenting on recommended plans or courses of action.
- The PC actively promotes objectivity in the cockpit by encouraging other crew members to speak up when they disagree with senior members; every crew member displays a sense of responsibility for adhering to flight regulations, operating procedures, and safety standards.

CREW-LEVEL AFTER-ACTION REVIEWS

E-16. This quality addresses the extent to which crew members review and critique their actions during or after a mission segment and during periods of low workload or mission debriefing. Specific goals include the following:

- The crew critiques major decisions and actions by identifying options and factors omitted and outlining ways to improve crew performance in future missions.
- The critique of crew decisions and actions is professional. Allegations are avoided; the emphasis is on education and improvement of crew performance.

CREW COORDINATION OBJECTIVES

E-17. Crew coordination elements and basic qualities are measured to determine if the program objectives have been met. The five crew coordination objectives are the following:

- **Establish and maintain team relationships.** A positive working relationship allows the crew to communicate openly and freely and operate in a concerted manner.
- **Conduct mission planning and rehearsal.** Explore all aspects of the assigned mission, and analyze each segment for potential difficulties and possible reactions in terms of mission requirements.
- **Establish and maintain workloads.** Manage and execute the mission workload effectively and efficiently with redistribution of task responsibilities as the mission situation changes.
- **Exchange mission information.** Establish intracrew communications using effective patterns and techniques that allow for the flow of essential data among crew members.
- **Cross monitor performance.** Cross monitor actions and decisions of other crew members to reduce the likelihood of errors affecting mission performance and safety.

STANDARDIZED COCKPIT PROCEDURES

E-18. Clearly defining a division of cockpit responsibilities ensures that duties that may distract the P* are transferred to the pilot (P). Clear division of cockpit responsibilities is of particular importance during the arrival and departure phases of flight. Because of different cockpit designs, units should modify these procedures based on unit aircraft equipment. All Army aircraft require two pilots for IMC flight. Appropriate verbiage and responsibilities serve as a guide to fully integrate the actions of the P* and P.

PILOT RESPONSIBILITIES

E-19. The P* is responsible for flying the aircraft. If autopilot equipped and it is coupled, the P* is responsible for ensuring that the autopilot correctly captures and maintains selected altitudes and courses. Unless required by a safety consideration, the P* shall avoid tasks that distract from the primary responsibility of flying by directing the other crew members to accomplish these tasks. Distracting tasks, especially those associated with departure and arrival, should be performed by the P, if possible. Managing the workload placed upon the P during periods of high cockpit workload is responsibility of the P*.

E-20. The P is responsible for cross monitoring the P* and accomplishing tasks that may distract the P* from his duties. The primary duty of the P is to keep the P* free to fly the aircraft. Basic P duties include the following :

- Maintain radio communications.
- Navigate – know at all times the position of the aircraft.
- Verify all navigational fixes for the flight.
- Change NAVAID and communications radio frequencies.
- Change transponder codes.
- Copy clearances, local weather broadcasts, and other flight information.
- Read and complete checklist items as required.
- Set/adjust pages, switches, and systems as required.
- Operate the FMS/GPS/onboard navigational system at the direction of the P* or as required for the flight.
- Change aircraft configuration at the direction of the P*, such as the following:
  - Power and propeller settings.
  - Flap selection.
  - Operating the gear handle.
  - Operating the weather avoidance equipment.
- Set and arm altitude on the altitude preselector (if installed).
- Take the following actions during IFR operations:
  - Ensure the correct altimeter setting and cross monitor the P* to assist in avoiding a misreading.
  - Note takeoff time.
  - Assist P* in determining correct holding entry.
  - Calculate and monitor times for holding and approaches.
  - When on approach, watch for the runway environment.
  - Be prepared to direct and assist the P* with the missed approach procedure, if required.

MANAGEMENT

Flight Director Panel

E-21. The P* and P must coordinate efforts to manage the flight director system. The P* determines and directs the P accordingly. The P makes changes to the altitude controls as required by newly assigned altitudes without direction of the P*. The P does not make other changes to the P*'s flight director system without P*'s direction. If the P is unable to assist, the P* may make minor changes to the flight director system. Examples include:

- Arming the approach mode.
- Selecting IAS or vertical speed (VS).

- Selecting heading (HDG) or NAV.
- Selecting standby (STBY).

E-22. Changes to status of the flight director system coupled to the autopilot are announced and mutually verified. When a selection is initiated, it is announced to the other pilot. P* announces when the flight director captures a selected mode.

Power Levers (Fixed Wing)

E-23. The P* does not relinquish control of the power levers to the P. The P is limited to assisting the P* by setting and maintaining the takeoff power as briefed. During the takeoff roll, if there is a need to abort the takeoff, the P* retards the power levers.

DEVIATIONS

E-24. Certain circumstances may require deviation from guidelines conveyed in this manual. Such deviations, when clearly communicated among the crew members, reflect good resource management and coordinated crew actions.

CHECKLISTS

E-25. The P and P* should use the challenge and response method of reading the checklist. This is the most positive way to proceed through a checklist because it allows for both pilots to remain aware of all checklist-related activities. Flexibility with this method is required. During periods of high cockpit workload (taxiing, departures or takeoffs, traffic patterns, descents, and approaches), the P* may not be able to respond in a quick and positive manner. As a result, the benefits of the challenge and response do not justify the additional workload that it places on the P*. Under these circumstances, the checklist should still be read aloud; however, the P now also provides the response. The P should only accomplish noncritical functions with command or acknowledgment. The operation of systems—such as landing gear, flaps, autopilot, FMS, and flight director mode selections—require P* participation, mandating a response of "Confirmed." For example, before landing, P initiates "Gear DOWN/confirm," and P* responds "Confirmed."

STERILE COCKPIT

E-26. The definition of a sterile cockpit is that only conversation required for safe aircraft operation is conducted. A sterile cockpit shall exist under the following conditions:

- From the start of the takeoff run through climb to a designated altitude, or the en route phase of flight when cruise altitude is less than the designated altitude.
- During descent from a designated altitude or the en route phase of flight into the terminal area for approach and landing.

TWO-CHALLENGE RULE

E-27. The two-challenge rule allows one crew member to automatically assume the duties of another crew member who fails to respond to two consecutive challenges or when aircraft control is in question. (For example, the P* becomes fixated, confused, or task overloaded or otherwise allows the aircraft to enter an unsafe position or attitude.) The P first asks the P* if he is aware of the aircraft position or attitude. If the P* does not acknowledge this challenge, the P issues a second challenge. If the P* fails to acknowledge the second challenge, the P assumes control of the aircraft.

E-28. Do not assume two challenges have to be made before control transfer. The two-challenge rule is the maximum. If the situation warrants, control transfer immediately or after one challenge. The pilot assuming the controls makes this decision. Challenges can also come from other crew members.

STANDARD CREW TERMINOLOGY

E-29. To enhance communication and crew coordination, crews should use words or phrases that are understood by all participants. They must use clear, concise terms that can be easily understood and complied with in an environment full of distractions. Multiple terms with the same meaning should be avoided. DOD FLIP and FAA manual 7110.65 contain standard terminology for radio communications. Operator's manuals contain standard terminology for items of equipment. Table E-1 is a list of other standard words and phrases that crew members may use.

Table E-1. Examples of standard words and phrases

Word or Phrase	Meaning
Abort	To terminate a preplanned maneuver (for example, an aborted takeoff).
Affirmative	Yes
Braking	Announcement made by the P* who intends to apply brake pressure.
Break	Immediate action command to perform a maneuver to deviate from the present ground track; will be followed by "RIGHT," or "LEFT."
Callout	Command by the P* for a specified procedure to be read from the checklist by another crew member.
Clear	No obstacle present to impede aircraft movement along intended direction of flight or while taxiing on the ground; followed by direction of movement (Clear right/left). Also, when preceded by the number one or two, indicates that the engine area has been visually checked for personnel or other hazards before engine start.)
Contact	Traffic in sight or establish communication with.
Correct	Confirms a statement as being accurate; do not use "right" to indicate correct.
Correcting	Statement that the P* is taking positive action to correct an out-of-tolerance flight parameter (drift or altitude).
Drifting	An alert of the unannounced movement of the aircraft on final approach or takeoff; will be followed by direction (drifting right or left).
Egress	Immediate action command to get out of the aircraft.
Execute	Initiate an action.
Expect	Anticipate further instructions or guidance.
Fire light	Announcement of illumination of the master fire warning light.
Go ahead	Proceed with message.
Hold	Command to maintain present position.
I have the controls	Used as a command or announcement by the rated crew member (RCM) assuming control of the flight controls.
Inside	Primary focus of attention is inside the aircraft.
In sight	Preceded by the word traffic, runway, obstacle, or descriptive term. Used to confirm that an object is positively seen or identified.
Maintain	Command to keep or continue the same.
Move forward/backward	Command to taxi the aircraft forward/backward, followed by distance. Also used to announce intended forward or backward movement.
My power	The P* resumes control of the power levers from the P (fixed wing).
Negative	"No" or "that is not correct."
Negative contact	Unable to establish communication with (followed by the name of the element).
No joy	Traffic or obstacle not positively seen or identified.
Normal	Condition as it should be. Airspeed check on takeoff roll.
Now	Indicates that an immediate action is required
Outside	Primary focus of attention is outside the aircraft.
Put me up	Command to place the P*'s radio transmit selector switch to a designated position or to place a frequency in a specific radio.
Report	Command to notify.
Right	Used to indicate a direction to the right.
Roger	Message received and understood.
Rotate	The P callout when the aircraft has obtained takeoff decision speed (V1).

Table E-1. Examples of standard words and phrases

Word or Phrase	Meaning
Say again	Repeat transmission.
Set power	Command by the P* for the P to set takeoff power or maximum available power during a go-around or missed approach (fixed wing).
Stand by	Wait. Duties of a higher priority are being performed.
Stop	Command to go no further; halt present action.
Talley	Traffic or obstacle positively seen or identified (will be followed by a repeat of the word traffic or obstacle and the clock position).
Traffic	Refers to any friendly aircraft that presents a collision hazard; will be followed by a clock position, distance, and reference to altitude.
Unable	Indicates the inability to comply with a specific instruction or request.
Up on	Indicates radio selected; followed by position number on ICS panel (Up on 3).
Verify	Request confirmation of information.
Wilco	I have received, understand, and will comply.
You have the controls	Used as a command or announcement by the pilot relinquishing the flight controls.
Your power	P returning control of the power levers to the P* (fixed wing).
You're up	Announces a specific radio or frequency selected. "You're up on 121.7 on number one."

CREW COORDINATION CALLOUTS

E-30. Bold type identifies the crew member who should initiate the call. In certain situations, it is initiated by the first crew member to observe or notice the event—and then the roles are reversed.

TAKEOFF

E-31. Table E-2 applies to an instrument takeoff.

Table E-2. Rotary and fixed wing instrument takeoff callouts

Action	P* Call/Response	P Call/Response
Collective increase to climb power (Crew brief specifies value)	**Climb power**	XX% (P calls actual value on torque display; continues to monitor and make calls as specified in brief until climb airspeed reached)
10 KIAS from briefed climb airspeed	Roger 10 knots	**10 knots prior**
Power levers advance	**Set power**	Power set
65 knots indicated (systems normal)		**Normal**
Airspeed at V1		**V1 Rotate**
Abnormal or emergency condition prior to V1 (identified by P)	Aborting	**Abort, Abort**
P* elects to abort prior to V1	**Aborting (state problem)**	Roger
Positive rate of climb (two indications)	After P call "Gear up"	**Positive rate** "Gear is up" or "Gear did not retract"
Airspeed at 105 KIAS (flaps at takeoff position)	**Flaps up**	Flaps up

CLIMB, CRUISE, AND DESCENT

E-32. If passing the 1,000-foot prior point and ATC communications are preventing the callout, either crew member may raise the index finger in view of the other to indicate the 1,000-foot prior point (table E-3, page E-10).

Table E-3. Climb/cruise/descent callouts

Action	P* Call/Response	P Call/Response
1,000 feet prior to level off	Roger	1,000 to go
Climbing through transition altitude	29.92 set left	29.92 set right
Descending through transition altitude or change to altimeter setting	XX.XX set (left or right as applicable)"	Altimeter XX.XX

ALL PHASES OF FLIGHT

E-33. Table E-4 applies to phases of flight.

Table E-4. Examples of calls/responses for all phases of flight

Observation	P* Call/Response	P Call/Response
100 feet prior to any altitude	Roger 100 to go	100 to go
Bank angle exceeds 30°	Correcting	Bank Angle
Airspeed deviates ± 10 KIAS	Increasing (decreasing) airspeed	Airspeed, XX knots low (high)
Altitude deviates ± 100 feet	Increasing (decreasing) altitude	Altitude, XX feet low (high)
Heading deviates ± 10°	Correcting right(left)"	Heading, XX degrees left (right)

INSTRUMENT APPROACH

E-34. Table E-5 applies to all instrument approaches except ground-controlled approach (GCA).

Table E-5. Examples of instrument approach calls/responses

Action	P* Call/Response	P Call/Response
Initial course/localizer movement	Roger	Course (localizer) alive
Course/localizer capture	Roger	Course (localizer) captured
Initial glide slope movement (precision approach)	Roger	Glide slope alive
Glide slope capture (precision approach)	Roger	Glide slope captured
FAF	Time	Time started
1,000 feet before DA/DH/MDA	Roger	1,000 to go
500 feet before DA/DH/MDA	Roger	500 to go
100 feet before DA/DH/MDA	Roger	100 to go

MISSED APPROACH

E-35. These callouts (table E-6, page E-11) apply when—

- Aircraft has reached DA/DH, MAP, MAWP at the published MDA and appropriate visual reference has not been called in sight.
- Wind shear is encountered and affects the safe operation of flight.
- If, after passing the FAF inbound, either the localizer, VOR, or GPS deviation indicator or glide slope reaches full-scale deflection or if RAIM annunciation appears.
- If, on reaching DA/DH or MAP, the aircraft is not continuously in a position from which a descent to land on the intended runway can be made at a normal rate using normal maneuvers permitting touchdown to occur within the touchdown zone.
- If, while circling to land, visual contact with the runway environment is lost by both pilots.

Table E-6. Examples of missed approach calls/responses

Action	P* Call/Response	P Call/Response
Straight-in approach–reaching missed approach point, runway environment not in sight	Roger, missed approach (followed by missed approach actions)	DA/DH, Time's up or MAP, negative contact, missed approach
Circling approach–visual contact with runway lost (crew member monitoring outside while circling initiates callout)	**Visual contact lost, executing missed approach (followed by actions)** Roger, missed approach	Roger, **Visual contact lost, execute missed approach**
Go around segment after P* initiates the power application	**Climb power**	Power set
After verifying two positive climb indications	Roger	**Positive rate**
Go-around segment after P* initiates the power application	**Set power**	Power set
After verifying two positive climb indications	Gear up	**Positive rate**
Flaps beyond approach	**Flaps approach**	Flaps approach
Airspeed reaches 105 KIAS	**Flaps up**	Flaps up
When time and altitude permit	**My power**	Your power

VISUAL TRANSITION FROM INSTRUMENTS

E-36. The P seeks outside references during the approach while cross-monitoring the P*'s instruments. Should visual reference deteriorate after a sighting call is made, call "visual contact lost." If the aircraft has not reached the missed approach point, the approach may be continued to DA/DH/MDA. If the aircraft has passed the MAP and visual contact is lost, call "missed approach," and complete missed approach actions.

E-37. Indicate to the P* when making the transition from instruments by stating the clock position along with a visual cue. The callout indicates that the P* can remain in constant visual contact with the runway environment from callout to landing. The P* must call "visual" before the aircraft continues below DA/DH/MDA. After such a call is made, the P assumes primary responsibility for monitoring instrument reference to touchdown and immediately calls out any deviation from normal operations. While at MDA on straight in or circling approaches, the P should call out any deviation in altitude or abnormal approach speeds. If level at MDA, the P* stays level at this altitude until calling "leaving MDA." During a circling maneuver when the runway is on the P's side, use appropriate callouts to direct the P* when to make turns with respect to the landing runway, traffic, or any necessary deviations (see table E-7).

Table E-7. Examples of calls/responses for instrument reference to visual

Action	P* Call/Response	P Call/Response
Appropriate visual references in sight	On instruments (or other intentions)	**Approach lights** (or other features identifiable with runway environment) **in sight continue approach** (or other recommended action)
Runway in sight	Runway in sight, visual	**Runway in sight** (clock position), **take over visually**
P* departs MDA to land	**Leaving MDA**	Roger

APPROACH DEVIATIONS

E-38. Table E-8 shows examples of calls/responses for approach deviations. The two-challenge rule applies to the callouts described in table E-8, page E-12.

Table E-8. Examples of calls/responses for approach deviations

Observation	P* Call/Response	P Call/Response
± one dot of glide slope	Correcting (up/down)	One dot (high/low) and increasing/decreasing
± one dot of localizer/VOR/GPS	Correcting (left/right)	One dot (left/right) and increasing/decreasing
± 5° on NDB approach	Correcting (left/right)	5° (left/right) and increasing/decreasing
± 10 kts from approach speed	Increasing (decreasing) airspeed	Airspeed ten knots low (high)
Rate of descent exceeds 1,000 ft per minute	Reduce sink rate	Sink rate (amount) increasing (decreasing/holding)

EMERGENCIES/MALFUNCTIONS

E-39. The primary action during emergencies or system malfunctions is to continue flying the aircraft. Table E-9 provides suggested callouts for these events.

Table E-9. Examples of emergency calls/responses

Observation	P* Call/Response	P Call/Response
Loss of an engine	Confirm engine failure number one/two	"Confirm engine number one/two has failed" or "Negative, number (opposite) has failed"
Other system malfunctions	State conditions or indications that lead you to believe that you have a problem	Confirm or deny suspected malfunction. (Make sure P* continues to fly and does not get distracted by emergency.)
Fixed Wing Specific		
Loss of an engine (one or two) by control pressures and/or instrument indications. Sequence begins after power is applied and aircraft stabilized.	Confirm engine number one/two has failed Did the propeller feather?	"I confirm engine number one/two has failed," or "Yes, number X prop feathered," or "No, it did not feather."
Propeller did not feather	Identify the number one/two (appropriate) prop lever P* visually confirms the correct prop lever has been identified "I agree, feather the prop" or "Negative, reidentify the number X prop."	P places index finger on appropriate prop lever. Number one/two prop lever identified. When directed by the P*, move prop to feather. Prop feathered.
Reaching designated airspeed, according to operator's manual	Flaps up	Flaps up

Glossary

14 CFR	Title 14 of the Code of Federal Regulations
AAF	Army airfield
AAR	after action report
AC	advisory circular
ACC	altocumulus castellanus (clouds)
acft	aircraft
ACSL	altocumulus (clouds)
ACTE	Aircrew Coordination Training Enhancement
ADAS	AWOS data acquisition system
ADDS	Aviation Digital Data Service
ADF	automatic direction finder
ADIZ	air defense identification zone
A/FD	Airport/Facility Directory
AFMAN	Air Force manual
AFOD	Army Flight Operations Detachment
AFSS	automated flight service station
aft	after
AFWA	Air Force weather agency
A/G	air/ground
AGL	above ground level
AHP	Army heliport
AIM	Aeronautical Information Manual
AIMS	ATCRBS, IFF, Mark XII identification system, and system
AIREP	air report
AIRMET	airman's meteorological information
AKO	Army Knowledge Online
ALSF	approach lighting with sequenced flashing lights
alt	altitude
ALTN	alternate
ALTRV	Altitude Reservation
AM	amplitude modulation
AMD	amended
AMDT	amendment
AMOCC	air mobility operations control center
ANDS	acceleration–north/deceleration–south

ANT	antenna
AOPA	American Owners & Pilots Association
AOR	area of responsibility
AP	Area Planning
APG	Aviator Procedures Guide
appr	approach
AR	Army regulation
ARINC	Aeronautical Radio Incorporated
ARNG	Army National Guard
ARTCC	air route traffic control center
ARTS	automated radar terminal system
AS	airspeed
A/S	all stops
ASOS	automated surface observation system
ASR	airport surveillance radar
ATC	air traffic control
ATCRBS	Air Traffic Control Radar Beacon System
ATCT	airport traffic control tower
ATIS	automatic terminal information service
ATM	aircrew training manual
ATNAVICS	Air Traffic Navigation, Integration, and Coordination System
ATS	air traffic services
auto	automated
AWC	Aviation Weather Center
AWOS	automated weather observing system
B	beginning time
BC	back course
bd	board
BDL	Bradley International Airport designator
BECMG	becoming
BFO	beat frequency oscillator
BIRDTAM	bird activity NOTAM
BKN	broken
BL	blowing (dust, sand, snow, and/or spray)
BMNT	beginning morning nautical twilight
BR	mist
C	Celsius
C2	command and control
C/A	course acquisition
cal	calibrated

CAS	calibrated airspeed
CAT	clear air turbulence
cat	category
CB	cumulonimbus (clouds)
CBMAM	cumulonimbus mammatus (clouds)
CCSL	cirrocumulus (clouds)
CDI	course deviation indicator
CDU	control display unit
ceil	ceiling
CFA	controlled firing area
CFACC	combined forces air component commander
CFIT	controlled flight into terrain
CFP	computer flight plan
CH	compass heading; cargo helicopter; ceiling height (METAR code)
chan	channel
CIG	ceiling (height above ground level to base of clouds)
CLC	course line computer
CLD	clouds
CLR	clear
con	control
CONUS	continental United States
COP	changeover point
CP	circular polarization
CPU	central processing unit
CRAFT	clearance, route, approach, frequency, and transponder (code)
CRS	course
CTAF	common traffic advisory frequency
CWA	center weather advisory
D	degrees; day
DA	decision altitude; Department of the Army
DAFIF	Digital Aeronautical Flight Information File
DC	direct current
DD	Department of Defense
dep	departure
DER	departure end of the runway
desg	designation
DEST	destination
DH	decision height
DINS	DOD Internet NOTAM Distribution System
dist	distance

DME	distance measuring equipment
dn	down
DOD	Department of Defense
DOTD	Directorate of Training and Doctrine
DP	departure procedure
DR	dead reckoning
DS	dust storm
DSN	defense switched network
dsnt	distant
DT	daylight saving time
DTG	date-time group
DU	dust
DUATS	Direct User Access Terminal System
DURGC	during climb
DZ	drizzle
E	ending time; east
EAS	equivalent airspeed
EENT	ending evening nautical twilight
EFAS	en route flight advisory service
EFC	expect further clearance
E-field	electric field
EGI	embedded global positioning system/inertial navigation system
elev	elevation
EM	electromagnetic
emerg	emergency
EOVM	emergency obstruction video map
ESA	en route safe altitude
est	estimated
ETA	estimated time of arrival
ETD	estimated time of departure
ETE	estimated time en route
EUCARF	European Central Airspace Reservation Facility
ex	example
F	Fahrenheit
FA	area forecast
FAA	Federal Aviation Administration
FAF	final approach fix
FAR	Federal Aviation Regulation
FAT	free air temperature
FAWP	final approach waypoint

FBO	fixed base operator
FC	funnel cloud
FCG	Foreign Clearance Guide
fcst	forecast
FDC	flight data center
FG	fog
FIH	Flight Information Handbook
FIR	flight information region
FL	flight level
FLIP	Flight Information Publication
flt	flight
FM	frequency modulation; field manual
fm	from
FMC	flight management computer
FMS	flight management system
FOE	fixation, omission, and emphasis
FPM	feet per minute
FPNM	feet per nautical mile
FR	from
freq	frequency
FROPA	frontal passage
FSS	flight service station
ft	feet
FU	smoke
FZ	freezing
FZRA	light freezing rain
G	gust
GCA	ground controlled approach
GCO	ground communication outlet
GHz	gigahertz
GLS	GNSS landing system
GMT	Greenwich Mean Time
gnd	ground
GNSS	global navigation satellite system
GP	General Planning
GPS	global positioning system
GR	hailstones
GS	small hail or snow pellets
GUS	ground uplink station
gyr	gyroscope

gyro	gyroscope
HAA	height above airport
HAL	height above landing
HAT	height above touchdown
HDG	heading
HEIL	high intensity runway lights
HF	high frequency
HFD	Hartford
Hg	mercury
HH	Coast Guard helicopter
HIRL	high intensity runway lights
HIWAS	Hazardous In-flight Weather Advisory Service
hr	hours
HSI	horizontal situation indicator
HZ	haze
Hz	hertz
IAF	initial approach fix
IAP	instrument approach procedure
IAS	indicated airspeed
IAWP	initial approach waypoint
IC	ice crystals
ICAO	International Civil Aviation Organization
ID	identification
IDENT	identification
IF	intermediate fix
IFE	instrument flight examiner
IFF	identification friend or foe
IFR	instrument flight rules
IIMC	inadvertent instrument meteorological condition
illum	illumination (moon)
ILS	instrument landing system
IMC	instrument meteorological condition
inc	increasing
inop	inoperative
INS	inertial navigation system
IP	instructor pilot
IPH	Instrument Procedures Handbook
IR	IFR military training route
ISA	International Standard Atmospheric
ITO	instrument takeoff

IVSI	instantaneous vertical speed indicator
JFC	Joint force commander
JP	jet propulsion
KHz	kilohertz
KIAS	knots indicated airspeed
KM	kilometers
kt	knots
L	left
LAA	local airport advisory
LAAS	local area augmentation system
LAHSO	land and hold short operations
LDA	Localizer-type directional aid
ldg	landing
LF	low frequency
LHA	general-purpose amphibious assault ship
LHD	multipurpose amphibious assault ship
LLWAS	low-level wind shear alert system
LLZ	localizer facility
L/MF	low/medium frequency
LMM	locator middle marker
LNAV	lateral navigation
LOA	letter of agreement
LOC	localizer
LOM	locator outer marker
LPH	landing platform helicopter
LR	lead radial
LTD	limited
LTG	lighting
lvl	level
MAA	maximum authorized altitude
MALS	medium-intensity approach lighting system
MALSR	medium-intensity approach lighting system with runway alignment indicator lights
MAP	missed approach point
MAWP	missed approach waypoint
max	maximum
MCA	minimum crossing altitude
MCS	master control station
MDA	minimum descent altitude
MEA	minimum en route altitude

MEF	maximum elevation figure
METAR	meteorological aviation report
MF	medium frequency
MFD	multifunction display
M-field	magnetic field
MH	magnetic heading
MHz	megahertz
MIA	minimum IFR altitude
MIFG	patches of shallow fog not deeper than 2 meters
MIN	minute
MLS	microwave landing system
MM	middle marker
MMLS	mobile microwave landing system
MN	magnetic north
MOA	military operations area
MOCA	minimum obstruction clearance altitude
MORA	minimum off route altitude
mov	moving
MR	moonrise
MRA	minimum reception altitude
MRAALS	Marine remote area automatic landing system
MS	moonset
MSA	minimum safe altitude
MSAW	minimum safe altitude warning
MSHP	mishap
MSL	mean sea level
MTR	military training route
MVA	minimum vectoring altitude
MVFR	marginal visual fight rules
N	north
N/A	not applicable
NACO	National Aeronautical Charting Office
NAD	North American datum
NAS	National Airspace System
NATS	North Atlantic Track System
NAUT	nautical
NAV	navigation
NAVAID	navigational aid
NAVAIR	Naval Air Systems Command
NCAR	National Center for Atmospheric Research

NCEP	National Centers for Environmental Prediction
NDB	nondirectional beacon
NEXRAD	Next Generation Weather Radar
NFDC	National Flight Data Center
NGA	National Geospatial-Intelligence Agency
NM	nautical miles
no	number
NOAA	National Oceanic and Atmospheric Adminstration
NOTAM	notice to airmen
NRP	national route program
NSA	national security area
NSN	national stock number
NSW	no significant weather
NTAP	Notices to Airmen Publication
NWS	National Weather Service
NYC	New York City
OAT	outside air temperature
OBS	omnibearing selector
OCONUS	outside continental United States
ODALS	outside directional approach lighting system
OIS	obstacle identification surface
OM	outer marker
onbd	onboard
ops	operations
OPTEMPO	operating tempo
OROCA	off route obstruction clearance altitude
OVC	overcast
OWS	operational weather squadron
P	pilot not on the controls
P*	pilot on the controls
PA	pressure altitude
pam	pamphlet
PANS-OPS	Procedures for Air Navigation Services-Aircraft Operations
PAR	precision approach radar
PC	pilot-in-command
PCL	pilot controlled lighting
PCN	planning change notice
PIREP	pilot weather report
PK	peak
PL	ice pellets

PMSV	Pilot-to-Metro Service
PO	dust/sand whirls
POB	persons on board
PPC	performance planning card
PPS	precise positioning service
PR	partial
pres	present; pressure
PRESFR	pressure falling rapidly
PRESRR	pressure rising rapidly
press	pressure
prob	probability (forecast)
P-static	precipitation static
PT	procedure turn
pt	point
pub	publication
pvt	private
PY	spray
QFE	atmospheric pressure at field elevation
QNE	standard altimeter
QNH	atmosphere pressure at nautical height
R	right
RA	rain
rad	radiation
RAIL	runway alignment indicator lights
RAIM	receiver autonomous integrity monitoring
RAMCC	Regional Air Movement Control Center
RAP	Research Applications Program
RAPCON	radar approach control
RCL	runway centerline lighting
RCM	rated crewmember
RCO	remote communications outlet
RCR	runway condition reading
REIL	runway end identifier lights
RF	radio frequency
rgnl	regional
RMI	radio magnetic indicator
RMK	remark
RNAV	area navigation
Rotor CLD	rotor cloud
RPM	revolutions per minute

RRS	Wiregrass (Midland City, Alabama) VORTAC
RSC	runway surface condition
RVR	runway visual range
RVSM	reduced vertical separation minumums
RVV	runway visual value
RWY	runway
S	south
SA	situational awareness
SARP	standards and recommended practice
SCSL	stratocumulus (clouds)
SCT	scattered
SEC	seconds
SFC	surface
SG	snow grains
SH	showers (precipitation)
SHRA	rain showers
SID	standard instrument departure
SIGMET	significant meteorological information
SKC	sky clear
sked	schedule
SLP	sea-level pressure
SM	statute mile
SN	snow
SOIR	simultaneous operations on intersecting runways
SPECI	special weather report
SPS	standard positioning service
SQ	squall
SR	sunrise
SS	sunset
SSALR	simplified short approach lighting system with runway alighment indicator
SSALS	simplified short approach lighting system
SSN	social security number
SSR	secondary surveillance radar
STAR	standard terminal arrival route
STAT	statute
STBY	standby
STOL	short takeoff and landing
STT	special tactics team
SUA	special-use airspace

SVFR	special visual flight rules (fixed wing)
T	true
TAA	terminal arrival area
TACAN	tactical air navigation
TAF	terminal area forecast
TAS	true airspeed
TCH	threshold crossing height
TCU	towering cumulus (clouds)
TDZE	touchdown zone elevation
TEC	tower en route control
temp	temperature
tempo	temporary
TERPS	terminal instrument procedures
TFR	temporary flight restriction
TH	true heading
TIBS	telephone information briefing service
tkof	takeoff
TN	true north
TRACON	terminal radar approach control
TS	thunderstorms (precipitation)
TSO	technical standard order
TSRA	thunderstorm with rain
TTS	time to station
TWC	The Weather Channel
TWEB	transcribed weather broadcast
twr	tower
UCN	urgent change notice
UH	utility helicopter
UP	unknown precipatation
UHF	ultra high frequency
U.S.	United States
USAASA	United States Army Aeronautical Services Agency
USAAWC	United States Army Aviation Warfighting Center
USAR	United States Army Reserve
USNS	United States NOTAM System
UTC	universal time coordinated
V	variable
VA	volcanic ash
VAFTAD	volcanic ash forecast transport and dispersion
var	variation

VC	vicinity
VCFG	fog in the vicinity
VCSH	showers in the vicinity
VDP	visual descent point
VFR	visual flight rules
VHF	very high frequency
vis	visibility
VLF	very low frequency
VMC	visual meteorological conditions
VNAV	vertical navigation
Vne	velocity never exceed (airspeed)
VOR	very (high frequency) omnidirectional range
VORTAC	very (high frequency) omnidirectional radio range tactical air navigation aid
VOT	VOR test facility
VR	VFR military training route
VRB	variable
VS	vertical speed
vsby	visibility
VSI	vertical speed indicator
VV	vertical visibility
VVI	vertical velocity indicator
W	without voice; west
w	with
WA	warning area
WAAS	wide area augmentation system
wea	weather
WMS	wide-area master station
wnd	wind
WGS	World Geodetic System
WP	waypoint
WRS	wide-area ground reference station
WS	report type designator for SIGMET
WSHFT	wind shift
WST	report type designator for convective SIGMET
wt	weight
WW	weather warning
WX	weather
Y	year
Z	zulu (time)

SECTION II – TERMS

aerodrome

Airfield; an area prepared for the accommodation (including any buildings, installations, and equipment), landing and takeoff of aircraft.

agonic line

A line drawn on a map or chart joining points of 0 magnetic declination for a specified year date.

air route surveillance radar

Air route traffic control center radar used primarily to detect and display an aircraft's position while en route between terminal areas.

Airport/Facility Directory

An FAA publication containing information on all airports, communications, and NAVAIDs pertinent to IFR flight; also known as A/FD.

annunciator

An electrically controlled signal board or indicator.

bezel

A rim that holds a transparent covering (as on a watch, clock, or headlight) or that is rotatable and has special markings.

circling approach

A maneuver initiated by the aviator to align the aircraft with a runway for landing when a straight-in landing from an instrument approach is not possible or is not desirable.

clearance limit

The fix, point, or location to which an aircraft is cleared when issued an air traffic clearance.

clearance void time

Used by ATC to advise an aircraft that the departure clearance is automatically canceled if takeoff is not made prior to a specified time. The aviator must obtain a new clearance or cancel the IFR flight plan if not off by the specified time.

common traffic advisory frequency (CTAF)

A designated frequency for the purpose of carrying out airport advisory practices while operating to or from an airport that does not have a control tower or an airport where the control tower is not operational. The CTAF is normally a UNICOM, MULTICOM, FSS frequency, or a tower frequency. CTAF will be identified in appropriate aeronautical publications.

cruise clearance

Used in an ATC clearance to allow an aviator to conduct flight at any altitude from the minimum IFR altitude up to and including the altitude specified in the clearance. Also authorizes an aviator to proceed to and make an approach at the destination airport.

decision altitude

A specified altitude in the precision approach, charted in "feet MSL", at which a missed approach must be initiated if the required visual reference to continue the approach has not been established. Also known as (DA).

DA will replace DH for Category I precision IAPs.

decision height

> A specified altitude in the precision approach, charted in "height above threshold (HAT) elevation", at which a decision must be made to either continue the approach or to execute a missed approach. Also known as (DH).

> ILS Category II and III approach DHs are referenced to AGL and measured with a radar altimeter.

deviation

> A magnetic compass error caused by local magnetic fields within the aircraft. Deviation error is different on each heading.

dew point

> The temperature at which a vapor (as water) begins or would begin to condense.

doghouse

> A mark on the dial of a turn-and-slip indicator that has the shape of a doghouse.

Doppler radar

> A radar system that differentiates between fixed and moving targets by detecting the apparent change in frequency of the reflected wave caused by motion of the target or the observer.

encoding altimeter

> An altimeter that sends signals to the ATC transponder, showing the pressure altitude the aircraft is flying.

established

> To be stable or fixed as, for example, on a route, route segment, altitude, heading, or published segment of the approach.

established on course

> The aircraft must be within half scale deflection for ILS and VOR/DME/TACAN/RNAV/GPS, or within ±5 degrees of the required bearing for NDB.

fixating

> Staring at a single instrument, thereby interrupting the cross-check process.

flight level

> A level of constant atmospheric pressure related to a reference datum of 29.92 inches of mercury. Each is stated in three digits that represent hundreds of feet. For example, FL 250 represents a barometric altimeter indication of 25,000 feet; FL 355, an indication of 35,500 feet.

flimsy

> A lightweight paper used especially for multiple copies.

height above airport

> The height of the MDA above the published airport elevation. This is published in conjunction with circling minimums; also known as HAA.

height above landing

> The height above a designated helicopter landing area used for helicopter IAPs; also known as HAL.

height above touchdown

> The DH or MDA above the highest runway elevation in the touchdown zone (first 3,000 feet of the runway). HAT is published on instrument approach charts in conjunction with all straight-in minimums.

instrument approach procedure

A series of predetermined maneuvers for the orderly transfer of an aircraft under IFR from the beginning of the initial approach to a landing or to a point from which a landing may be made visually; also known as IAP.

isogonic lines

Lines drawn across aeronautical charts connecting points having the same magnetic variation.

Kollsman window

A barometric scale window of an altimeter referenced for changing altimeter settings.

lenticular

A type of cloud, shaped like a lens.

localizer

A directional radio beacon that provides to an aircraft an indication of its lateral position relative to a predetermined final approach course.

lubber line

A fixed line on the compass of an aircraft that is aligned with the longitudinal axis of the aircraft.

Mach number

The ratio of the velocity of a body (as an aircraft) to that of sound in the surrounding medium (as air).

magnetic bearing

The direction to or from a radio transmitting station measured relative to magnetic north.

magnetic heading

The direction an aircraft is pointed with respect to magnetic north; also known as MH.

marker beacon

A transmitter that directs its signal upward in a small, fan-shaped pattern. Used along the flightpath when approaching an airport for landing, marker beacons indicate, both aurally and visually, when the aircraft is directly over the facility.

middle marker

VHF marker beacon used in the ILS. When the NDB compass locator is collocated with an MM, it is shown as LMM on instrument approach charts.

millibar

A unit of atmospheric pressure equal to 1/1000 bar or 100 pascals.

minimum descent altitude

The lowest altitude, expressed in feet above MSL, to which descent is authorized on final approach or during circle-to-land maneuver in execution of a standard IAP where no glide slope is provided; also known as MDA.

missed approach

A maneuver conducted by an aviator when an instrument approach cannot be completed to a landing. A pilot executing a missed approach prior to the missed approach point (MAP) must continue along the final approach to the MAP. The pilot may climb immediately to the altitude specified in the missed approach procedure.

missed approach point

A point prescribed in each instrument approach procedure at which a missed approach procedure shall be executed if the required visual reference does not exist.

movement area

The runways, taxiways, and other areas of an airport/heliport that are used for taxiing/hover taxiing, takeoff and landing aircraft, exclusive of loading ramps, and parking areas.

MULTICOM

A mobile service, not open to public correspondence use, used for essential communications in the conduct of activities performed by or directed from private aircraft.

outer marker

VHF marker beacon used in the ILS. When the NDB compass locator is collocated with an OM, it is shown as LOM on instrument approach charts.

pascal

A unit of pressure in the meter-kilogram-second system equivalent to one newton per square meter.

pitot pressure

Ram air pressure used to measure airspeed.

pitot-static head

A combination pickup used to sample pitot pressure and static air pressure.

precipitation static

A form of radio interference caused by rain, snow, or dust particles hitting the antenna and inducing a small radio-frequency voltage into it; also known as P-Static.

precision approach radar

An instrument approach in which ATC issues azimuth and elevation instructions for aviator compliance, based on aircraft position in relation to the final approach course, glide slope, and distance from the end of the runway as displayed on the controller's radar scope; also known as PAR.

radials

Courses oriented from a VOR or TACAN station.

relative bearing

The number of degrees measured clockwise between the heading of the aircraft and the direction from which the bearing is taken.

reverse sensing

When the VOR needle indicates the reverse of normal operation. This occurs when the aircraft is headed toward the station with a FROM indication or when headed away from the station with a TO indication.

rigidity

The characteristic of a gyroscope that prevents its axis of rotation tilting as the Earth rotates.

rime

An accumulation of granular ice tufts on the windward sides of exposed objects that is formed from supercooled fog or cloud and built out directly against the wind.

special-use airspace

Airspace in which certain activities are subject to restrictions that can create limitations on the mixed use of airspace. Consists of prohibited, restricted, warning, military operations, and alert areas.

St. Elmo's fire

A corona discharge that lights up aircraft surface areas where maximum static discharge occurs.

standard rate turn

>A turn of three degrees per second.

transmissometer

>An instrument that measures the transmission of light through a fluid (as the atmosphere).

uncaging

>Unlocking the gimbals of a gyroscopic instrument, making it susceptible to damage by abrupt flight maneuvers or rough handling.

UNICOM

>A nongovernment air/ground radio communication station that may provide airport information at public use airports.

VFR Over-The-Top

>A VFR operation in which an aircraft operates in VFR conditions on top of an undercast.

VFR-On-Top

>ATC authorization for an IFR aircraft to operate in VFR conditions at any appropriate VFR altitude.

victor airways

>Except in Alaska and coastal North Carolina, the VOR airways are predicated solely on VOR or VORTAC navigation aids; they are depicted in blue on aeronautical charts.

VOR test facility

>A ground facility which emits a test signal to check VOR receiver accuracy. Some VOTs are available to the user while airborne, while others are limited to ground use only.

waypoint

>A designated geographical location used for route definition or progress-reporting purposes and defined relative to a VOR/DME station or in terms of latitude/longitude coordinates; also known as WP.

ZULU

>Time zone indicator for Universal Time.

References

The bibliography lists field manuals by the new number, followed by the old number, when applicable. These publications are sources for additional information on the topics in this field manual. Most joint publications can be found at http://www.dtic.mil/doctrine/s_index.html. Most Army doctrinal publications are available online at http://www.train.army.mil/. Federal Aviation Administration publications can be found online at http://www.faa.gov/regulations_policies. Air Force publications can be found online at http://www.e-publishing.af.mil. Marine publications can be found online at https://www.doctrine.usmc.mil.

SOURCES USED

These are the sources quoted or paraphrased in this publication.

AIR FORCE PUBLICATIONS (AIR FORCE MANUAL)

AFMAN 13-220, *Deployment of Airfield Operations*, 1 May 1997

AFMAN 15-124, *Meteorological Codes*, 30 October 2001

ARMY PUBLICATIONS

AR 95-1, *Flight Regulations*, 3 February 2006

AR. 95-2, *Airspace, Airfields/Heliports, Flight Activities, Air Traffic Control, and Navigational Aids*, 29 December 2006

DA PAM 25-30, *Consolidated Index of Army Publications and Blank Forms*, 1 January 2007

DA PAM 738-751, *Functional Users Manual for the Army Maintenance Management System—Aviation (TAMMS-A)*, 15 March 1999

FM 1-120, *Army Air Traffic Services Contingency and Combat Zone Operations*, 22 May 1995

FM 1-230, *Meteorology for Army Aviators*, 30 September 1982

FM 1-564, *Shipboard Operations*, 29 June 1997

FM 3-04.301, *Aeromedical Training for Flight Personnel*, 29 September 2000

FM 3-52.3, *Multi-service Procedures for Joint Air Traffic Control*, 17 July 2003

DEPARTMENT OF DEFENSE PUBLICATIONS/JOINT PUBLICATIONS

DOD 4500.54-G, *DOD Foreign Clearance Guide.* 5 January 1992

DOD FLIP AP/1B, Military Training Route

FEDERAL AVIATION ADMINISTRATION (DEPARTMENT OF TRANSPORTATION) PUBLICATIONS

AIM, *Aeronautical Information Manual (AIM): Official Guide to Basic Flight Information and ATC Procedures*, 19 February 2006

FAA Advisory Circular 90-45A, *Approval of Area Navigation Systems for use in the U.S. National Airspace System*, 21 February 1975

FAA Advisory Circular 150/5220-16C, *Automated Weather Observing Systems (AWOS) for Non-Federal Applications*, 13 December 1999

FAA Order 7110.65, *Air Traffic Control*, 16 February 2006

FAA Order 7110.10, Flight Services, 3 August 2006

FAA Order 7210.3, Facility Operation and Administration, 3 August 2006

INTERNATIONAL CIVIL AVIATION ORGANIZATION (ICAO) PUBLICATIONS

ICAO Document 7910, *Location Indicators,* June 2006

MARINE PUBLICATIONS

Marine Corp Warfighting Publication (MCWP) 3-25.8, *Marine Air Traffic Control Detachment Handbook,* 1 November 2004

DOCUMENTS NEEDED

These documents must be available to the intended users of this publication.

ARMY PUBLICATIONS

DA Form 2028, *Recommended Changes to Publications and Blank Forms*

DEPARTMENT OF DEFENSE PUBLICATIONS/JOINT PUBLICATIONS

DD Form 175, *Military Flight Plan*

DD Form 175-1, *Flight Weather Briefing*

DD Form 1613, *Pilot's Compass Correction Card*

DD Form 1801, *DOD International Flight Plan*

FEDERAL AVIATION ADMINISTRATION (DEPARTMENT OF TRANSPORTATION) PUBLICATIONS

FAA Form 7233-4, *International Flight Plan*

FAA Form 7233-1, *Flight Plan*

READINGS RECOMMENDED

These sources contain relevant supplemental information.

AFMAN 11-217, Volumes 1 and 2, *Instrument Flight Procedures,* 3 January 2005

AR 34-4, *Army Standardization Policy,* 15 March 1984

AR 40-8, *Temporary Flying Restrictions Due to Exogenous Factors,* 17 August 1976

AR 40-501, *Standards of Medical Fitness,* 27 June 2006

AR 95-10, *Department of Defense Notice to Airmen (NOTAM) System,* 1 August 2004

AR 385-10, *The Army Safety Program,* 29 February 2000

AR 385-95, *Army Aviation Accident Prevention,* 10 December 1999

AR 600-105, *Aviation Service of Rated Army Officers,* 15 December 1994

AR 600-106, *Flying Status for Nonrated Army Aviation Personnel,* 8 December 1998

DOD FLIP, *Planning and En Route Publications*

FAA-H-8083-3A. *Airplane Flying Handbook,* 2004

FAA-H-8083-15. *Instrument Flying Handbook,* 2001

FAA-H-8083-21. *Rotorcraft Flying Handbook,* 2004

FAA-H-8083-25. *Pilot's Handbook of Aeronautical Knowledge,* 2003

FAA-H-8261-1. *Instrument Procedures Handbook,* 2004

FAR Part 1. *Definitions and Abbreviations,* 1 March 1992

FM 1-02, *Operational Terms and Graphics,* 21 September 2004

FM 1-100, *Army Aviation Operations,* 21 February 1997

FM 1-203, *Fundamentals of Flight*, 3 October 1988

FM 3-04.300, *Flight Operations Procedures*, 26 April 2004

FM 3-04.508, *Aviation Life Support System Maintenance Management and Training Programs*, 23 April 2004

FM 3-52, *Army Airspace Command and Control in a Combat Zone*, 1 August 2002

FM 3-100.2, *ICAC2 Multiservice Procedures for Integrated Combat Airspace Command and Control*, 30 June 2000

FM 5-19 (FM 100-14), *Composite Risk Management*, 21 August 2006

FM 7-0, *Training the Force*, 22 October 2002

FM 7-1, *Battle Focused Training*, 15 September 2003

FM 7-15, *The Army Universal Task List*, 31 August 2003

Naval Air Systems Command (NAVAIR) 00-80T-112, *NATOPS Instrument Flight Manual*, 15 October 2002

TC 1-210, *Aircrew Training Program Commander's Guide to Individual, Crew, and Collective Training*, 20 June 2006

TC 1-211, *Aircrew Training Manual Utility Helicopter, UH-1*, 9 December 1992

TC 1-218, *Aircrew Training Manual Utility Airplane C-12*, 13 September 2005

TC 1-237, *Aircrew Training Manual, Utility Helicopter, H-60 Series*, 27 September 2005

TC 1-238, *Aircrew Training Manual, Attack Helicopter, AH-64A*, 23 September 2005

TC 1-240, *Aircrew Training Manual, Cargo Helicopter, CH-47D*, 12 September 2005

TC 1-248, *Aircrew Training Manual, OH-58D, Kiowa Warrior*, 12 September 2005

TC 1-251, *Aircrew Training Manual, Attack Helicopter AH-64D*, 14 September 2005

TM 1-1500-204-23-1, *Aviation Unit Maintenance (AVUM) and Aviation Intermediate Maintenance (AVIM) Manual for General Aircraft Maintenance (General Maintenance and Practices) Volume 1*, 31 July 1992

TM 1-1500-204-23-2, *Aviation Unit Maintenance (AVUM) and Aviation Intermediate Maintenance (AVIM) Manual for General Aircraft Maintenance (Pneudralics Maintenance and Practices) Volume 2*, 31 July 1992

TM 1-1500-204-23-3, *Aviation Unit Maintenance (AVUM) and Aviation Intermediate Maintenance (AVIM) Manual for General Aircraft Maintenance (Maintenance Practices for Fuel and Oil Systems) Volume 3*, 31 July 1992

TM 1-1500-204-23-4, *Aviation Unit Maintenance (AVUM) and Aviation Intermediate Maintenance (AVIM) Manual for General Aircraft Maintenance (Electrical and Instrument Maintenance Procedures and Practices) Volume 4*, 31 July 1992

TM 1-1500-204-23-5, *Aviation Unit Maintenance (AVUM) and Aviation Intermediate Maintenance (AVIM) Manual for General Aircraft Maintenance (Propeller, Rotor, and Powertrain Maintenance Practices) Volume 5*, 31 July 1992

TM 1-1500-204-23-6, *Aviation Unit Maintenance (AVUM) and Aviation Intermediate Maintenance (AVIM) Manual for General Aircraft Maintenance (Hardware and Consumable Materials) Volume 6*, 31 July 1992

TM 1-1500-204-23-7, *Aviation Unit Maintenance (AVUM) and Aviation Intermediate Maintenance (AVIM) Manual for General Aircraft Maintenance (Nondestructive Testing and Flaw Detection Procedures and Practices) Volume 7*, 31 July 1992

TM 1-1500-204-23-8, *Aviation Unit Maintenance (AVUM) and Aviation Intermediate Maintenance (AVIM) Manual for General Aircraft Maintenance (Machine and Welding Shop Practices) Volume 8*, 31 July 1992

TM 1-1500-204-23-9, *Aviation Unit Maintenance (AVUM) and Aviation Intermediate Maintenance (AVIM) Manual for General Aircraft Maintenance (Tools and Ground Support Equipment) Volume 9*, 31 July 1992

TM 1-1500-204-23-10, *Aviation Unit Maintenance (AVUM) and Aviation Intermediate Maintenance (AVIM) Manual for General Aircraft Maintenance (Sheet Metal Shop Practices) Volume 10*, 31 July 1992

TM 1-1500-328-23, *Aeronautical Equipment Maintenance Management Policies and Procedures.* 30 July 1999

TM 1-1510-218-10, *Operator's Manual for Army C-12C, C-12D, C-12T, and C-12C2 Aircraft.* 4 September 2001

TM 1-1520-237-10, *Operator's Manual for UH-60A Helicopter, UH-60L Helicopter, EH-60A Helicopter.* 17 April 2006

TM 1-1520-238-10, *Operator's Manual for Helicopter, Attack, AH-64A Apache.* 22 December 2005

TM 1-1520-240-10, *Operator's Manual for Army CH-47D Helicopter*, 30 June 2006

TM 1-1520-248-10, *Operator's Manual for Army OH-58D Helicopter*, 15 March 2005

TM 1-1520-251-10, *Operator's Manual for Helicopter, Attack, AH-64D Longbow Apache*, 29 March 2002

TM 1-1520-253-10, *Operator's Manual for Army Models UH-60Q Helicopter, HH-60L Helicopter*, 17 April 2006

TM 55-1520-210-10, *Operator's Manual for Army Model UH-1H/V Helicopters*, 15 February 1988

Joint Pub 1-02, *Department of Defense (DOD) Dictionary of Military and Associated Terms*, 12 April 2001

NATO Standardization Agreement (STANAG) 2999, *Use of Helicopters in Land Operations-Doctrine-ATP-49(D), Volume 1*, 18 May 2005

STANAG 3805, *Doctrine for Joint Airspace Control-AJP-3.3-5(A)*, 5 April 2006

Index

References are to page numbers except for illustrations, which are listed by figure or table numbers.

www.ingramcontent.com/pod-product-compliance
Lightning Source LLC
LaVergne TN
LVHW081323060426
835511LV00011B/1818